werewolf

The Architecture of Lunacy, Shapeshifting, and Material Metamorphosis

Edited by Caroline O'Donnell and José Ibarra

For Lúnasa

Contents

an OMG project,
in collaboration with Martin Miller

Foreword

Peter Eisenman

"Werewolf. Where wolf? Wear wolf. Beware, wolf.

There were so many possibilities that, in the end, I did not know if I were man or I were wolf."[1]

In the 1960s, Jacques Derrida introduced one of the most important concepts for architecture, film, painting, and literature: *undecidability*. The philosopher described it as a moment in which meaning, wholeness, and presence were uncertain. Inevitably, in any text, there are points of ambiguity and complexity that disrupt any thought-to-be-stable meaning that an author might intend. The more abstraction and complexity, the more space for undecidability, and the more room for the meaning to be a mental construct. In this sense, architecture is about the invisible. It is about clues that only architects can see. As such, we can read compression, tension, movement, and even implied planes continuing beyond corners. We can experience the stressed space between what we expect to be there and what is there. In the physical world, things are hidden in plain sight.

In Michael Haneke's *Funny Games* (2007 and 1997), there is a tension which comes from what we do not see. Everything on the surface looks fine; a soft-spoken young man dressed in white comes to the door and asks a woman if he can borrow some eggs. He is given the eggs and says his goodbyes. In the next scene, the eggs have fallen to the ground, but we do not see the eggs dropping. Instead, we see an apologetic, clumsy man with cracked eggs at his feet. This methodology of off-screen action repeats consistently throughout the film. In fact, very little happens on the screen, at least when compared to what happens in the mind of the viewer; a projected reality based on experience and speculation. It is the tension between what is expected and what is shown that produces an anxiety in the spectator.

For Jasper Johns, such undecidability manifests differently. In his piece *Flag* (1954–1955), we encounter a familiar object that has been strangely altered and defamiliarized—the viewer can sense that something is wrong. The canvas is not the same proportion as the American flag's familiar ratio. From experience, we know that the flag has been trimmed. There is a tension between the physical and the virtual, an incredible edge stress that is produced between our knowledge of what the painting should be and what the painting is.

Architecture is about signs, not things. It is language. And consequently, the possibility of any reading implies abstraction. This book's three guiding terms—lunacy, shapeshifting, and material metamorphosis—are all misnomers and misunderstandings. *Lupacy*, perhaps. Or *form*-shifting.[2] These might be better terms. What *is* interesting for me about the book's concept, "werewolf," is its embedded possibility to appropriate multiple meanings, its ability to be set up as a critical discourse, inscribed within Derrida's idea of undecidability. When we read a text, the images are as problematic as our minds can conjure. In a movie, the transformation from man to wolf is rather banal—even comical, at times. The image that we can generate in our minds is much more unsettling, and consequently, it can become much more problematic.

Charles Sanders Peirce described the difference between the linguistic signs: symbol, icon, and index. For him, the symbol is an arbitrary referent requiring cultural agreement, while the icon is visually similar to the object. An index, on the other hand, is the only sign that has a physical and temporal relationship with the object. A footprint in the sand, a scratch, a drop of blood … these are traces, marks, imprints, and clues to a former presence (and current absence) of the referent. Haneke's *Code Unknown* (2000) is an interesting model for this because we cannot deduce who the killer is in the plotline. We follow leads but each one invalidates the other, which destabilizes the expectation of a typical "whodunit" plot. The premise becomes undecidable. In other words, legibility is frustrated, and linear narrative is gone.

The murder mystery is the most modern form of literary discourse because the clues are indices. Clues depend on traces or marks of a presence that is no longer. A crime scene is a series of abstract marks that requires the mind of the detective—and that of the reader—for deducing the meaning. The solution involves a tracing back in time to the moment of the event.

In O'Donnell's practice, CODA, several projects suggest an architectural equivalent. The 2013 MoMA PS1 winning entry, *Party Wall,* is not interesting because of its environmental or material qualities. It is interesting because there are clues at work that also play with the project's own notions of being. *Party Wall* spells out "wall" in its own shadow in a way that provokes the questions: is it a wall? And, what is the constitution of a wall, anyway? This play between a word and a physical object is

the beginning of undecidability in three-dimensional form. In this case, the form of the object has nothing to do with aesthetics. The project is shaped in a specific way only to give formal meaning. In doing so, it avoids the possibility of someone saying, "I like it," because the project has no option but to look the way it does. Thus, the material and color are irrelevant. CODA took a basic shape, eroded it, and produced meaning that was both the object itself, and the sign of the object.

I argue that in architecture, *ducks* are the product of modernism, and *decorated sheds* are the product of postmodernism. *Party Wall* reinvigorates this Venturi Scott Brown proposition, producing a type that is a third condition, somewhere in between, or even beyond a duck and a decorated shed. The project is not quite a decorated shed, even though it is all sign, and it is not quite a duck, as it lacks a formally symbolic meaning. Typologically, it falls outside of these two seemingly dialectical terms. CODA, in this project, is on to something that is both conceptual and phenomenological. For example, James Joyce deals with language in a supposedly phenomenological way, but it is actually abstract. The sounds (and thus, the meanings) are garbled. The question in architecture has been how to problematize meaning by the language of disturbance, erosion, or transfiguration. Similar to Joyce's spaces of literature, experience is not just physical, it is conceptual. The column is not simply the thing itself, it is also the sign of the column. It is simultaneously the phenomenon and its abstraction as a sign function.

Against this background, the difference between semantics and syntax is relevant. While *semantics* is about the meaning of words, *syntax* is about the relationship between words: that is, the context of a word in regard to the other words around it. The latter term literally means "composition" in Greek. Ferdinand de Saussure, Derrida's mentor, wrote regarding syntax that: "The idea or phonic substance that a sign contains is of less importance than the other signs that surround it."[3] And Derrida, himself, believed that the omnipresence of context was fundamental to undecidability: "One can perhaps come to recognize other possibilities in it by inscribing it or grafting it onto other chains. No context can entirely enclose it."[4] Since every utterance is repeated in a different context, each reading and writing is evolved because of its changed context.

In the same way, context is important for architecture. There are different approaches to contextual projects: Leon Krier's *New Urbanism*, Colin Rowe's *Contextualism*, O.M. Ungers's *Green Archipelago,* Aldo Rossi's *Analogous City*. The question today is how to make context thematic and abstract, or how to make it operate in an undecidable or disturbing way within an architecture. The possible readings of *Party Wall* only occur because the context of the museum courtyard forces the possibility of multiple readings. Context is a serious contingency in any architecture.

Between the 1960s and 1980s, a transition occurred from a strictly formal reading of context to one with semiotic possibilities. Relationships between pure geometries were no longer sufficient to explain the complexities of the world and of architecture. The epistemology that related some stable state of form to some progressive mode of an ideal universe, seen as an absolute condition, was questioned. Pure geometry was disrupted and dislocated through the introduction of fractal mathematics and topology. Opposite to the prescriptive codes of classical architecture and the Cartesian geometry of modernism, the generative use of geometries today has emerged from new relationships with nature, biology, and ecology. D'Arcy Thompson's *On Growth and Form* influenced generations of architects, from Le Corbusier onwards, but our understanding of nature today is far more complex than demonstrated in Thompson's transformations. Avalanches, tectonic movement, clouds … we have begun to think about global systems, dynamic organizations that involve form in a space-time continuum. These new natures have restructured our thinking about architecture today.

In this new ecological world, undecidability performs differently. Undecidability is still possible today through dismantlement, deterioration, and materiality. The object is not only a *being* in the Hegelian sense, but a being *in the process of becoming other* through such disturbances. John Hejduk, for example, invented a whole series of student exercises with fruit and vegetables that deteriorated over the course of the semester: the mold was about an intellectual and conceptual exercise, not a phenomenological one.

Undecidability's disruption allows for misreading. Aside from the slew of double-entendre project titles in the book, from *Tripe* to *Zimmer*, the name CODA is also intentionally misreadable. It suggests a code yet to be deciphered. Or a manuscript

as in the codex, which in some cases, notably in Leonardo da Vinci's, was written backwards, from right to left, such that it could only be read using a mirror, which prompted a different kind of reading. This produces strangeness and the possibility of new effects. A coda is also the end of a piece of music coming from *cauda*, which is Latin for tail.

Does the werewolf have a tail? Or a tale to tell?

Introduction

Caroline O'Donnell and José Ibarra

It was fascinating to watch her skull change shape—as though the hands of an invisible sculptor were kneading and molding the living clay, squeezing the very bony structure into new conformations. The elongated head seemed miraculously shorn of curls for the moment, and then the fine fur sprang up, the ears flared outward, the pinkish tips twitched along a thickened neck. Her eyes slitted upward, while the features of the face convulsed, then converged into a protuberant muzzle. The grimace of involuntary rictus became a snarl, and fangs jutted forth.[1]

The werewolf is defined by her[2] liminality, her existence in a state of *becoming*. While the vicious actions under the power of the moon—the biting and eating of human flesh, the howling, the baring of teeth—are startling, it is perhaps the creature's transformation that is most fundamental. This metamorphosis rocks our image of an ordered, cultured world, and of our place in it as stable and fixed. The werewolf blurs the boundaries of human, animal, and monster in a way that seems to leave the doors tantalizingly open to the wilderness and to the wild.

As early humans co-evolved alongside wolves, oftentimes in fear of the furry marauders, they recognized parallels between the two species. Inevitably, they began to venerate the speed and ruthlessness of the wolf and, in many ways, "to desire some appropriation of its power for themselves."[3] In Native American culture, entering a lupine trance could yield a "wolf trot," allowing the tribesmen to cover hundreds of miles without interruption.[4] And in Norse mythology, the transformation into a wolf-like state was desirable for battle. A poem by Snorri Sturluson recalls Þorbjörn Hornklofi's account (ca. 872) and describes a combat in which the heroes are becoming lupine:

Savage berserker roaring mad,
And champions fierce in wolf-skins clad,
Howling like wolves; and clanking jar
Of many a mail-clad man of war.[5]

Indeed, the revered shapeshifter, preying at the boundary of civilization, appears in the folklore of countless cultures. In Europe, the wolf-human existed in innumerable variations: *lupo mannaro* (Italy), *hombre lobo* (Spain), *vrykolakas* (Greece), *varulf* (Sweden), *faoladh* (Ireland), and so on. In Ancient Egypt, *Anubis*, the god who ushered souls

into the afterlife, was himself half-man and half-wolf. And in other cultures where the wolf is not a common predator, other animals replaced it: werejaguars (pre-Columbian Mesoamerica), weretigers (India), and wereleopards and werelions (Africa). These mythical creatures emerged from very real beasts; the relentless predators who lurked in the shadows at the edge of early settlements.

Between the late sixteenth century and early nineteenth century in France, over 1,600 death certificates note the wolf as the cause of death, though the real number is likely higher.[6] Of these, half are estimated to have been rabid wolves infected with "canine madness."[7] Rabid wolves tend to develop extraordinary strength and violent behavior, and these transformed creatures were regarded, at the time, not as the result of a disease but as "monstrous creatures endowed with supernatural powers."[8] The wolf, already wild, was even wilder as it crossed the boundary from animal to monster.

Throughout the nineteenth century, myriad gothic horror novels told tales of the human-become-wolf, endowed, in the process, with all the traits of the beast: "a shaggy covering of fur, glowing eyes, long canine teeth, and razor-sharp claws … cunning, craftiness, swiftness of movement, bestial ferocity, and unbridled cruelty."[9] One century later, the dawn of cinema brought with it a new popularized werewolf whose diverse origins in pulp fiction converged into a more homogeneous character with, at times, somewhat comic or kitsch connotations. In these more recent times, the full Moon has become the accepted trigger for the transformation, a relationship not essential in earlier fiction. Common to all definitions, however, is the werewolf as an ambivalent creature, unsatisfied with *being*. The werewolf is, whether voluntarily or otherwise, always driven toward *becoming*.

While humans compared themselves to wolves and dreamt of an ability to devolve wolfward, architecture fantasized about achieving the order and perfection displayed by man. Architecture has long favored *being* over *becoming*, thing over event, such that any association of architecture with impermanence is thought to challenge its longstanding affiliation with a universal perfection—especially the perfection embodied by the static human figure encased within platonic shapes. What new architectures might arise if that alignment with *man-in-geometry* were to be exchanged for *werewolf-in-the-wild*?

Werewolf: The Architecture of Lunacy, Shapeshifting, and Material Metamorphosis is a monographic manifesto[10] that departs from the prevalent architectural models of inert *objectness* and proposes a shift toward working with today's dynamic political and ecological climates, morphing and adjusting in response to shifting scenarios and surroundings.

The first part of this book begins with architecture's pervasive lineage of man as ruler—both master and measure—of space. Chapter 1 moves from human to animal to monster and arrives at a new model for architecture in which fluctuation and indeterminacy are fundamental. As the animal becomes monster, three characteristics that define the werewolf are translated into analogous conceptual frameworks and architectural propositions: *lunacy* considers natural triggers for transformational events, *shapeshifting* explores formal variation—whether literally, in physical space, or metaphorically, through perceptual means—and *material metamorphosis* investigates physical and chemical changes to matter. Finally, this chapter juxtaposes lupine tales of trickery and deception with architecture's linguistic trajectory. This unpacking of the book's conceptual framework is followed by chapter 2, which studies the arc of dynamic architecture through twentieth- and twenty-first-century case studies. These building precedents support an argument for transformation and responsiveness as an imperative for architecture today.

Following these chapters, a series of contributor essays explore contextual responsiveness, materiality, form, and perception in the blurry zone between architecture and werewolves. Kari Weil addresses literary transformation through Kafka's *The Metamorphosis*, Spyros Papapetros investigates the lunar affect upon architecture from Renaissance cosmology through modern ecology, Jesse Reiser delves into primordial instincts and their risks and rewards, Greg Lynn discusses mechanically dynamic architecture, and Jimenez Lai explores the material and perceptual logics of furriness.

The second part of this book presents a series of experiments and forays into the world of transformation that look directly at werewolf theory in practice. These are selected built and unbuilt works of CODA (and its sister practice, OMG) ranging from objects to pavilions to buildings, all using lunacy, shapeshifting, and material metamorphosis as design principles.

The third and final part of this book collects various insights on the origins of these lycanthropic notions, as well as the architectural associations to werewolves. This section starts with an interview with O'Donnell that traces her own transformation from wain to woman to wolf, and features an appearance by her OMG partner, Martin Miller. Then, a survey asks historians, theorists, designers, and building users about the role of werewolves and other monsters in architecture. Finally, these transcripts are followed by two additional essays by O'Donnell. These texts were written and published years before *Werewolf: The Architecture of Lunacy, Shapeshifting, and Material Metamorphosis* was conceived, but they serve to reveal underlying relationship between the shapeshifting monster and the theories presented in this book by looking at architecture through economy, ecology, and psychoanalysis.

This *festigraph* is bookended with essays by Peter Eisenman and Cynthia Davidson, whose contributions to architecture have given shape to many of the ideas here, either by direct correspondence or by opposition.

Ultimately, all these words and projects respond to one fundamental prompt: what would it mean for architecture to be, sometimes, lycanthrope?

The human fascination with the monster comes not so much from her beastliness but from her transformability, indefinability, and behavior outside the norm. The werewolf encounter is exhilarating not so much due to the contact with a wild animal but rather, as Herbert de Vries has noted, "with one that has transgressed a boundary between nature and culture."[11]

What is architecture when it exists in a state of *becoming*, between nature and culture?

From Caged Human to Cageless Monster

Caroline O'Donnell and José Ibarra

Human within Geometry

> *Without symmetry and proportion, there can be no principles in the design of any temple … as in the case of a well-shaped man.*[1]

Da Vinci's drawing of the Vitruvian Man, which traps the figure of a man inside the pure geometries of a square and a circle (as if one platonic shape were not constraint enough), is one of several visualizations of the human's relation to a transcendental order, as proposed by Vitruvius in his *Ten Books of Architecture*. This notion can be traced further back, at least to Aristotle and Plato, who advised that a speech or a poem should have a coherent unity, similar to that of the body: "so as to enable the work to produce its own proper pleasure like a living creature which is one and a whole."[2] The belief in the human figure as the ultimate model of perfection, and its use as a mirror of proportions and order in the built world, abounds in early cultures: from the ancient Egyptians who used a grid to draw the perfect human, to Sanskrit texts that referenced the body in relation to building dimensions, or the Malay *Ilmu Taju* system, where the female arm-span gave proportions to architecture.

Renaissance reinterpretations of the "well-shaped man … designed by nature,"[3] reinforced a belief that "all the art of science and reason are drawn from a well-composed and proportioned human body."[4] Both textually and graphically, they served not only to affirm the rules of proportion and order but, more insidiously, to represent an architecture that was modelled after the image of a man: perfect, fixed, and static.

This figure-within-figures lingered over our understanding of the body, of architecture, and the desire for order that unites them, well into the twentieth century. From Ernst Neufert's prolific publications of measured man in 1935, originally published as *Der Mensch als Maß und Ziel* (Man as Measure and Goal), to Kiesler's *Biotechnique* man in 1939, and most famously Le Corbusier's *Modulor* in 1943, in which the architect drew a "grid … designed to fit the man placed within it,"[5] the naked male figure contained within a geometric system persisted. The message continued even with Henry Dreyfuss's rendition, which added the figure of the female and the child, in the family centric 1950s. And though architecture today no longer faithfully applies the rules of proportion that a Renaissance or mid-twentieth-

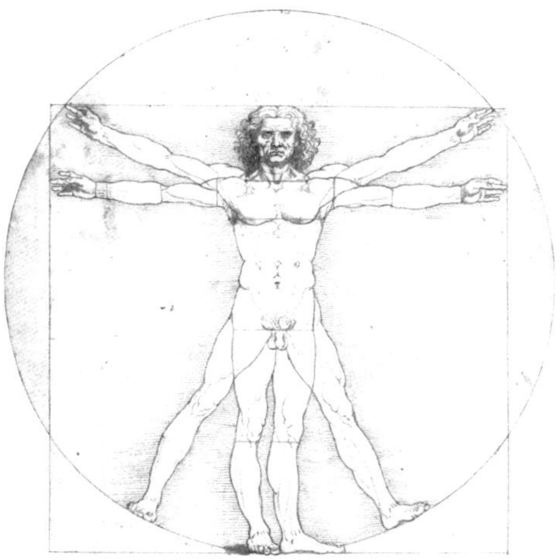

Vitruvian Man, Leonardo da Vinci, c. 1490.

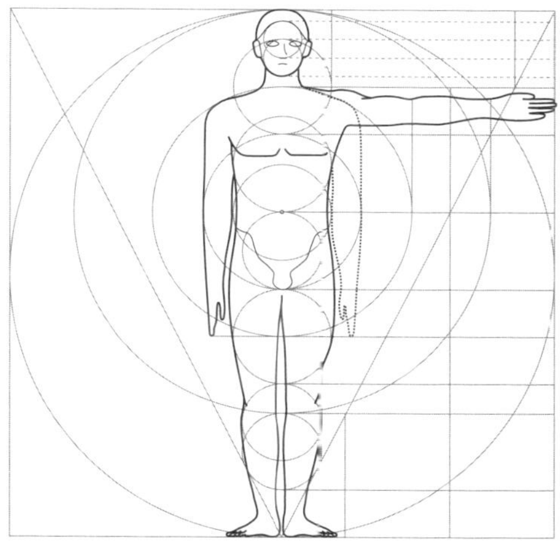

Drawing after Neufert's *Man as Measure and Goal.*

century architect may have been inclined to do, the fundamental notion of a static and ordered architecture endures.

Human to Animal

An animal looks at us and we are naked before it. Thinking, perhaps, begins here.[6]

Since Aristotle's *History of Animals*, the human has been made different from the rest of the animal kingdom by calling attention to its "unique" ability to think and reason. In recent years, this distinction has been put under scrutiny, creating a rift in thinking that has come to be known under many names, of which, for now, "post-humanism" will do. Post-humanism points to the inevitable redefinition of humanity's place in nature, in which the human is only one species among many. In *Thinking Animals*, Kari Weil describes the turn to animals in art as well as in literary theory as an attempt to envision "a different understanding of what we humans are and consequently to enlarge or change the possibilities for what we can think and what we can do in the world."[7]

This idea is not new and some of its architectural roots can, too, be traced to Renaissance architecture. In contrast to Leonardo Da Vinci and Giorgio Martini's focus on the human, Leon Battista Alberti saw animals as analogous to architecture,

carrying with them an embodiment of natural principles of organization and order in their part-to-whole relationships, as well as in their consideration of climatic and site-related givens.[8] Alberti wrote, for instance, that "the supports of ancient buildings were generally even in number, as animals support themselves on an even number of feet; but the apertures were generally odd in number, in the same way that the mouth is a single opening in the face."[9] Three hundred years before Jean-Baptiste Lamarck and Charles Darwin put forth their theories on evolution and variation, Alberti had already drawn an analogy between buildings and living beings in their "fitness and adaptation to the tasks they must perform."[10]

It was not until the evolutionary revolution of the mid-nineteenth century,[11] precipitated by Darwin, Lamarck, and others, that the animal's inevitable challenging of the human gained traction. In 1917, D'Arcy Thompson demonstrated visually the mathematical relationship between species in which no type was ideal. Instead, every morphological possibility hypothetically existed along a smooth continuum.

As biological research in genetics progressed, the evolution analogy, which had long been influential to architects, was certainly fueled in the late twentieth century by the digital turn. Architects began to use dynamic animation software and design evolutionarily, perhaps rooted in Peter Eisenman's explicitly operative and indexical design iterations. For instance, Greg Lynn's juxtaposition of Eisenman's indexical operations with Thompson's fish transformations led to his designs for a series of *Embryological Houses* (see Lynn's essay in this volume), which spearheaded a

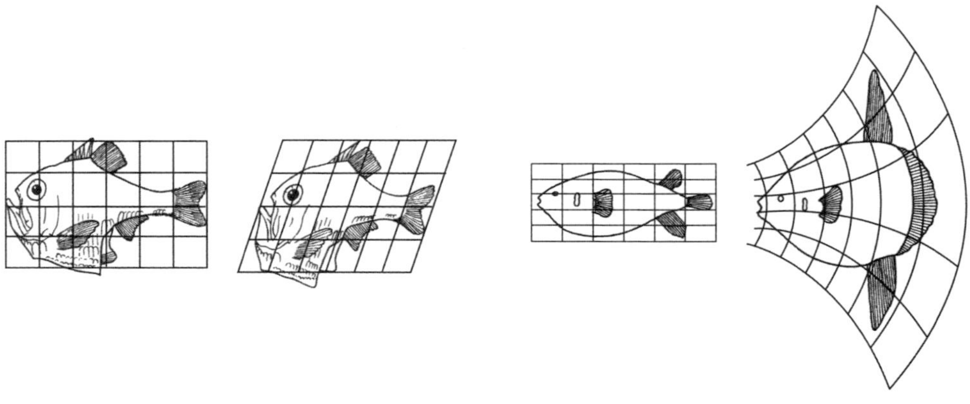

Evolution of body form. D'Arcy Thompson, in *On Growth and Form*, ed. by John Tyler Bonner.

turn toward digitally generated architecture. Here, design, evolution, and selection processes aligned with their biological counterparts. The language of evolution seeped quickly into architectural discourse, as terms like *species* and *brood* replaced mainstays like *typology*. Besides, we all embraced software and programming languages with names like Rhinoceros, Grasshopper, Python, and Kangaroo without hesitation.

Catherine Ingraham elucidates the logic of the animal analogy in architecture. Pushing beyond the shallow metaphor, she proposes that animal and architecture form a useful alignment because they are both *object* and *other*. "Architecture," Ingraham writes, "'animalizes' itself by maintaining a distinctness as object apart from the realm of the inhabiting subject. Alberti might have agreed … This is the distinctness of a "living object," all of whose parts have been classified and named, but whose primary presence in the world is one of form. Architecture would thus act *as* animal in the sense that it makes culture and is made by culture in much the same way as the post-human animal: by filling in the place of a speechless simplified other."[12]

Where Ingraham's argument is for the inclusion of animal-thinking, this text pushes beyond that, into monster-thinking. Why inhabit the circle and square with another animal, when the monster could devour its geometric cage and its singularity in time?

Animal to Monster

The slip from architecture-as-animal to architecture-as-monster occurred in short order after the initial introduction of the animal. Alberti himself warned the architect of the "errors of excess," which would push architecture to the limits of its species and produce a "monster with limbs disproportionate."[13] Throughout architectural history, the reference to the monster has been no compliment.[14]

However, while the animal aligns with the human in reinforcing an architecture of order and balance, the monster, existing as it does in a category distinct from that of the animal,[15] may provide an opportunity to rethink architecture's stasis. Reiser + Umemoto have noted, "Making architecture anthropocentric in order to deal with movement and change in fact makes it much more limiting."[16] We may consider that

making architecture zoocentric does the same. The monster, however, is perhaps the liberating figure, which augments and extends the performance of the body, but does not represent it.

Fifteenth- and sixteenth-century monsters were collages of incongruous parts, often comprising multiple species. In some cases, the species remains consistent, but scales or numbers of parts are distorted: the monster of *Spalt*, for example, has two heads, four arms, and four legs—a geometric doubling that maintains the singularity of the species. In other instances, the monster is a hybrid composed of multiple species; the monster of *Ravena* is a human body with a horn, wings, and a single avian foot. The Berlin *Papyrus with Sphinx sketch* demonstrates the multiple distinct regulating lines necessary to represent the three species—lion, human, and goddess—that combine into one whole chimeric creature in the Sphinx. Erwin Panofsky calls the result "monstrous" due to this heterogeneity; things together that should not be.[17]

Today, monsters are understood as genetic manipulations, whether by addition or deletion, that operate in many ways like the medieval predecessors mentioned previously, only now the editing is at a much smaller scale, and at the level of the genotype rather than the phenotype.[18]

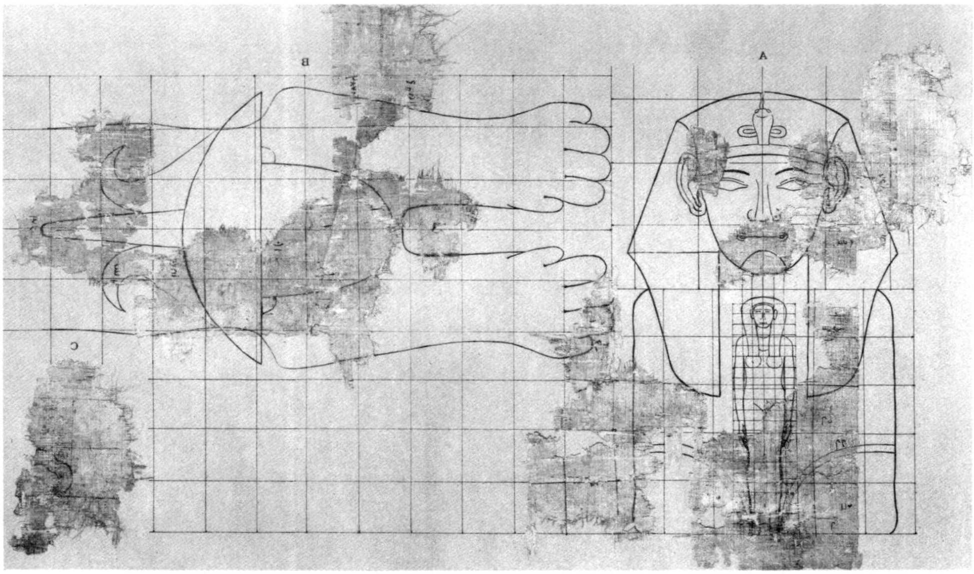

Papyrus with Sphinx sketch, (304-282 BCE). Papyrus, 33.7 x 57.2 cm.
From the Ägyptisches Museum und Papyrussammlung, Staatliche Museen, Berlin, Germany.
Photo courtesy of bpk, Berlin / Sandra Steiss /Art Resource, NY.

Alternatively, rather than occurring in a single creature as an incongruous combination of species at the same time, the werewolf exists as multiple creatures that manifest as a singular species at different times.[19] This kind of monster can adapt physically, through form and material, to specific environmental conditions and it can acquire superior intellect, strength, and cunning—all qualities that are desirable to the static human in many ways. This time-driven process of transformation was named "becoming" by Gilles Deleuze and Félix Guattari, whose animal theory questions the accepted definitions of what it means to be human "by replacing notions of exterior form and function with notions of affects and intensities and flows of movement as a means to describe and value life."[20] Their theory places emphasis less on the animal itself and more on *becoming* animal.

The shapeshifting monster is of interest to architecture as a model that is against stasis and ideal outputs, and is instead for states of becoming that privilege performance. Opposed to what Sanford Kwinter has called architecture's "thinkable space of measure, management, and mastery,"[21] an alternative model would be one that does not try to protect from an exterior world, but instead is conceived in response to it; a model that is transformative, responsive, and reactive to those inevitable stimuli. Kwinter describes the flipside of the finitude and regularity of the "thing" as the "event," which is driven by contingency and volatility. Such a world is more aligned with the savagery *beyond* the Vitruvian lines of the circle and square: the natural world, which is "wild, indifferent, and accidental … a ceaseless pullulation and unfolding, a dense evolutionary plasma of perpetual differentiation and innovation."[22] This state of "becoming-ever-different" produces, according to Kwinter, not only wildness, but also novelty.

Three Points for a Werewolf Architecture

one. **Lunacy**

> *Even a man who is pure in heart*
> *And says his prayers at night*
> *May become a wolf when the wolfsbane blooms*
> *And the autumn Moon is bright.*[23]

Of the many transformational creatures that exist in mythology, the werewolf is among a subset of creatures that change in response to external stimuli.[24]

The earliest werewolf literature originates in antiquity, when metamorphosis from human to animal was a common literary trope. In Virgil's *Eclogue* (39BCE) a warlock eats magical herbs to transform himself into a wolf, and in Ovid's *Metamorphosis* (8CE) Lycaon is transformed by Jupiter into a wolf as a punishment for serving human flesh at dinner. The first mention of the Moon as a possible motivator in the transformation is in Petronius's *Satyricon* (55CE) when a young soldier, passing by a graveyard on a moonlit night, removes his clothes, urinates on them, turns into a werewolf and runs off to ravage the livestock.[25]

Although today the Moon is again the popularly accepted trigger for the werewolf metamorphosis, earlier lore and literature mention the lunar body infrequently, and in many cases, they refer specifically to the tides rather than to the Moon itself as the motivator for change. The transformation has been stimulated by a range of surprising objects and events: another werewolf's bite, drinking water out of a wolf's print, eating a wolf's brains, drinking from a lycanthropic stream, and picking or wearing certain flowers.[26] Countless works also have the transformation occurring with no specific trigger. This is certainly the case in what is commonly accepted as the very first work of werewolf fiction, *The Lay of the Bisclavret*. This is a twelfth-century tale by Marie de France, where the werewolf transforms due to forces beyond his control on a weekly schedule.[27] In this tale, a man of great repute is trapped in the state of a wolf by his wife, who knowingly steals his clothes during one of his transformations so that he cannot return to human form.

Oftentimes, there are multiple triggers working together. In the 1893 story by Count Stenbock, *The Other Side*, Gabriel becomes transformed by flowers, moonlight, a lycanthropic stream, and the presence of other werewolves: "Then the Moon breaking from a cloud shone with unusual brilliance, and he saw, stretching before him, long reaches of strange blue flowers each one lovelier than the last … and his heart was filled with longing for what he knew not, and the Moon shone, and the nightingale sang. But on a sudden a black cloud covered the Moon entirely … and through the darkness he heard wolves howling and shrieking in the hideous ardour of the chase, and there passed before him a horrible procession of wolves (black

wolves with fiery red eyes) and with them men that had the heads of wolves and wolves that had the heads of men."[28] Soon enough, Gabriel looks at his reflection in the stream and realizes that he has become one of them.[29]

However, since George Wagner's *The Wolf Man* (1941),[30] the transformation of the werewolf has become almost exclusively synonymous with the icon of the full Moon. In that film, Gwen recites the poem that begins this section to the unsuspecting soon-to-be werewolf, Larry. Subsequent films, from Roy William Neil's *Frankenstein Meets the Wolf Man* (1943) to Anthony Waller and John Landis's horror comedy, *An American Werewolf in London* (1981), as well as the spate of contemporary werewolf television serial dramas, have reinforced the role of the Moon in motivating the transformation to the extent that the contemporary werewolf is inextricable from its lunar trigger today.[31]

This motivation to change by time and force outside of the self is one of the key elements in the werewolf's selection for this *festigraph*, where transformation is not caused solely by an internal imperative—this is to say, it is not autonomous. Instead, the architectural transformation is responsive and reactive to external motivators and stimulators; it responds to environmental contexts.

Lunacy implies more than relations to the Moon: the term also alludes to insanity and other mental pathologies. In fact, the earliest studies of neurological and psychiatric diseases believed these illnesses to be linked to the phases of the Moon.[32] The werewolf, too, exists in a schizophrenic state: a creature not only of split body, but of split mind. In his 1955 book on schizophrenia, *The Divided Self*, psychologist R.D. Laing writes that, for the schizophrenic, "The body is felt more as one object among other objects in the world than as the core of the individual's own being."[33] When the boundaries distinguishing an object from its environment become too blurry, a psychic break occurs.

From the ecological perspective, the same feeling of loss of distinction is registered. In *Hyperobjects: Philosophy and Ecology at the End of the World*, Timothy Morton mentions a schizophrenic defense in the context of a similar object/background blurring. He explains the psychotic break as a fair reaction to the closeness and pervasiveness of everything relative to the self: "The need to distance in the face

Drawing after *An American Werewolf in London,* drawn by Philippe Lapierre, 2020.

of threatening proximity."[34] Morton describes the self, the earth, and the biosphere as "viscous surfaces from which nothing can be forcibly peeled … no away on this surface, no here and no there."[35] Everything is part of everything else, boundaries are blurred and lost, figures lose their outlines and become backgrounds, as in R.C. James's famous image of the Dalmatian in the dappled light of the tree. The spots of light on the ground become equal to the surface of non-spotted dog—best viewed, according to perceptual psychologist R.L. Gregory, in moonlight—and our perception slips uncomfortably between object and background.

This loss of figuration connects back to Deleuze and Guattari's writing on Franz Kafka, where metamorphosis is related to language: "Metamorphosis is the contrary of metaphor. There is no longer any proper sense or figurative sense, but only a distribution of states that is part of the range of the word. The thing and other things are no longer anything but intensities of deterritorialized sound … It is no longer a question of a resemblance between the comportment of animal and that of man … The animal does not speak "like" a man but pulls from the language tonalities totally lacking signification … To make the sequences vibrate, to open

Dalmatian, ©R.L. Gregory, *The Intelligent Eye* (Weidenfeld & Nicolson, 1970), 14.
Photograph by R.C. James.

the word onto unexpected internal intensities—in short, an asignifying *intensive utilization* of language."[36] These deterritorialized sounds constitute the basis for an architecture that *becomes with* its environment. In other words, it is the relationship—and blurriness—between object and field, or between building and context, that gives new meaning to architecture through an aesthetic and ecological responsiveness that works with nature.

Werewolf architecture hopes to be schizophrenic, to be metamorphic instead of metaphoric, to dare to lose clarity between object and background, to be one amongst others, instead of being an isolated and independent unit in the world. As Morton reminds us in *Hyperobjects*, this ecological enmeshing already exists: "Objects entangle one another in a crisscrossing mesh of spacetime fluctuations."[37] It is an embracing of this entanglement that distinguishes werewolf architecture.

And sure enough, an architecture that is responsive, dynamic, and degenerating, may also need to be a little mad.

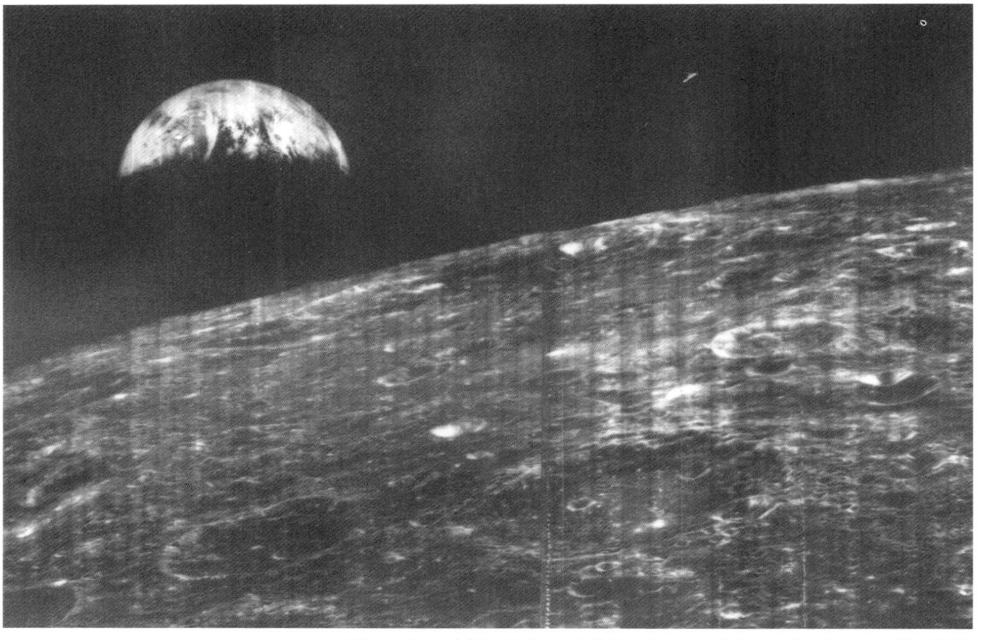

First photo of Earth from the Moon, Lunar Orbiter 1, August 23, 1966.
Courtesy of NASA.

two. **Shapeshifting**

> *His handsome countenance elongates into one of a savage and brute-like shape; the rich garment which he wears becomes a rough, shaggy and wiry skin; his body loses its human contours, his arms and limbs take another form; and, with a frantic howl of misery, to which the woods give horribly faithful reverberations, and with a rush like a hurling wind, the wretch starts wildly away … no longer a man, but a monstrous wolf!*[38]

Shapeshifting is oftentimes a monster's formal response to a dynamic world. Humans change their erect spine to werewolves' quadruped configuration, their noses become elongated snouts, their teeth transform into fangs, and their nails stretch into claws—all favoring specific acts of running, hunting, mauling, and so on. These geometric contortions of bending, stretching, compressing, and twisting occur at multiple scales and on different axes. The shape of the wolf here is not engaged for the hell of it. Form is per*form*ance. The morphological reconfiguration allows the creature to be faster, to bite harder, and to rip better to shreds.

The shifted shape, albeit with performative intent, has semantic consequences through its formal modification. The fearful wolf silhouette is an icon that incites terror in anyone who sees it. The vicious jaw, teeth, and claws are not only the tools of our future being-eaten, but also the signs of them.

In some tales, however, there is no stretching of skin and popping of bones to morph between creatures. Instead, both forms exist at once, one inside the other. This is the case in the Irish tale of the werewolves of the Kingdom of Ossory, where the form of the human is found inside the form of the wolf. According to the legend, every seven years two people from the kingdom are exiled "from their territory and their bodily shape." The story tells of a priest who was forced to spend a night in the Meath woods because of a long journey. There, the priest was approached by two wolves who claimed to be human, and who asked him to deliver last rights to the she-wolf of the couple, who happened to be very ill. To prove their humanness, the male "pulled all the skin off the she-wolf from the head down to the navel, folding it back with his paw as if it were a hand. And immediately the shape of an old woman, clear to be seen, appeared."[39] While the shape does not exactly shift in this case, the two forms co-exist. When one form is revealed, it is the meaning (or function) assigned to the creature that changes.

This notion is explained through the concept of *affordance*, which is borrowed from perceptual psychology. The term was coined by James J. Gibson to describe the perception of the performance of an object; what it can do. Gibson describes this as a fundament of perception, an animalistic means of survival: the wolf can eat me (or, conversely, I can eat the human). The role of affordance in architecture has a long history but is most active in *Architecture Parlante*,[40] a movement in which architecture aimed to communicate the function of a building. For instance, Claude-Nicolas Ledoux's *House of the River Inspector* is a hollow cylindrical form wrapped around the gushing channel, or his *Oikèma* is a brothel in the shape of a penis. Ledoux's mentor, Germain Boffrand, had insisted that buildings should not only *have* meaning, but that they should *express* that meaning.[41] More recently, *Learning from Las Vegas* (1971) presented a similar typology—an architecture that communicated its function through its form: the *duck*. The duck idea originated in a duck-shaped shop that sold, as the text-sign confirmed, "Fresh killed ducks and other fowl." As with Ledoux, the exterior form expressed the program of the building (i.e., selling duck). Venturi and Scott Brown's *duck* was explained through its comparison to the *decorated shed*, a non-descript and functional volume with a highly representational and two-dimensional façade. Whereas the decorated shed split the sign and the enclosure into two separate parts, the duck united the two: the architectural form *was* the sign itself.

Using Charles Sanders Peirce's three types of sign (icon, symbol, index), Peter Eisenman challenged this semantic understanding of an architectural language that communicates program and proposed instead a syntactical reading, one that considered meaning through relationships with other parts.[42] Yet Eisenman's sign returns, in its own ways, to affordance. Perhaps the key example of this is in his *Wexner Center for the Visual Arts* in Columbus, Ohio, where a column-like element is suspended over the entry stair. Grids of columns and beams frame the space. A skeletal corridor that projects from the entry into the interior warns of this system even before the visitor has entered. Their regular placement and identical white forms make for a familiar scene in which both the structural and organizational systems are legible. Yet the attribution of "structure" to the columns is called into question when, in the atrium, one column clearly hangs freely above the floor as if unfinished. By functional standards, this column is purposeless. This provokes reconsideration of the meaning of such a column and potentially those around it that, in fact, do meet the floor.

Rosalind Krauss comments on the role of the sign here: "The non-supporting column is understood as a signifier ('a signal or notation') whose significance depends, at least in part, on the knowledge of everything that it is not."[43] Eisenman's process, and indeed his point, hinges upon the setting up of rules related to the performance of the column that is assumed as a result of its placement in the context of other similar columns. The relationship of the non-supporting column to the supporting columns that surround it is at once broken and intact. The incorrect preconception of the viewer is revealed as the observer perceives its non-supporting function and its meaning is called into question. Resolution of the incongruous column reveals what Eisenman set out to demonstrate: a syntactical understanding of architecture is one that refuses to consume the object in one complete optical bite and instead as a series of interrelated and meaningful pieces, or "traces," of its own "process of becoming."[44]

In this sense, Eisenmanian *becoming* is an evolution in the process of formation, as rocks *become* through heat and pressure but are, in our temporal experience, static.

Mentem non Fornam plus pollere, Alciato, Andrea, Woodblock Print, 1531.

For Eisenman, the becoming occurs through the design process, as iterative accretions or morphological forces cause deformations in the evolving geometry, and the trace of these operations remains embedded in the final form.

Rooted in, but also counter to, this approach, werewolf architecture considers the possibility that these and other morphological transformations continue both physically and perceptually in the final object, in real time, and in response to the surrounding environment.

three. **Material Metamorphosis**

> *Where was the stiff gray hair? The jet-black steel-strong nails? And what was the odd fifth thing that jutted out from his paw at right angles? … Where was his long snout, the bristling whiskers, the flat head, the pointed ears? … He must rid himself of this soft pelt, this hairlessness that made him sick at his stomach just to touch it with his too soft pads.*[45]

Bruce Elliott's "Wolves Don't Cry" is a short story told, unusually, from the perspective of a wolf who changes into a man. *Lobo*, the story's protagonist, is distraught by the disorientation of life in color, lack of raw meat, and the two-leggeds' expectations that he "encumber his legs in cloth that flapped and got in the way, or balance precariously on his hind legs." He expresses the material advantages of the wolf's rough pads and fur over the human's horrid smoothness and softness.

Material transformation is a trademark of the werewolf mutation: from clothed, glabrous skin, to lustrous, shaggy fur; human becomes wolf. In Ancient Rome, werewolves were described as *versipellis,* meaning "turn skin." Later, in medieval times, witches who were accused of also being werewolves were suspected of having two-sided skin: human skin on the outside and wolf fur on the inside (their skins were turned inside out for verification);[46] and in Navajo culture, a "skin-walker" is a witch who has the ability to transform into an animal, often a wolf. Fur is highly functional in allowing the wolf to stay warm, to camouflage, and to protect herself in wildernesses beyond the pasturelands of civilization. But fur also signifies a liberation from the smooth and ordered confines of human norms.

In what is perhaps the best-known werewolf story, though technically not so for many, *Dr. Jekyll and Mr. Hyde*'s duality is mirrored by their house: on the front street, a splendid façade appropriate for one of London's greatest doctors; on the other, trash and squalor, a "blistered and distained door" in a "discolored wall" displaying "the marks of prolonged and sordid negligence."[47] While many have observed the Freudian parallels between the house's duality and that of the eponymous pair,[48] less obvious is the fact that the house, itself, is undergoing its own material metamorphosis. It is important to notice that this material duality offered more than an aesthetic shift in the building: it politicized the house by creating an image of what good and evil "looked" like. Moreover, it rendered visible how a decentering of the human is perceived as "disdained" and "discolored," when in fact it is simply different and perhaps even more aligned with nature.

Seemingly at odds with the formalist theory of the previous section, architectural phenomenologists have long argued for the subjective, sensorial experience over the objective, intellectual legibility of space. Seen through the phenomenological lens, it is architecture's materiality, skin, and tactile qualities that dominate its legibility. In *The Eyes of the Skin*, for example, Juhani Pallasmaa writes of a peculiar exchange that takes place in the architectural experience: "I lend my emotions and associations to the space and the space lends me its aura, which entices and emancipates my perceptions and thoughts. An architectural work is not experienced as a series of isolated retinal pictures, but in its fully integrated material, embodied and spiritual sense.[49]

While formalists like Eisenman even strove to photograph their dematerialized architectural forms in minimal contexts, in many cases in the snow, phenomenologists like Juhani Pallasmaa, Kenneth Frampton, Peter Zumthor, and others argued that the material grain, and its perception through the senses, was precisely the locus of the meaning of the work. Returning to Gibson's ecological theory, the separation of the formal and material worlds seems artificial; affordances depend on both. Indeed, the nauseating success of Méret Oppenheim's *Object* lies in the incongruous triangulation of the form, materiality, and function of the cup and saucer: the form affords drinking, but the furry materiality opposes it.

In architecture, materiality and the articulation of the part over the whole provide as much legibility as its formal systems. This communication of meaning need not be subjective: materials and components can tell objective stories about a material's provenance or a component's fabrication in which traces of their coming-into-being operate indexically.

Werewolf architecture introduces furriness into the lexicon of contemporary architecture, where material and component have as much meaning as form. Further, the inclusion of materiality is also an inclusion of time: as materials change over time, in their composition and combination, a renewed respect is necessitated, not only for *becoming*, but its opposite, *entropy*, through weathering, decomposition, and dismantling.

Object, Méret Oppenheim, Paris, 1936.
Fur-covered cup, saucer, and spoon, Cup 4 3/8" in diameter; saucer 9 3/8" in diameter; spoon 8" long, overall height 2 7/8".

The Art of Perceptual Trickery

A domesticated girl that's all you ask of me
Darling it is no joke, this is lycanthropy
Moon's awake now, with eyes wide open
My body is craving, so feed the hungry

S-O-S she is in disguise
S-O-S she is in disguise
There's a she-wolf in disguise,
Coming out, coming out, coming out.[50]

While duplicity is fundamental to her character, a werewolf often struggles to conceal her transformative tendencies. In a human state, hints of *otherness* leak out in the form of extra-bushy eyebrows, low-set ears, long fingernails, and general hairiness, especially on the hands and feet, but it is often not until after the transformation that those clues make sense.

In Clemence Housman's 1896 story, "The Were-wolf," White Fell is a disarmingly beautiful woman who uses her innocent appearance to enter a country house and beguile the family. Though there are clues to her true nature, the family does not suspect the sweet feminine beauty to be associated with the paw-prints and sounds of the wolf that they believe to be outside: "She was a maiden, tall and very fair. The fashion of her dress was strange, half masculine, yet not unwomanly. A fine fur tunic, reaching but little below the knee, was all the skirt she wore; below were the cross-bound shoes and leggings that a hunter wears. A white fur cap was set low upon the brows, and from its edge strips of fur fell lappet-wise about her shoulders; two of these at her entrance had been drawn forward and crossed about her throat, but now, loosened and thrust back, left unhidden long plaits of fair hair that lay forward on shoulder and breast, down to the ivory-studded girdle where the axe gleamed."[51] White Fell convinces the family, through her initial appearance, that she is one thing. And while they should know better, she lulls them into a false sense of security, which makes her eventual revelation all the more shocking.

This perceptual trickery underlies all three of the werewolf traits of lunacy, shapeshifting, and material metamorphosis through an "aha" moment. This event is

akin to the joke, the setting up of one scenario only for a second one to undermine it.[52] The architectural joke, like the hanging "column" in Eisenman's *Wexner Center*, relies on the expectation of a certain situation—in this case, that all columns "should" touch the ground. The disruption of that fallacy has the effect of being funny because it makes the observer rethink all other columns by questioning their ontological enclosures of existence: after all, what is a column?

Endlessly setting up an expectation and overturning it, werewolf architecture is always in this "aha" realm: in the moment of getting a joke. It *was* something, now it *is* something else. For the werewolf, this liminal status, "precisely *neither man nor beast*,"[53] "between the forest and the city,"[54] and between nature and culture,[55] motivates a set of diverse and dynamic conditions. Being "between" allows one to be malleable and lithe while reacting to the dynamism of the world, breaking free from the constraints of a pure geometric cage and from fixed and idealized form.

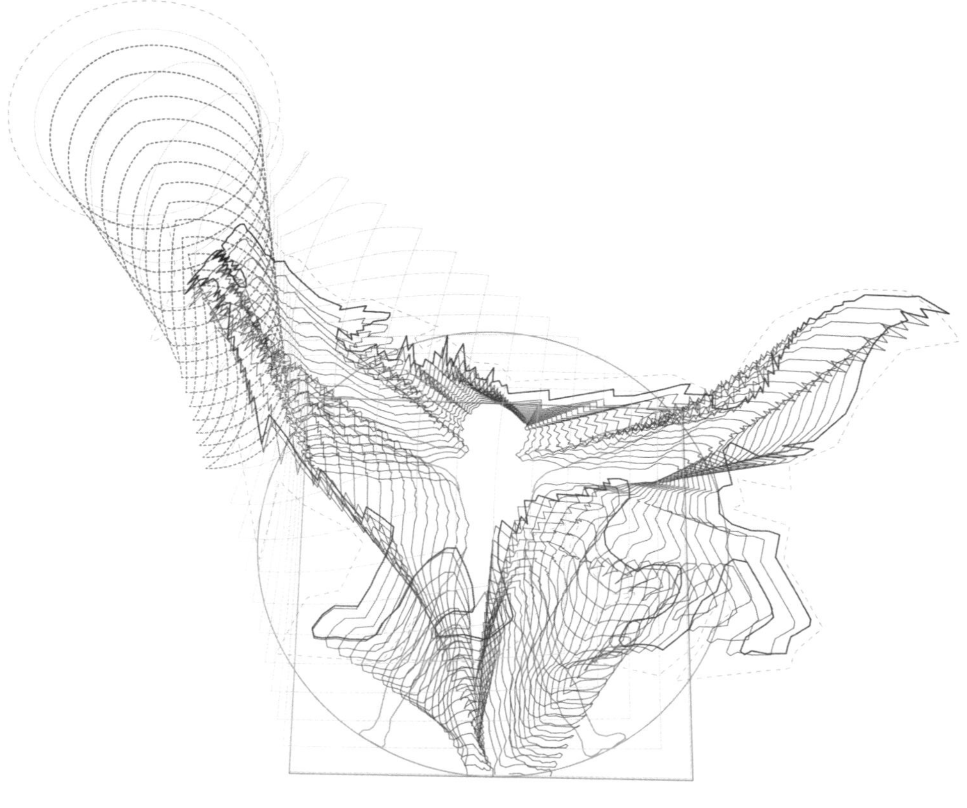

From Strategy to Tactic

Caroline O'Donnell and José Ibarra

You could build a fortification, but an umbrella and a handshake might be enough.[1]

In a misremembered quote from Reyner Banham's 1957 studio brief, an alternative to architecture's seemingly inevitable permanence and solidity is proposed in two parts: the first, a device that is minimal, flexible, and responsive to climate and need; the second, a barely tangible agreement, more concept than matter. In the fiction conjured by the statement, these two fleeting devices function as well as, if not better than, the bricks-and-mortar alternative.

The fortress is the ultimate example of a static object, having as its primary goal the function of exclusion. Thick walls resist the impact of catapults, battering rams, trebuchets, and cannon fire. Its articulated geometries, including bastions, moats, trenches, and battlements, counter any attacks. Here, exclusion is aimed toward an enemy. Yet, all architecture could be considered an act of exclusion in some sense: isn't protection from vermin, friends, thieves, and weather a fundamental necessity of any basic shelter, after all?

If Banham's handshake (or treaty, in the original version) solves the problem of the invading enemy, his umbrella (or hat) is the least amount of equipment needed to exclude the rain. This basic device is highly specific in its usefulness. It is agile, nimble, and responsive. The fact that it retracts when *not* raining is perhaps as important as its appearance when needed. The handshake or treaty, likewise, is not physically present at all times. Both are cunning and tactical responses to dynamic and unpredictable external forces.

Banham applied this train of thought to architecture in his essay, "A Home is Not a House," pondering what the role of traditional architecture might be in the new mechanized age:

> *When your house contains such a complex of piping, flues, ducts, wires, lights, outlets, ovens, sinks, refuse disposers, hi-fi reverberators, antennae, conduits, freezers, heaters—when it contains so many services that the hardware could stand up by itself without any assistance from the house, why have a house to hold it up?*[2]

Implied here is the notion that mechanical systems are not architecture—they are outside of the discipline—yet they threaten, in Banham's fantastical scenario,

to overpower and make redundant the bricks and mortar of architecture proper. Similarly, while architecture has always been dynamic and transforming in some ways (drawbridges are raised, doors swing, windows open, chimneys vent, louvers rotate, elevators lift, heaters pump, electricity flows, toilets flush, roofs leak, materials erode, ivy grows, damp rises, termites attack, and so on), buildings that are entirely dynamic are oftentimes considered a cultural threat to architects.[3] Existing as it does, outside a multifarious norm, transformative architecture might be to the discipline what the monster is to the species.

In fact, if architects think of architecture as "having evolved from the elemental human defiance against nature,"[4] then an evolution that welcomes nature must produce an organism beyond the normal. And while defiance against the dynamic forces of nature has typically produced an architecture of order and stasis, it follows that the embracing of nature should produce much more malleable responses.

The creators of dynamic devices that disrupt architecture's unyielding status quo have often come from disciplines outside of architecture proper. In 1893, for instance, Thomas Edison built the *Black Maria*, a moving stage set enclosure, fixed

Black Maria Motion Picture Studio, Thomas Edison, 1893. Smith Archive / Alamy Stock Photo.

on a giant horse-powered turntable. The *Black Maria*'s rotation was necessary in order to align the stage with the direct sunlight—the only medium bright enough for the requirements of film—while its envelope protected the scenes from wind and rain. Moving the building itself allowed the heavy cameras to be fixed relative to the stage. This building followed a series of cinematic devices developed by the same inventor, including a kinetograph (motion picture camera) and a kinetoscope (viewing cabinet). Although it technically qualifies as architecture, the *Black Maria* is more primitive machine: scaled-up camera meets vernacular horse-powered mill.

The heyday of mechanically responsive buildings designed by architects cannot be dissociated from the space race of the 1950s and 1960s, which peaked with the first manned moon-landing in 1969. As Lydia Kallipoliti writes, "The house was promoted as a performative machine, capable of providing its own energy and food … [and] delivered as NASA's gift to the optimization of architectural design."[5] Spurred on by futuristic visions on one hand, and unemployment on the other, groups like UK-based Archigram proposed radical visions of the *Walking City,* the *Plug-in City*, and the *Instant City* (1964), featuring balloons, ambulatory buildings, reconfigurable pods, and so on, in anticipation of the inevitable technological future of the space age.[6]

Cedric Price's *Fun Palace* (1961), another fictional project born in the UK, featured an infinitely reconfigurable series of boxes on tracks, to be rearranged depending on program. Groups like Ant Farm (USA) and Haus-Rucker-Co (Austria) worked with inflatables, prosthetics, pods, and other pop-up typologies. And certainly, these groups endeavored to separate themselves from architecture. Ant Farm, for instance, described itself as an "art agency that promotes ideas that have no commercial potential,"[7] while Price notoriously had a business card stating that he was "Anti-Architect No.1."[8]

Following these vintage visions, the twenty-first century has toned down the mechanization and used more subdued, even clunky, means to produce dynamism: Lebbeus Woods's *Horizon Houses* (2000), which either roll under the force of gravity (*Wheel House*) or are jolted into new relationships with the ground by seismic force (*Star House*); OMA's *Prada Transformer* (2009), which is gracelessly reoriented by two cranes based on programmatic alternatives; Bureau Spectacular's mechanically rotated

Phalanstery Module (2008), and manually rotated *White Elephant* (2011); and Ward Shelley and Alex Schweder's *Reactor Module* (2016), a house on a single hinge that tilts and rotates based on the interaction of two humans.

In parallel with the initial rise of mechanization, but also presumably borne as a consequence of witnessing the vulnerability of Earth from space, and realizing its limited resources, was the Whole Earth Movement. Set against the various environmental crises of the 1960s and 1970s, the movement was spearheaded by architects like Ian McHarg and John McHale, who envisioned a path for architecture that would work *with* nature. McHale saw the spaceship as a "microminiaturized version of the Earth itself, a simulated planetary vehicle for the larger human community,"[9] and a model for how we might rethink our behavior with respect to the environment. While mechanically leaning sustainable trends have been born out of this thinking, so too has another trend in which the acceptance of nature and its transformative forces are central. This more phenomenal branch begs for a consciousness of time, process, and place, by exhibiting tactile layers of accretion and dissolution through weathering, decomposing, melting, rotting, and so on.

Natural dynamism operates at a slower speed and with a different motivation than the mechanical or animal-powered formal change, instead generating material or chemical changes. While the mechanical transformations of the late twentieth century were overwhelmingly motivated by programmatic reconfigurations, this slow dynamism is a rather passive response to an inevitably dynamic exterior: wet, dry, sun, shade, wind, lee, animals burrowing, plants rooting, and so on.

Although architecture proper continues to obsess about repairing, cleaning, anodizing, sealing, painting, and generally limiting the decay of building materials, a new generation of architects have embraced the accruing dirt (Lydia Kallipoliti, R&Sie(n), Anna Heringer), rust (Herzog de Meuron, Peter Zumthor), soot ("Shou-Sugi-Ban" techniques), weeds and roots (David Benjamin), and water (Diller Scofidio + Renfro); as well as the eroding forces of the weather (stpmj, Emerging Objects), of pests and wildlife (Nikole Bouchard, Joyce Hwang), or the generative forces of draft animals (R&Sie(n)/François Roche), and herbivores (Ensamble Studio).

The search for entropy and the push back against mechanization brings us, strangely, back to Banham. In his "A Home is Not a House" essay, Banham reprimands

humans for having two static ways of dealing with the environment: either they avoid it by hiding in a cave, or they interfere with it by lighting a fire. Instead, Banham ponders, could we create an architecture that is not static, but as supple as the nature just beyond the controlled conditions of the cave or the campfire? "Unlike the living space trapped with our forbearers under a rock or roof," he writes, "the space around a campfire has many unique qualities which architecture cannot hope to equal—above all, its freedom and variability."[10] This state of intermediacy—of being in-between something or at the verge of becoming something else—neither caters for interior nor exterior conditions exclusively, but rather privileges responsive ways in which architecture might occur in that space between caves and campfires.

If architecture began with the recognizable entity of a body inscribed in two idealized geometries—floating in unknown abstract space, contained, and made stationary—Banham's various metaphors may just help shift the focus toward becoming rather than being, operating in an active physical and temporal reality and no longer in a static geometry. This dynamic thinking might serve to reactivate the discipline, shifting its gears from reliability, durability, and stasis, to instability, impermanence, and fluctuation.

Architects have only to claim the agency of handshakes and umbrellas, the agency of the zone around the campfire: the agency of the werewolf.

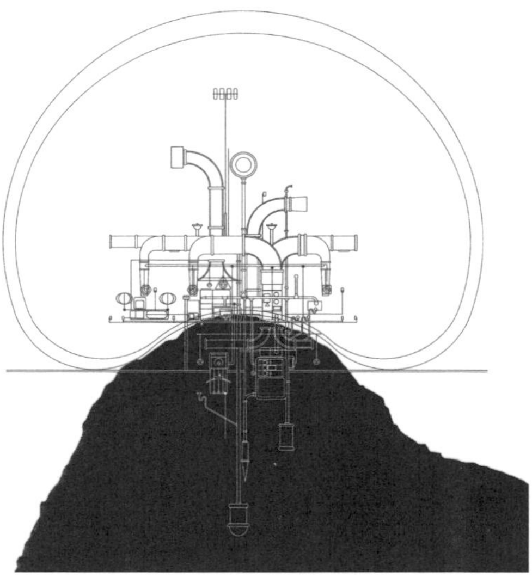

Drawing after Reyner Banham's *Anatomy of a House.*

Perceptual Metamorphoses: Becoming With

Kari Weil

The fearful transformation of a werewolf haunts Ursula Le Guin's short story, "The Wife's Tale." "He was a good husband," the wife asserts in the first line, even as she and the narrator slowly come to accept the truth behind the telltale signs of something amiss in his appearance. She sees a different look in her "mate's" eyes as he returns from hunting, then spots a strange smell that stays in his hair, and finally witnesses the actual "changing." She notices it first in the feet: "they grew long, and fleshy, and white. And no hair on them." And then the "hair begun to come away all over his body," his ears also disappeared, his mouth flattened, teeth whitened and finally, "he stood up on two legs." To the ultimate surprise of the reader, the husband has become "the hateful one," a human.[1]

"The Wife's Tale" is a reverse werewolf story that plays with the reader's expectations and how we misread or ignore conflicting signs of evidence, such as the hair turning to flesh rather than vice versa. Such misreading may be likened to the tendency we humans have to screen out distracting stimuli and to focus on what we expect or want to see before us. We expect the persistence of our world and this can lead to a comical "aha" moment when a scenario is reevaluated in a new context. Such perceptual screening can make it difficult for a human to understand what the biologist Jakob von Uexküll called an animal's particular "Umwelt" or world view, as it also makes it easier for us to interfere in that world.[2] Instead, non-human animals, like the wife in the story, are less likely to screen out conflicting stimuli.[3] The proverb, *Homo homini lupus est* (man is a wolf to man) draws attention to our intentional beastliness toward other humans, but sidesteps the fact of our continuing disregard for and destruction of the *Umwelten* of other animals. Our understanding of wolf behavior has changed greatly since ancient times and especially since Thomas Hobbes, who drew on the proverb for his understanding of warring societies. We now understand wolves' pack mentality to be responsible not only for their documented sociality and ability to cooperate on a variety of tasks, but also for the very possibility of co-evolution between canids and humans.[4]

The literary tradition of human-animal transformations dates back at least to Ovid's *Metamorphoses* in the eighth century. The fifteen books of the *Metamorphoses* follow various transformations of human to animal or inanimate nature, as well as from animal or fungus back to human. Ovid focuses on both the causes and effects of these transformations, which are often violent.

In the twentieth century, Franz Kafka's own *Metamorphosis* tells of a similar transformation. The hard-working salesman, Gregor Samsa, awakens one morning to find himself turned into a "monstrous vermin," for reasons which are never given.[5] This calls attention to a major difference between the two authors. For Ovid, metamorphoses are most often imposed by a god or higher power as a punishment for an act committed. Gregor's metamorphosis is evidence of what is often referred to as the Kafka-esque—awful and frightening situations which occur with no apparent cause. One may be turned into an animal, trapped in an endless burrow, or arrested and put on trial without justification, with no logic or moral that can explain this fate, nor help with finding a "way out."

Kafka's stories are often read as allegories for the way the Law and its servants act in fundamentally unjust ways, locking up or condemning persons for no other reason than the way they look. Such readings do not address the function of the animal or animals with which so many of Kafka's stories are filled. Are they merely metaphors for humans who are not accepted as such, or who are not regarded as fully human? To be sure, in "becoming animal," Gregor instigates a series of transformations in his family, his living quarters, and ultimately in himself that expose the limitations and even cruelty of their previous, bourgeois lifestyle, and hint at the possibility of a new way to live.

But metamorphosis is not metaphor, or so claim Gilles Deleuze and Félix Guattari in an essay on what they call "becoming animal."[6] This is a concept, or more precisely a "real" process, that can undo or "deterritorialize" our understanding and image of the human by replacing taxonomies of exterior form and function with the less visible and more sensible forces of affect and movement. To become animal is to value life for the intensities of felt experience over any identifiable act or essence. Indeed, it is to challenge the very notion of identity since "becoming produces nothing but itself."[7] It is an endless process that never arrives at being, that is at being one, nameable thing or state. Thus, one does not even become "an animal," an idea confirmed by the original German of Kafka's story, which describes Gregor with a double negative. He is transformed into an "**un**geheures **un**geziefer" animal: that is, neither measurable nor fit for sacrifice. Such is the monster whose proportions and purpose are regarded as indeterminate, and whose ongoing betweenness or unrecognizable shapeshifting is the very image of becoming.

The monstrous liminality, what Deleuze and Guattari see as the productive potential of becoming animal, becomes clearer if we contrast Gregor's metamorphosis with that of Red Peter, the ape in Kafka's "A Report to the Academy."[8] Red Peter was wounded and captured by a well-known merchant. His only chance to escape captivity and find "a way out" is to prove his humanity by becoming recognizably human. In this, he succeeds brilliantly by smoking, spitting, drinking red wine, and finally, learning to converse as "an average European."[9] Whether an act of self-education or assimilation (the story is often read as an account of the pressures to assimilate on the part of Jews like Kafka), Red Peter's transformation is essentially an act of imitation, not one of generative discovery. "There was no attraction for me in imitating human beings; I imitated them because I needed a way out, and for no other reason."[10] For this, he was forced to "whip" his "ape nature" out of him. As an ape, he admits, he may have known that "spacious feeling of freedom on all sides."[11] By contrast, he describes the so-called "human freedom" as a "mockery of Holy Mother Nature," like the "self-controlled movement" of acrobats swinging on trapezes which, he says, would surely rouse the laughter of the apes they claim to resemble. [12]

Ultimately, Red Peter's goal was "not to stay motionless."[13] It is significant that it is precisely a newfound sense of movement and of space that Gregor Samsa comes to experience in his "becoming animal," if only briefly. In the first of the three parts of *The Metamorphosis,* we witness Gregor's efforts to deny his bodily transformation so that he can get to work, as his family, and especially his father, are filled with both fear and pitiless abjection of the son's changed image and voice. Toward the very end of the same part, however, after Gregor's father has essentially locked him into his room, he begins to adapt to his changing body and to experience new physical pleasures which were denied to him as human.

> *Without remembering that he was still unaware what powers of movement he possessed … he fell down with a little cry upon all his numerous legs. Hardly was he down when he experienced for the first time this morning a sense of physical comfort; his legs had firm ground under them; they were completely obedient, as he noted with joy; they even strove to carry him forward in whatever direction he chose.*[14]

Slowly, Gregor's new physical comfort extends to new kinds of recreation and a "blissful absorption" in hanging from the ceiling; "it was much better than lying on the floor; one could breathe more freely; one's body swung and rocked lightly."[15] Gregor's sister, Grete, comes to Gregor's aid by slowly removing the furniture in his room, if not investing in a form of "niche thinking"[16] by opening herself and Gregor to the unexpected, so as to enable him to adjust to a new *Umwelt.* Creative in his adaptation to his environment, and newly intuitive of the ways the other creatures in that environment (i.e., his family) respond to him, Gregor-as-monster slowly immerses himself in a sensate world with an intensity that was previously unknown to him. This monstrous liminality becomes fully apparent in his reaction to his sister's violin playing: "Was he an animal that music had such an effect upon him? He felt as if the way were opening before him to the unknown nourishment he craved."[17] But as Gregor slowly crawls out to partake in that "nourishment," the horrified reaction of the boarders who have been brought in to compensate for Gregor's lost wages and their threats to leave without paying rent, are too much for the family to bear. Even Grete admits that having to support this creature is unjust. Her argument is rational, even, one might say, a model of utilitarian ethics that calculates what is right by what will produce the greatest good or happiness for the greatest number.

> *"He must go," cried Gregor's sister, "that's the only solution, Father. You must try to get rid of the idea that this is Gregor. The fact that we've believed it for so long is the root of all our trouble. But how can it be Gregor? If this were Gregor, he would have realized long ago that human beings can't live with such a creature, and he'd have gone away on his own accord."*[18]

If the creature were Gregor, he would act rationally. By rational calculation, he would conclude that the interests of his family outweigh his own and that he must leave to free them of the responsibility to care for him. The changed creature does not deserve to live, and neither can his death, as the term "ungeziefer" (unclean animal) suggests, be called a sacrifice. There is, of course, much more to Kafka's story, but what is important to underscore here are the implicit warnings of the dangers of holding onto and prioritizing a particular idea or image of the world and its inhabitants—what has been claimed as the exclusive capacity of humans. We see with Red Peter how the "gradual enlightenment" of his becoming human amounts

to an imitation of required, yet ironically degenerate, behavior. What Gregor's family enforces, and what the son must ultimately accept, is the choice between what Deleuze and Guattari characterize as a "re-oedipalization," a return to recognizable, defined, and "useful" familial roles under paternal authority, or death. Simply put, an identity, whether of persons or things, is meant to persist, not to change.

Such are the dangers of the Anthropocene ruled by "the hateful one," and fueled by a utilitarian and capitalist mentality that turns so-called vermin or monsters to waste; not waste that can be recycled or turned to productive use, but trash that must be eliminated. This is why the term Anthropocene is often coupled with that of the Capitalocene and in the past years, the field of animal studies has grown in response to their interrelated concerns.

As the concept of the Anthropocene challenges and changes the status and meaning of the human in the world, so does it bring us to rethink our presumed difference(s) from other beings. We can no longer scientifically prove our exceptionalism. What had previously been thought to distinguish humans from non-human beings has been shown to be possessed by at least some species of non-humans. While many legal and ethical theorists would try to prove the moral standing of non-human animals on grounds that they are like us and share our capacities for consciousness, thinking and language, others seek to know and to celebrate their differences, their capacities for ways of living and being in the world that our reasoning can only begin to fathom. In my own "Report on the Animal Turn," I situate Deleuze and Guattari's "becoming animal" within what I call a counter-linguistic effort to affirm ways of knowing or being that do not depend upon our flawed systems of language and representation. We may know the breed, color, and name of certain animals, but they know us through scent, movement and/or touch; signs that may not even exist for us. To be sure, such efforts might require that we learn to "write like a rat," as Deleuze and Guattari suggest, and to think outside the taxonomic and aesthetic traditions that rendered non-human animals visible within the newly illustrated volumes of 18th-century naturalists. If, however, we also aim for our efforts in this regard to be ethical, then it is imperative that the productive possibilities of "becoming animal," or becoming itself, not be regarded for the knowledge and future of human life alone. As Donna Haraway writes, "if we appreciate the foolishness of human exceptionalism then we know that becoming is always becoming *with,* in a

contact zone where the outcome, where who is in the world, is at stake."[19]

Becoming with Gregor is precisely what his family refused. They could put up with him only as much as was "humanly possible," only so long as he could contribute to the accepted image of the human household and its short term, monetary foundations. That said, Kafka gives little indication of the consequences of their refusal. In 1924, the Anthropocene had yet to be named. Reading the story now, however, it is difficult not to be reminded of the unintended deaths and extinctions of countless species that our built environments and lifestyles have produced. And to think this through is to question how we might rethink and become with those others whose lives we affect and who affect ours. "We become with each other or not at all," Haraway declares, thus confirming recognition of "becoming with" as an ethical demand.[20] Indeed, this demand becomes even more relevant when we recall von Uexküll's notion of the *Umwelt*, for as distinct as the *Umwelten* of different species are (and even of different individuals within species), as much as we focus on the bubbles created by our distinct ways of perceiving and responding to meaningful cues, the fact is that our physical worlds intersect; our constructions become signs which others perceive and interpret. Semiosis is not the property of humans alone, but a principle of life itself. Biosemiosis and zoosemiosis are the very processes that account for niche construction and the fact that, as evolutionary biologist Richard Lewontin pointed out almost forty years ago, organisms do not passively adapt to their environments, but actively construct important components of their niches.[21]

This perception of meaning in the animal world was described as "affordance" by ecological psychologist James J. Gibson in the 1960s.[22] Gibson defines the affordance of an object as "what it offers the animal, what it provides or furnishes, either for good or ill."[23] This "functional meaning" refers to a set of "action possibilities" that are latent in the environment and exist independently of an animal's ability to recognize them, but nevertheless are always related to and dependent upon the animal's capabilities.[24] Jakob von Uexküll's notion of *Umwelt* suggests., alternatively, that the meaning is not intrinsic to the thing but *bestowed* upon it by the animal, or "*acquired* by virtue of having been drawn into that creature's activity."[25] Thus, rather than the animal fitting to its environment, the animal fits its "perceived" environment to itself and gives it meaning through use.[26]

We are all animals who perceive, interpret, and respond to each other and to our shared environments—some in expected, some in novel ways. If Deleuze and Guattari regard becoming as a kind of writing or, perhaps, semiosis, it is one that expands and explodes all accepted or recognizable signs so that "all forms come undone, as do all the significations, signifiers, and signifieds."[27] In this regard, then, we can understand monsters as no more (and no less) than emergent identities, creatures reading and writing in new ways, as they adapt their behavior to novel signs within their environments and become with other-beings. Monsters, like Gregor, are co-creators of hybrid *Umwelten,* and their ways of reading may offer pathways to thinking beyond the static anthropocentric (and capitalocentric) interpretations that we have imposed on the world. Rather than fearing or devouring the werewolves (or werevermin, and all those associated with such names), we need to learn to *become with* them and to be drawn affectively into a world that lies beyond our recognition. In this way, we will be better able to sense, if not to understand what is needed for monsters to flourish in the worlds they newly effect, and so for the rest of us animals along with them.

Lunar (Re)Turns: Cosmology, Ecology, and Extraterrestrial Influence

Spyros Papapetros

Perhaps the condition described as "lunacy" always had an undisclosed architectural affect. The Moon's purported "influence" on humans, an invisible power exercised on an earthly subject by an extraterrestrial object, generates a sequence of unprecedented spatial and formal effects whose covert architectural significance relies on their aberrant topological as well as typological potentials. The historical overlap between the reinvention of the lunacy discourse and the reemergence of the mythic story of the werewolf in the nineteenth century reveals that the transformative effects attributed to the Moon extend beyond individual psychological behavior or bodily morphology; both project into juridical territory to demarcate boundaries between collective bodies of society while at the same time disrupt established classifications in the epistemic areas of natural history and the evolutionary hierarchy of species. This seemingly antithetical effect, at once implacably normative and malleably transgressive, informs lunacy's bipolar constitution in modernity, as well as its veiled legacy within the space of modern design.

Space, in terms of both proximity and distance, is the defining quality in lunacy's power. The Moon is the optically largest object among celestial bodies visible from the Earth. It was always too close, as well as too far, as it remained unreachable until the second half of the twentieth century. Its uncanny proximity would transform the lunar sphere into a curious "double" to the body of the Earth, creating an array of sympathetic analogies with the living inhabitants of the terrestrial surface manifested in its capacity to sway their volatile behavior and mood by the periodicity of its illumination. The volatility associated with the Moon stands in total contrast to the fixity of the stars, whose distances could be coherently mapped on the night sky as figurative animal representations or organized in abstract mathematical relations, and whose harmonic laws informed Pythagorean and Neoplatonic doctrines of proportion. As stated in Rudolf Wittkower's *Architectural Principles in the Age of Humanism*, these macrocosmic correspondences were reflected on the proportional systems devised by Renaissance architectural theorists.[1] According to Reyner Banham, a faint echo of such Renaissance cosmological principles had a belated "influence" on some unrealized designs of mid-century architects following the publication of Wittkower's book in 1949.[2] These proportional analogies, hovering between modernity and the Renaissance, reflect a number of contemporary anxieties about the precarious order of the world after WWII, as well as the imminent collapse of modern architecture.[3]

These historiographic correspondences also demonstrate that such seemingly far-fetched cosmological associations between earthly designs and their extraterrestrial surroundings are periodically triggered by real historical events on Earth that are about to occur, or that have already happened. This is the legacy of a long series of researches on the cultural and iconographic survivals of micro-macrocosmic doctrines conducted by the scholars of the Warburg Library, originally in Hamburg and after 1933 in London, where Wittkower's studies of Neoplatonic influences on architecture were developed. Fritz Saxl, the first director of the Warburg Institute in London, had lectured on the survival of images of the "microcosm and the macrocosm" from pagan antiquity to medieval Christianity and Renaissance humanism.[4] Per Saxl, what was once a matter of religious belief based on the correspondences between stars and humans had transformed into a series of images that were often devoid of their ancient meaning. Soon after, the same cosmological correspondences would turn into a set of practical guidelines informing matters of earthly life of both public and personal importance. The founder of the Warburg Library, Aby Warburg demonstrated in his great essay on Luther and the reformist culture of prognostication that a devout Protestant leader of the sixteenth century would still rely on the opinions of astrologists. Such a leader would consult nativity charts and zodiac calendars before resolving to wage war against his enemies or for determining whether his newborn daughter was destined to become a nun or eventually get married.[5] Warburg's essay described Luther's religious revolution during an era that also witnessed a major social uprising in the 1525 "Peasant's War." Written between 1915 and 1918, the scholar's history of Northern Renaissance astrology also reflected the unprecedented turbulence of Warburg's contemporary era, which witnessed Germany's defeat in the Great War as well as the Bolshevik revolution in Russia. These world-changing events preceded the author's personal decent into madness. While confined in Ludwig Binswanger's psychiatric sanatorium in Kreuzlingen, the scholar appeared to regurgitate the mental split of historical as well as mythological figures in his Luther story, most forebodingly, the murderous melancholy of Saturn, the volatile planet god.[6]

Along with the anthropomorphic figures of the stars, another category of hybrid beings was key in the production of prophesies about the future: namely, monsters, which in 16th-century iconography are often linked to practices of religious

prognostication and political propaganda. A key passage in Warburg's essay[7] describes the "prodigious" Sow of Landser, a monstrous swine with one pig head, two trunks, and eight trotters, which appears in a well-known engraving by Dürer.[8] The collision of two animal bodies in one monstrous creature (de)monstrates not only an ontological but also a spatial disparity caused by the sow's ostensible inability to move forward. The hypothetical movement of its upper legs rooted close to its head and spine appear to resist progress by attempting to run backwards while dangling upside down in the air. The religious representation's ominous teratological sign exists not only in the assemblage of animal limbs but on the contradictions of the spatial directions of its multiple animal appendages, half of which do not meet the ground. However, within the intricate architecture of Warburg's text, the monstrous Sow of Landser and its directional aporias also serve as a resolution that facilitates movement. The cultural historian uses the multi-limb creature as a narratological device to introduce a twist in his plot. As soon as the sow appears, the essay moves from the discussion of prophesy in texts and letters by reformist authors debating the astrological advantages of Luther's birth date, to the discussion of art and specifically the work of Dürer, whose prior involvement in discourses of prophecy

Engraving of *The Monstrous Sow of Landser*, Albrecht Dürer, c. 1496.

finds its most intricate expression in his well-known engraving of *Melencolia I* and its brooding allegorical figure posing under (what Erwin Panofsky has read as) a "lunar rainbow."[9] The iconological shift from animal monstrosity to human pondering and scientific reflection leads Warburg's essay to its Faustian conclusion describing the polarity between "magical practice and cosmic mathematics" manifested in the "modern scientist['s]" attempts to "insert the conceptual space of rationality between himself and the object."[10] The sow's impossible movement ultimately creates an oscillating motion as well as a rift between magic and reason that runs through several modern eras. This is the unstable tectonic legacy of the stars that is not present in Wittkower's history of "harmonic proportions."[11]

As shown in the microcosmic images assembled in Warburg's *Mnemosyne* Atlas, put together by the scholar and his collaborators in the 1920s, several practical (and more down to earth) correspondences between stars and humans would survive well into the early modern era. For instance, astrological calendars indicating the appropriate time for extracting a tooth or performing bloodletting were hung in barber shops of Northern Europe as late as the early eighteenth century.[12] However, while these mundane medical interventions authorized by the stars aimed to ameliorate the condition of an ailing human, the social practices associated with lunacy in the modern eras of the late eighteenth and nineteenth centuries mainly intended to confine, restrict, and ultimately ostracize the body of the psychologically distressed person legally proclaimed "lunatic."[13] While the influence of the moon in the misdoings and irrational psychological behavior of a person were soon scientifically rejected, the terms "lunatic" and "lunacy" persisted. These terms became imbedded in juridical and medical terminology informing a number of "lunacy laws" in the course of the nineteenth century, addressing criminal or other delinquent behavior that abided well into the twentieth and even the beginnings of the twenty-first.[14] Only in December 2012, then-president Barack Obama signed legislation approved by the U.S. House of Representatives that eliminated the word "lunatic" from language contained in federal laws.[15]

Divested from property or any form of personal agency, "lunatics" were assigned to local madhouses and later private or public asylums, where they lived in often appalling conditions. Once again, issues of distance and proximity appeared to play an important role in the volatile state of "lunatic" patients. [16] As social historians

have amply demonstrated, "lunacy" marked dividing lines in terms of race, ethnicity or heritage, gender, social, and economic status, and was often presented as "cause" in criminal investigations.[17] These strict dividing strategies represent lunacy's social architecture, which was then replicated in the spatial divisions of its building institutions. Within the walls of the lunatic asylum, the uncontrollable influences of the Moon as well as the territorial contests in economic and political power represented by the body of the "lunatic" would be enclosed and rigorously regulated in the institutional space of the asylum.[18] As the several institutional histories of madness written by Michel Foucault and then a series of social and architectural historians have demonstrated, the "lunatic asylum"[19] and later on the federal- or state-owned mental hospital managed to simultaneously control and preserve "madness" by replicating the mechanisms of its spatial paranoia in a series of perfectly rational geometric designs that often overlap with the typology of prisons.†

If we go back now to the nineteenth century, which generated the epistemological rift running through lunacy's modern reinvention, we may be able to discover an alternative motive for the reemergence of the werewolf myth closely associated

† To offer an example of the architecture of the lunatic asylum and its development into the mental hospital, instead of citing the voluminous literature, I will attempt a chronological as well as slightly (auto) biographical digression, which is deliberately demoted to the equivocally privileged margin of a long footnote, similar to those Freud used to insert in his text while revising his essays. During the course of my Princeton seminar on *The Architecture of Psychoanalysis*, which produced the essay "Diagram as Remedy" by a young Caroline O'Donnell, republished in this volume, and which consisted of a series of close readings of diagrams and texts by Freud probing the spatial and tectonic strategies of psychic operations, the class also watched a film. It was the 1948 Hollywood melodrama *The Snake Pit*, based on the homonymous novel by Mary Jane Ward of 1946—a rare depiction on the big screen of the application of Freudian psychoanalysis in the treatment of schizophrenia in mental hospitals in the United States and whose representation of traumatic psychological disturbances enjoyed particular popularity after the end of the war. The film's narrative is not only orthodoxly psychoanalytic, punctuated by a series of flashbacks zooming on the traumatic experiences of the main character, a female patient named Virginia Cunningham suffering a memory loss, but also rigorously architectural, as the story follows the trajectory of Virginia's assignment in the various wards of the mental hospital she has been confined independently of her own volition. Much like Freud's own diagrams, the film projects on the screen a hypothetical floor plan made of solid and dotted lines through which the audience can reconstruct a medical chart of Virginia's psychological condition as she is being moved across the entire sequence of the hospital's hierarchy of secluded wards in the female-only institution. The wards are numbered from 1 to 33, according to the inmates' professionally assessed mental state, yet it is not clear how they are arrayed or connected. As she makes progress in her psychoanalytic treatment, Virginia moves up to the highest wards closest to no. 1, but when she suffers a violent relapse, she is demoted to ward no. 33 at the lowest level of the hospital, the so-called "snake pit," housing the most mentally infirm patients, for whom there appears to be no cure. Virginia ultimately escapes the confines of the snake pit and is released from the hospital via the successful application of the transference she experiences with her convivial analyst who, under the gaze of a portrait of Freud hanging on the wall and constantly surveying the analytic process

with the moon's volatility, in which the same epistemic cleavage acquires an ontological character. The history of nineteenth-century science marks a period of reclassification when the practice of natural history was succeeded by the new discipline of biology in which all categories of life, including function, form, and space had to be (archi)tectonically reinvented. However, the scientific facts as well as myths of monstrosity informing the werewolf story portent that the formalization of these living processes also contained the possibility of their radical undoing. The dynamic capacity of living space served once more as the instigator. The course of human and animal evolution outlined in Darwin's *Origin of the Species* transformed the "strife for life" into a "strife for space," the contest among all species for spatial dominance through territorial expansion. Later evolutionists extended the same territorial struggle among the individual parts of every living organism, whose external limbs and internal organs had to fight for their survival via the organic processes of atrophy and hypertrophy regulating the morphological development of all animal species.[20]

Rudiments, the formal and spatial remnants of anterior organizations, were

from the upper top of the camera frame, unveils to her the origin of her trauma, which lies, predictably, in her childhood experiences with her father. Next to this authorized interpersonal transference between analyst and analysand, the film also depicts a spatial form of transference when the wards of the asylum

Drawing after the scene of Ward no. 33 in *The Snake Pit*, drawn by Philippe Lapierre, 2020.

essentially a form of innate monstrosity that was more or less present within every living organism, and which revealed a closer proximity among species distanced in the evolutionary scale. As Darwin's 1872 study of "expression in men and animals" illustrated, there were common traces in humans with different animals. Several species of apes appeared to "laugh" or "chuckle" when overjoyed or "weep" with tears when distressed. Similarly, hidden connections to cats and dogs became evident every time people's hair bristled because of their anxious condition or when they exposed their "canine tooth" while "sneering" in defiance.[21] Darwin's inclusion of the photograph of an "insane woman" in order "to show the condition of her hair" and numerous other photographs of psychiatric patients among the illustrations in his book, which references several medical reports from "lunatic asylums" in Sussex and elsewhere in Britain, displays the purported linkages of these animal remnants with psychotic conditions ascribed to persons doomed by law as "lunatics."[22] Following Darwin, madness and lunacy were "expressions" not simply of human emotional states, but the side effects of animal-to-human evolution. The transgressive psychological state associated with lunacy was no longer conditioned by the periodic beaming of the moon, but by the animal lineage of humans. Such animal origins were no longer connected with the astrological figures of the planets yet could be retraced in evolutionary histories of life that extended to the geological

are swiftly replaced by those of Virginia's family house or the concert hall where she (re)met her future husband via series of "whip camera pans." Spaces that are geographically and chronologically distant in real life appear to rhyme and interlock on the screen, as happens in Freud's dream narratives via the psychic operations of "displacement" and "condensation." This spatial fluidity is in total contrast with the insularity and unyielding rigidity of the asylum's ward enclosures always blocked by locked doors and demarcated by other less solid, yet equally impermeable, spatial prohibitions similar to those described by Freud in the second chapter of *Totem and Taboo*. For example, in the snake pit of ward no. 33, inmates are made to walk around a carpet, which none of them is allowed to step on—a spatial prohibition that unavoidably instigates a riotous transgression by one of the elderly patients, Emma, who dares to break course and perform a defiant song and dance on the carpet before being promptly removed by the nurses. Virginia's final release from the hospital and transition into so-called free life is marked by the fact that, much to her surprise, the doors are now unlocked. The vertical turning of the handle and horizontal rotation of the door leaf unfold as a revolving miracle registered on the screen by the opening of the mouth and rolling eyes on Olivia de Havilland's ecstatic physiognomic expression. Unsurprisingly, the hospital's deceptive "open access" policy ultimately leads to Virginia's rehabilitation as a married housewife in mid-century America that could be equally confining. In all their crudeness and subtlety, *The Snake Pit*'s detailed descriptions of life inside a modern mental hospital reveal the architectural legacy of lunacy in modern spaces—a type of architecture that is ecstatically split between the fluidity of spatial transference and the rigidity of institutional confinement. Also, an architecture that ends up replicating the typology of the schizophrenic condition it attempts to cure by the very layout and contested territoriality of its enclosures.

history of planet earth. And the lunar affect was now imbedded within evolutionary time.

Werewolving is an extreme case in the roman of evolution. As the various literary versions of the legend describe in graphic detail, during this process, the entire body of a human transforms into that of a wolf,[23] the ancestor of the dog preceding its domestication, whose familiar and occasionally uncanny countenance punctuates Darwin's descriptions of animal behavior, including personal experiences with his own canine(s).[24] The almost instantaneous transformations in the body of the werewolf could reverse hundreds of millennia of human and animal evolution in the space of a few minutes or even seconds. Animal remnants formerly eclipsed from the human body, such as sharp teeth and extensive hair growth, would resurface to reclaim their place. This not simply a shape- or form-shifting transformation, but also a space-altering reorganization. Such spatial reorganization involves not only a single living organism, whose skull, neck, appendages, and trunk become abnormally elongated, but also an entire group of animal species, whose bodies would aberrantly shift places in the taxonomic charts of evolutionary classification via the designing imagination of the werewolf storyteller.[25]

One of the most radical as well as fundamentally architectonic transformations in the body of the werewolf is the (re)turn from bipedalism to a quadruped state, in which all four appendages of the animalized human come into contact with the earthly surface. In Frederick Kiesler's unpublished book manuscript, *Magic Architecture: The Story of Human Housing*, the architect sketches an imaginative evolutionary narrative in which the origin of the first architectural site, the cave, coincides with the emergence of the human being standing in two feet.[26] According to Kiesler, *protohumans* enter the cave in all fours by a small aperture and only gradually *dig* their way up creating the interior of the cave. While doing so, they use the cave's semi-formed enclosure as an orthopedic mechanism for standing upright (reminiscent of Lacan's *trote-bébé* in his "Mirror Stage" essay). Per Kiesler, it is as much the human that creates the cave and reshapes it into a living space, as it is the cave that supports the vertical erection of the human. In his earlier project for an unrealized exhibition for New York's Museum of Natural History in 1944, Kiesler proposed to diagram the deep "geological" history of human and animal evolution. The architect would organize all plant and animal organisms into a vertical stratification. The illustrated chart moves

from seaweed, starfish, and a worm placed at the bottom to multi-leg creatures and quadruped mammals further distanced from the ground, placed in the middle along with a marsupial capable of standing on two feet. At the top there is an animal creature climbing up vertically on a tree along with a bat flying on air.[27] Significantly, humans do not figure among earthly bipeds but are elevated onto aerial space inside a Leonardo-like "flying-machine," morphing into a modern airplane and hovering among the ominous bats. The "modern magic man" of contemporary technology has fully emancipated himself from the earth in order to attack his fellow humans from a distance and seize their territorial space with his telekinetic weapons.[28] Evidently, Kiesler's evolutionary stories of bodily and built architecture reflect the cosmic anxieties of the mid-1940s triggered by massive aerial assaults culminating in the throwing of the atomic bomb, during which the manuscript of *Magic Architecture* was drafted.[29] If in Warburg's studies of astrological prognostication, written during the Great War, stars and comets could only signal a universal catastrophe, in Kiesler's evolutionary narratives, written at the end of World War II, aerial objects made by human hands had the material agency to realize a worldwide disaster.

Yet, if these space-altering transformations were associated with the "magic" of either Renaissance astrology or the mid-twentieth-century techno-politics of global superpowers and their respective world-transforming historical transitions, what would be the equivalent historical changes triggering the lycanthropic and other "shape-shifting" effects in the contemporary architecture of the last two decades that have informed the architectural projects in this book and others like them?[30]

Architectural theorists have reviewed the animated blobs of contemporary architecture as the offspring or aftereffect of the hypertrophic economy of the 1990s: the former's explosive forms mimicking the booming or inflated "financial bubbles" of the latter.[31] It would appear that the 1990s displaced politics in favor of formal liberation. However, a cultural critic viewing things through a more recent perspective could also read the same agitated structures as omens of the expansive economic deflation and larger resource and environmental crisis that precipitated in the following decade. This divided legacy cladding a cultural with a morphological rift traverses the work of CODA and its collaborators and may be the most essential "shifting" strategy underpinning their design projects.

It would be hard to miss the evolutionary analogies in designs like the *Urchin* circus or the environmental references in a project such as *Primitive Hut* (a collaborative work under the banner of OMG). The spinal and other skeletal twistings of *Urchin* renegotiate the standing or vertical with the recumbent or horizontal positioning of the body. While doing so, the project retraces continuities with a series of ambient animal bodies like that of the urchin, a marine organism with no visible trunk that is able to anchor and protect itself on account of its spiky appendages. These projects, in their correspondences with animal and vegetal forms, reference not only a *prehuman* but also a *prearchitectonic condition*—a state that precedes the origins of human or built architecture, yet exists in natural objects and continues to survive as remnant following the establishment of human building.[32] The memory of the *prearchitectonic* state informs a project like the *Primitive Hut* pavilion, which marks the theoretical and historiographic origins of architecture via a modular structure with a palpable drive to return to nature and thus *unbecome* architecture through the process of material decay. This project does not display the spectacular morphological effects of the werewolf's explosive transformation but a slow transubstantiation occurring in the very sap of the vegetal branch, which gradually distances itself from the hexagonal module.

These are the effects of a self-inflicted "lunacy" within the very pores of vegetal and architectural matter, which show the alternative environmental benefits of decay within the built environment as opposed to its constant disavowal via restoration practices. As shown by the enduring legacy of D'Arcy Thompson's *On Growth and Form*, scientists and designers alike were obsessed with the formal as well as economic capabilities of growth throughout the twentieth century.[33] On the contrary, the shape- and space-shifting alterations that occur inside each of the slowly rotting units of *Primitive Hut* bring to light the enormous formal and tectonic capacities of decay and degeneration when these two natural processes become absolved of the negative cultural connotations imposed on them by late nineteenth-century medical science and discriminatory politics of social and biological determinism. As shown in Thompson's statistical illustrations, growth cannot only be programmed by a series of scientific principles but also measured and diagrammed in charts, tables, and graphs, by the means of which progress becomes an object of design. But what kind of design can objectively predict or delineate the trajectory of decay, which, by

definition consists of a series of accidents, including a series of unpredictable twists and turns, during the organism's vertiginous free-fall from its hypothetical "peak" condition?

Progressing in its slow decay and thus following the principles of a *regressive* form of evolution, *Primitive Hut* ultimately builds a void, similar to the one shown in the engraving of the frontispiece of Laugier's 1755 *Essai sur l'architecture*. In this work, the raised arm and finger of the antique allegorical figure points to none of the four tree columns or the classical pediment, but to the central *gap* that *supports* the natural/artificial structure. Like every story of origin, which by necessity entails an eschatological aspect, architecture's foundational myth projects the *framing* of its own dissolution. That would be the alternative ecological endpoint brought forward by OMG to Laugier's enlightenment perspective, which for some architectural historians of the postwar period marks the origins of "functionalist" modern architecture.[34]

In a more Warburgian reading of the same iconographic *scene*, the originating myth of rational architectural construction is uncannily close to its antique mythological and often irrational foundation. Such reading could also reveal a clandestine link

---

‡ A more recent cinematic example that links the foundational architectural model of the hut with the allegorical theme of melancholia can be found in Lars von Trier's *Melancholia* (2011), which also describes a pronounced cosmological and eschatological perspective. Here, Melancholia is a planet that is on a collision course with the Earth, and whose precipitous approach toward our planet causes severe depression on one of the two main characters of the film, Justine (played by Kirsten Dust). In the first part of the film, Justine appears constantly under the light of the moon, as she bathes naked under the moonlight during the night of her wedding. However, Justine is no old-fashioned "lunatic," but a modern-day "depressive," on whom the intense influence of the moon and the approaching Melancholia are manifested by the gravitational effects of *dropping*, which have both physical and ethical repercussions. Justine first drops her sexual inhibitions as she initiates a brief sexual intercourse with one of the wedding guests and then drops on her knees to urinate on the soil as the full moon beams on her ecstatic face; then she drops out of her marriage and at the same time drops her boss's requests and quits her high-profile job. By the beginning of the film's second part, she can barely open her falling eyelids, get out of bed, and stand on her two feet to take a taxi to the "castle" of her sister's family—an opulent chateau in the forest, actually located in Sweden. Ultimately, it is a much humbler architectural structure that marks Melancholia's arrival in the film's apocalyptic conclusion. I refer to the conical hut made of tree branches, cut and leaned together by Justine and her young nephew, which is described in the film as a "magic cave," yet resembles a prehistoric or traditional tent, such as the *lavvu* constructed by the Sami indigenous people in the North of Europe. This improvised cave-tent has, however, no fur-skin cladding. This brings the tent even closer to the ahistorical models of the conical hut made of tree branches that we see in nineteenth-century architectural treatises, such as the Viollet-le-Duc's *Histoire de l'habitation humaine* (1875), whose proposed architectural prototype distances itself from the pedimented classical temple of Laugier and, via an anthropological detour, returns to the arboreal model of Vitruvius, according to whom humans join the branches of trees to form their first abode, following a fire that at some point breaks out in the forest. In its conflation of the cave (by name) and the tent (by structure), the "magic cave" of von Trier's *Melancholia* merges two of the foundational prototypes in histories and theories of architecture

between the allegorical figures in the engravings of the forest setting of Laugier's frontispiece and the moonlit landscape of Dürer's *Melencolia*.‡ But if while writing his essay on reformist prophecy, Warburg would become increasingly agitated by the catastrophic events of World War I and Kiesler's *Magic Architecture* would be tinged by the shadow of the aerial assaults of World War II, a twenty-first-century renaissance of cosmological thinking in architecture would perhaps be triggered not by the breakout of a Third World War (even if that, too, certainly remains in the cards), but by the global ecological catastrophe, the unfolding of which we alarmingly witness every day.[35] In this contemporary ecological predicament, the material deformations and devolutionary contractions manifested in recent architectural projects, such as those by CODA and OMG, could be retroactively diagnosed as vigorous pathological reactions triggered by the Anthropocene side of lunacy and its cataclysmic environmental impact.[36]

Given the heavily tinted institutional history of "lunacy," another term could perhaps be coined or recycled to denote the source of contemporary architecture's ecological impetus for shape-shifting deformations that could eventually flesh out its alternative

---

from Kiesler all the way back to Vitruvius into a single symbolic enclosure. But here this primal cave-tent signals less the beginnings of human civilization but its very end, as it is made with the explicit purpose of housing Justine, her sister, and her nephew, who are the only surviving characters around the "castle" during Melancholia's inevitable collision with the Earth. However, von Trier is not Warburg, so there is no sign of redemption in his apocalyptic cosmological prophesy. The film's final scene stages a veritable massacre, where both the body of Justine and the skeletal enclosure of the magic cave instantly explode the moment that Melancholia falls upon the Earth and triggers a spectacular global conflagration. On a philological and art historical (end)note, the prophecy of a similar universal conflagration (*ekpyrwsis*) signaling the end of the world is in fact mentioned by Plato and recited by mysticist Neoplatonist philosophers, as mentioned in Edgar Wind's *Pagan Mysteries in the Renaissance* (London: Penguin, 1967,

Drawing after the final scene in *Melancholia*, drawn by Philippe Lapierre, 2020.

cosmological potential. And yet in spite of its rightful deletion from official legal documents, "lunacy" has survived in the scientific as well as popular literatures of the last decades. Numerous articles have been written by medical and other scientific experts investigating the physiological and psychological impact of the Moon's shifting attraction to Earth across a wide variety of recurring human adversities, from criminal arrests and mental hospital admissions to injuries among football players, whose frequency is tested across the spectrum of the lunar calendar.[37] Via the implementation of statistics, "lunacy" is once again subjected to rigorous numerical analyses evoking the cosmological mathematics of the Renaissance episteme of prognostication. Today, the findings of scientists tend to refute the Moon's impact on human affairs and thus corroborate the prescription of "lunacy" as a myth or a rudimentary superstitious belief as had already been proclaimed by nineteenth-century psychiatrists.[38] However negative, these recent scientific assessments of lunacy offer a novel chemical reconceptualization of the old magical or alchemical affliction as a potentially environmental malaise. For example, we learn that because human bodies consist of approximately eighty percent water, the Moon could potentially have an effect on a "cellular scale" on people, similar to the effect exercised by the "gravitational pull" between the Earth and the Moon on the tidal cycles of the Earth's oceans.[39] Other theories focus on bodily changes affected by "gravitational changes" caused by the lunar rotation "on the earth's electromagnetic field," yet most scientists reject the impact of such gravitational effects on humans as negligible.[40] Nevertheless, these studies recast the "lunar affect" as an impalpable cosmic stressor, whose almost imperceptible impact adds to the environmental stress we experience every day in our urban settings. Even if physiologically miniscule, the inorganic traces of the Moon's magnetic influence on our chemical composition serve as proof that our bodies still vibrate sympathetically with both the fluid and the solid inorganic matter of the universe and that, as medieval cosmologists claimed, all human offspring of the earth are in a way "children of the planets."[41] One

135, n. 22), who also associates the same "supreme conflagration" with the myth of Saturn swallowing his children—a darker side of Neoplatonist philosophy, entirely absent in Wittkower's historiography of harmonic proportions. On a different and less gloomy (end)note proposed by contemporary astro-science, following the "Giant Impact" or "Big Splash" hypothesis, the debris left from a similar interplanetary collision between the Earth and Mars formed the Moon (see, Dana, Mackenzie, *The Big Splat, or How Our Moon Came To Be* [Hoboken, NJ: Wiley, 2003]). Following its collision with Melancholia, the Earth as we know it will no longer exist, yet another moon may be born from such cosmic impact; but this new lunar origin is not projected by von Trier.

can only hope that such heightened cosmic sensitivity, which in past architectural studies remained largely contemplative, could also translate into urgent political and environmental action.[§]

[§] Such calls become even more prescient apropos the new line of proposals by federal and private agencies for a second moon landing. Such plans follow the fiftieth anniversary of the first human arrival on the Moon performed by U.S. space forces in 1969, which effectively expanded the Darwinian "struggle for space," from the surface of the Earth to outer space, in a quest for cosmic territorial dominance. Critics have dismissed these extraterrestrial colonizing efforts as another "lunacy" due to their exorbitant expenditure, the funds for which could instead be used to counter the pressing economic and environmental challenges experienced by several territories on Earth. The latest news about the Moon's own "volatile lunacy" announced by geoscientists is that its seemingly dry mass is actually "damp," as it contains traces of water, which could be construed as the remnant of a primeval form of life. Such recent scientific discoveries could further feed speculations about the origin of future life on the Moon evolving the presence of humans. Should it ever happen, the gradual colonization of the Moon would mark the cosmic expansion of anthropocentric lunacy on the very surface from which lunacy allegedly originated. In other words, lunacy would return to the Moon, closing the circle of its diachronic trajectory from antiquity to modernity while exposing its human bias, as well as the idiopathic reflex that connects the destiny of the Earth with its singular satellite body. For a reaction to the first moon landing, see Stephen Minot "The Lunacy in that Lunar Trip" *North American Review*, 254: 3 (Fall 1969), 2-5. For a reappraisal of Minot's views in 2010, see Richard Natale, "Past Perfect: Continuing the Lunacy," *The North American Review*, 295:3 (Summer 2010), 48. For the presence of water in the Moon, see the editorial "Volatile Lunacy" (no author), *Nature Geoscience* 7 (June 2014): 389. For recent discoveries on the Moon's magmatic "dampness" see Tim Elliot, "Galvanized Lunacy," *Nature* 490: 18 (October 2012), 346-7.

Awry of the Plan

Jesse Reiser

When you start working, everybody is in your studio—the past, your friends, enemies, the art world, and above all, your own ideas—all are there. But as you continue painting, they start leaving, one by one, and you are left completely alone. Then, if you are lucky, even you leave.[1]

To paraphrase, great work requires nothing short of transcendence—to silence rational thought, to lose oneself, to be intuitive, and to think through *things* instead of concepts. One must disband the walls of one's creative identity and give way to chance encounters and circumstances, like devolving from Dr. Jekyll to Mr. Hyde, where more primordial instincts emerge. Far from hyperbole, such is the task and ecstasy of creative labor: to accept the malleability and transience of one's identity to create something foreign and new.

Architecture is unique in its discomfort with intuition, which finds safe harbor in nearly all other artistic disciplines. For better or worse, architecture has largely tasked itself with the design of a more reasonable world, providing a justification for every form and supposedly rescuing humanity from the abyss of absurdity and irrationality. From the pervasive orthogonal grid to the curvilinear distortions of D'Arcy Thompson, architecture has historically asserted itself over materials and routines, preempting the behaviors of both and taming the messiness of the world in a manner to make one less nervous.

True to this ethos, the modernist project dealt almost exclusively with the currency of order, control, and top-down hierarchy. As demonstrated by Ludwig Mies van der Rohe, material expression was often limited to "accidents" that could be controlled by geometry, as seen in the polished, book-matched slabs of once-amorphous onyx in his Barcelona Pavilion. In other projects, one literally rises from the ground toward the architecture in an unfailingly dramatized experience, in which the "leaving of the earth" toward the ideal space of architecture, like rising toward the heavens, places the architect in the place of a god, separating light from shadow and order from disorder, and creating architecture as though the world had not already been made.

"The architectural revolution is achieved," declares a proselytizing Le Corbusier in *New World of Space*, before explicating his five points, like commandments, to a presumably uninitiated audience. His prophecy continues by introducing his Modulor

as “a measuring instrument of tremendous importance which may be used for everything,”[2] as if one’s relationship to all around, large and small, could be reduced to a single system. What is compelling here is less Le Corbusier’s drive toward reason and order, as outlined in these theories, but more that they immediately follow, and are purported to embody, a long, meandering explanation on the mystical and ineffable foundations of architecture. As if all emotion could be reduced to neurochemistry, Le Corbusier’s attempts to codify ineffability through systems of structure and proportion seem similarly reductive, at odds with the better, intuitive angels, which perpetually grace his best work.

Thus, even those in the twentieth century who purported to attack “order” remained seduced by its cleanliness and rationality. As Le Corbusier’s late curvilinear gestures were often read against a dominant grid, Eisenman’s 1990s forays into geological form and the “index” likewise stamped grids over fluid forms. One can debate the potency of the resulting architectures, but that architectural theory is, historically, more an articulation of rules than sensibilities goes almost without saying. Reason and order, both geometric and rhetorical, permeate our discourse like a religion, as if architecture could not exist without precise geometrical description or practical justifications—be they natural law, economic efficiency, or the demands of the client—often voiced with a distressing righteousness.

Time has only compounded these sentiments. The twenty-first century has seen a shift in its models of architectural production toward ones that privilege algorithmic thinking, hoping to justify any and all results while amassing vast quantities of potential options. Such alternatives are commonly understood to be without error, as they are the outcomes of computer algorithms and the products of hyper-rational procedures. These results improve workflows immensely, but they often don’t “look” or “feel” good. Regardless of technological advances, it is easy to tell whether an architecture is algorithmically generated or crafted with instinct and skill. Resulting compositions of the latter kind exhibit an incontrovertible intelligence seemingly more native to the stuff of architecture, which remains paradoxically beyond an algorithm’s reach. Computers can do much, but produce architecture they cannot, at least not alone.

It is with no small sense of irony that the results of sophisticated computation could be rejected so readily by dumb instinct, as they have been and continually are. And

as such computational advances have been perpetually justified by their similarity to biological models, it seems that, as they are no match to the evolved human instincts against which they are judged, computation's ties to biological evolution are in error. This is because biological evolution creates tendencies through random mutations—the "arbitrary play" of biochemical bases—for no purpose whatsoever. Contrary to goal-driven computation, any advantages gained through biological evolution are incidental, without rational reason or purpose, toward compounding degrees of beauty, complexity, and variety.

Nonetheless, if biology has taught us anything in the past century, it is that the supposedly dark, irrational, and instinctual world of beasts is in fact a bastion of unimaginable ingenuity and diversity from which we, "enlightened" humans, can only hope to take some sampling of inspiration through mimicry or benefit through husbandry. Responding to the immediate environmental conditions and constraints at hand, the world of beasts reminds us that intelligence is less an ability to justify and rather a reflex toward appropriate action. Indeed, when it comes to matter and materials, no doubt the sensitivity of manipulative action is more consequential than the nuance of thought. This is not to say that words and ideas do not matter, but rather to say that analysis alone a great work cannot make. And it is through practice that we may embrace our more instinctual, primordial roots, which themselves are the products of evolutionary refinement and conditioning.

Of course, losing oneself in the ecstasy of work is no excuse to plea insanity or abdicate responsibility.[3] Architecture requires much in resources and much is required of it in practicality, distinguishing it from other creative disciplines. Uncomfortably poised between art and engineering, the dual demands for rational systematization and novelty placed upon architecture are perhaps its defining generative conflict. Indeed, the best architecture is always both of this world and foreign to it, seemingly a product of both materials and the mind, somehow always bridging a gap between humankind, its routines, and the primordial world from which it emerged.

Accordingly, like the *uomo terribile* Michelangelo, an architect might best thrive in a world between beasts and humankind, between the divine rationality and instinctual play, and consider oneself a discerning outsider to both worlds. Not unlike the werewolf, an architect might embrace animalistic impulses without fear

of reprisal, only considering the consequences of her actions when confronted with the persisting, enlightening sun and a recognition of her own amnesia. Such is to entertain an architecture more instinctual and performative, never belonging to one single state, yet always becoming. A metamorphosis like this might not only generate new things and events in our world, but it could evolve the way in which we, after returning from our state of delirium, think.

Shape Shifting: Intelligent Animism

Greg Lynn

Architecture is a discipline of stasis. Movement is not only minimized due to practical considerations of stability, but it also challenges the assumption of timelessness that is fundamental to the discipline, both in the search for pure space outside of the particularities of historical style, as well as the desire for literal permanence. More specifically, stasis has been intimately linked with architecture in at least five significant ways: *permanence*: the assumption that buildings should be built for eternity; *usefulness*: the assumption that buildings are built for only one purpose; *typology*: that there are persistent underlying organizational and spatial principles that endure across styles and the vicissitudes of context and methods of construction; *verticality*: that gravity and therefore structural forces flow perpendicular to the surface of the earth; and *inertness:* that buildings are designed in static orthogonal coordinate space and experienced as one moves through them but never actually moving their occupants.

As a counterpoint to inertial design, take the case of the hull of a sailboat. The form is designed with multiple orientations to the true wind direction in mind, yet it does not change its shape literally. The virtuality of its shape has several points of sail optimized in a single surface. Not coincidentally, this example is required to respond to the forces of its motion through a fluid medium. Many of my own projects included in the book *Animate FORM* in the 1990s were designed in animation software where the coordinate space for modeling was supplemented by the ability to model global and local forces as well as making forms and spaces both movable and deformable.[1] I adopted the conventional position back then that the use of these tools "does not mandate that architecture should change its shape."[2] Architecture, like the hull, need not *literally* move, but instead, its design captures multiple forces in its shapes that, when positioned in space, instigate motion by virtue of their position and contour as people—or even the eyes—move through and around them. This version of a baroque argument of sculpture was literally animated by a new regime of modelling and simulation tools when they first became available for architectural design. It was understood and developed by Sanford Kwinter, Jeffrey Kipnis, Charles Jencks and others discussing morphogenesis in regard to the development of the form and body plan of organisms as they unfold from simplicity to adult complexity. The approach to design was seen as folding contextual or extrinsic information into a surface or surfaces where they would unfold dynamism visually and spatially

when moved through, primarily as an interior. Forms were derived in response to particularities of their future performance as defined by the design of forces that moved and deformed them.

Following this interest in design with dynamic forces came a second interest in animation and that was the design of series in time, as freeze frames of morphological unfolding, for example. The intention was to shift the architectural conversation away from the established architectural notion of typology toward an idea of an architectural species or brood,[3] in which there was no ideal—as had been engrained by such scholars as Colin Rowe[4] and Rudolf Wittkower[5] in their renowned theories on Palladian Villas—but rather a mutable and unlimited unfolding of instances of a design.[6] I asked, "might there be another way to respect particularities and differences without 'returning our inquiry' to universal types," one characterized by "more pliant systems of description," and including "a system of local affiliations outside itself"?[7] My proposition was that, instead of occurring spontaneously in a vacuum of static space, an animate architecture should originate in a dynamic environment of multiple and simultaneous pressures and movements. Rather than designing for a single outcome, architecture could be designed in such a way that autonomous spatial and material decisions would diversely unfold based on the externalities of a particular site.

The Embryological House was the most succinct example of this approach, where more than 50,000 houses were designed simultaneously. The project was founded on a family of interchangeable and compatible curves that were used to loft a control surface. These curves were designed with different inflections in their twelve control points so that they would always result in a faired and continuous surface (as far as I know, neither I nor anyone in my employment has ever examined all 50,000+ forms). Architecture here was not the fish or crustacean trapped within the grid by D'Arcy Thompson, it was the grid itself. This project was a critique of Rudolph Wittkower and Colin Rowe's notion of an ideal villa: there was no single referent that was deformed but, instead, a collection designed at once.

In "The Renewed Novelty of Symmetry,"[8] a key concept presented was symmetry-breaking, a phenomenon first observed in the late 1800s by William Bateson, who pointed out that symmetry was not a sign of order but the indication of a lack

of information. He showed, through a focus on mutations that exhibited higher degrees of symmetry than normal growth, that the absence of information as an organism grows reverts to growth by mirror symmetry. For example, there are two mutations around the thumb: the first consists of four additional fingers mirrored where a thumb would be, and the second is double thumbs, mirrored one to another. I had previously assumed symmetry-breaking was the violation of symmetry due to external constraints of site or function, as I was taught to think of symmetry as ideal order. With Bateson's text from the 19th century, I learned that symmetry was a sign of disorder or the lack of information and it was a method of growth to be used when there was no other external or internal information to guide growth otherwise; it was a generic default, not an organizing principle. Bateson was dissatisfied with Darwin's inability to account for mechanisms of mutation and the fact that organisms lived in gradient environments but did not evolve in a gradient fashion related to such environments. The term Bateson coined for the information that would break symmetry with higher ordering was "genetics." Today, as we learn how much differentiation is possible by tiny fractional differences of genetic

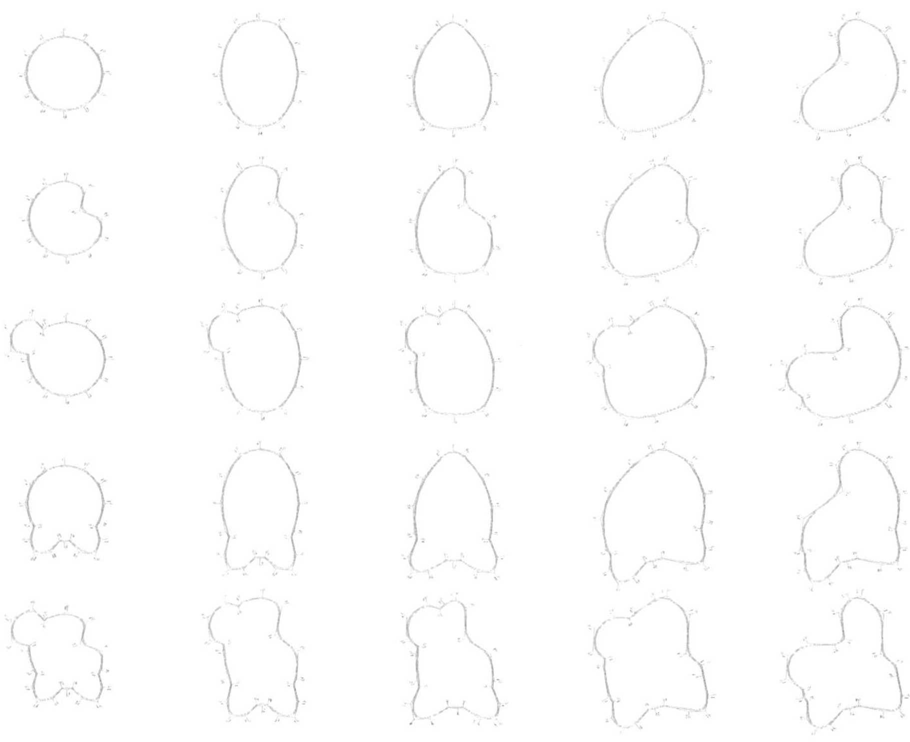

Embryological House, Greg Lynn, (1997-2001). Courtesy of Greg Lynn/FORM.

information, Bateson's insights are all the more poignant as with small amounts of genetic sequential variation radical degrees of variation are generated. What came to be called "Bateson's Rule" was extensively employed in the study of flat worms and their regenerative growth as well as appendages on insects with special regard to beetles.

The architectural idea that symmetry equals order is immediately overthrown when one reads virtually any reputable biological text written after 1900. In the biological sciences, symmetry is known to be a sign of the rudimentary; a default in the absence of order or logic. Architecture had managed to get away with over one-hundred years of ignorance, not confronting what every other science had discovered—that symmetry is, actually, *disorder*. This is most simply observable in worm regenerative studies: a worm cut at the frontal or sagittal end will grow two tails. This insight was the genesis of the models and drawings of the "Stranded Sears Tower" that preceded my use of animation software.

In many ways, there was a parallel between evolutionary thinking, the computer, and the procedural nature of formalism in processes like Peter Eisenman's *Frankfurt Biozentrum Competition* that I worked on during the Summer of 1988. In fact, Peter was himself a computer. He set a procedural process of iterative transformations and then ran them over and over again. He began any house diagram with a cube, then he sliced it, voided it, rotated it, and, after a number of iterations, he reached the final product, in which the trace of the process was indexed.

And so, the digital project began the way that it did because of the iterative process that Eisenman had established, and not the other way around. Both the hull and house models are static in their final state and were arrived at by a series of formal iterations. Yet, they differ from one another in two important ways: firstly, the hull's iterations are performative, while the houses are formal. Secondly, the hull's motivations are from exterior forces, as opposed to the house's self-referential geometric motives.

In 2008, I returned to these ideas of animation, in particular the key statement—that the use of animation software to model forms in a dynamic space of forces and deformable and movable surfaces did not mandate that buildings should literally

change their shape. I questioned that assumption. In a world in which robots and dynamic systems had become much more integral, I wondered, *what if we consider that architecture should change its shape?*

Eisenman/Robertson Architects. *Schematic representation of a DNA sequence for Biozentrum, Biology Center for the J.W. Goethe University, Frankfurt am Main, Germany.* 1987, electrostatic print on paper with pen notations, 28 x 21.5 cm, DR1999:0646. Peter Eisenman fonds. Canadian Centre for Architecture.

Architecture is, of course, already animate. Elevators, escalators, sliding doors, sunshades that respond automatically to changing light levels, etc. At times, it would appear that an alien being is making decisions in buildings without asking its inhabitants. In the 21st century, our living environments have become more mobile, with increased intelligence, sensing, and processing capabilities. As designers today, we must harness that potential of dynamic deformable environments combined with an awareness of our surroundings, leading to an intelligent responsiveness. We must embrace dynamism not as a technical add-on, but as inducted into the language of architecture.

The next frontier of architectural innovation is not form but *performance*: intelligent dynamism. Typically, form has been thought of as static and ideal, rather than dynamic with variable performance.

In the last few years, I have been interested in how to animate environments. As a counterpoint to the *Embryological House*, the *RV (Room Vehicle) Prototype* is a house that evolves within its own lifetime. It can be moved in two axes and with its motion, some of the furniture disappears into pockets embedded in the walls/floor/ceiling, while other furniture rotates out for use. The furniture becomes vehicular. The space becomes active. A robot spins the house in the X/Y plane and rolls the house in the Z axis. This robot is controlled by a simple downloadable app.[9] Following the moving building elements and the rotating furniture is the founding of *Piaggio Fast Forward* and the development of the mobile carrier "gita." Gita is a lightweight, intelligent technology that follows users with pedestrian etiquette. It is something between robot, furniture, and vehicle, whose spherical shape was dictated by its wheels, as well as the need for a slippery form for moving through pedestrian landscapes.

These projects are similar to CODA/OMG's *Zimmer*, which uses moving components to reorganize the entire spaces of the house, as well as other mechanized projects. But it is not only in mechanization that the dynamics of an environment should be explored. In *Animate Form* I wrote that "techniques for obsolescence, dismantling, ruination, recycling and abandonment through time warrant exploration." Here, in these pages, and after 20 years, that exploration has begun.

This essay was adapted from a 2017 conversation with Caroline O'Donnell & José Ibarra.

Hair Dos and Don'ts:
A Brick Problem

Jimenez Lai

82

The contrasting graphic techniques of the two *The Lion King* films demonstrate a jarring shift in representation between 1994 and 2019. In the first film, the individual hair strands are invisible, but the flattened, cartoon surfaces depicting a low-resolution[1] hairstyle for each animal exaggerates their attitudes. These smooth surfaces make up the animals' fur, which the viewer perceives to be comprised of many parts only by way of the tufts at the edge. In the second film, a high-resolution attempt at realism demanded the articulation of individual hair strands at the expense of the characters' ability to emote.[2] The fur is made up of so many highly defined individual parts that it appears continuous and approaches verisimilitude. This contrast, paralleled in architecture, highlights a compositional problem: easy "parts" with easy "wholes" or difficult "parts" with no "wholes." The former prioritizes the legibility of a "hairstyle" silhouette to convey character, while the latter emphasizes the quality of an individual hair strand to display technological mastery.

This perceptual "experience" of surface, whether one whole or many parts, is elucidated by perceptual psychologist James J. Gibson. In *The Ecological Approach to Visual Perception*, Gibson states that "the perception of surfaciness depends on the proximity to one another of discontinuities in the optic array."[3] In other words, there needs to be a certain density of parts for one to perceive a surface instead of an array of many parts. In Gibson's experiments, which involved imperfect wall surfaces and a series of black and white rings, discontinuities were seen as the grain or density of a given surface. When the density was high, a continuous surface was perceived.

The Lion King film comparison of both conditions—the *whole* hairstyle dominating in the first movie, and the individual *parts* making up the whole in the second one—shows the inherent duality of fur-as-surface and fur-as-array. The 1994 fur is always flat and never multiple. By contrast, the 2019 fur, which is a product of the digital age, employs a topographic skin that is populated with a series of interrelated primary and secondary hairs. Adult Simba's mane consists of 700,000 strands of hair in which 1% are "lead" hairs and guide the movement of any surrounding tresses.[4]

Architecture has always had a hair problem, too. The single follicle (or part) must necessarily negotiate with the hairstyle (or whole). As an irreducible, atomized absolute, the strand of hair is architecture's default single-pixel part that aggregates into a greater whole. It is one fraction of a modular, standardized, repeatable,

Drawing after *The Lion King* (1994), drawn by Philippe Lapierre, 2020.

rearrangeable, and replaceable system usually guided by an additive process. One ubiquitous example of this is the unit of the brick, which defines the scales and resolutions of an object, whether such object is as small as a wall or as large as a city. Rather than having any character of their own, architecture's hairs are only masterful and complete when they make up a hairstyle. Such hairs can be clay, terracotta, and mushroom bricks, but other times concrete masonry units, pillows, rooms, lawn chairs, skateboard off-cuts, and even megapixels. The hair versus the hairdo is a conceptual problem at the core of every compositional endeavor.

Drawing after *The Lion King* (2019), drawn by Philippe Lapierre, 2020.

Much like film and animation, architecture has experienced a digital transformation in the last 30 years. In many cases, this transformation has moved away from the raster and toward the vector, assigning directionality and movement to architecture's parts. This suggests that component-based architecture has begun to swirl and coif in ways that make it behave even more like hair. As Caroline O'Donnell points out in *Niche Tactics: Generative Relationships Between Architecture and Site*, Tim Ingold's diagrams of a human's relationship to the earth and sky are best understood when one studies the effect of wind, weather, and land unto the human. Unlike an "exhabitant,"

After Tim Ingold, in "Earth, Sky, Wind, and Weather."

an "inhabitant" of the earth has an orientation, a gait, and hair to interface with the environment. This tactical relationship to context can also be perceived in ecologically responsive architecture, where a favoring of the edge condition of a given whole increases the legibility and performance of the architecture.

The turn of the 21st century saw technological advancement in rapid prototyping. This allowed architects to explore new territories and conceive previously impossible forms without the computer. The *Blobwall* (2005) by Greg Lynn, for example, is composed of highly customized parts made possible by CNC robot arms. This digital turn transformed the software vector process into physical hardware. CNC machines, laser cutters, waterjet cutters, and other interfacing output systems all worked better with vectors, instead of raster, files. Limited by the size of the output constraints of the machines, as well as the software that handled the file types, designers began to place more emphasis on the complexities of each part, rather than the image of the eventual whole. Lynn's early career, particularly given his focus on the qualities of curves and splines, was a natural fit in the cultivation of vector-based projects. In his essay, "Multiplicitous and Inorganic Bodies," he describes the animated cut of the Statue of Liberty as a series of successive curves. The generative nature of developing the body based on the geometric properties of the vector was critical to the early practitioners during the digital turn.

Meanwhile, those whose work followed the raster logic had a different relationship with the digital project. For instance, Jesse Reiser and Nanako Umemoto were producing collages. Their 1989 *Aktion Poliphile* series was an aggregation of found objects in large raster clusters. To collage is to derive new meanings from parts with old meanings—the part-to-part relationship of the clusters to convey semiotic associations. Therefore, a collage cannot be broken down into smaller bricks and its context is indispensable in order for the (collaged) architecture to become characters.

The clusters were recognizable images in themselves, which allowed them to obtain new meanings when rotated, interrupted, or surrounded by new meanings. The collage was more difficult to translate using the early rapid-prototyping technology, and it would take another decade or two for technology to catch up to the raster logic.

Greg Lynn's *Toy Furniture* series in 2008 marked a significant transition point from which designers sought to find bricks, rather than make bricks. Similar to a collage where the image is composed of found objects, Lynn curated the bricks instead of prototyping them. Perhaps Lynn foresaw the problems ahead in the over-articulation of the single follicles with *Blobwall*; either the bricks needed to be simpler to produce, or the wholes must become more legible for the architecture to work. The zero-sum game of spending all efforts in the design and fabrication of individual parts contributes very little to a larger output or a project's reading across multiple scales. In the toy series, Lynn's solution was to simplify the parts by aggregating modified plastic toys and turning them into compression members for furniture.

In an age where the design focus is placed on the over-articulation of the individual hair strands, the awareness of the haircut can be lost on the designers themselves. Jason Payne's *Raspberry Fields* (2010) might be a perfect example of overly articulated parts with no vision for wholes. In *Raspberry Fields*, a highly customized, individually

Raspberry Fields in *Rawhide: The New Shingle Style* exhibition at SCI-Arc, Jason Payne, 2011. Photograph by Joshua White / JWPictures.com.

Blob Wall, Greg Lynn, (2005-2009), Permanent collection of The Canadian Center for Architecture. Courtesy of Greg Lynn/FORM.

weather-curled cedar shingle is used to compose a pitched-roof. The logic of this approach is described by Payne as a "hair problem."[5] In this case, the scale of the strand (part) is the design problem, not the hairstyle (whole). This design approach is symptomatic of the early digital era, where the lasercut bed or the CNC machine becomes the space to design special bricks, instead of designing at the scale of the full composition. *Raspberry Fields* is almost literally splitting hair—it is a hair project that disregards the haircut, defaulting the decision of the overall haircut toward a slightly morphed postmodern vernacular pitched-roof house that the designer, apparently, did not intend to produce.[6] Being too invested in the details results in projects that cannot see the forest for the trees. The first decade in the 21st century has brought with it a field of over-articulated trees with hardly any understanding of a forest—a "difficult parts with no wholes" problem.

Opposed to Payne's project, the *House of the Suicide* by John Hejduk has no hair and only the haircut. The scale from which Hejduk conceived of this project is at the architectural scale, and not at the scale of the brick. This project spends no effort on the articulation of the "how" of each component, instead just focusing on the "what," or the full object. The shape of the hairdo is the only graphic to read. The materiality of the hair has no traces of the individual follicle. Whereas Payne's *Raspberry Fields* resembles the high-resolution of the 2019 *Lion King*, the *House of the Suicide* is the low-resolution 1994 cartoon.

At the architectural scale, buildings are shapes that make up a city's skyline. They lose all hair once they start reading as the silhouettes of haircuts. As Robert E. Somol notes in his article, "12 Reasons to Get Back into Shape," the idea of shape is expendable, adaptable, fit, empty, arbitrary, intensive, buoyant, projective, and illicit. "Shape," he writes, "eliminates information, is often low resolution, and is in this sense a 'cool' medium."[7] Most importantly, shape is easy, "avoiding the rhetorical excess of geometric form or expressive mass, shape exhibits the immediacy of the graphic."[8]

Designs like MOS's *Afterparty* (2009) or CODA's *Party Wall* (2013) might be the beginning of a different story about the digital transformation of architecture. While the former is literally hairy, the latter is conceived as an aggregation project using CNC-fabricated parts. In *Party Wall*, the concept does not revolve around the mass-

customization of individual components. Instead, the pavilion's parts came from the off-cuts of industry-standard skateboards transformed to achieve a dual legibility of array and surface. In other words, CODA found "bricks" that had already been produced. Put simply, *Party Wall* is both hair and hairdo—a wall guided by a raster logic that makes a new composition out of found objects. The use of the digitally fabricated leftover toggles the viewer's attention from the part to the whole so that neither dominates. Instead, one flicks back and forth between object and field. *Party Wall* alludes to but reroutes architecture's place in the digital realm, continuing an important disciplinary conversation about collage and the as-found.

Picking up where Lynn left off with the *Toy Furniture* series, CODA's *Urchin* (2016) reopens the part-to-whole dialogue between the hair and the hairdo by aggregating found-objects. In *Urchin*'s case, the problem of the eccentric part is also tested with more familiar and readily available everyday items in the form of lawn chairs. Akin to Reiser + Umemoto's collage problems, this update to the hair-and-hairdo problem transcends the technical difficulties of the individual digital part, instead prompting the viewers to look for unexpected redeeming qualities in the objects that are all around us. It is not only a simple and made-new part, but also a generous acknowledgment about the beauty of an existing object. Where Duchamp saw the

Afterparty, MOS Architects, 2009. Photograph by Florian Holzherr.

urinals for the fountains, CODA saw the chairs for *Urchin*. Moreover, compared to the over-articulated hair of Payne's or the easy hairdo of Hejduk's, CODA attentively works with both the part and the whole, creating a new graphic language that is able to mediate between multiple scales and resolutions. In other words, both the hair and the haircut are simple, legible, and intrinsic to the architecture. It is also easy to slip between the two, to be between object and field in a way that the 2019 *Lion King* could not. *Urchin* is an easy-whole made from easy-parts.

The more literally furry, *Combust*, begins life as a hairy object, where the hair is generated by hundreds of matchsticks penetrating a thin surface. Like a chrysalid undergoing a state of metamorphosis, the model is liberated by being set on fire. Here, *Combust* switches its operation to be more like the *House of the Suicide*, where all hair is lost and only the outline of a shape remains. As this model disappears into the flame, it recalls the way that the hair on Akira Toriyama's cartoon character, Goku, turns from the many parts into a graphic whole the moment he goes "Super Saiyan" for the first time. This easy outline describes the metamorphosis of the character transformation.

Finally, in OMG's 2017 pavilion *Primitive Hut*, hair and hairdo become literal. The pavilion's hairs are not minimally milled and notched components. Instead, the hair is the wild and unruly shag bursting through the roof in the form of four maple trees. This living hair is in a constant state of change in color, density, and scale, across seasons and years. This move to a more literal understanding of transformation marks the transition from the representation of hair to a literal living, growing, and shedding material.

The story of the raster logic in the digital age is an ongoing saga, especially where the collage of the found objects interface into and out of the computer much more easily. In the 2014 symposium, "Firmness, Commodity, & Delight," organized by Joanna Grant and Kevin Pazik at Princeton University, Mark Foster Gage and Andrew Kovacs presented their respective 2014 Helsinki Guggenheim competition entries. The first architect worked with an approach that he described as "kitbashing," in which license-free digital models from 3D-warehouses were aggregated together. During this time period, Gage was experimenting with outputting the digital matter into the physical realm through the CNC-cutting of

marble. Not unlike a bas-relief, Gage collapsed a Minion next to a Hello Kitty next to a pile of other pop-culture objects. The second architect achieved a similar effect by purchasing inexpensive commodities (with architectural qualities) at a dollar store, and physically gluing the found objects together. In both cases, the result was a flattening of hundreds of found objects, not dissimilar from a judgement scene on a Gothic cathedral façade in which Jesus Christ, Hercules, and other historical, mythical, and invented figures collapse with one another. For both Gage and Kovacs, the collage was not about deriving new meanings or creating thought-out hairstyles, but rather about maximizing the spatial potentials yielded by the aggregation of individual strands of hair.

Whereas the aggregation of the found part in Kovacs's case was physical, Gage worked on his found objects within the digital space. What this meant was that, while the part-to-part relationship of Kovacs's physical aggregation would have to undergo a tectonic process of gluing objects that cannot physically merge into one another, Gage's kitbashed digital matter could merge with no consequences. The mathematical implications of a group of objects with no possibility for overlap juxtaposed with a seamlessly merged Venn Diagram was a striking moment in the recent history of hair problems in architecture. Additionally, Kovacs organized his physical objects mostly in plan, while Gage's Boolean union of the found parts was largely elevational. This suggests that the application of the individual unit was choreographic and

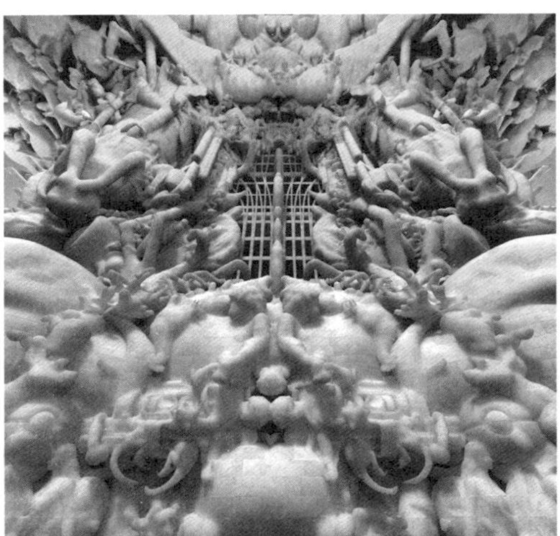

Proposal for the *Helsinki Guggenheim*, Mark Foster Gage Architects, 2014.

Proposal for the *Helsinki Guggenheim*, Office Kovacs, 2014.

programmatic for Kovacs, while Gage's bas-relief in elevation was a continuation of the flattened communicative narrative used in ancient façades.

The distinction between the collage of digital and physical found objects renders visible the advantages of harnessing the intelligence of things that already exist. Aside from simplifying architecture's modes of production without sacrificing the novelty of form, this strategy enables the re-seeing of the found objects based on their qualities and opportunities in a new context—or, as Gibson puts it, it allows for an understanding of the affordances of such objects.

In *Party Wall*, *Urchin*, *Combust*, and *Primitive Hut* (as well as *Evitim*, which uses the offcuts from *Primitive Hut*), the objects are certainly found ones, but the story pushes deeper into the nature of the part itself. CODA asks us to think beyond the dollar store and into the manufacture and provenance of the object, as well as into the future trajectory of the part when it enters into a future state, usually of waste. The tension between object and field traps us in a mind game between the wasted object and the extravagant whole, architecture's pleasure and pain in one glimpse. Only then is the struggle between hair and hairdo balanced: finally, a third *Lion King* emerges that is both legible in part and in whole, allowing the lion to have its essential outline and its necessarily furry texture, while being able to emote.

Party Wall

Not a Wall
MoMA PS1 Young Architects Program (YAP), winner
PS1, Long Island City, NY, USA
commissioned by MoMA
with support from Cornell Architecture/AAP
2013

Responding to a brief that serves two diametrically opposed constituencies, this project deploys the notion of the party wall: a common wall shared by two adjacent buildings. The first part of the brief requires shade, seating, water, and as much free floor area as possible to accommodate thousands of jovial dancers at the Saturday "Warm-Up" parties at MoMA PS1. The second part, in many ways, asks for the opposite: more intimate seated gatherings on the other days of the week to accommodate lectures, movies screenings, dinner parties, and so on. *Party Wall* acts as shared device for both groups by storing 300 benches as its skin. When the museum courtyard is filled with a horde of dancers, the benches are stowed in the façade. When a smaller performance is happening, the requisite number of benches can be removed and located on an appropriate "stage." For example, 39 benches can be removed from the cinema screen and laid out on the deck in front of it to create seating for a movie night. Or, for larger gatherings, like a fashion show, all 300 benches can be removed, and all stages used simultaneously. The true technical definition of *Party Wall* is intended: a wall shared between different users, each one with

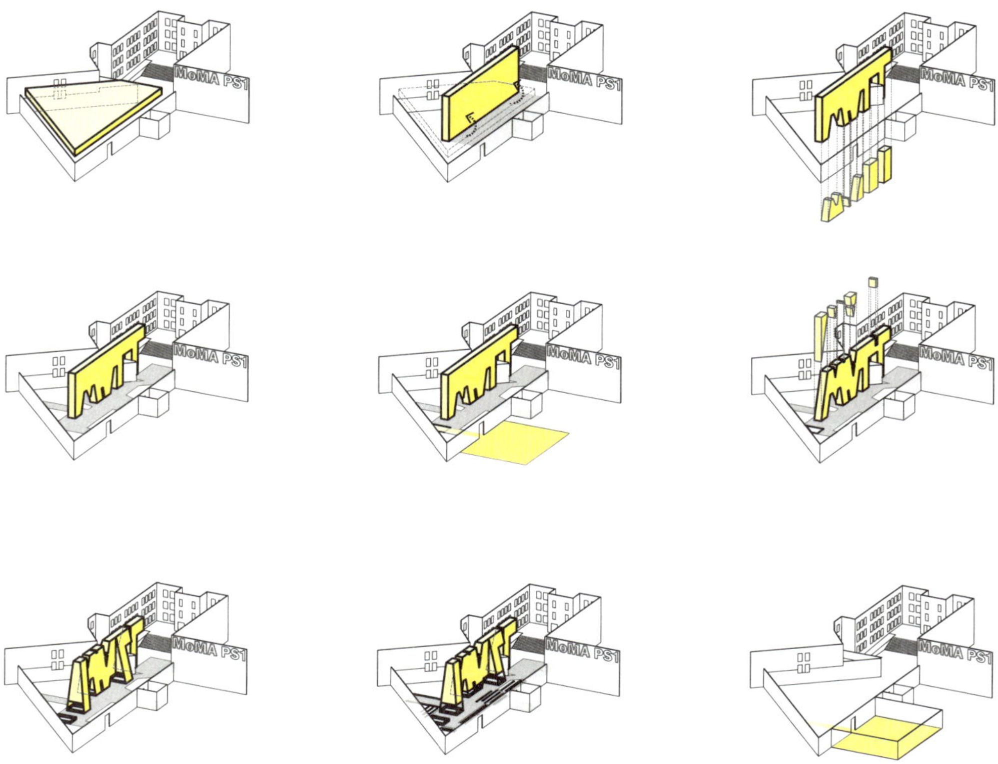
MoMA PS1
MoMA PS1
MoMA PS1
MoMA PS1
MoMA PS1
MoMA PS1
MoMA PS1
MoMA PS1
MoMA PS1

different needs and desires, and each one with different readings of the piece. The wall is constantly in flux, as its skin's components are removed and rearranged, and its users make up the final material in the project.

Long Island City, the home of MoMA PS1, is populated by many vintage signs. That architecture is a sign has been well documented, most notably by Robert Venturi and Denise Scott Brown, who famously classified buildings as ducks or decorated sheds. In either case, the building was always a sign. The only distinction was whether or not the decoration was applied or inherent to the form. This dialectic is reminiscent of *architecture parlante* ("speaking architecture," in English)—that is, that architecture can say something. However, architecture that communicates too often says something about itself; it is egocentric and narcissistic. Those familiar with Peter Eisenman's essay, "Aspects of Modernism: Maison Dom-ino and the Self-Referential Sign," understand the architectural sign as self-referential—one reinforcing the autonomy of the discipline. Capitalizing on the parched Corbusian diagram of *Maison Domino*, Eisenman's close reading of the column, slab, footing, and stair placements is an astounding investigation into the meanings of such signs. Still, one might wonder if, in this way, the treatment of the sign runs the risk of becoming *too* self-absorbed.

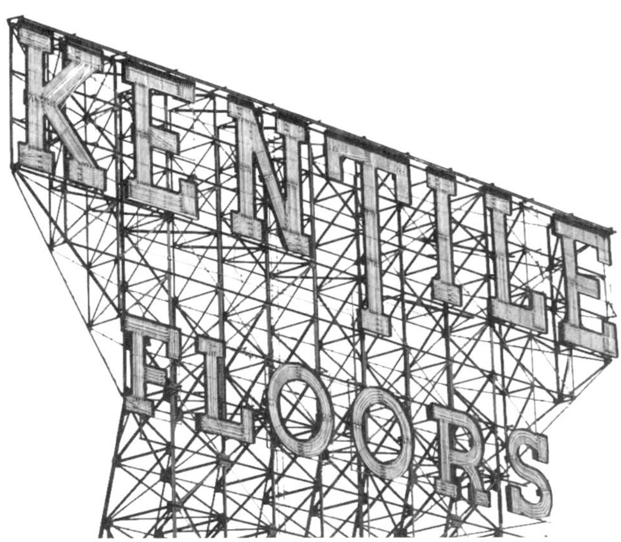

As an alternative, *Party Wall* wonders if what architecture says could be not just about itself, but also about its relationships to the world. Aiming for both popular and architectural audiences, the project rejects the architectural sign's seemingly inevitable self-centeredness. Crucially, the sign is not legible if one attempts to read the object on its own. As both an architectural and literal sign, the pavilion does not communicate by itself but relies directly on its context to produce a hint of its true meaning: under certain lighting conditions, at certain times of day, at certain times of year. The clue to understanding most fully the concept at work appears as a shadow in text on the ground. Read: WALL.

Party Wall is all-wall at the top, existing as a continuous linear element. Yet, at the bottom, it stands only on four splayed feet and allows passage through the space it encloses. The object-as-itself and the object-as-named are productively conflated: a non-wall spells the name of its ambition on the pavement. A wall, or not a wall? *Ceci n'est pas un mur.* In fact, the very form of the letters that make up the sign disrupt the object's ability to be what it says it is, only to provoke endlessly this question of what it really is.

When coupled with the larger context of billboards and signs that proliferate like grazing beasts around the site, the object becomes more sign than wall. It is a sign that points to something other than itself. The play between sign and signified is tossed back and forth. The joke may even be too subtle or too superficially easy (as in the news headlines: "'Party Wall' at MoMA PS1 Is More Than Just a Pun (It's Two Puns)" and "This is Not a Wall"). In this sense, *Party Wall* evades categorization as a Venturi Scott Brown duck-type, because it does not say what it does. Beyond that, it is syntactical with its environment, and thus represents a progression that extends beyond both semantic duck and syntactic Dom-ino. Like the joke, it plays with the manipulation of expectation and transformation on a number of levels.

Kelly Chan, "'Party Wall' at MoMA PS1 Is More Than Just a Pun (It's Two Puns)," in *Blouin Artinfo*, March 15, 2013.

Justin Allen, "This is Not a Wall," in *Domus*, July 2, 2013.

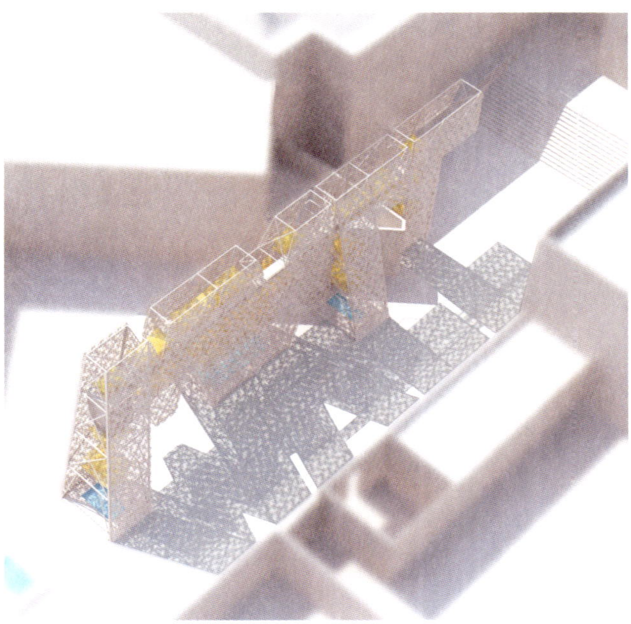

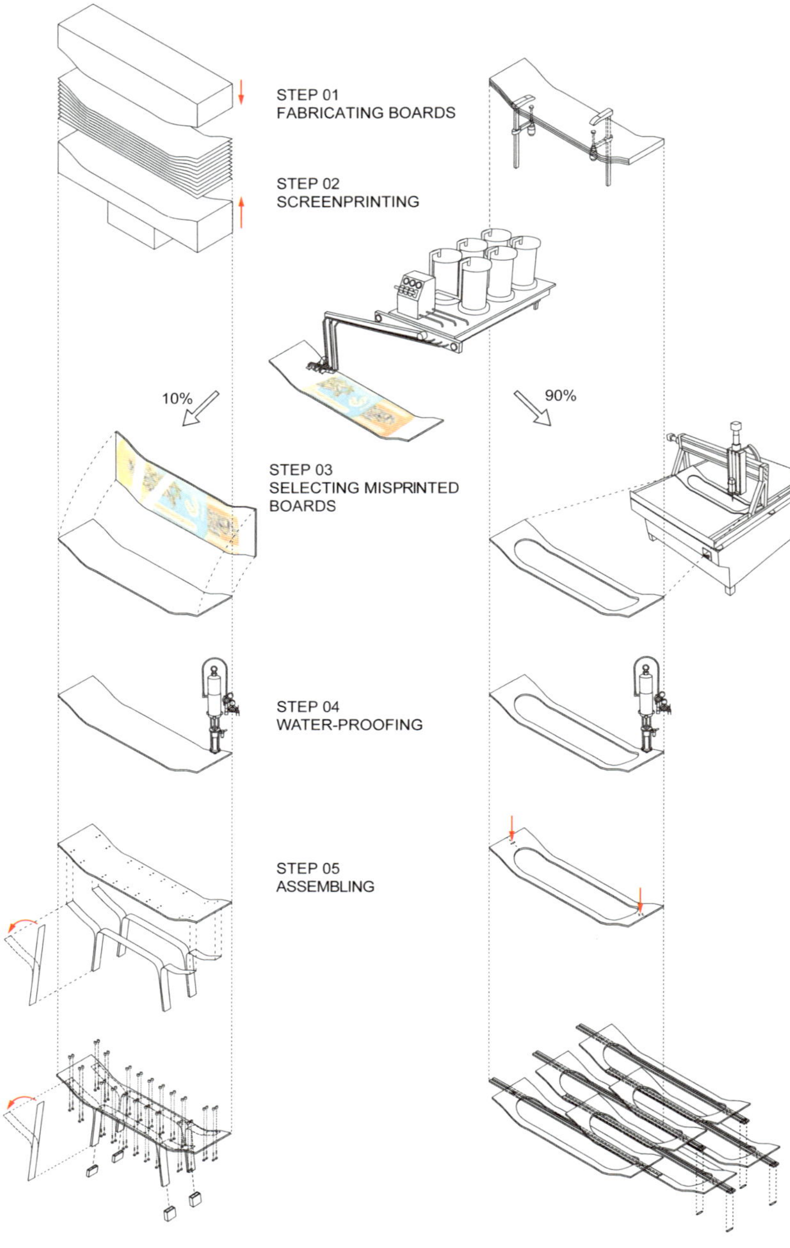
STEP 01
FABRICATING BOARDS
STEP 02
SCREENPRINTING
10%
90%
STEP 03
SELECTING MISPRINTED
BOARDS
STEP 04
WATER-PROOFING
STEP 05
ASSEMBLING

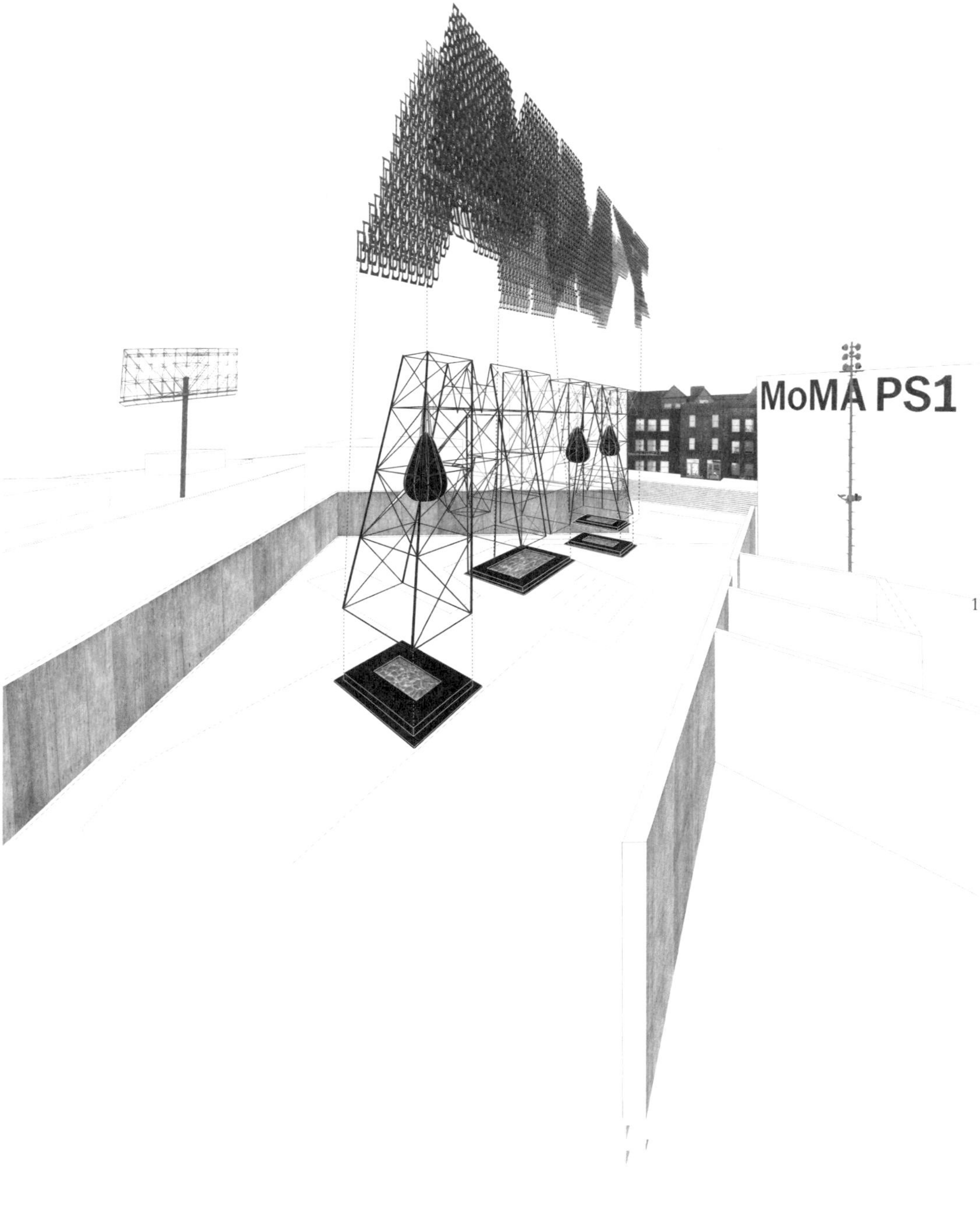
MoMA PS1

Party Wall uses two types of byproducts from eco-friendly Ithaca company, Comet Skateboards. For their typical longboard manufacturing sequence, Comet uses sustainably harvested plywood sheets that are heat-pressed together with a custom resin developed with the Cornell Center for Materials Research. These 4' x 1' curved boards are first printed and then CNC-milled in a range of shapes and patterns. About 90% of the waste comprises the leftovers from the milling process: curved rectangular panels with a longboard-shaped void, called "bones." *Party Wall*'s façade weaves these bones together into a double-layered screen that gives the pavilion its skin. The remaining 10% of Comet's waste comprises misprinted boards that do not reach the milling step and are therefore uncut. These panels, printed on one side, are used as the seats for the benches on the lowest layer of the façade.

The structure is also made of leftovers. In this case, unused 4" x 4" x ¼" steel L-profiles from a project by Banker Steel were made usable after a re-engineering process led by Silman. Various other components—pools, pumps, lights—were returned to

their manufacturers to be resold after the dismantling of the pavilion. Many of the longboard panels were donated to an artists' community to use as dividing screens, while some of the water bags were given to a farm in New Jersey.

At the finer scale, the weaving together of longboard off-cuts into a pattern sets up a similar tension at the level of the façade. The original expectation of a digitally designed woven fabric is overthrown as the voided longboard shape becomes apparent. Mounted on the base of the façade, the solid boards afford enclosure and architectural pediment. When removed, they afford sitting (with legs, we call them benches) or playing (with "soft-trucks," they revert to a strange kind of skateboard). Working backward, the bench reveals its other affordances by its underside print, which in turn hints at the façade components as a series of functional cuts, and a chain of events which potentially conjures the origins of the material and its many transformations (and affordances) throughout its own, diverse life cycle.

Party Wall: View of shadow from above.
Photograph © 2013 Zachary Tyler Newton.

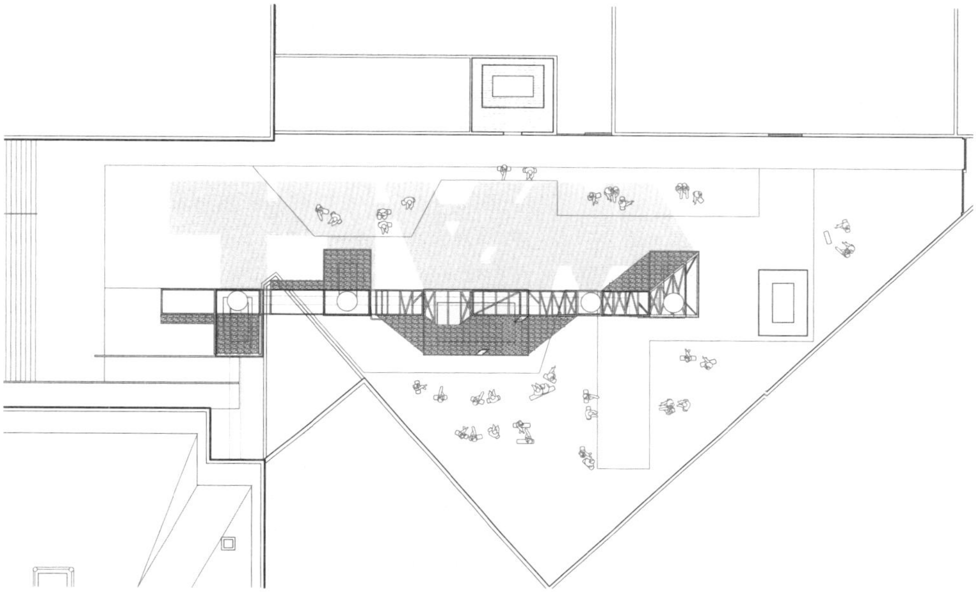

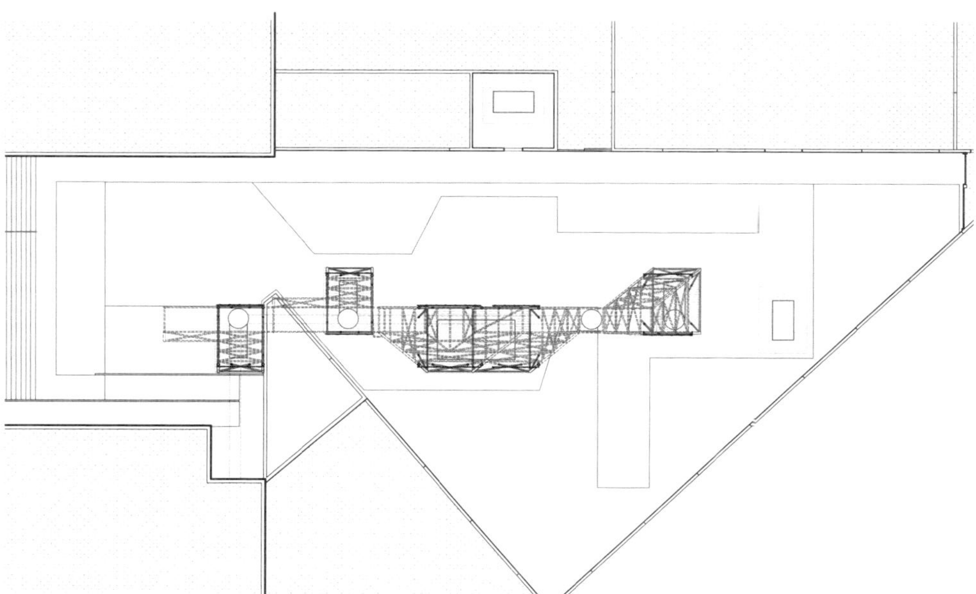

MoMA PS

left: *Party Wall: View of unattached benches from above.* **Photograph © 2013 Zachary Tyler Newton.**

left: *Party Wall: View through upendded W*. **Photograph by Brent Solomon.**
right: *Party Wall: View from dancefloor*. **Photograph by Brent Solomon.**

Party Wall: View from PS1 at night. Photograph © 2013 Zachary Tyler Newton.

Party Wall in action. **Photograph © 2013 Zachary Tyler Newton.**

Party Wall Skin at dusk. Photograph © 2013 Zachary Tyler Newton.

Tripe

An Offally Little Library
The Buffalo Architecture Foundation Little Free Library competition, winner
Riverside Community Garden, Buffalo, NY, USA
with support from Cornell Architecture/AAP
2018

In the culinary world, "nose-to-tail" refers to a practice in which the whole animal is used, without discarding the parts that are typically considered waste. Whereas *Party Wall* used found objects, *Tripe* began with the premise that it is possible to design one's own waste. By carefully arranging the necessary parts in a cut file, the leftovers can be, like tripe, as useful as the originally desired output.

Tripe, meaning "stomach lining," is typically considered waste or low-grade meat in the processing of an animal. The term also means "hole" in Greek (*tripa*).

In the mini-library, the leftovers from the production of 36 reading stools are designed so that the "waste"—plywood sheets with multiple cut-outs—becomes a functional screen. The voided layout of seat-parts, leg-parts, and structural connectors, which combine to make stools, is interspersed with square voids to house compartments for seven waterproof book boxes. The pattern also includes cut-outs for the storage of the stools, which can be reinserted into the screen when not in use. In this way, the

programmatic organization and the porosity of the piece can be adjusted depending on activity and numbers.

While most mini-libraries are simply containers for books, this project argues that a library is more than shelves—in addition to bookcases, a library is a space to sit and read with others. Part reading room, part book-stack, and part stage, *Tripe* contains over 600 books that circulate around Buffalo's Riverside neighborhood. Local children visit the space to borrow and return books, and to read, perform, and play.

The planting boxes extant on the site are echoed in the installation via a small planting box within the structure. The red tulips planted in this box serve as a bookend to the garden's productive landscape, and as a nod to *Tripe's* red interior. The red-revealing cut-outs are indexed by a reverberation of lines that are offset from the openings in a gradient. These lines transform from one cut-out shape to the next, created by the same CNC-milling process used to extract the shapes. This technique, inspired by the Mexico '68 Olympic Games logo—a recognizable image that came to be associated with a student-led revolution—produces its own pattern within the cutout pattern, while at the same time revealing a secondary pattern in the grain of the wood.

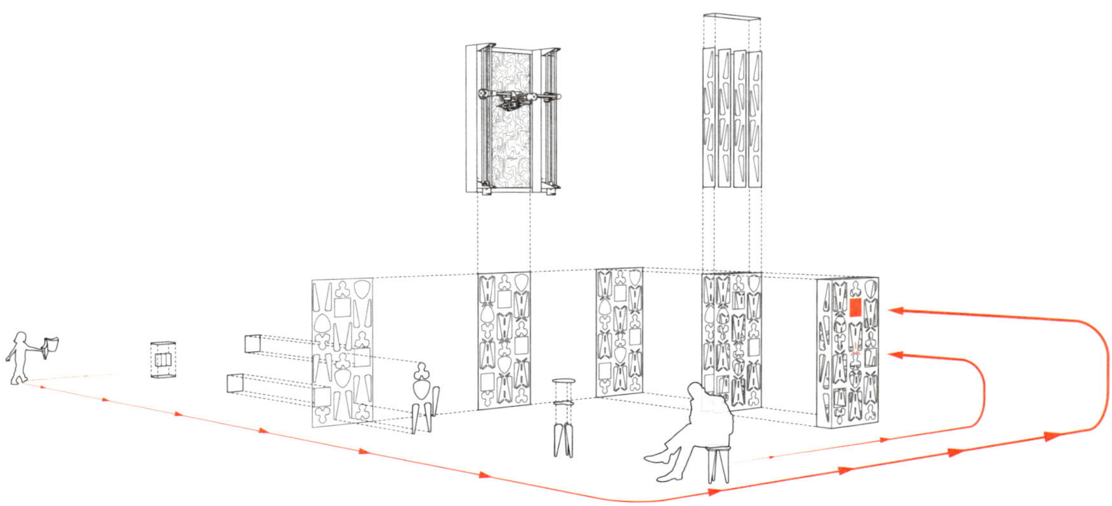

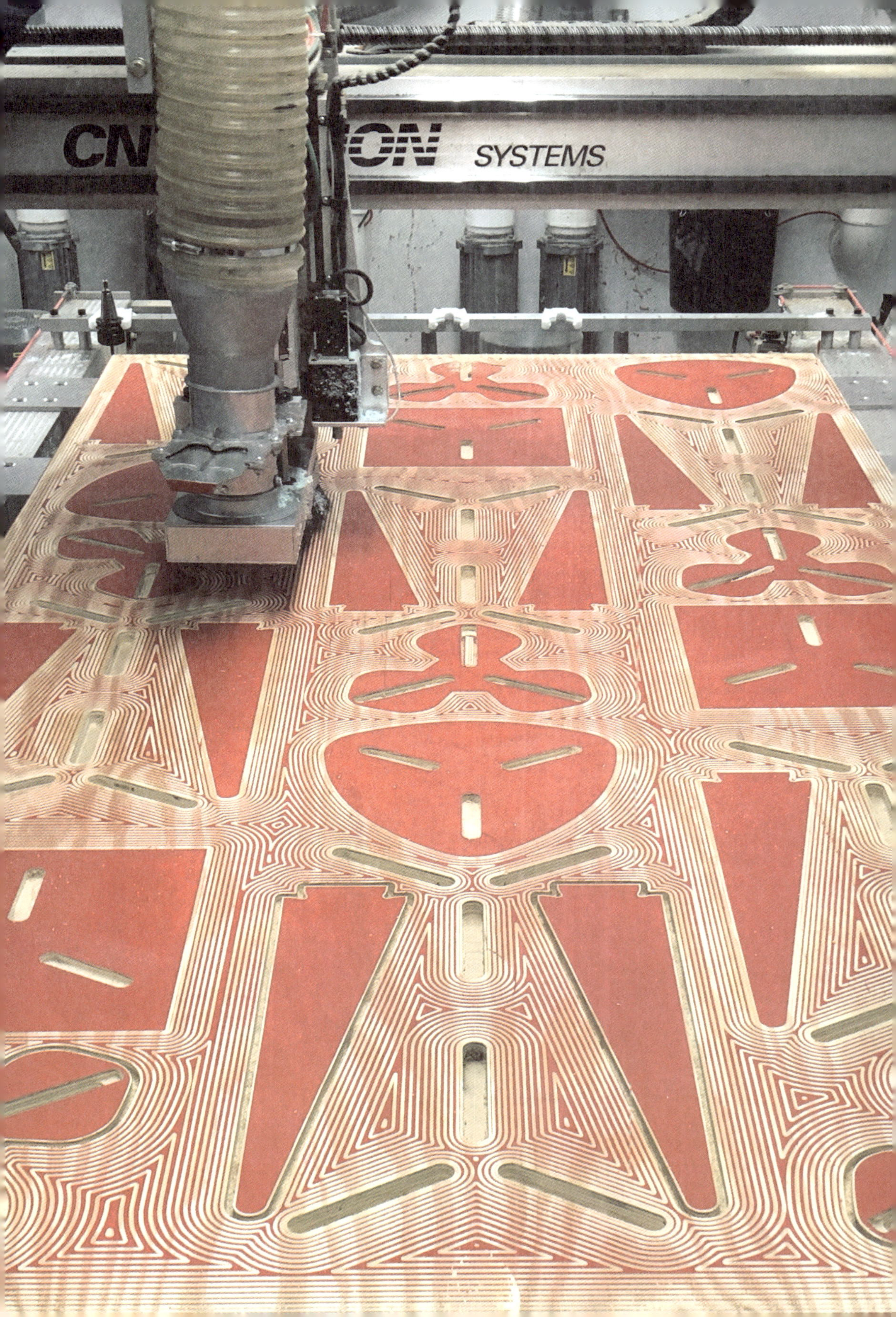
SYSTEMS

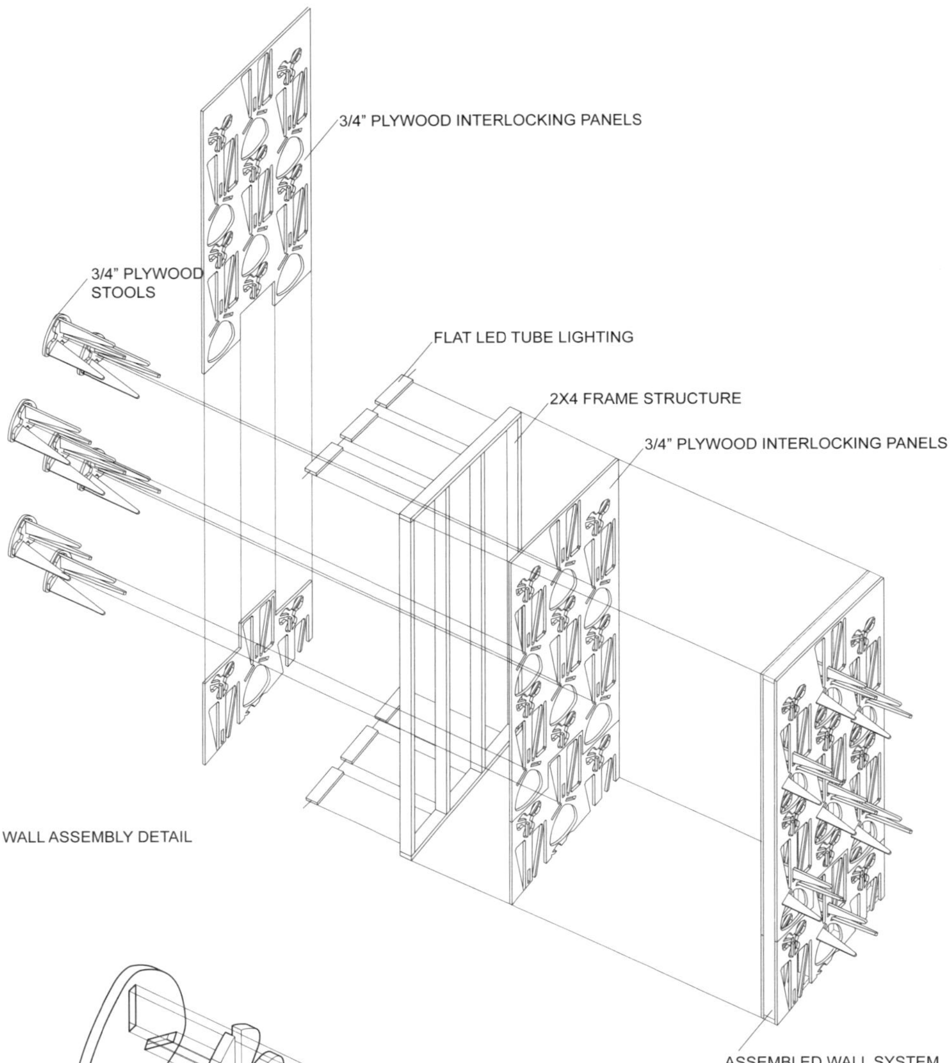

WALL ASSEMBLY DETAIL

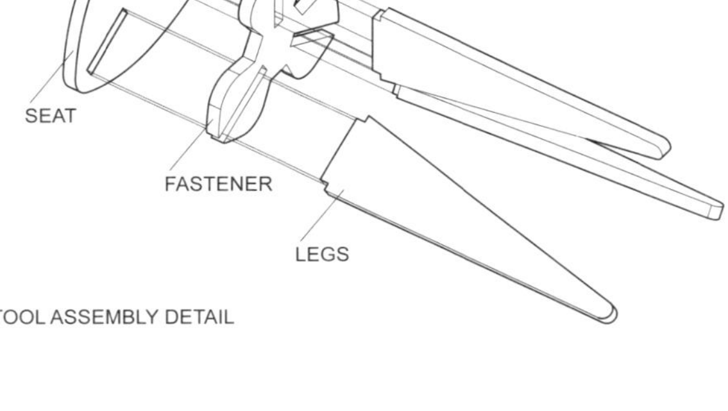

STOOL ASSEMBLY DETAIL

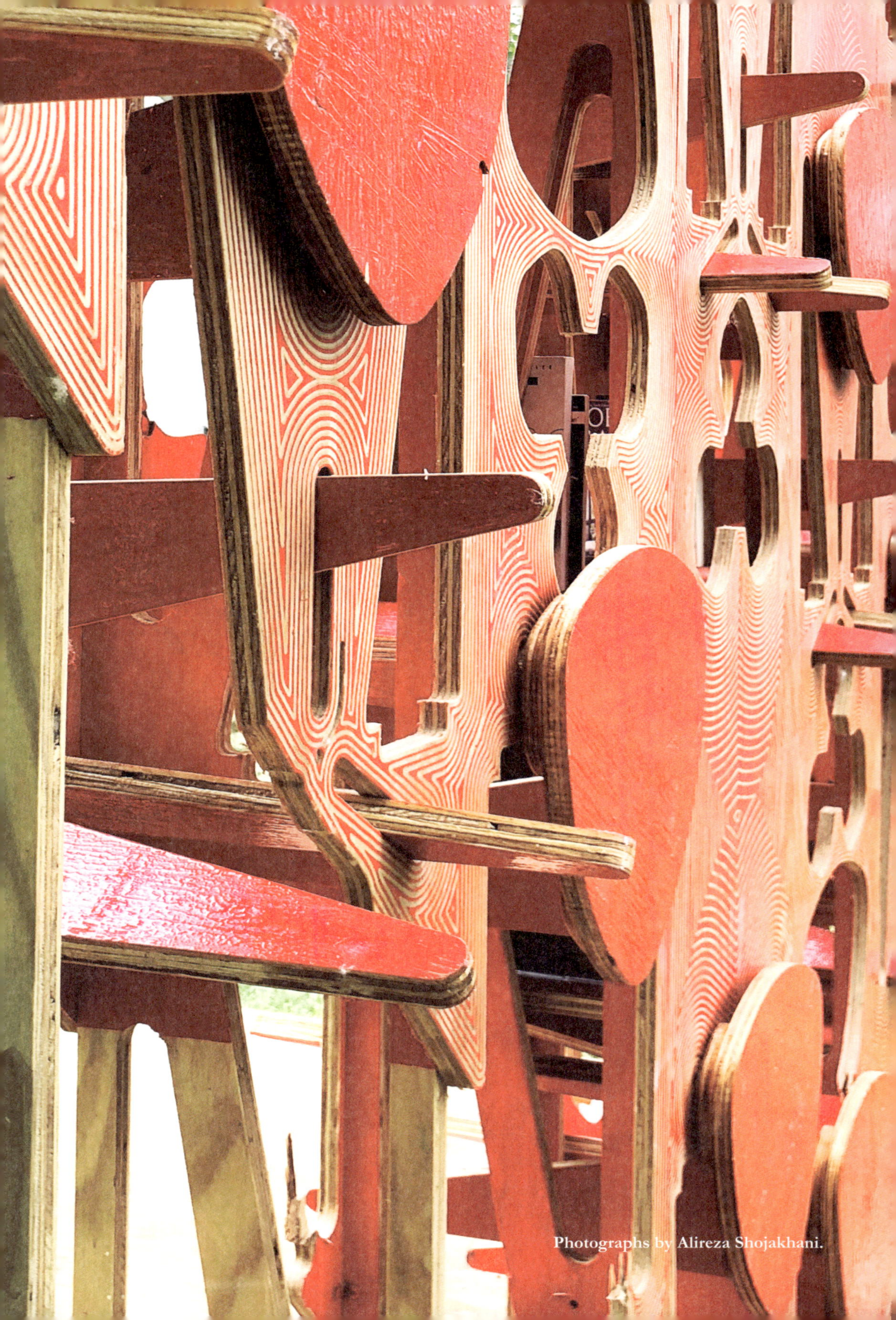

Photographs by Alireza Shojakhani.

Photograph by Alireza Shojakhani.

THE OPPOSITE OF ME
JODI PICOULT
THE SOUTH BEACH DIET
LittleFreeLibrary.org
Take a Book · Return a Book
Happy Birthday or Whatever
Annie Choi
WALT DISNEY PRODUCTIONS presents
GOOFY'S GAGS
Hansel and Gretel
Hansel and Gretel
STEP INTO READING
PIT CREW PUPS
OF THE LONGHOUSE
BETTY BAKER
PICTURES BY ARNOLD LOBEL
MINNIE ROCKS
HAPPEN

Photographs by Alireza Shojakhani.

Bloodline

A Self-consuming Grill Pavilion
Schloss Solitude, Stuttgart, Germany
supported by Akademie Schloss Solitude 2008-2011
exhibited in Tjaden Gallery, Cornell University, Ithaca, NY, USA
with support from Cornell Council for the Arts and Elise Jaffe + Jeffrey Brown
2011

Through an analysis of the parent-child relationship of a pair of umbilically connected baroque palaces, *Bloodline* proposes a third in the lineage. This pavilion exposes not only the barely concealed monstrosity of the second palace, but also foregrounds the idea of real-time evolution through the new form itself.

Bloodline is a small pavilion in a forest outside Stuttgart, Germany, within the grounds of the eighteenth-century Schloss (Castle) Solitude. The pavilion begins as a cube, clad with *grillholz* (local

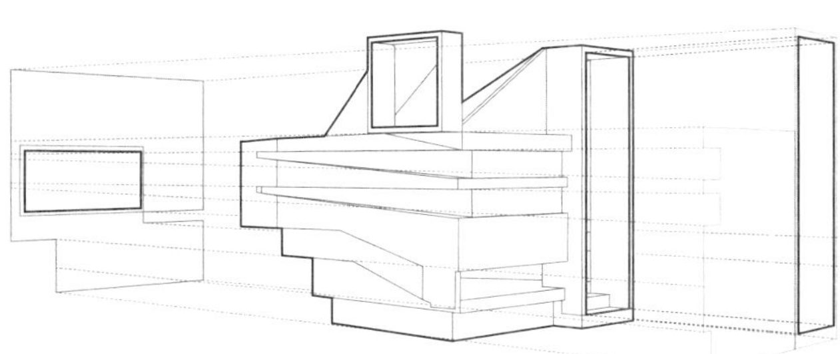

barbecue wood), which conceals a more complex space for food preparation and grilling. The exterior *grillholz* cube is consumed as the grill is used, gradually revealing the asymmetric "fire-space" inside. This space is derived from a few necessary parameters: a door, a serving window, a grill, and a chimney. Between these key components, a lofted surface creates the necessary shelves and work benches.

At first glance, Schloss Solitude appears to be as perfect an example of baroque architecture as its parent castle, Schloss Ludwigsburg. However, hidden beneath an ordered façade, a sinister and degenerate architecture is concealed. Its "fire-spaces" are misshapen volumes with openings through which the castle's servants viewed the world of the aristocrats from behind the fire. As the third in the lineage, *Bloodline* is located on its own unoccupied axis and asks: how can the third castle reveal the DNA of the original two? Or, could this pavilion render visible

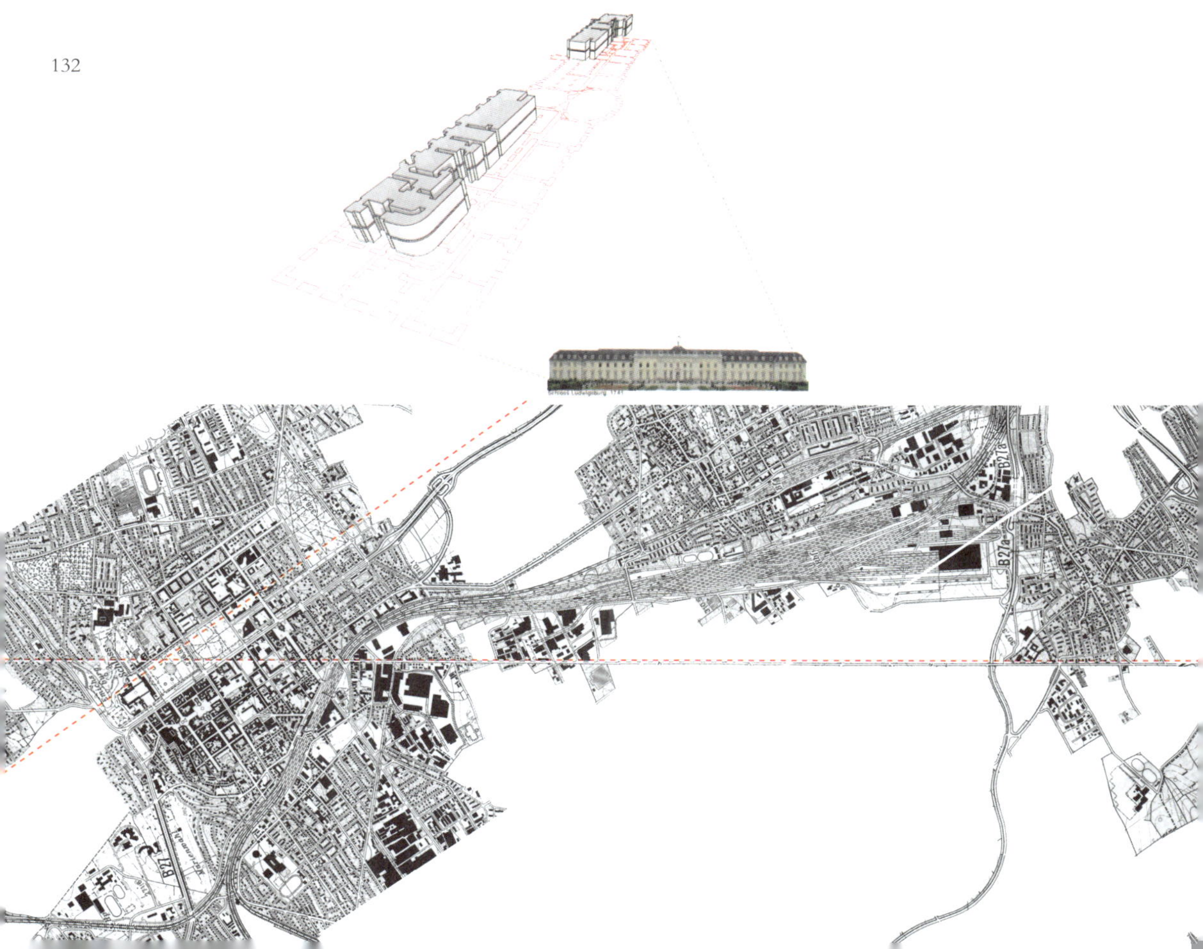

the opposing logics of perfect form and functional monstrosity through degeneration and change?

The shedding and consumption of *Bloodline*'s own skin is an exploration of architecture's potential transformation from animal to monster. While the animal evolves from generation to generation, the monster is able to transform swiftly before the eyes: *Bloodline* reveals its own evolutionary transformation in real time. As a perfect cube, the pavilion represents the architects' preconception of an ideal form. In this case, the project uses a material that is chromatically connected to the comparably pure form of the adjacent palace. As it transforms, the de-purification of the form and material corresponds to the revelation of the potential reinterpretation of cladding-as-fuel. After all, wood affords appropriate enclosure from one perspective, but it affords burning—and grilling—from another. The grill activates the cube's program and changes the project from pavilion to barbecue.

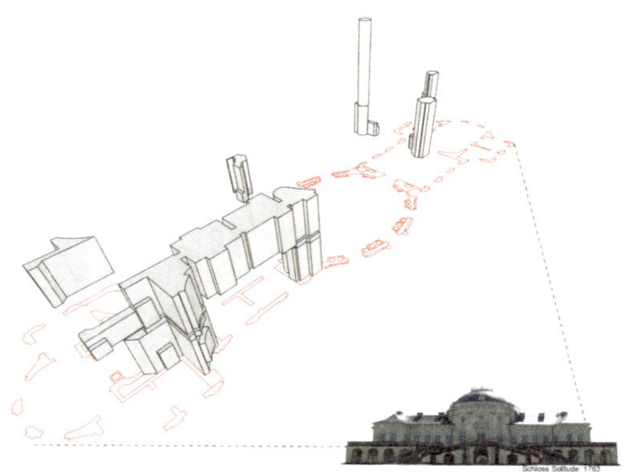

Bloodline's formal qualities are also in flux. On the one hand, the grill window's alignment with the forest axis (which was previously missing its requisite "castle"), or the chimney's alignment with the prevailing wind, both point to factors outside the project itself. On the other hand, the folds of the skin point to its internal functional needs, such as fire safety equipment, grilling tools, and food and ash storage. Use, interaction, and consumption cause the form to evolve and become a tool that provokes new readings of an object in a dynamic dialogue with its niche.

This approach is situated somewhere between indexical formal theory, in which dynamic diagrams result in a static but legible form, and material practices, in which change over time is fundamental. As James Lowder has described it: "the processes behind the formal erosion of the skin are not conceptual in nature and occurring in a virtual space, but rather are the actual physical and material processes based on the forces of program in a literal temporal field." As an ecdysic spider periodically sheds its skin, or a chameleon adapts to unpredictably changing backgrounds while preserving its integrity as an organism, this active, open, and tactical—if indeterminate—project is engaged with its context both in principle and in practice.

James Lowder, "Skin Problems," *The Expanding Periphery and the Migrating Center*, 103rd ACSA Annual Meeting Proceedings, Edited by Lola Sheppard & David Ruy.

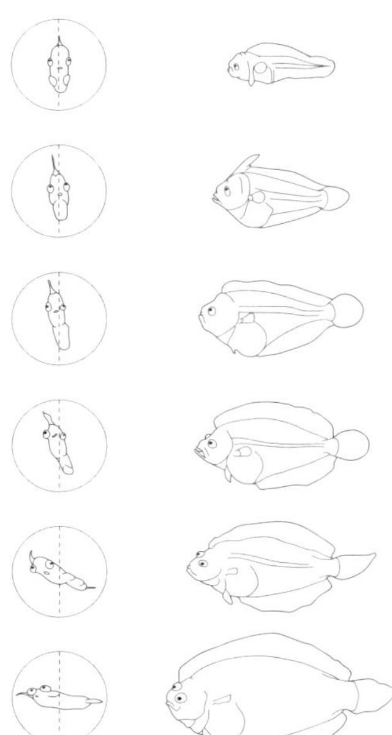

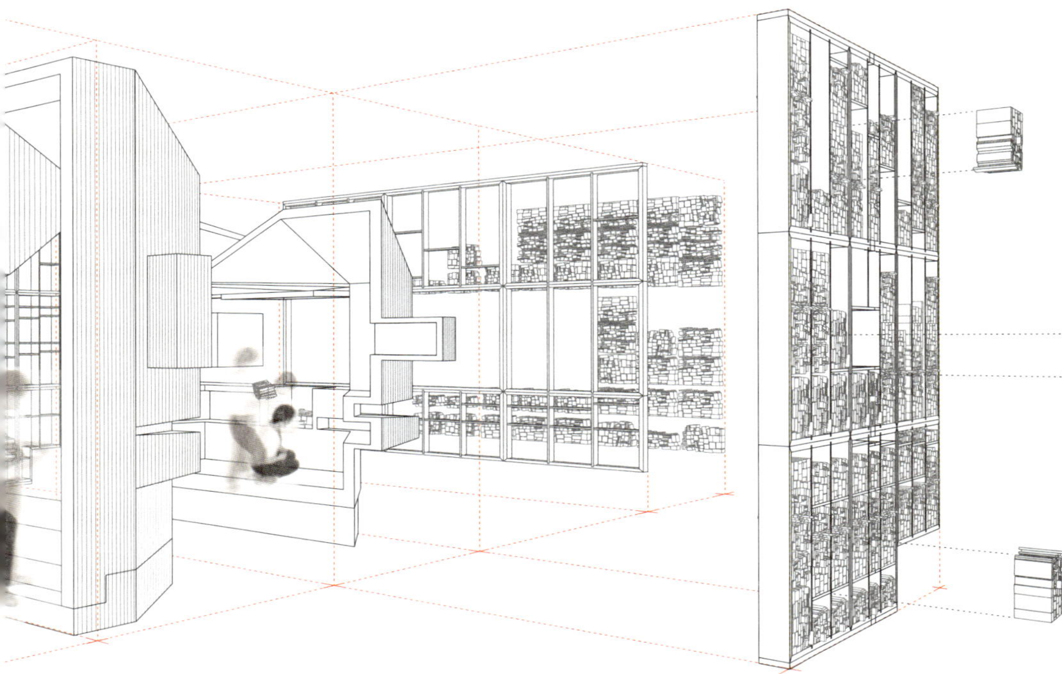

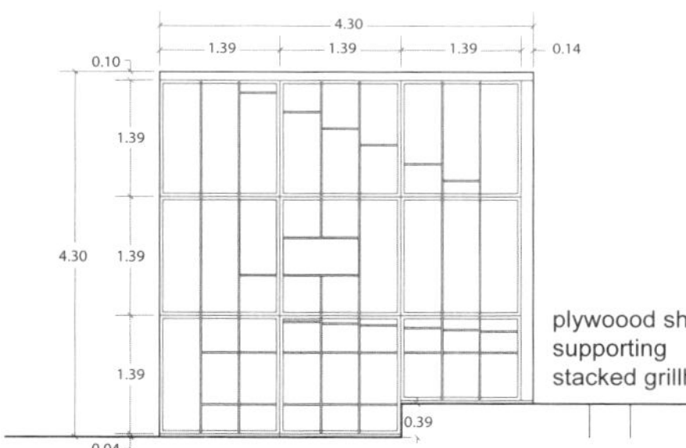

NORTH-WEST ELEVATION T=0

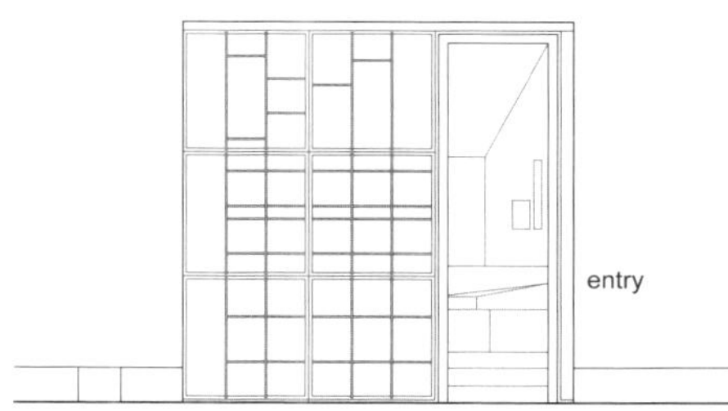

NORTH-EAST ELEVATION T=0

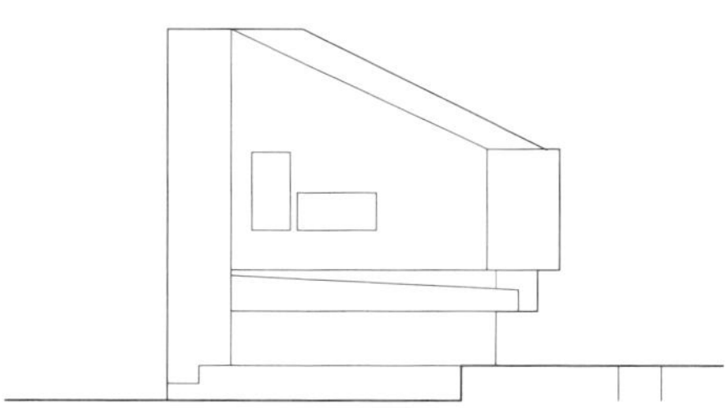

NORTH-WEST ELEVATION T=2

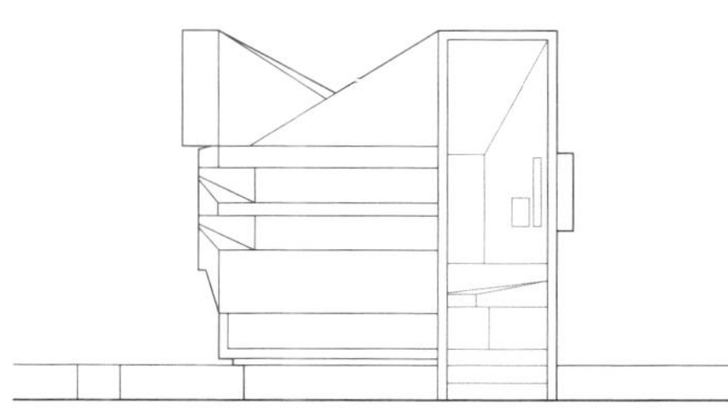

NORTH-EAST ELEVATION T=2

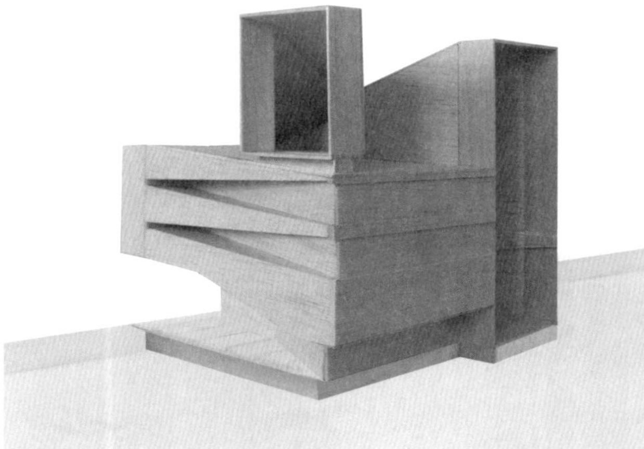

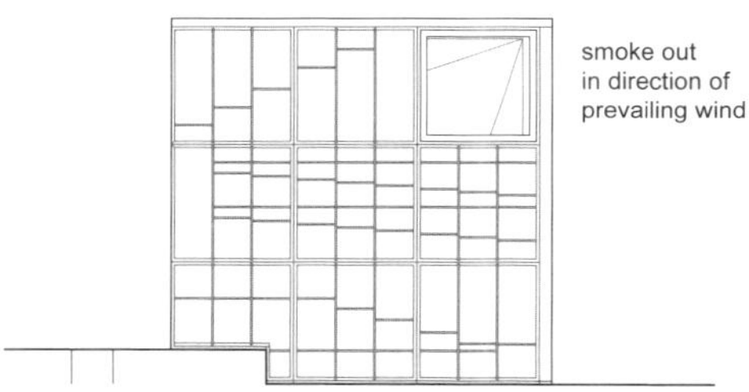

SOUTH-EAST ELEVATION T=0

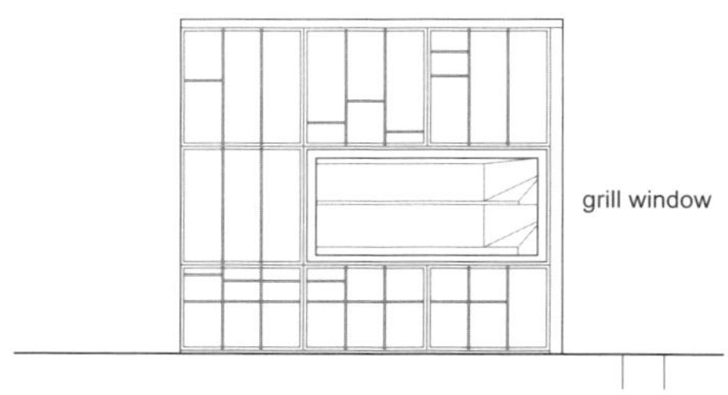

SOUTH-WEST ELEVATION T=0

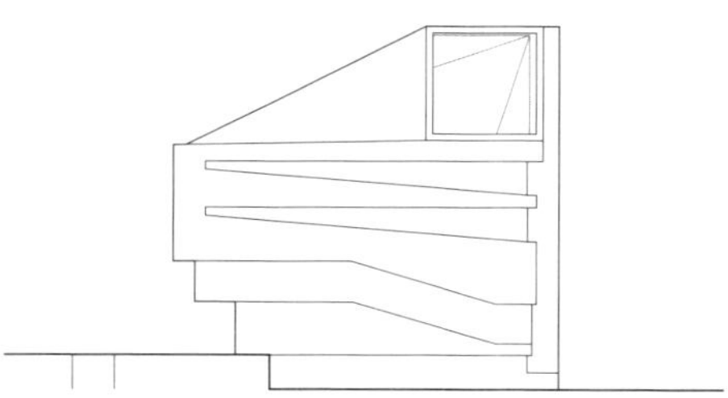

SOUTH-EAST ELEVATION T=2

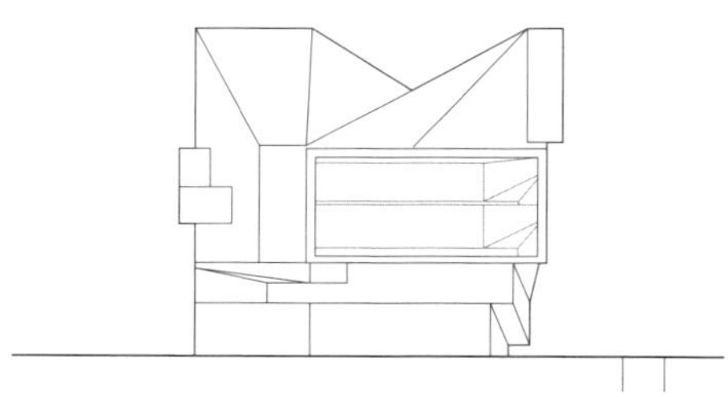

SOUTH-WEST ELEVATION T=2

Combust

An architectural bust
in "Bust"
commission for an exhibition curated by William O'Brien Jr.
Jai & Jai Gallery, Los Angeles, USA
2015

Combust manifests several lycanthropic traits that are central to CODA's practice: context as a generator of legible form, perceptual manipulation and surprise through material misuse, and transformation through interaction. Here, the match is both what makes the bust, as well as what un-makes it. The transformation is thus irreversible—once combusted, there is no return to a former state.

Combust draws in its environment, twisting, posturing, and opening in response to local infrastructure: the smoke detector and the light source. The tense dialog between face and sensor is palpable when, as the viewer moves toward and around the bust, the material is understood not only as wooden sticks but as phosphorus-tipped matchsticks, always threatening to ignite and cause the sensor to sound. In its stand-off with the sensor, the bust's promise of imminent fire implies a future, albeit burnt, doppelgänger.

Whereas the typical bust is closed and convex, *Combust* reveals an uncharacteristic double-sided faciality and thinness most akin to

GENERIC BUST:
BASE-NECK-HEAD,
BILATERAL SYMMETRY

BUST ABSTRACTION

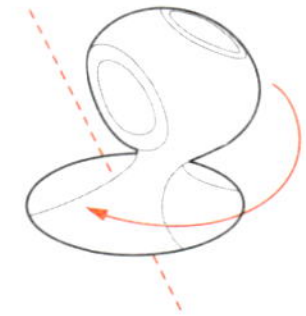

BUST ROTATES IN X-AXIS
TO RECOGNIZE THREAT

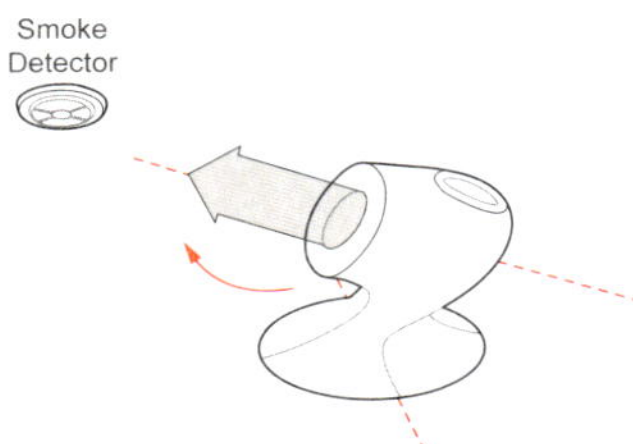

BUST ROTATES IN Z-AXIS
TO CONFRONT CEILING THREAT

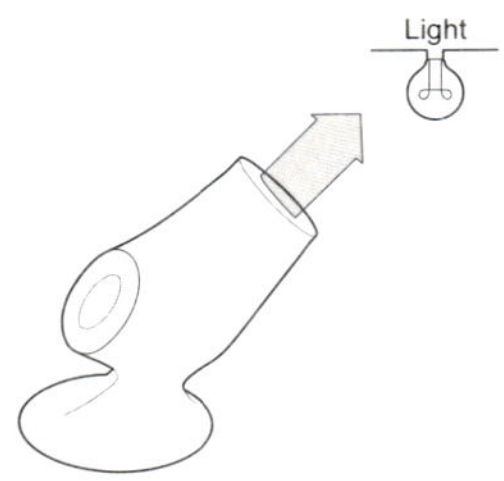

BUST OPENS
TOWARD LIGHT SOURCE

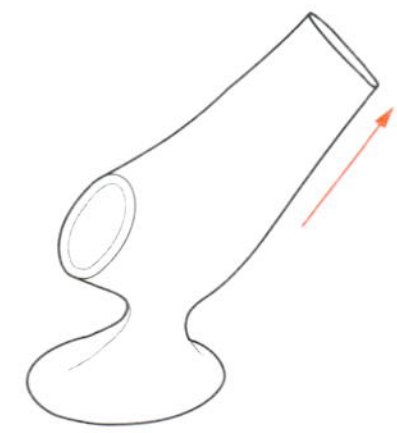

BUST ELONGATES

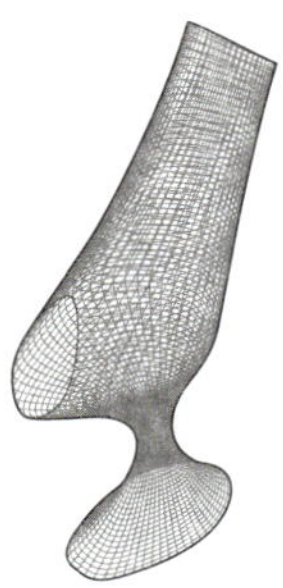

BUST INTERIOR SURFACE MOLD
WITH DISTROTED GRID LAYERED IN
PAPIER-MÂCHÉ

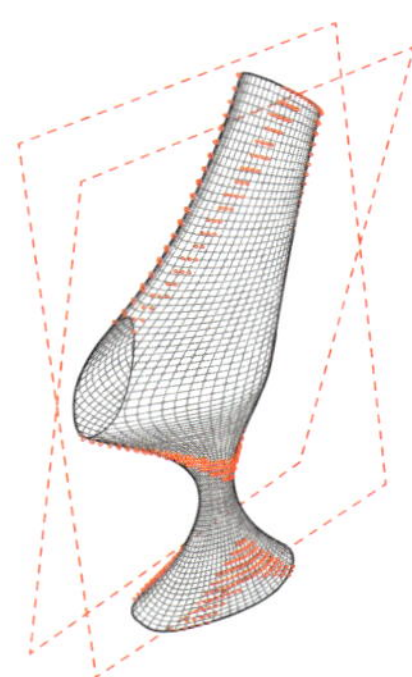

BUST OVERLAID WITH SALTIRE

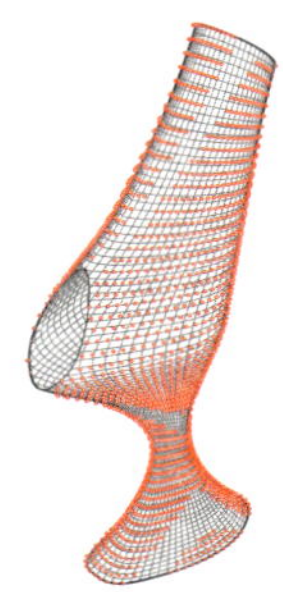

BUST POPULATED WITH POINTS

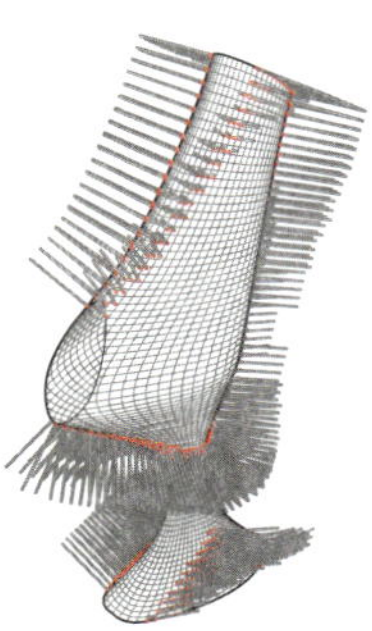

SALTIRE POPULATED WITH
WHITE CIGAR MATCHES

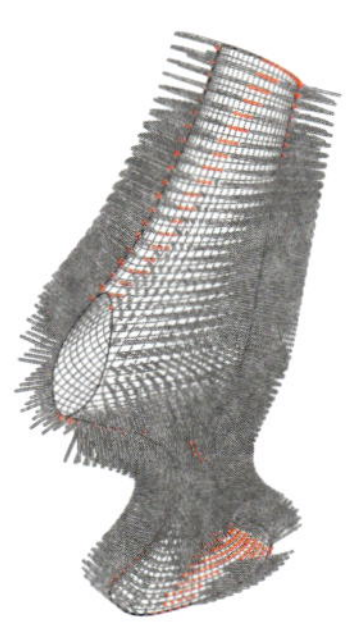

SKIN POPULATED

SET ALIGHT

that of flags. Reinforcing this, an internal saltire created by longer and thicker white cigar matches is legible in color (interior) and depth (exterior). In this case, *Combust*'s hypothetical burning is meant as a political and symbolic gesture. Where saltire-bearing flags serve as reminders of oppression, invasion, and slavery, *Combust* serves as an act against these transgressions.

Combust's 2,000 matchsticks, 200 cigar matches, and papier-mâché surface were exhibited at the Jai & Jai Gallery in Los Angeles, along with nine other busts. Commissioned by William O'Brien, Jr. in 2015, all ten busts were limited only by size and some presumed "bustiness." O'Brien explained his curatorial motives thus: "The conception of a bust within an architectural context privileges certain architectural concerns—such as those related to form, figure, façade, hierarchy, orientation, exteriority, interiority—while diminishing many other architectural considerations that must ordinarily be addressed when designing buildings."

Janelle Zara, "On View> Los Angeles or BUST: New exhibition features full-frontal forms," in *Archpaper*, September 4, 2015

In 2019, *Combust* was finally set alight. Flames were sucked inward into the voided face, as heat, fire, and smoke poured out of the chimney in an extreme demonstration of the stack effect. In a

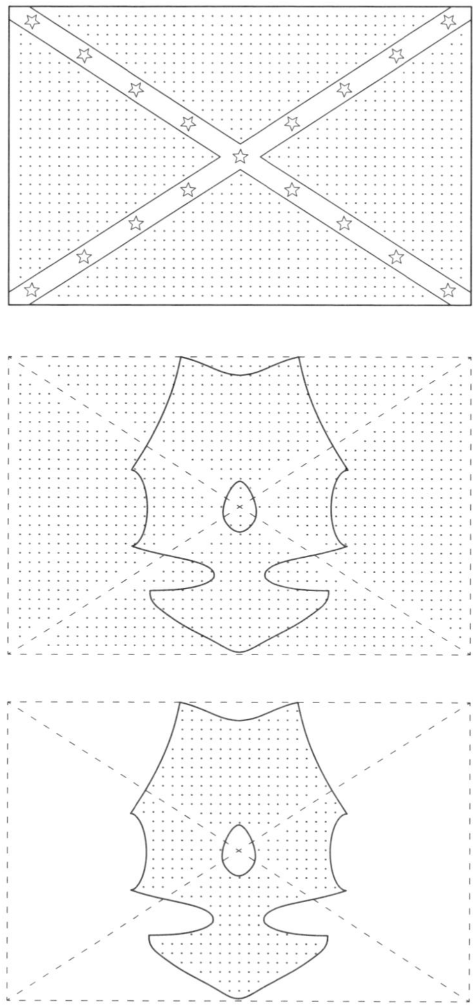

glorious one minute and thirty-nine seconds, as the room turned orange, the cigarsticks and matchsticks became black and curled. The Samson Fire Alarm Apparatus read BREAK GLASS, OPEN DOOR, PULL HOOK DOWN. But as they continued to stare at each other, like twin cyclopes, nobody did. Later, in the rubble, the balding and ashen husk held little of its former stateliness.

She burn'd with love, as straw with fire flameth,
She burn'd out love, as soon as straw out-burneth.

William Shakespeare,
The Passionate Pilgrim,
1599.

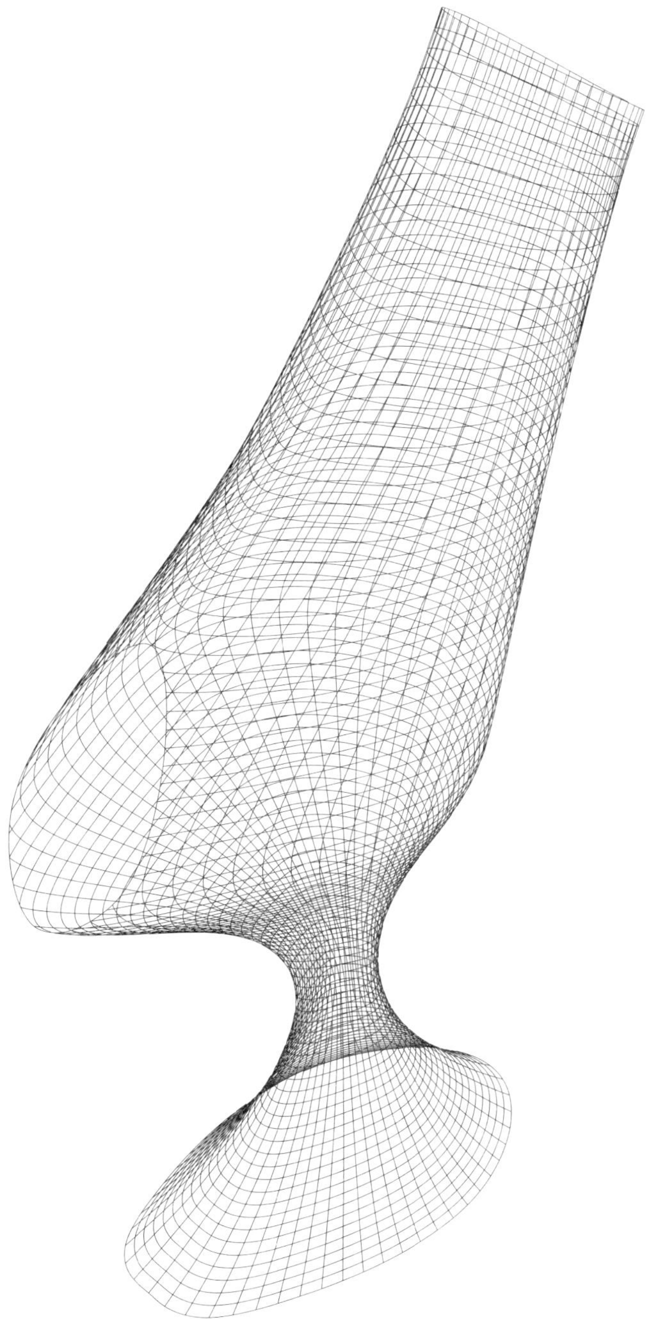

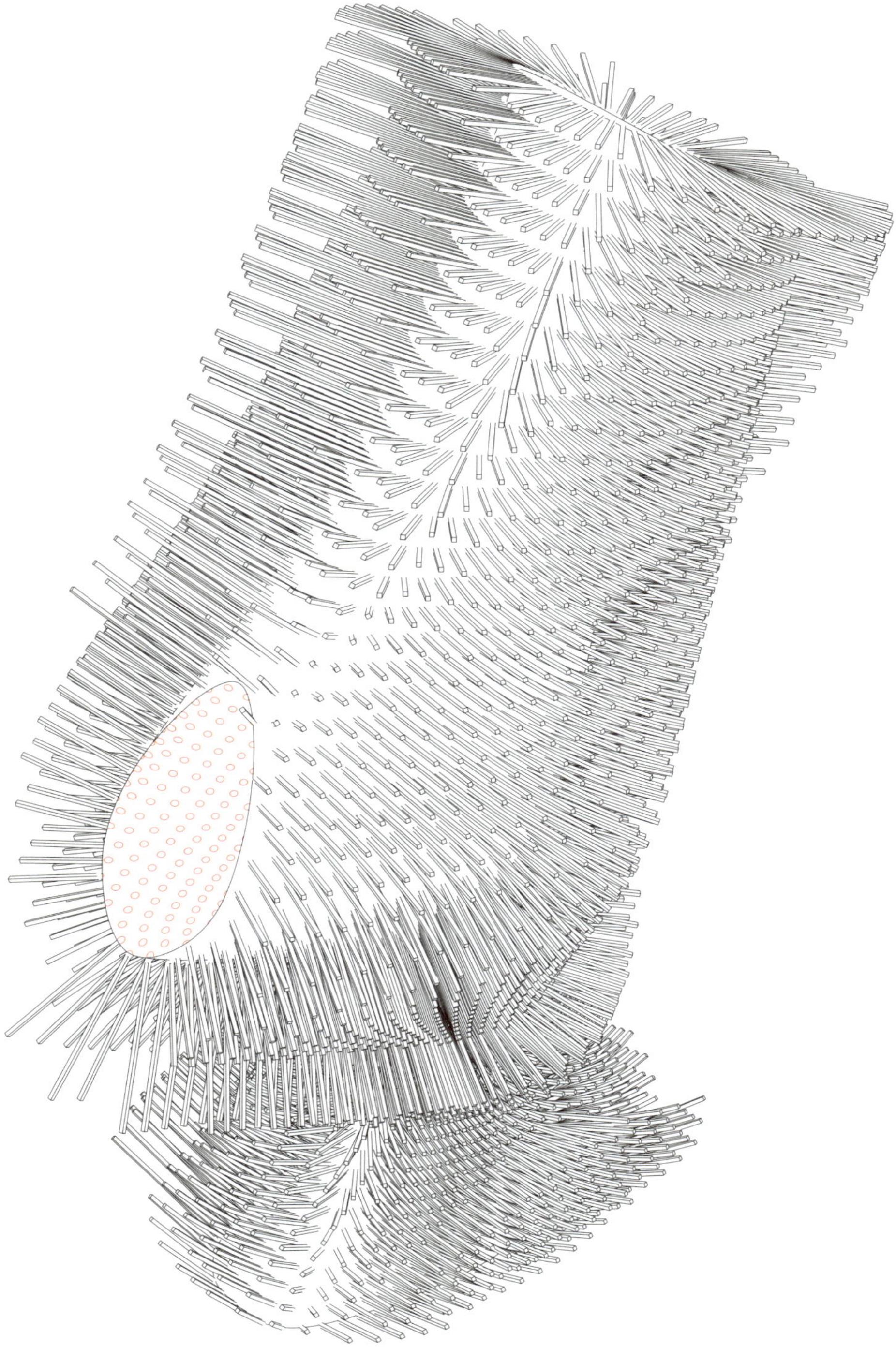

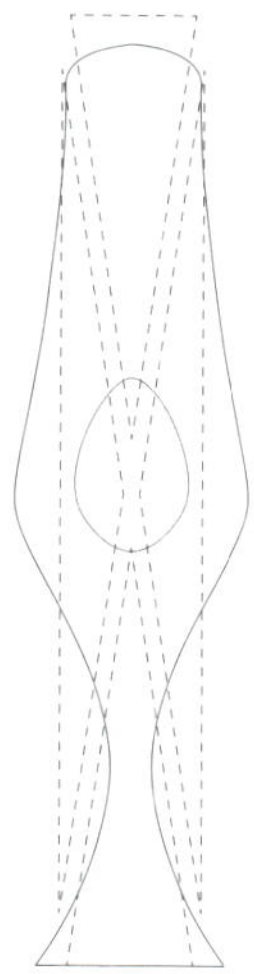

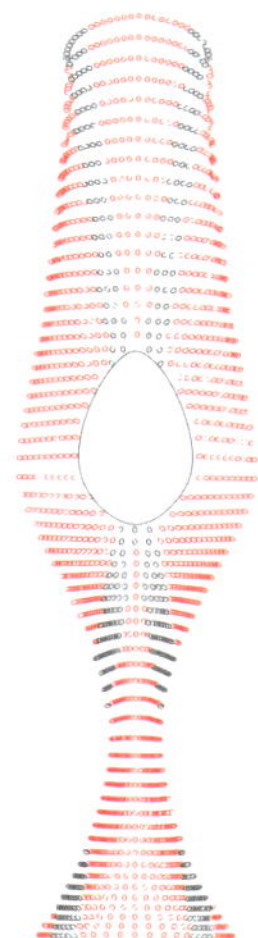

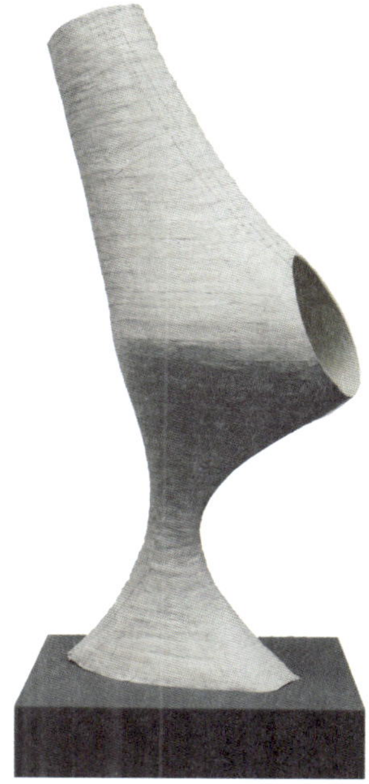

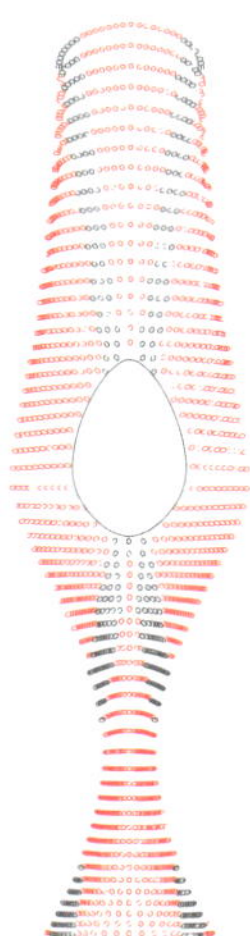

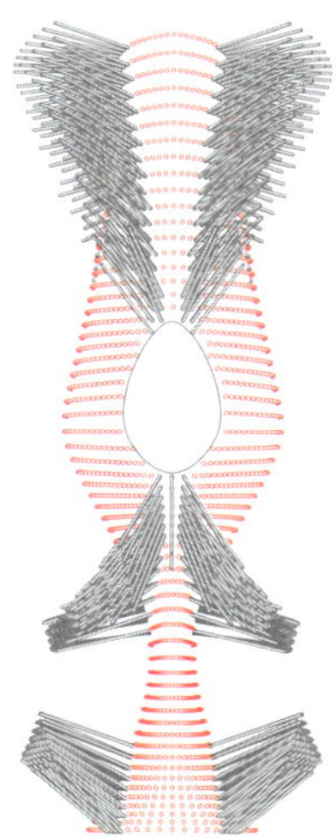

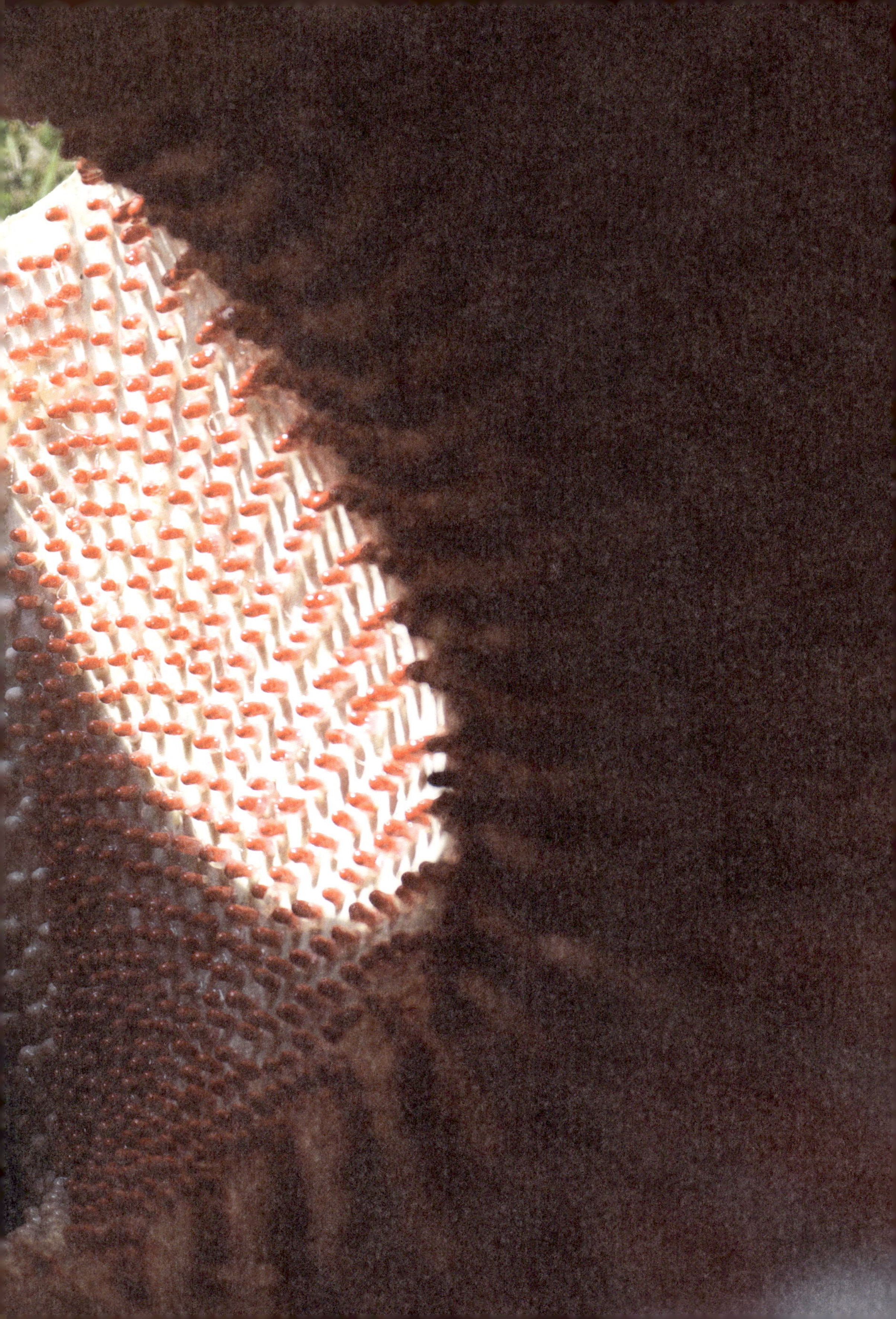

Combust, **courtesy of Jai & Jai Gallery, LA, 2015.**

Charolina House

A Recycled House
in collaboration with **Dillon Pranger**
private commission
Danby, NY, USA
2018–2019

Karolina's childhood home transformed itself on Christmas Eve of 2017, when a massive fire destroyed everything and left only the charred husk of a log cabin. The timber structure was completely blackened on the exterior, and everything else, except a few hastily rescued objects, was gone.

Karolina dreamed of a new house that would remind her of her destroyed family home. She also wanted to live in tune with the natural environment, so the new house needed to engage in circular material economies, renewable energy, rainwater collection, and so on. The proposed design plays on this ambivalence between the image and memory of the house, on the one hand, and the overturning of that image for harnessing the resources of the site, on the other.

Formally, the roof profile reads as a stereotypical house at the front. At the rear, the profile inverts itself to create a valley for water collection. The south-oriented façade and overhang allow solar energy to fall on the large reused glass façade in the winter

months, while shading it in the summer. Additionally, a circular opening in the porch roof allows a single maple tree to grow through the building and, together with several other adjacent maples, to mark the house as existing *within* nature rather than in isolation from it.

Similarly, the choice of materials plays an important role in accentuating that ambivalence. The reuse of the charred timber of Karolina's original home on the new façade is just the beginning of a list of materials that are reused and recycled: the floor slab makes use of the slab of an existing shed on the property, the insulation is denim, the structural timbers are reclaimed from a local barn, the kitchen surfaces use local unrecyclable Saratoga Springs bottle tiles, the windows are reused, and the interior surfaces are finished with mycelium bricks.

The organization of the interior shifts all of the wet programs to the rear of the house, where the water is collected via the roof inversion. A bathroom and kitchen on the ground level are covered with a loft-level sleeping area. The rest of the house is a double-height space that operates as a flexible living area and artist's studio. The east wall punches outward to accommodate the stair, chimney, and storage area.

Karolina's home. Photograph by Karolina Grunberg.

In the use of the charred skin, the old house literally becomes the new house. It contains Karolina, her art practice, and her collection of rescued objects, but it also opens itself up to the world and allows nature to shape it. The roof's response to the rainfall pushing downward and the tree expanding outward are in conflict with the stereotypical image of a house with a pitched roof and a porch. It is precisely this conflict between the expected and the reactive that makes the project intentionally uncanny.

Both homely and unhomely, this house is not just a nostalgic ghost of a past house, but a phoenix, reborn from its own ashes, drawing vitality and energy from its surroundings.

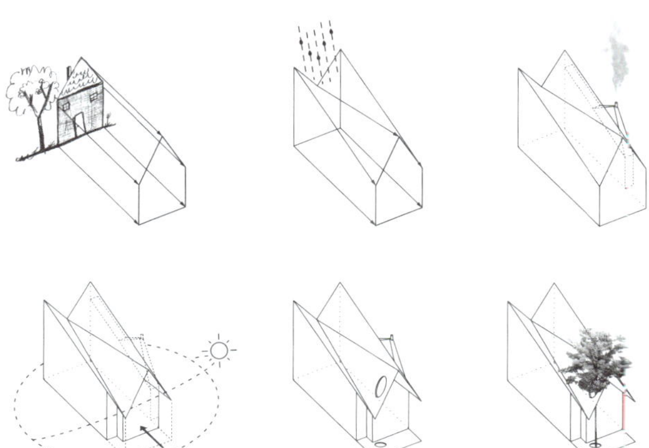

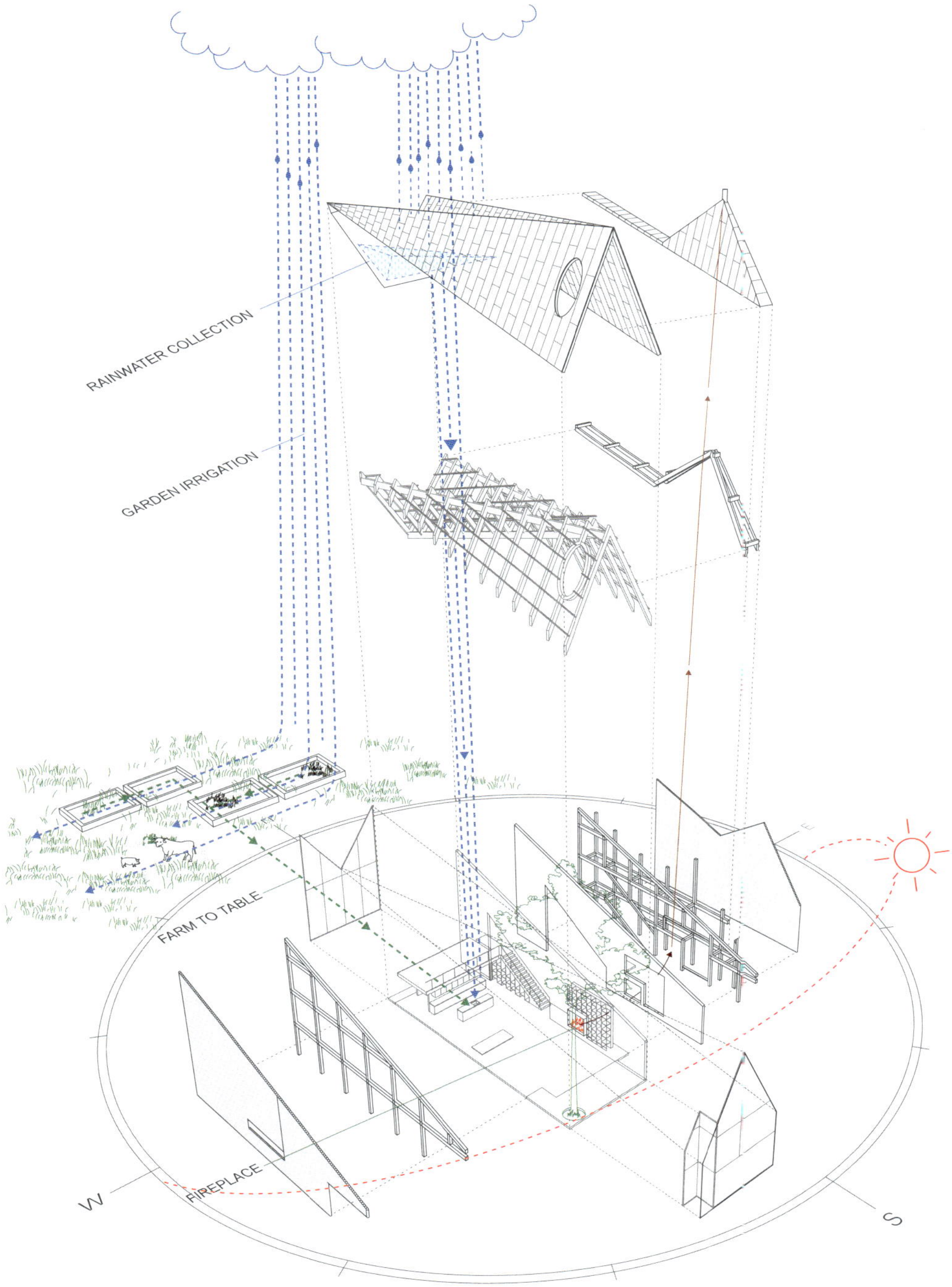

RAINWATER COLLECTION
GARDEN IRRIGATION
FARM TO TABLE
FIREPLACE
W
S

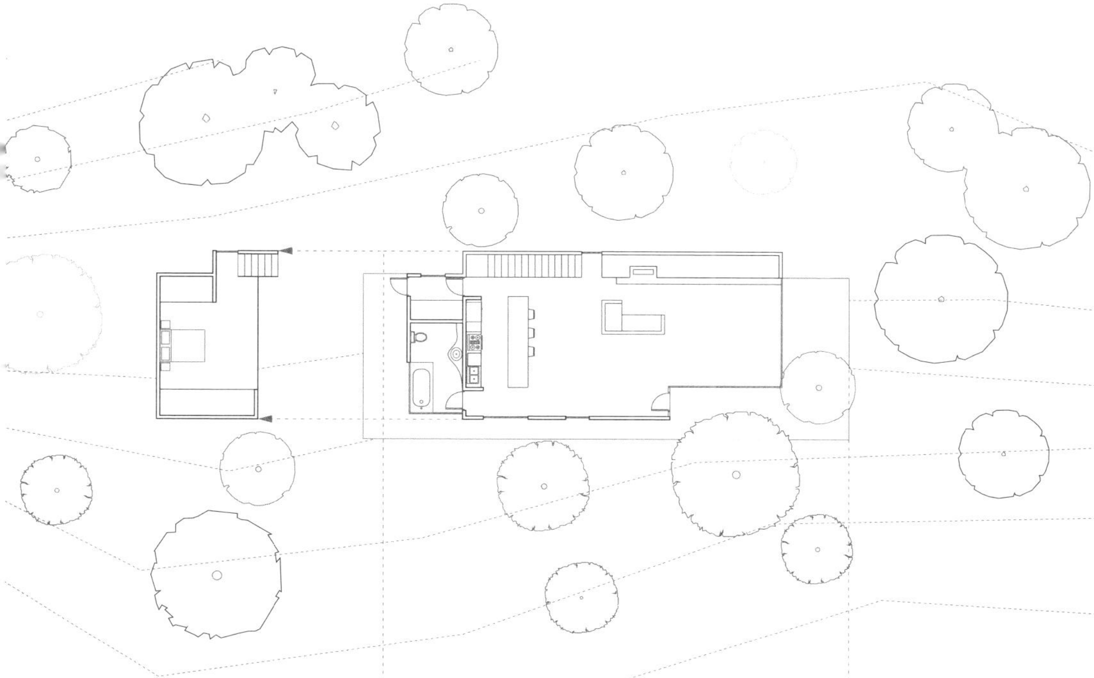

170

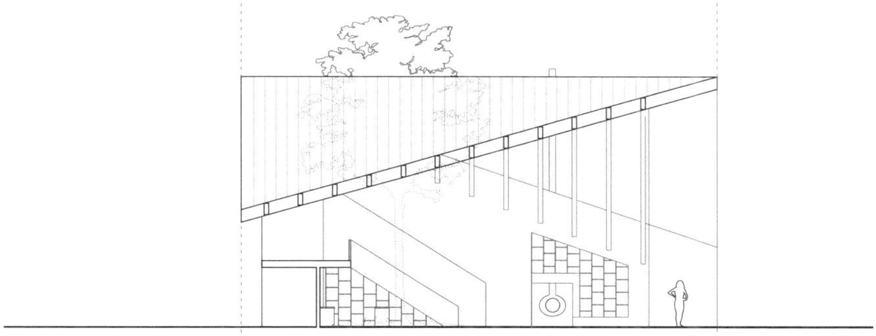

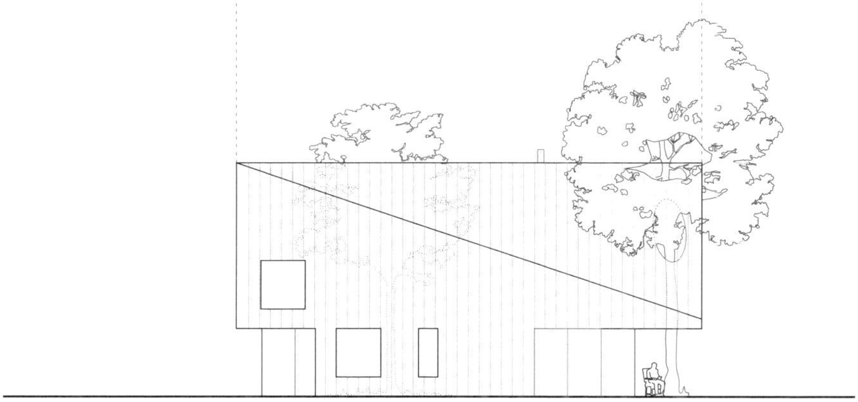

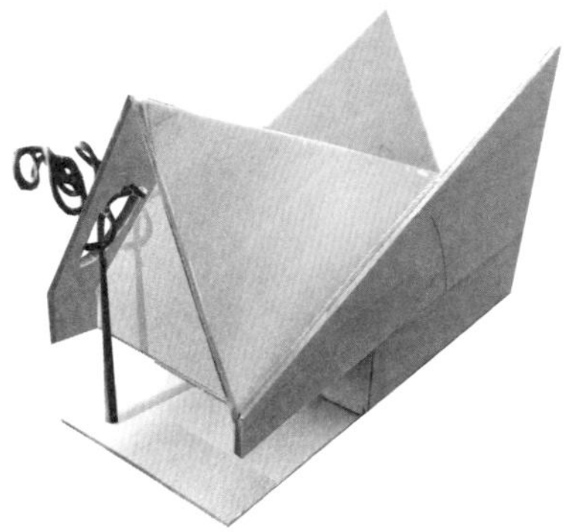

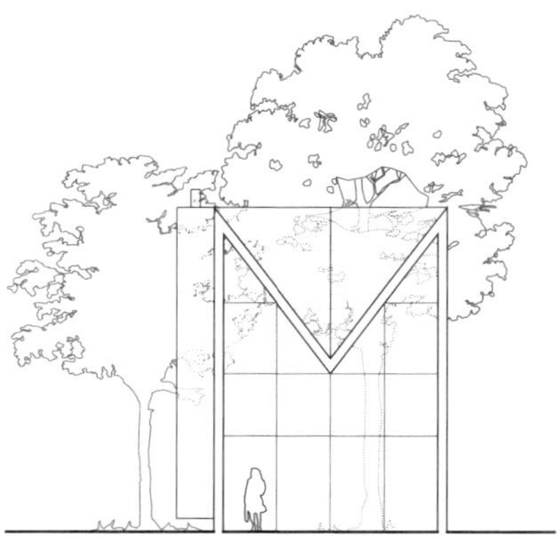

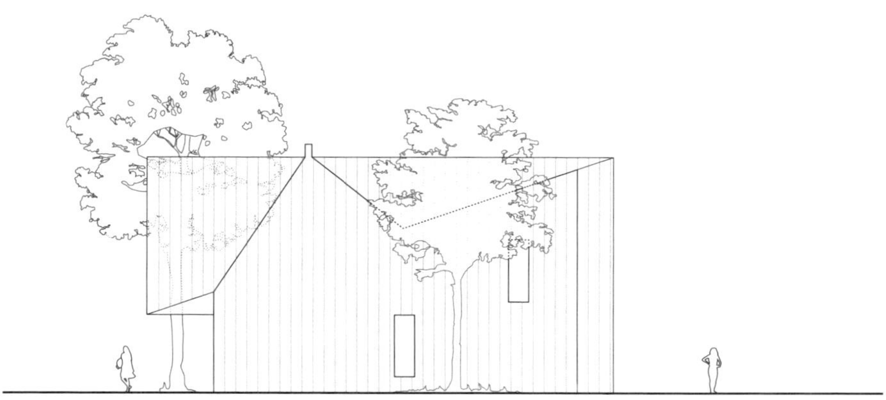

Salt Inc.

An Inclusive Addition
Constance Saltonstall Foundation for the Arts
private commission
Ithaca, NY, USA
2016–2020

Salt Inc. compresses five desired spaces into three, functioning by time-sharing the main spaces with multiple programs, depending on use and season. At times, this addition is intended to provide accessible studio space for one of the artists in a five-person artists' residency, along with accessible cooking and dining spaces. At other times, the addition should function as a public gallery for one of the foundation's frequent open-houses.

This transformation, from a private and contemplative setting to a public state, is achieved through a series of rotating walls and shutters. On the interior, the studio/gallery and dining room/gallery are separated/joined by a large rotating wall. On the exterior, a series of barn doors and shutters open and close to give privacy to the studios during public events and to form a backdrop for the performances.

Salt Inc. is conceived as a folded surface that first wraps around the existing studio building, then clads the façade of the new addition, and then folds diagonally to form an outdoor amphitheater.

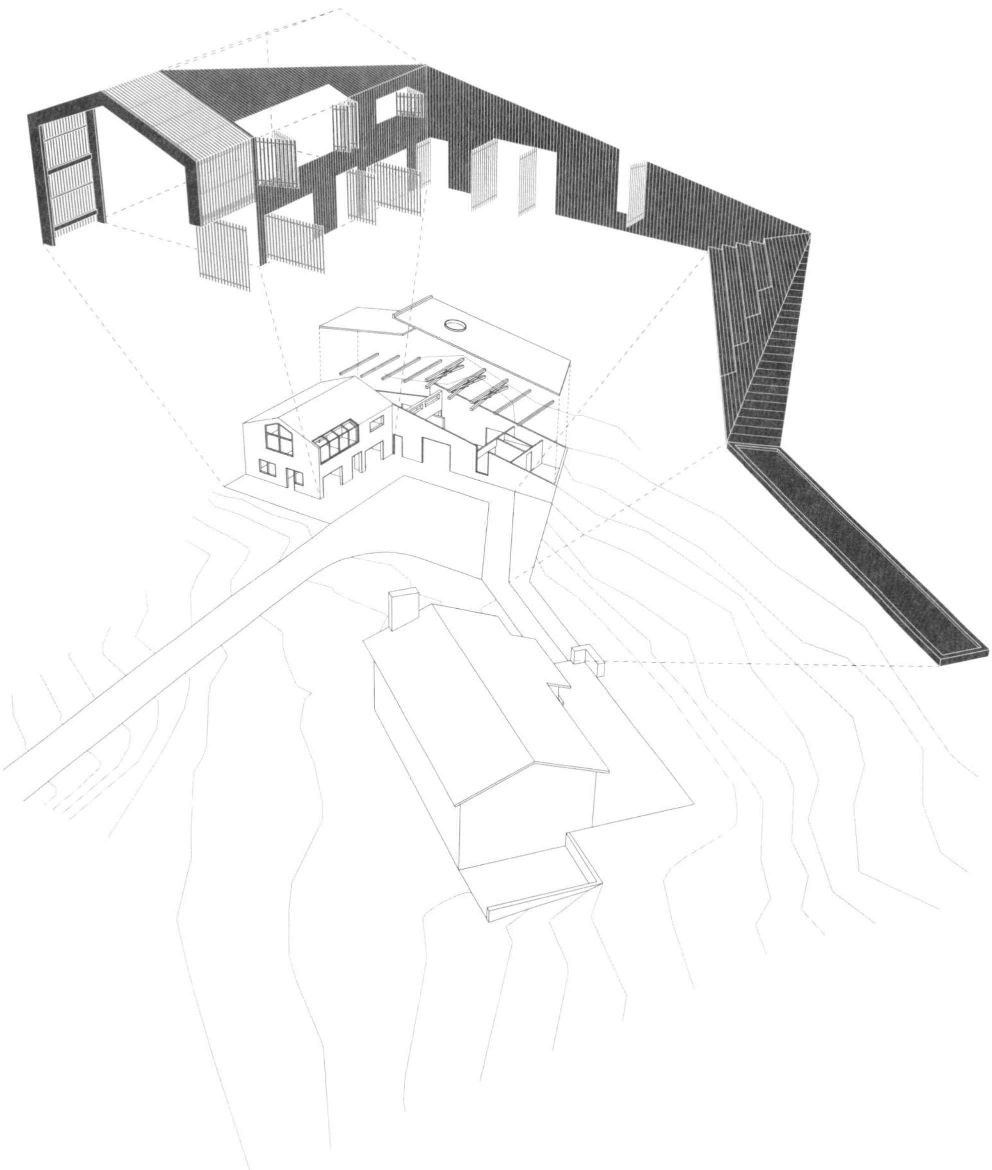

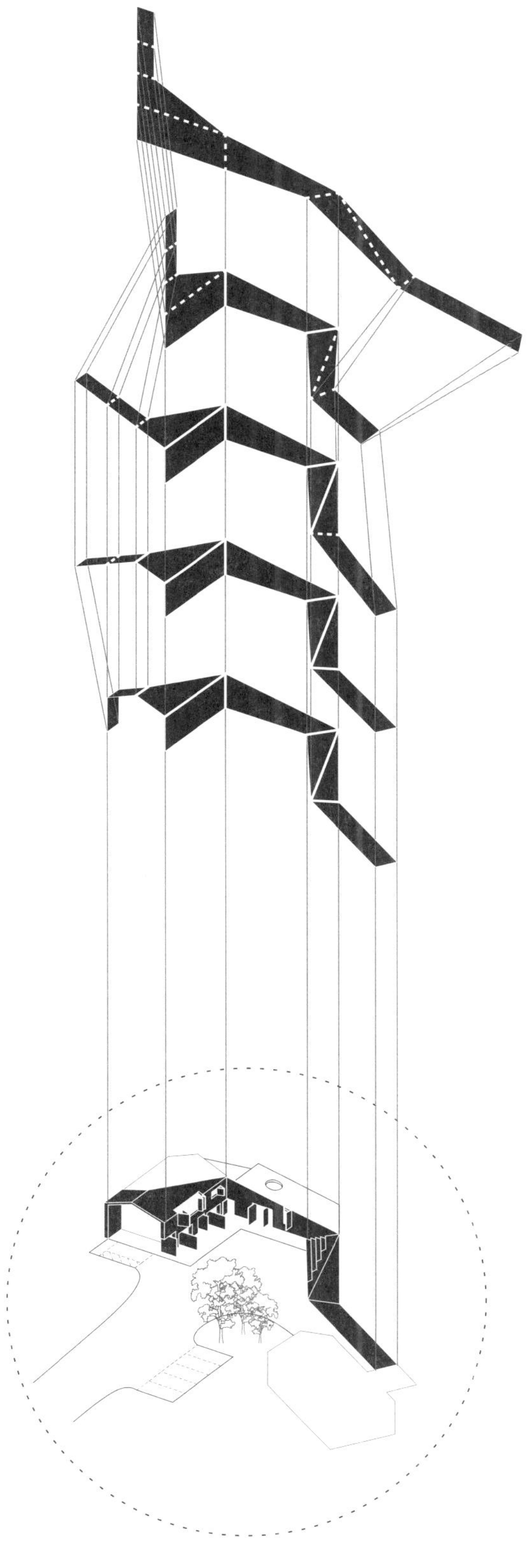

Finally, the skin folds diagonally once again to lie horizontally along the ground, creating a tail that leads the way to the existing, main house. In this way, the addition ties together the two existing buildings—studio and main house—on the site.

The outer skin uses the Japanese technique of yakisugi (charring), where wood is carbonized by burning to produce a waterproof and sun-resistant layer. The combustion neutralizes the cellulose that attracts insects and bacteria, requiring minimal maintenance thereafter. Yakisugi connects the fragments of buildings on the site, without literal mimicry, to the material of the main house, which is a dark gray-brown stained wood. Built in 1980 as a residence for its founder, Constance Saltonstall, the modest house is domestic yet stoic.

The opening and closing of shutters on the façade animates the exterior and reinforces its two states. When the artists are busy working and the public is absent, screens can be open and the gallery door closed. When the festivals take place, the artists' screens can be closed for privacy from the courtyard and the gallery door open to welcome the public.

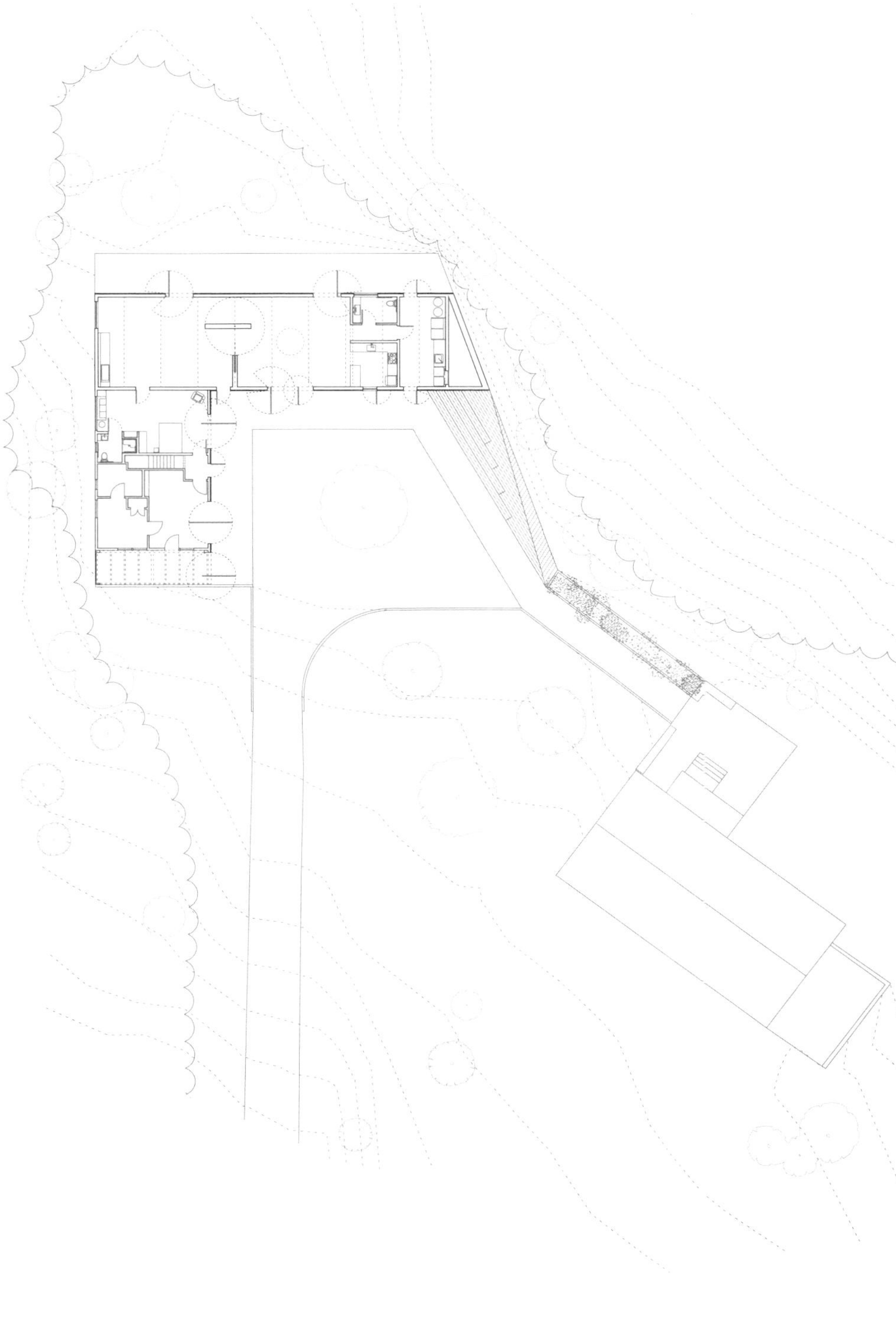

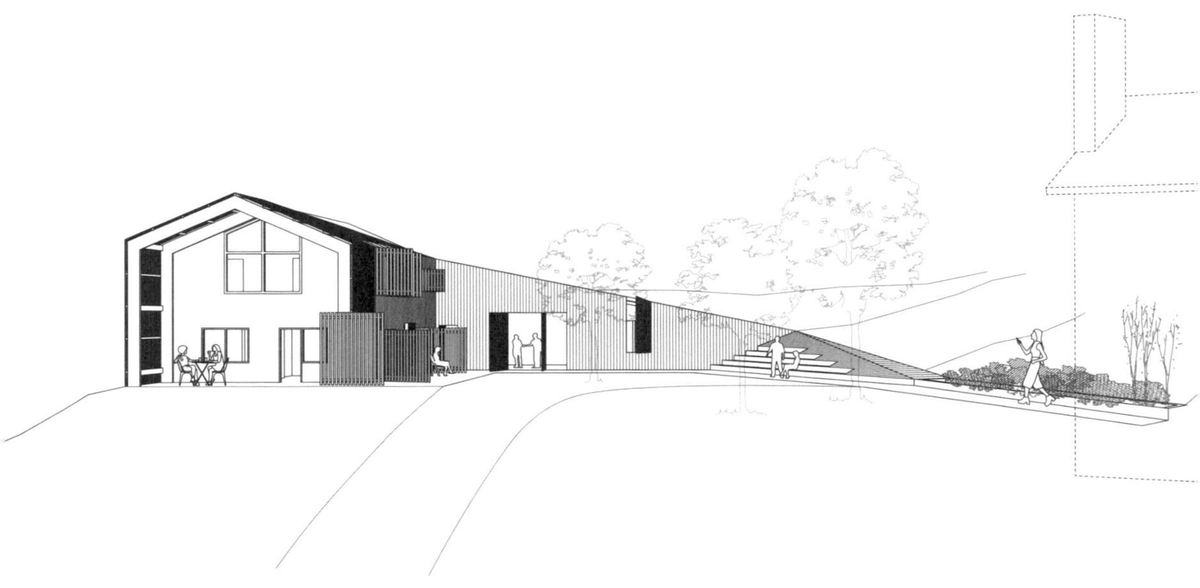

Melt

A Change of State Space
Minus-20-Degree Art and Architecture Winter Biennial Competition, loser
Flachau, Austria
2015

Designed for the *minus20degree biennial art and architecture festival* in Flachau, Austria, where installations are tasked with using the elements of the winter landscape, *Melt* is a device that harnesses water's transformative potential. Using this ubiquitous material's changing states (solid as ice or snow, liquid as water, and gaseous as steam), the device structures the reformation of a space in constant seasonal flux: both formally and programmatically. Although its material remains the same, its states are ever-changing.

The device consists of a double V-shaped roof trough, skewered by a diagonal chimney shaft, with a stove at its base. Made entirely of plate steel, the device is set into a steel and wood deck. Before the onset of winter, logs are stacked between the base and the roof to create a small enclosure. Through the entrance, a hearth is visible, inviting a user to enter and warm up by burning the wood-stack skin. The heat produced by the fire warms the metal chimney and transfers the heat to the concave roof, where snow has been collecting. The snow, now melting, transforms into water and makes its way to the lowered tip of the roof trough. Dripping

slowly onto the hot metal chimney shaft, the water sizzles and turns into steam. At this point, the pavilion becomes a sauna.

The sauna loses its enclosure as the wood is used up. Yet, as the temperature falls over the winter months and precipitation continues, the roof collects snow and creates a dam at the eaves to stimulate the formation of icicles. The enclosure line, having been consumed in the fire, is now reinstated by the icicles. This line, now vertical, spiky, and glistening, is distinct from the previous diagonal generated by the wood stack, and creates a new interior space where steam continues to be produced but is no longer contained.

After the last snow has melted, the final naked form creates a dialogue with Flachau's industrial heritage and reveals the structural and formal properties of the device. *Melt* is tilted in the direction of the prevailing wind in order to shelter the original entryway and facilitate ventilation through the chimney. Similarly, the precise cut of the chimney void through the mass of snow in the vessel both calibrates the location of the drip back onto the chimney shelf but also re-centers the device's center of gravity. Although formally precarious, *Melt* is gravitationally grounded.

Throughout the progression of the winter festival, the pavilion goes through of series of state changes, prompted by its use and the environmental conditions of the site. While the device has no moving parts, it relies on the weather to generate the raw material and the ice formations, gravity to generate movement in water and ice, and thermodynamics to generate steam and smoke. The form is merely a framework that allows the dynamic systems to do their work. Dynamism also occurs through human work (the physical moving of the logs) and combustion (the burning of the logs to generate heat). As the device anticipates weather and is designed to exaggerate the effects of those conditions, it also anticipates a range of changing programs. The base of the pavilion, which is acting as a counterbalance to the cantilever structure, is designed to accommodate these changing programs throughout the seasons.

A mock-up tests the relationship between form, temperature, and material. The details of the ⅛th-scale construct are designed to promote the formation of icicles. These begin to create their own enclosure along the edge of the container in the winter, while the drip, chimney, and stove components produce steam.

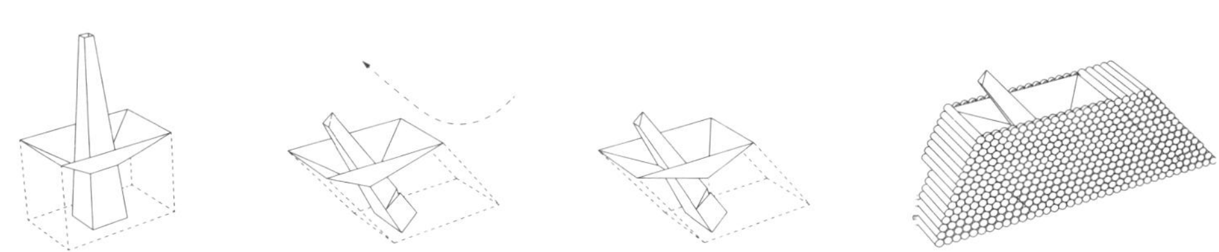

SPACE + VESSEL + CHIMNEY

TILT FROM PREVAILING WIND

SKEW VESSEL TO OFFSET DRIP

COVER WITH LOGS, BURN LOGS, REPEAT ...

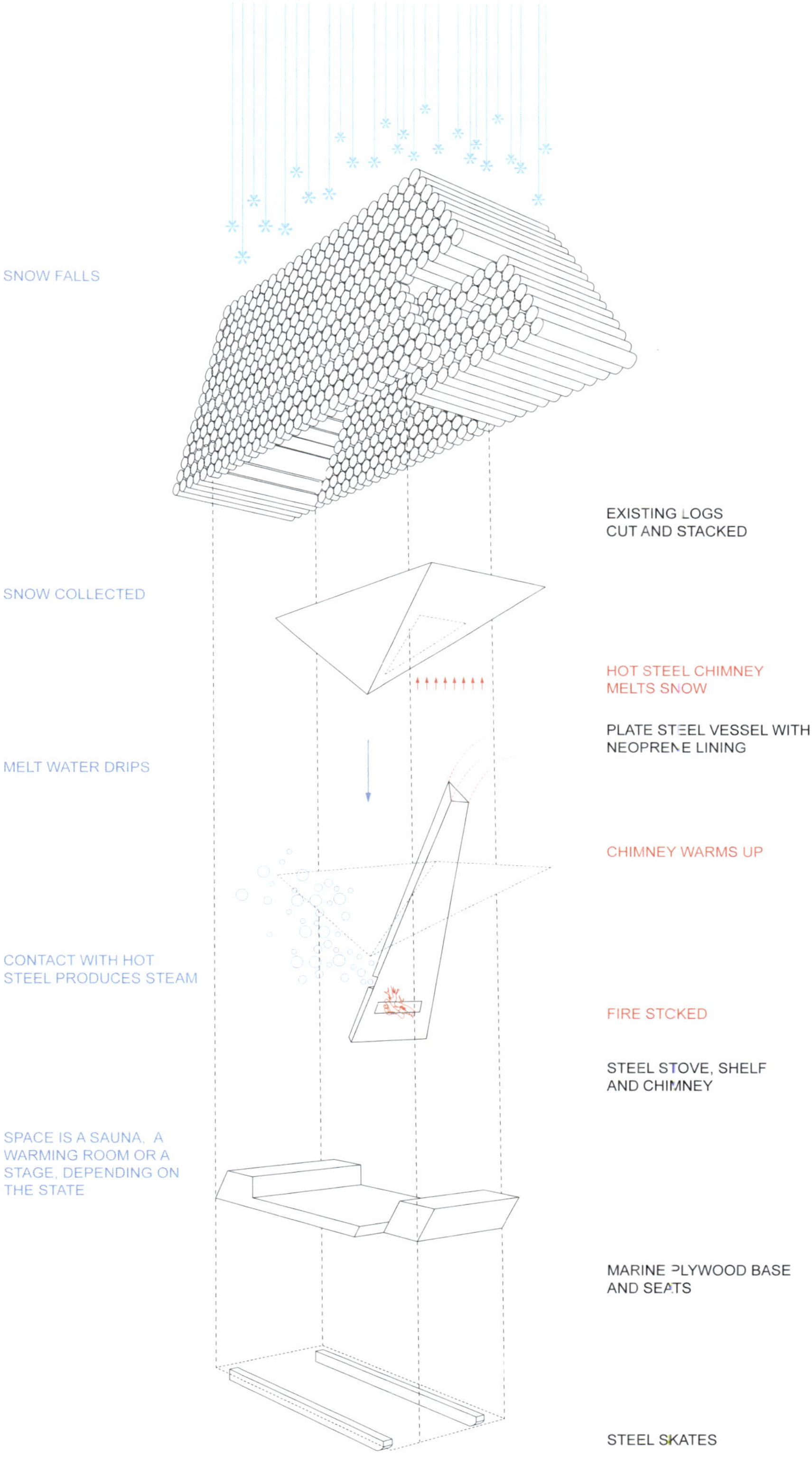
SNOW FALLS
EXISTING LOGS
CUT AND STACKED
SNOW COLLECTED
HOT STEEL CHIMNEY
MELTS SNOW
PLATE STEEL VESSEL WITH
NEOPRENE LINING
MELT WATER DRIPS
CHIMNEY WARMS UP
CONTACT WITH HOT
STEEL PRODUCES STEAM
FIRE STCKED
STEEL STOVE, SHELF
AND CHIMNEY
SPACE IS A SAUNA, A
WARMING ROOM OR A
STAGE, DEPENDING ON
THE STATE
MARINE PLYWOOD BASE
AND SEATS
STEEL SKATES

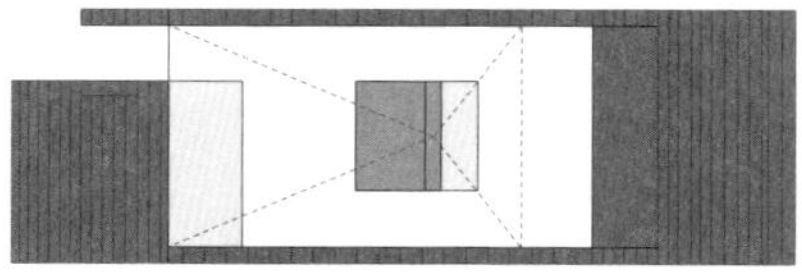

GROUND LEVEL PLAN: BEFORE

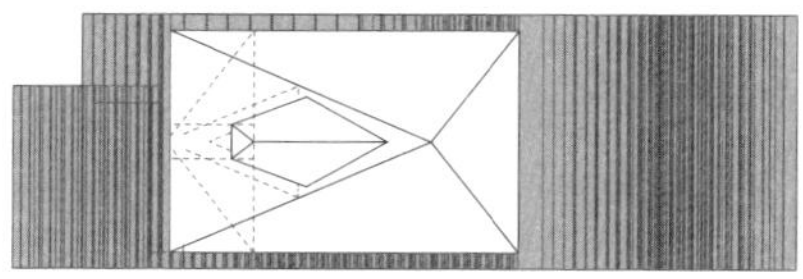

ROOF PLAN: BEFORE

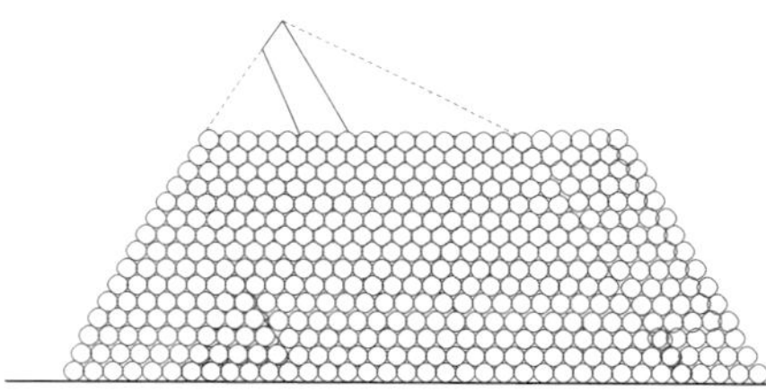

LEFT ELEVATION: BEFORE

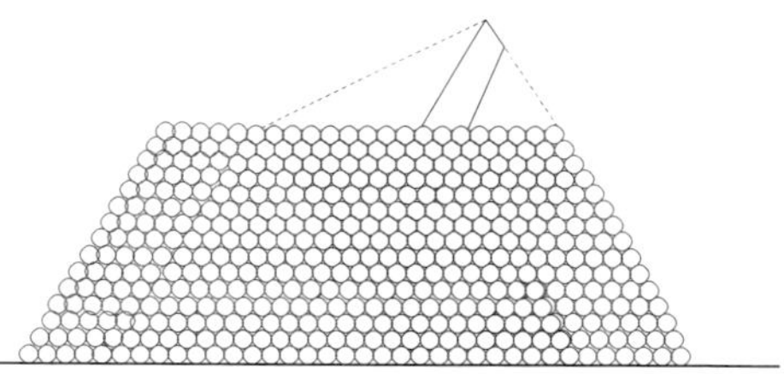

RIGHT ELEVATION: BEFORE

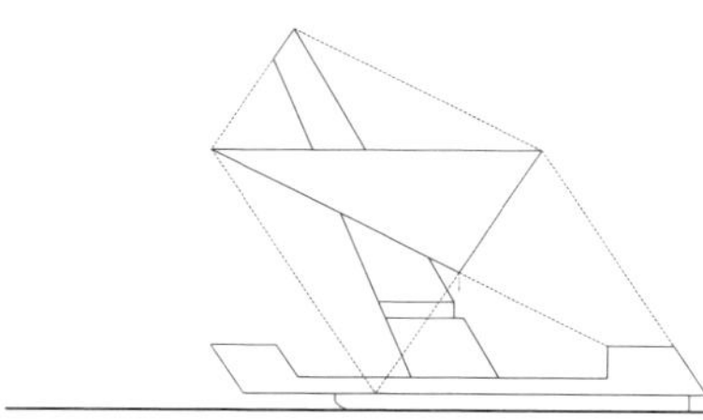

LEFT ELEVATION: AFTER

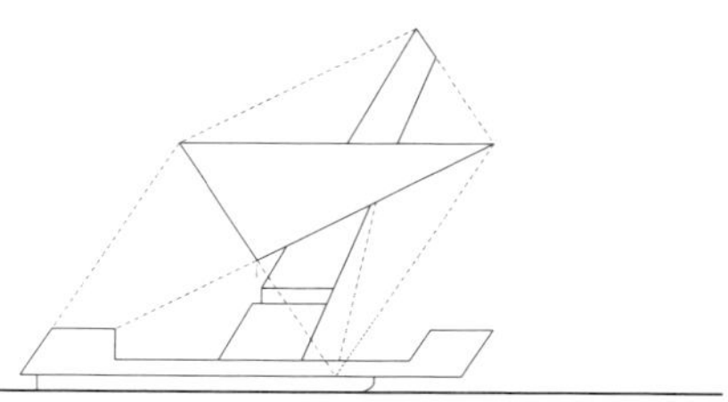

RIGHT ELEVATION: AFTER

Crossing

A Potato Pavilion
in collaboration with **Samantha Martin-McAuliffe** and **Irene Kelly**
Competition for the Irish exhibition at the Venice Architecture Biennale, loser
Venice, Italy
an experimental material installation
2018

Since the segregation of Ireland in 1921, the border has been, at times, heavily militarized and, at other times, invisible, especially since the establishment of the Single Market in 1993. Many productive farms straddle the perimeter, and trade between Ireland and the UK is a large component of both economies. Consequently, rather than a line, the Irish border is, in fact, an edible landscape comprised of agricultural tracts, hedges, and waterways. The openness of the border, both conceptually and literally, has been called into question by the UK's 2016 decision to exit the EU.

Crossing presents the Irish border as a thriving, fuzzy, hedge-like boundary that at first appears impenetrable, but ultimately allows way via a *kissing stile*: an S-shaped passage through a hedge that is used to allow humans, but not livestock, through. The stile works because the exit is not visible from the entrance, so even though the distance is short, the meandering path requires an amount of belief (or knowledge) to enter into it.

The structure of the installation is an intricate lattice of components, heat-formed using hemp potato sacks and a custom bioresin that uses potato starch and other aggregates. This recipe builds on a material innovation by Cornell material scientist, Anil Netravali, who used soy as the base for a thermoset resin. Crucially, the scientists speculated on the possibilities of replacing the soy protein with starch and carried out initial studies. According to Netravali et al.: "Starch is a highly hydrophilic biomaterial with weak mechanical properties rendering it useless for commercial applications. A fully "green" water based process is presented to crosslink corn (cereal) and potato (tuber) starch to enhance mechanical properties as well as lower hydrophilicity. In addition, malonic acid, a green, plant based water soluble and relatively inexpensive polycarboxylic acid, was used as the crosslinker. The reactivity of potato starch toward esterification and crosslinking was found to be higher than that of corn starch owing to the inherent differences in the granule morphology and internal structure of the two starches."

Chabba, Matthews, & Netravali, "'Green' composites using cross-linked soy flour and flax yarns," in *Green Chemistry*, 20th May 2005: rsc.org/greenchem

Dastida & Netravali, "'Green' crosslinking of native starches with malonic acid and their properties," in *Carbohydrate Polymers*, 14 July 2012.

For *Crossing*, this experimental potato starch recipe replaces the more developed soy protein resin, while hemp potato sacks substitute the flax yarn. This combination creates a fully potato-based component. In its finished state, this material resembles amber, and its transparency allows for a design that explores variations in contour, porosity, and visibility—all attributes inherent to the Irish border. As one moves around, and in changing light conditions, the installation shows varying transparencies and a constantly shifting porosity, all possible through an introduced variation in the components that make up the project. This gradient creates a variegated porous surface of self-stacking components ranging from spiky and closed to flat and open.

The key ingredient—the potato—is also intrinsic to Irish history and culture. At the same time, the technology embodies a radical and experimental approach to form-making that characterizes contemporary Irish design.

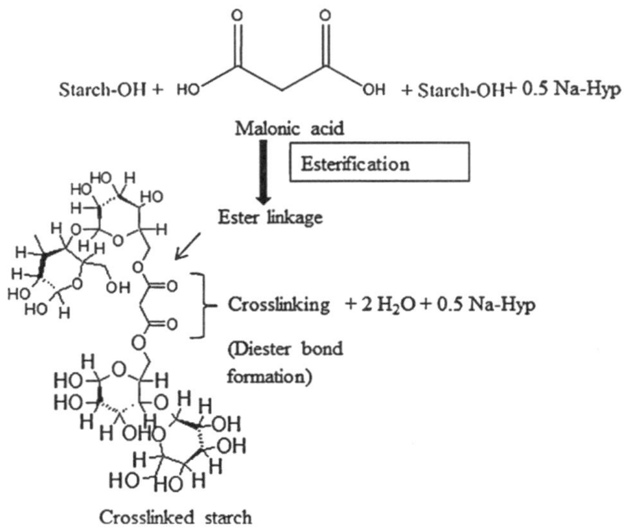

Importantly, this installation encompasses both production and consumption processes: potato plants act as ballasts that weigh down the structure. These plants will continue to grow throughout the six-month exhibition. In lieu of display panels with informational text and images about architecture in and related to the borderlands, visitors are offered a favorite Irish potato snack: crisps (chips) packaged in bags, which double as texts for the exhibition. Each project featured in the exhibition is presented on one waxed brown paper bag which, upon consumption of the crisps, can be unfolded and retained by the visitor.

In drawing on natural materials to construct this exhibition, the living and organic materials need not be flown home but can continue to nourish through continued production and composting in Italy. As the potato plants grow, the potato chips will be consumed, and the resin will decay through moisture in the air. As such, the installation is porous, fragile, productive—very much alive.

Unconvinced, the Irish jury awarded the pavilion to another team which explored the "Free Market" towns of Ireland.

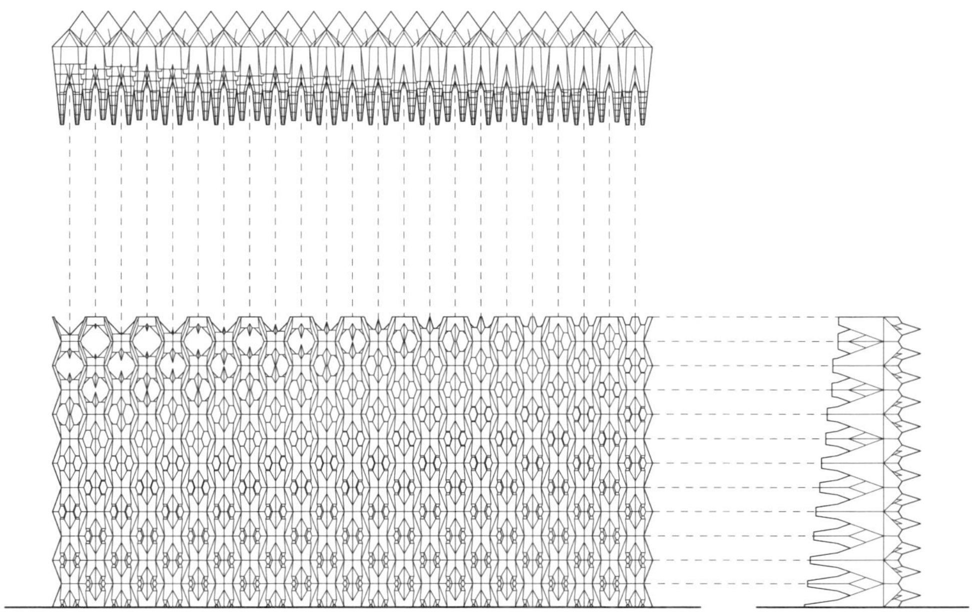

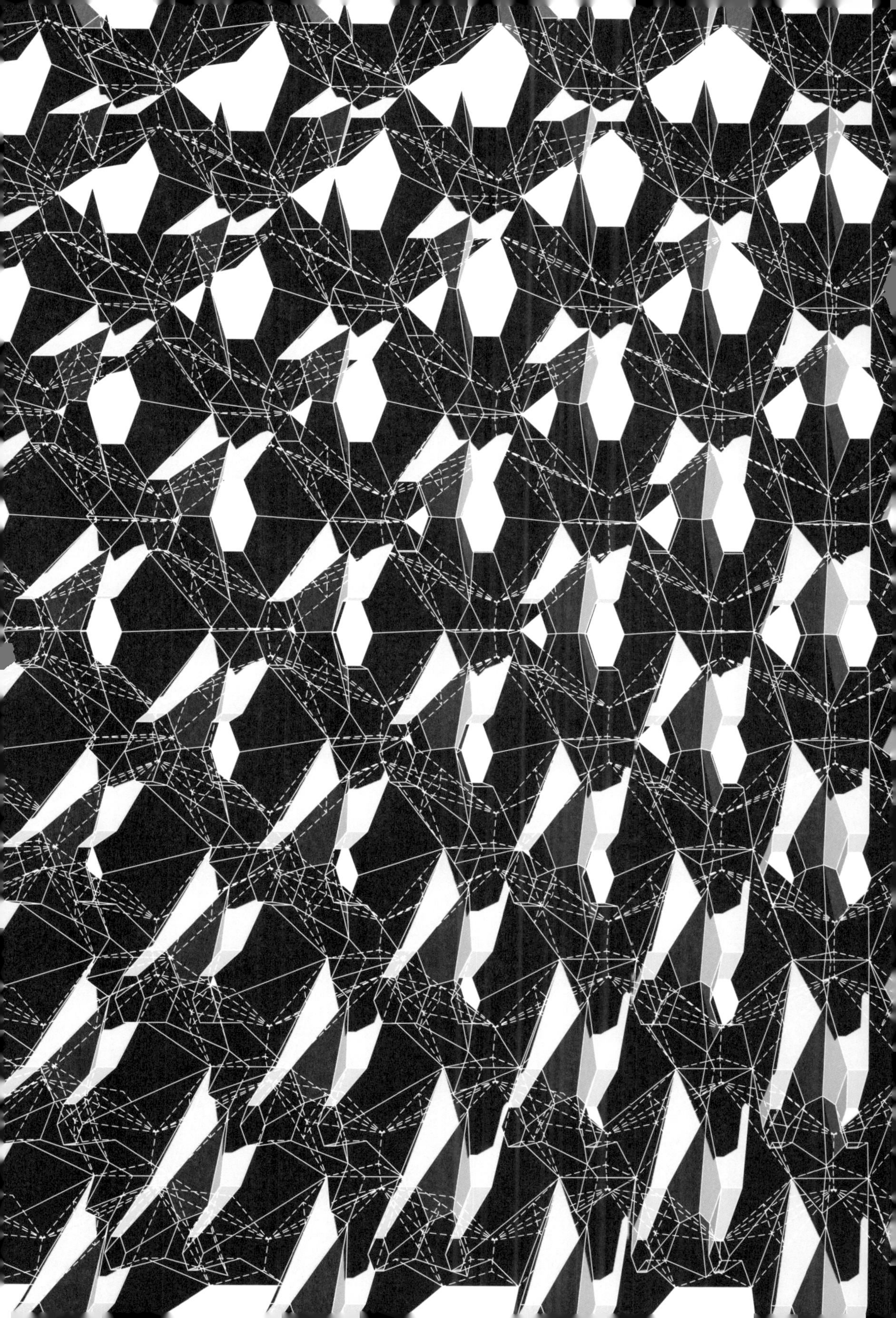

omg!

Primitive Hut

A Growing and Decomposing Pavilion
An OMG project: in collaboration with **Martin Miller**
Art OMI, Ghent, NY, USA
commissioned by Art OMI
with support from Cornell Architecture/AAP
2017

Primitive Hut is a temporary pavilion that questions architecture's relationship with time through an exploration of growth and decomposition. The structure transforms between states of solid mass, frame, and void while, through its decay, it nourishes the trees that will replace the departing geometric form with a living organism.

Built around four pre-planted red maple saplings, the structure comprises two parts: one structural lattice of plywood components and one decomposing lattice made from a custom recipe of bio-resin, hemp, and sawdust (extracted from the fabrication of the plywood components). The lattices are infilled with decomposable manure cylinders. The parts are tuned to decompose at varying rates throughout the seasons, opening up four doorways so that the interior of the structure will become inhabitable, and eventually, the structural remainder will be twisted and lifted as the trees grow.

Primitive Hut recalls Charles Eisen's frontispiece for Marc-Antoine Laugier's "Essai sur l'architecture." This 1755 engraving speculates on the primitive human's first house as one that harnessed the potentialities of the environment and blurred the lines between nature and architecture. Laugier was reacting to contemporaneous work by baroque and rococo architects, whose ornamental use of pilasters and pediments was, in his mind, a shameful use of the orders in a decorative rather than functional way. Laugier argued that we should look to nature not as something to mimic, but as something that would demonstrate the basic rules of architecture. In other words, that we should imitate how nature operated, not how it looked.

Primitive Hut. Front elevation, front, courtesy of Travis Nissen.

Frontispiece to 2nd edition of *Essai sur l'Architecture,* Marc-Antoine Laugier, 1753.

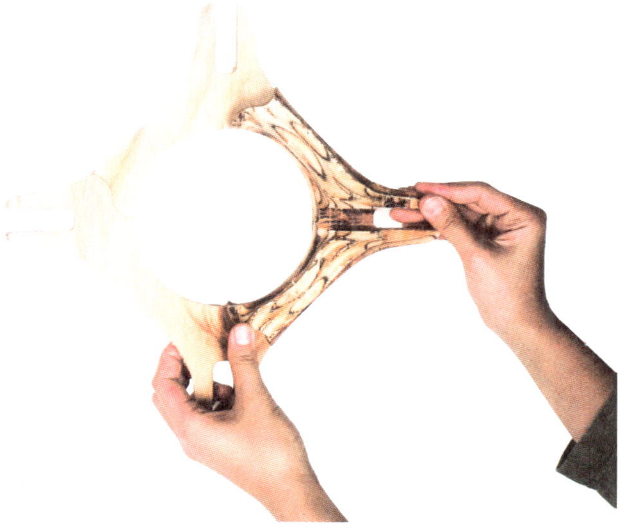

Laugier asked us to imagine a primitive man in his primitive environment with only instincts to guide him. To shelter himself, he must build a hut. The *petit cabane rustique* has four branches connecting four trees set in a rectangular plan. Above, diagonal branches meet at a point, though it is not clear if these branches have been placed by the primitive man or if they are part of the primitive tree. Leaves cover the roof, and again, there is ambiguity as to whether those leaves are growing or cut and placed artificially by the primitive man. This ambiguity intentionally blurs the boundary between artifice and nature and underscores Laugier's most important point that, "in order to be an art, and not a mechanical craft, architecture must follow not the external appearance of nature but her laws."

Marc-Antoine (Abbé) Laugier, *An Essay on Architecture*, London (1755), 9.

Laugier shifts the thinking of his time from mimesis to emanation (from *looking like* to *acting like*) and also rejects ornament for its own sake in favor of function (or structure). He writes: "the parts of an architectural order are the very parts of the building. They therefore must be employed in such a way that they do not only decorate the building but constitute it. The existence of the building must depend to such a degree of their union that one cannot take away any of its parts without causing the collapse of the edifice." While this well-known image shows the iconic form of the house formed by the tree branches, the house is not yet

Marc-Antoine (Abbé) Laugier, *An Essay on Architecture*, London (1755), 10.

formed and implies both a future and a past state of growth and decay.

Primitive Hut plays directly with all of these ambivalences. The component design builds on traditional notched-wood joinery (such as the Norwegian *stavkirke*) to create interlocking parts that require no glue. Each component is CNC-milled on two sides, which combine with sibling parts to create a notched element that can slide into another component. In total, 5,000 milled parts combine into 2,000 components.

The ribbed surface of the components results from the single passage of a drill bit over the material. Whereas today many digitally fabricated objects are smooth as a result of surface

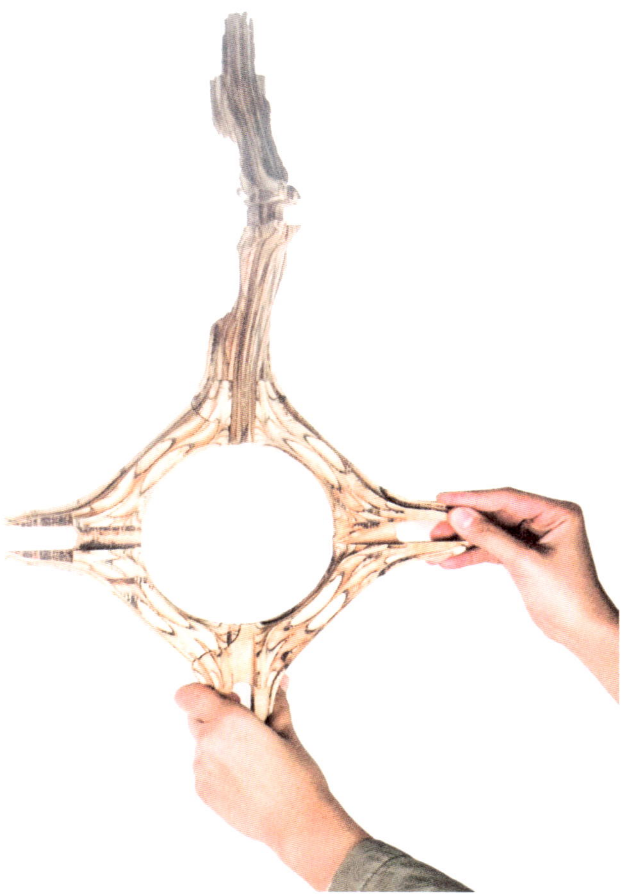

generating software, *Primitive Hut* intervenes in the fabrication process between the software and the tool, to produce a more efficient process whereby the number of passes by the mill tool is vastly reduced. The end result expresses the material's layers and produces an effect of exuberance through efficiency. This refinement and control of the robotic CNC tool seeks not only to optimize the fabrication process, but also to embrace the expression of the tool itself, resulting in a form embedded with the trace of the digital craftsperson.

The macro-cellular solid is designed as a structural lattice, which maximizes volume while minimizing material. This system was developed in collaboration with Cornell's Department of Aerospace Engineering and NASA's research into Digital Cellular Solids (with Daniel Cellucci). The resultant lattice geometries have higher performances than traditional assemblies.

Primitive Hut is a temporary pavilion contractually required to be removed after some years. Whereas other pavilions in OMI's Architecture Field would need to be physically removed, this one will remove itself, leaving only the trees and some clues of its former presence within their branches.

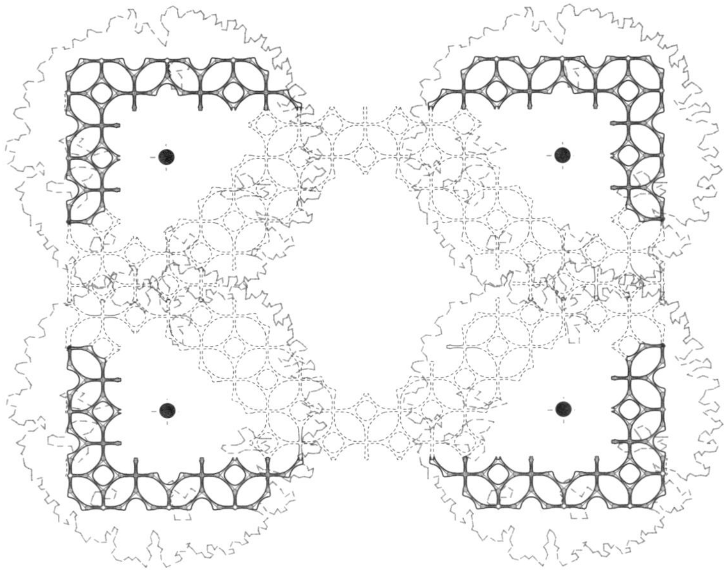

Primitive Hut. Plan, courtesy of Travis Nissen.

Primitive Hut. Elevation, front, courtesy of Travis Nissen.

Primitive Hut and Sweet Lou, a mixed-breed rescue dog from Louisiana who enjoys a paleo diet and long walks amidst ever-changing architectures. **Photograph by Leigh Strimbeck.**

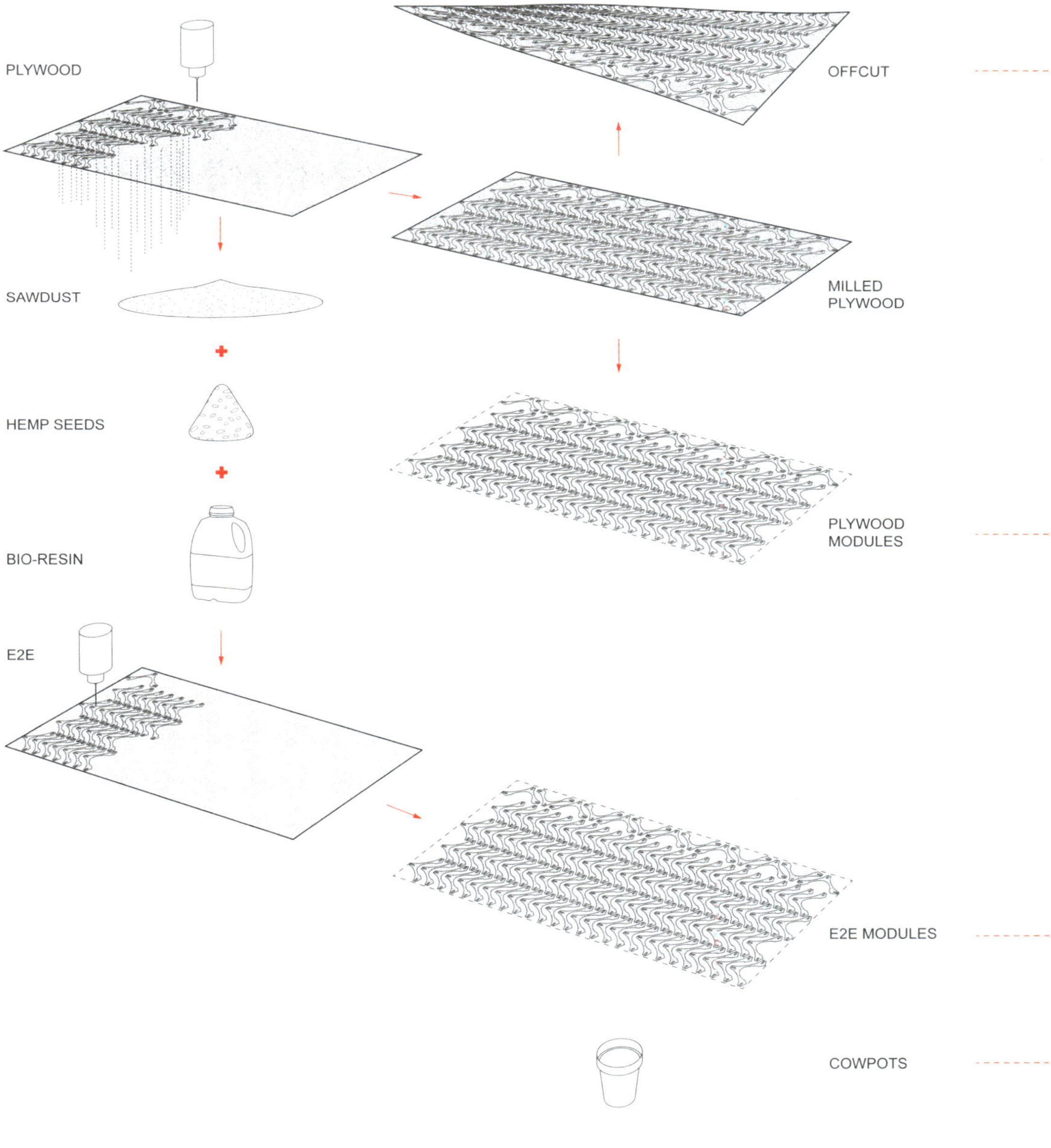
PLYWOOD
SAWDUST
HEMP SEEDS
BIO-RESIN
E2E
OFFCUT
MILLED
PLYWOOD
PLYWOOD
MODULES
E2E MODULES
COWPOTS

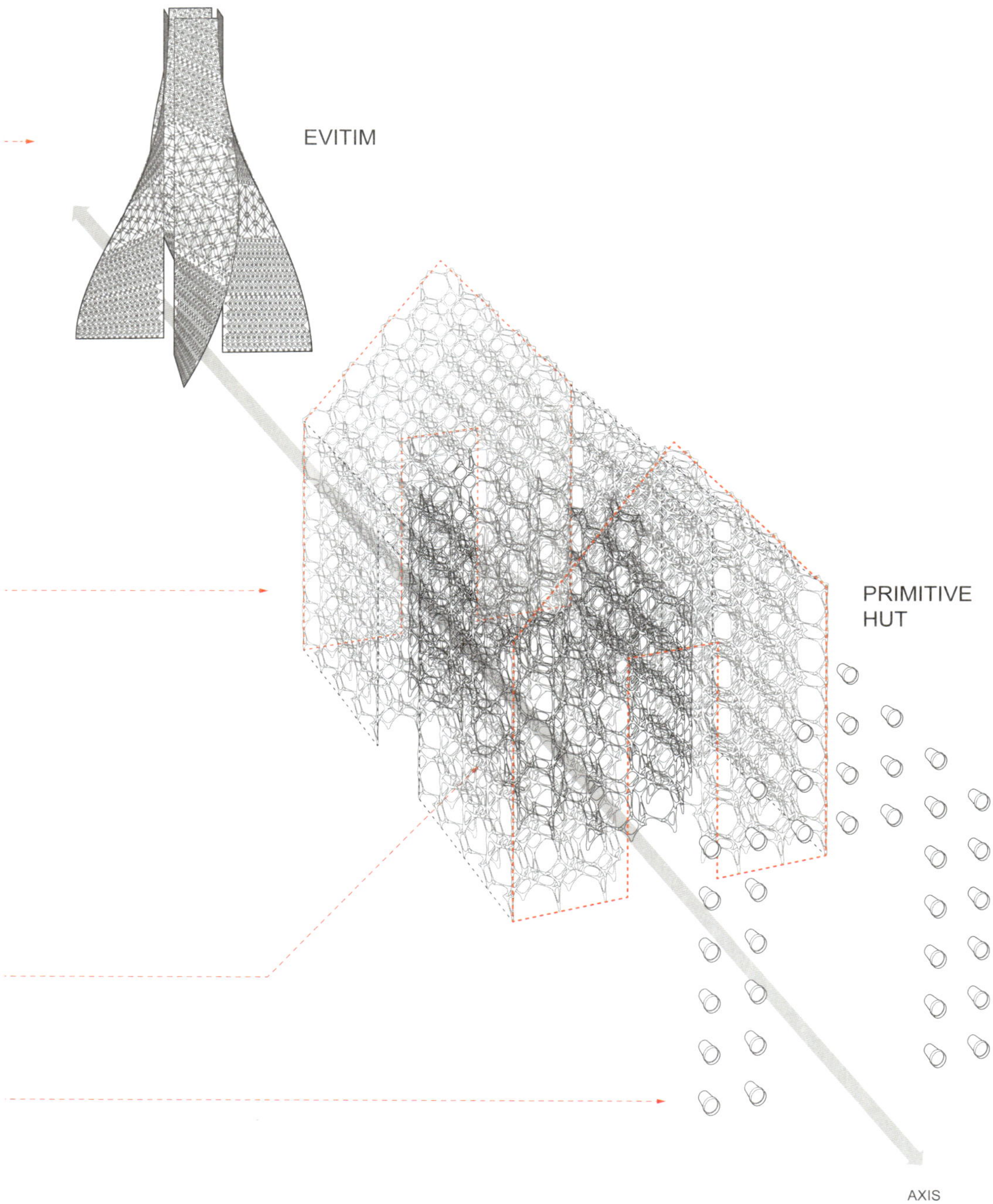
EVITIM
PRIMITIVE
HUT
AXIS

omg!

Evitim

A Pavilion of Leftovers from Primitive Hut
An OMG project: in collaboration with **Martin Miller**
Art OMI, Ghent, NY, USA
commissioned by Art OMI
with support from Cornell Architecture/AAP
2018

Evitim is the familiar name for Tuh *Evitim*irp—that is, *Primitive Hut* spelled backwards.

The pavilion, which is located adjacent to *Primitive Hut* in the Architecture Fields at Art Omi, is built using the CNC-mill's byproduct from the fabrication of the structural (non-decomposing) components for *Primitive Hut.* The leftovers are 8' x 4' plywood sheets with multiple cut-outs, which render the panels flexible. Using the leftover sheets' inherent desire to be twisted, the tower's skin peels outward from top to bottom, creating four openings that relate to its sister pavilion's openings.

The peeling away of the curvilinear from the orthogonal is an orthopedic analogy, in which the complex relationship between the curved and the straight can be read against one another.

The frontispiece to Nicolas Andry's book *Orthopédie* (1741) is an apt partner to Laugier's frontispiece. Published four years apart, the two illustrate a tendency that mirrors a contemporary

position: to look to nature not for imitation but as a model for operation. The engraving shows a stake tied at regular intervals to a deformed, curvilinear tree. Andry coined the term Orthopædia from "two Greek Words, viz. Orthos, which signifies straight, free from deformity, and Pais, a Child. Out of these two words I have compounded that of Orthopædia, to express in one Term the Design I Propose, which is to teach the different Methods of preventing and correction of Deformities of Children."

Nicolas Andry, *Orthopédie* (1741), quoted in F.N.L. Poynter, "Christener of Orthopaedics" (review of a facsimile edition of *Orthopædia*), *The British Medical Journal* 2, no. 5248 (1961): 360.

The power struggle between the built and natural forms is constantly blurring and changing at all times. In the same way that *Primitive Hut* shows its ambivalence to the natural and the artificial, *Evitim* expresses its duality between the orthogonal and the curvilinear (or organic) forms.

The double-curved beam is produced by laminating layers of 3/32" plywood to create a custom 4-inch-thick and 24-foot-tall twisted beam. At the top, this wooden beam connects to the steel tower. At the bottom, it connects to a steel foot rotated by 90 degrees. The two edges are re-stitched together using the plywood sheets, made malleable by the removal of components for *Primitive Hut.*

L'orthopédie ou l'art de prévenir et corriger dans les enfants les difformités du corps, Nicolas Andry, 1749.

Evitim & *Primitive Hut* at Art Omi Sculpture & Architecture Park, Ghent, NY.
Photograph by Alon Koppel. Courtesy of Art Omi.

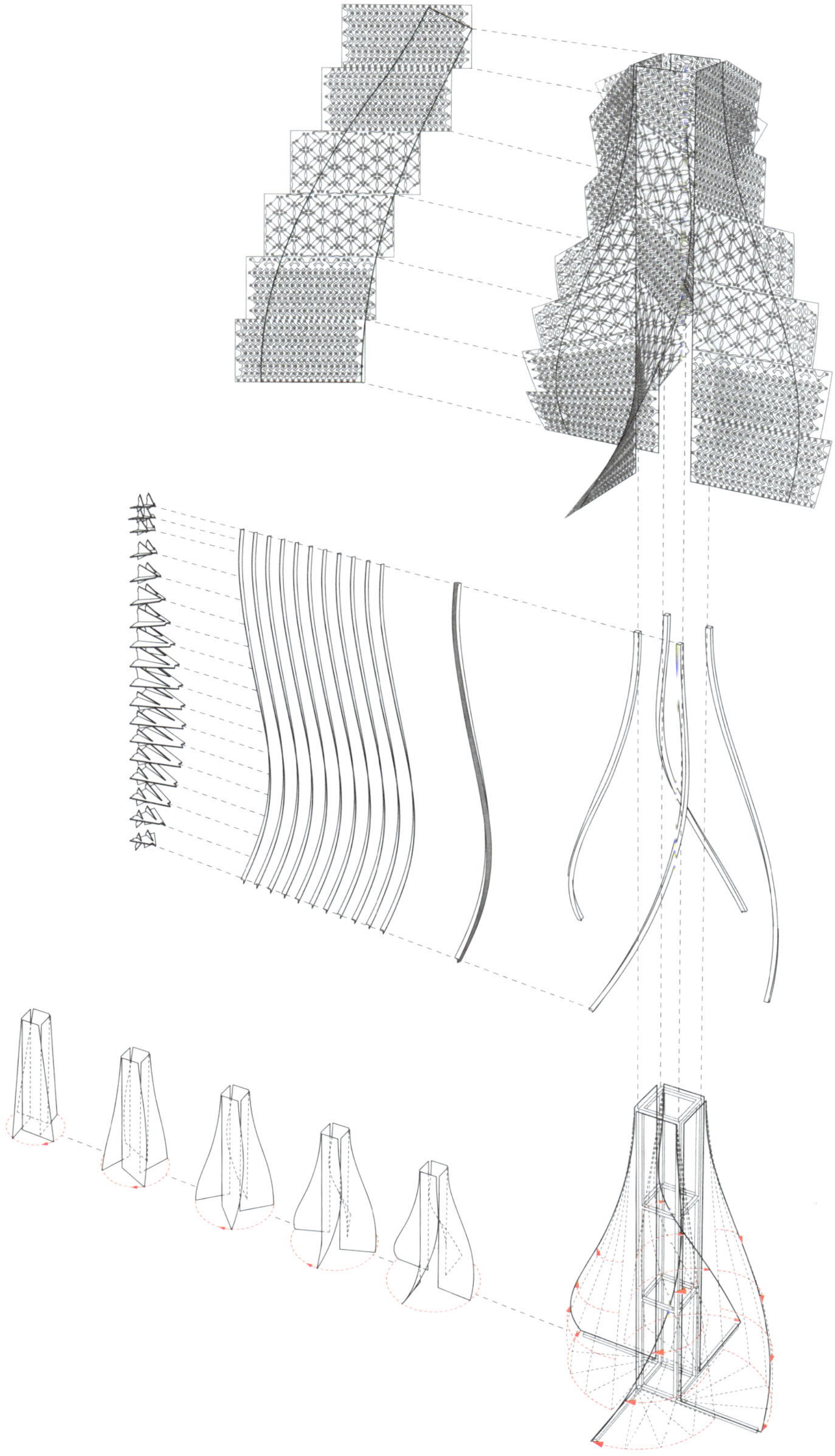

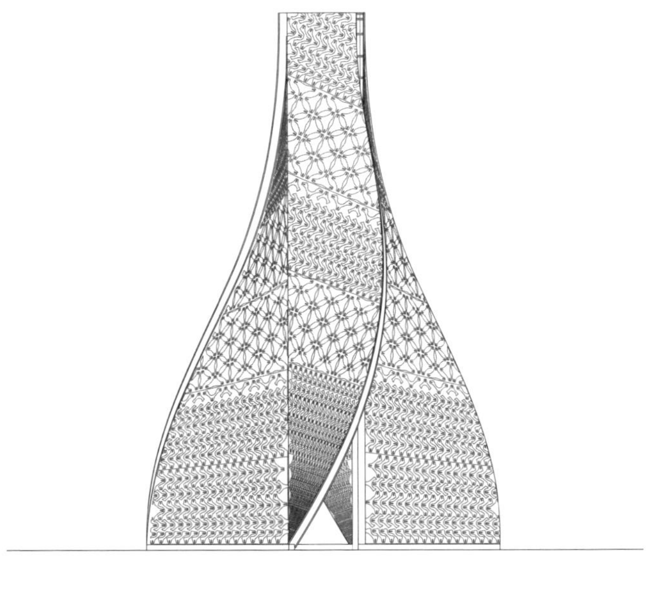

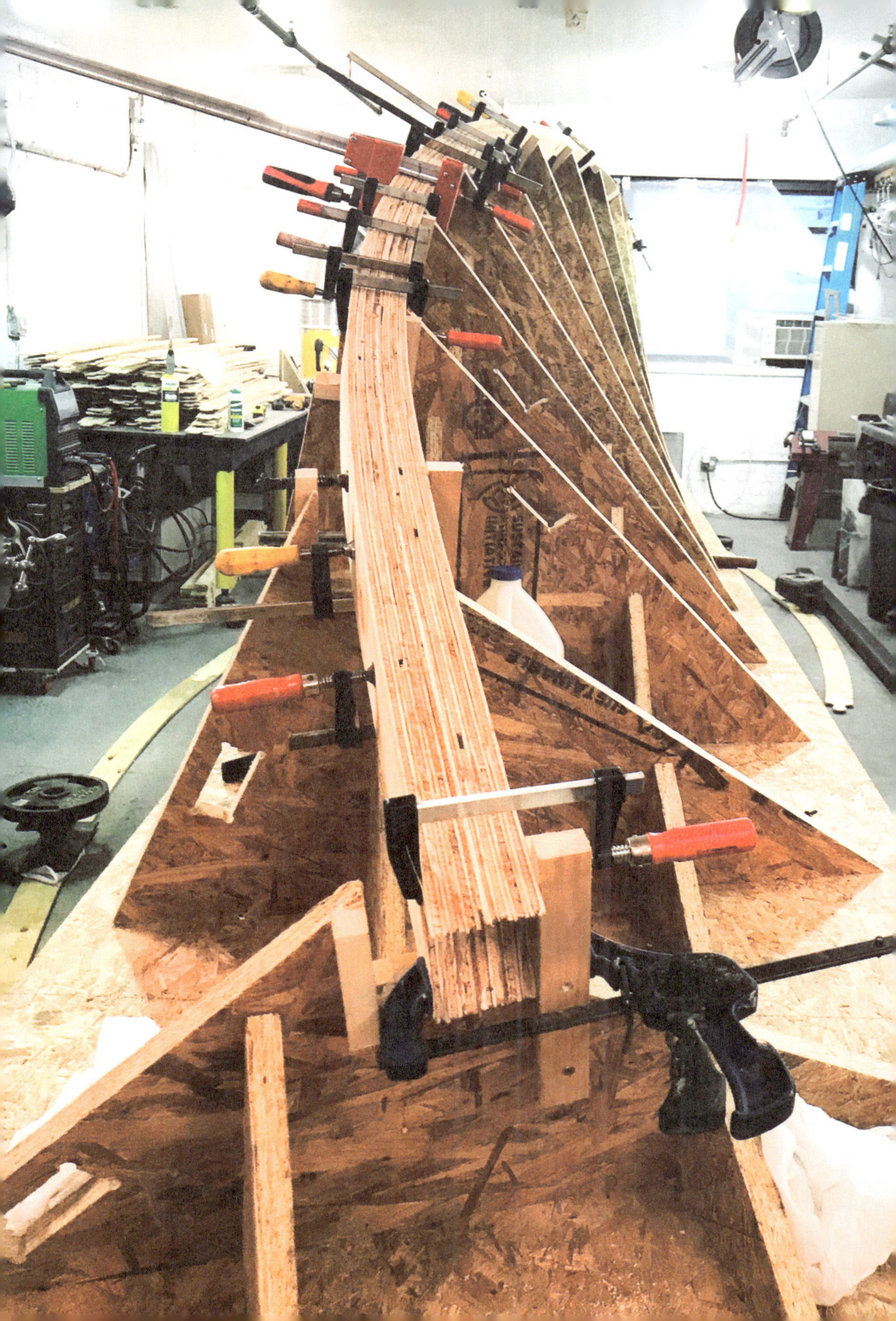

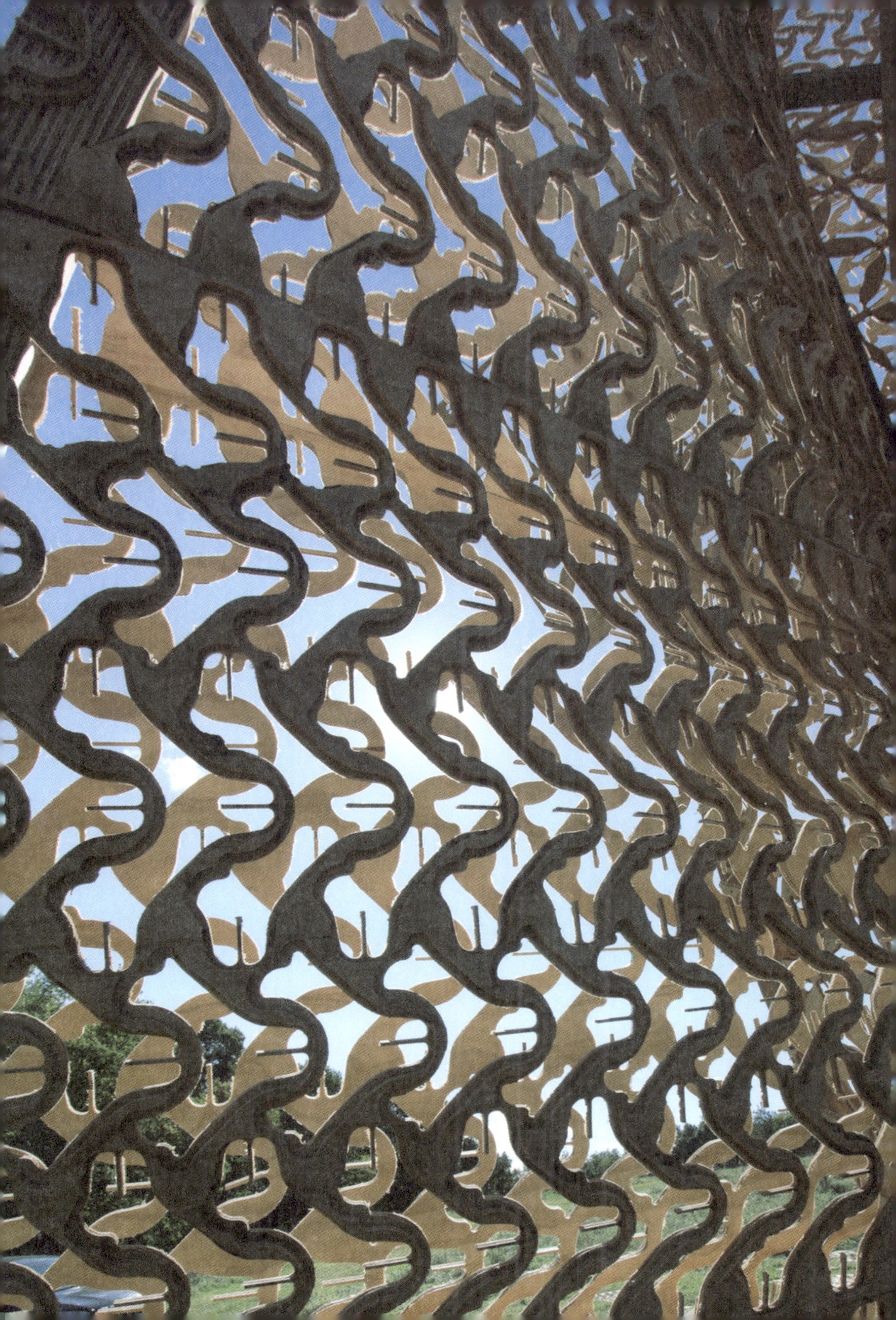

Urchin

An Impossible Circus
Cornell Arts Biennial Competition, winner
Cornell University, Ithaca, NY, USA
with support from Cornell Council for the Arts and Cornell Architecture/AAP
2016

According to James J. Gibson in *The Ecological Approach to Perception,* an *affordance* is a primary perception of the function of an object: "what it offers the animal, what it provides or furnishes, either for good or ill." Affordances exist as "action possibilities" latent in the environment, in relation to and dependent upon the animal's capabilities. It is the function of an object, Gibson proposes, that is perceived before the color, form, or shape of such an object. For example, the physical properties of flat, horizontal, rigid, and extended afford standing or walking: they are walk-on-able. However, an affordance does not reside completely in the object, but rather in the relationship between the object and its perceiving body. Affordance, Gibson posits, "cuts across the dichotomy of subjective-objective and ... is equally a fact of the environment and a fact of behavior ... [Affordance] is both physical and psychical, yet neither."

James J. Gibson, *The Ecological Approach to Visual Perception* (New Jersey: Lawrence Erlbaum Assoc. Inc. Publishers, 1986), 7.

James J. Gibson, *The Ecological Approach to Visual Perception* (New Jersey: Lawrence Erlbaum Assoc. Inc. Publishers, 1986), 129.

The common plastic chair affords sitting—a familiar act with a familiar object. *Urchin*, in its up-ending and aggregation of the

everyday object, defamiliarizes the chair and cancels the original affordance. The chairs beyond the first row are no longer sittable. This gives room for their other non-functional qualities to emerge. For instance, the spikiness of their legs, the translucency of their material, their curvilinearity, their whiteness, and so on. Existing in a new and aggressive relation to the body—becoming bristling skin rather than objects of human servitude—are the objects even chairs anymore?

Built from 360 plastic deck chairs, *Urchin* aims to question the role of the everyday object: from the typical use that affords sitting to an aggregation that becomes skin-like. In other words, the object's features are no longer understood in terms of their function but in terms of their form as, due to their rotation away from the ground, they lose their relationship with the human body. *Urchin* changes based on the viewer's perception. From far away, the pavilion might look like a prickly donut or a sea urchin. From up close, one realizes that the skin is, in fact, nothing but the familiar patio chair.

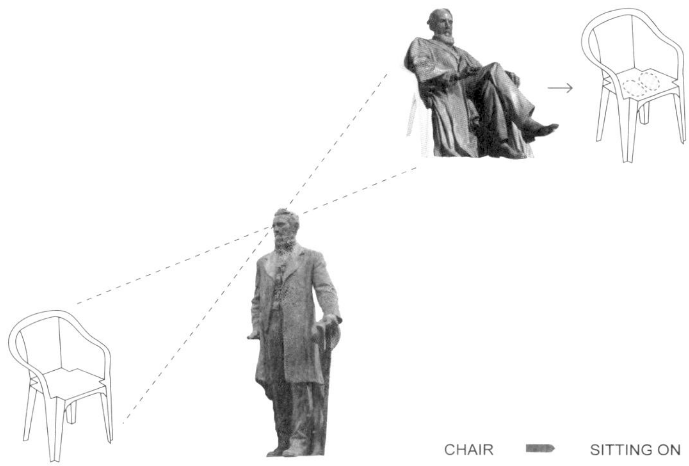

250

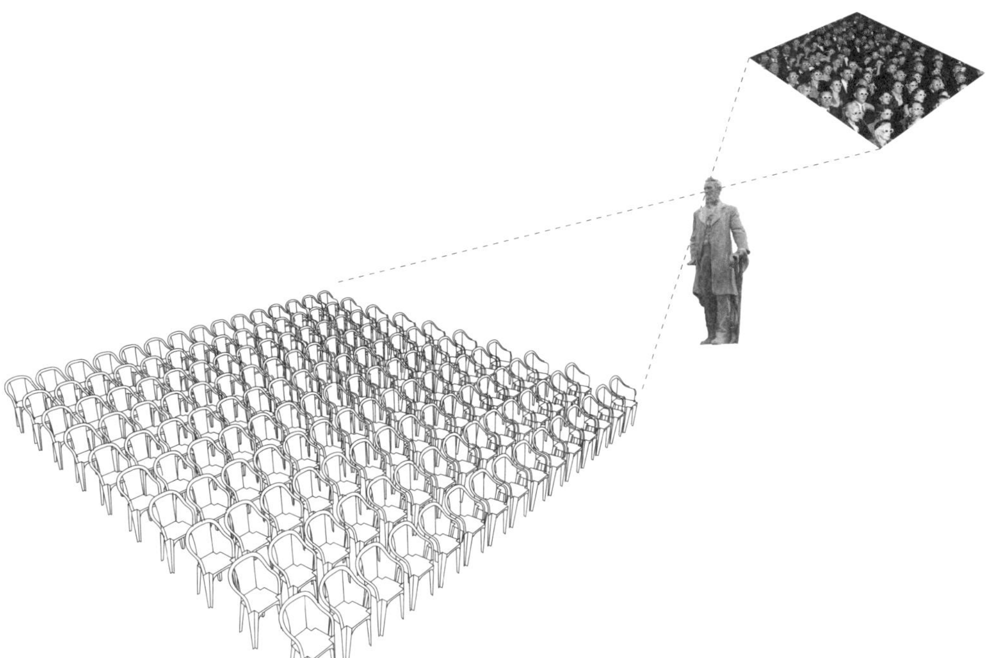

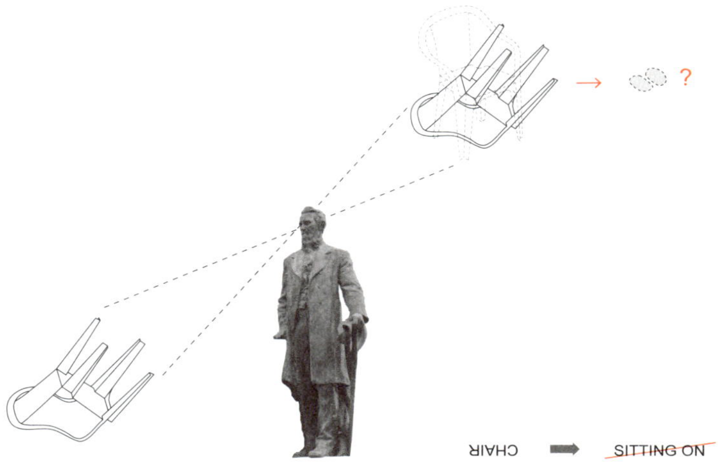

251

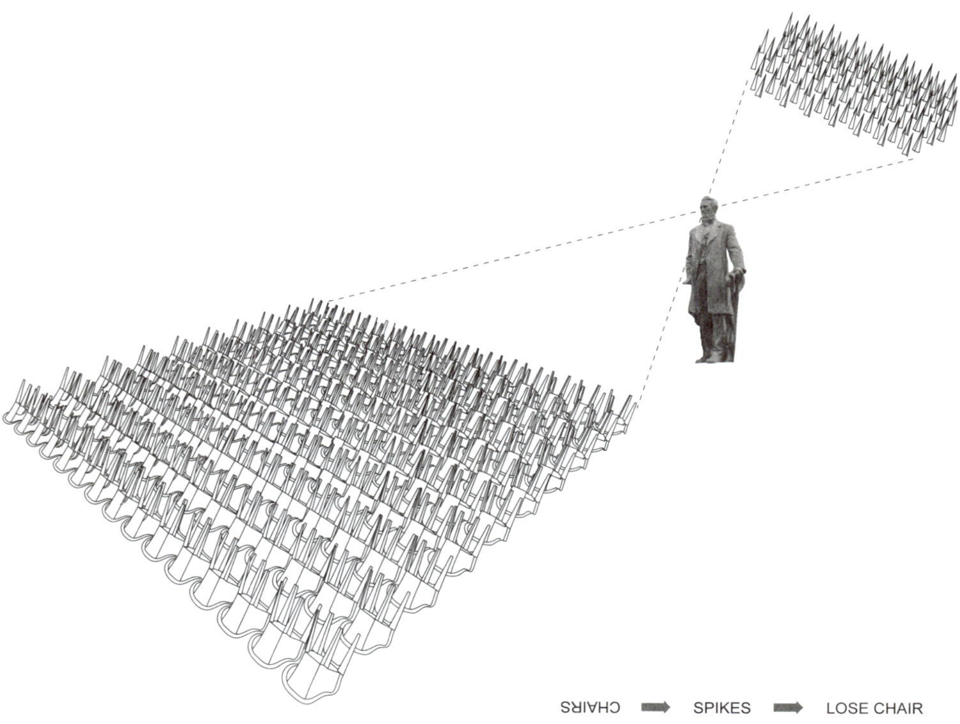

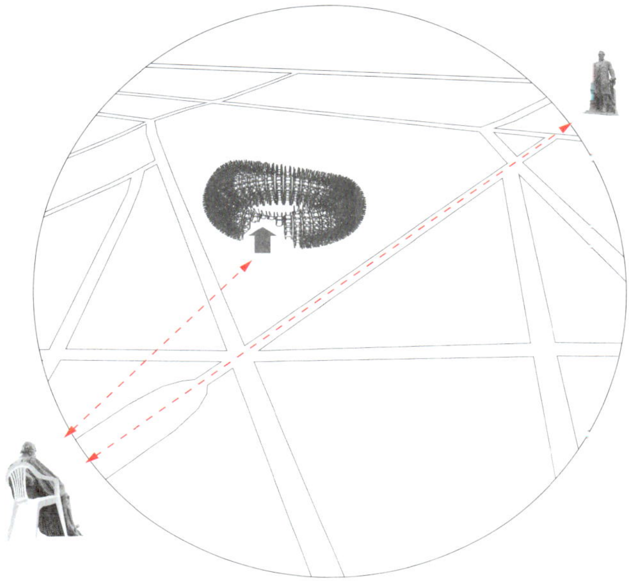

Or is it?

Such a coming into being is not a physical transformation, but an affordance transformation. Progressively, the viewer realizes the expected relation of the body to the object and, at the same time, the impossibility of that relation.

Located on the Arts Quadrangle at Cornell University, the design responds to the presence of two statues of the university's founding fathers: A.D. White and Ezra Cornell. White, seated, becomes complicit in the ring of (also white) chairs as the pavilion

opens to the axis of his body, and he becomes the original audience member.

While each plastic chair is identical, it is the changing dimensions of the steel rod connecting them that allows the changing curvature. Every third chair, a dog-spike anchors the pavilion into the ground.

The 360 chairs that make up the pavilion had been earmarked by *The Home Depot* as end-of-season surplus to be donated to their charity distributors, *Good360*. Once there, they were to be assigned to *Starfish*, a charity that provides materials and funding to girls' education in The Gambia. Urchin intervened in this process before the chairs went to be stored but continued the cycle by reconnecting them with *Starfish* after the pavilion's deconstruction. Due to the minimal incisions of the five "ear-piercings," the chairs could be easily disconnected, cleaned, and shipped. Today, they reside in a school in Banjul.

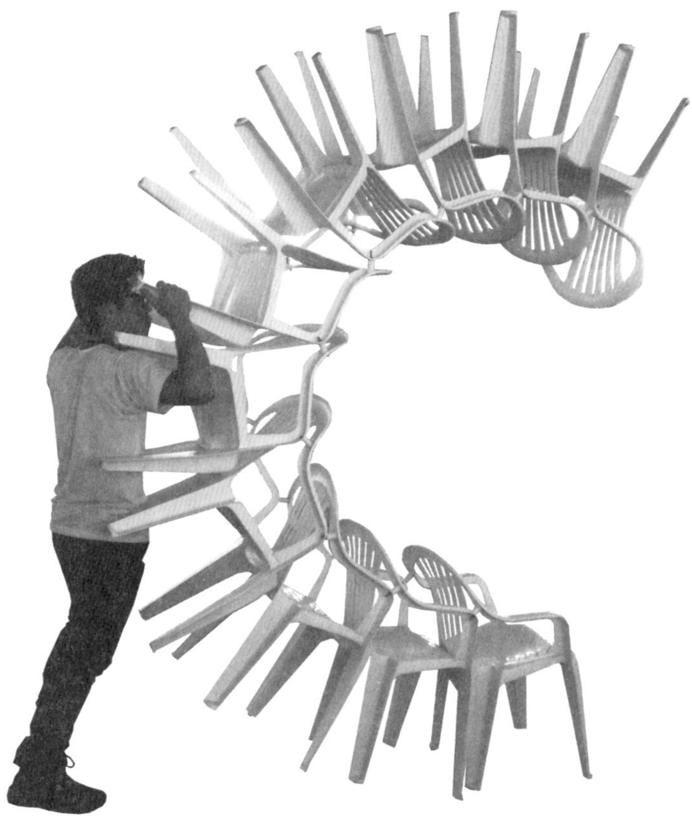

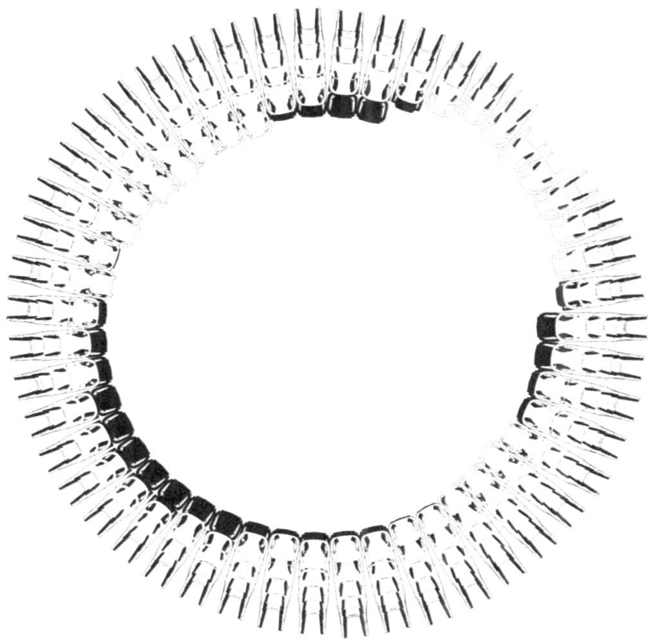

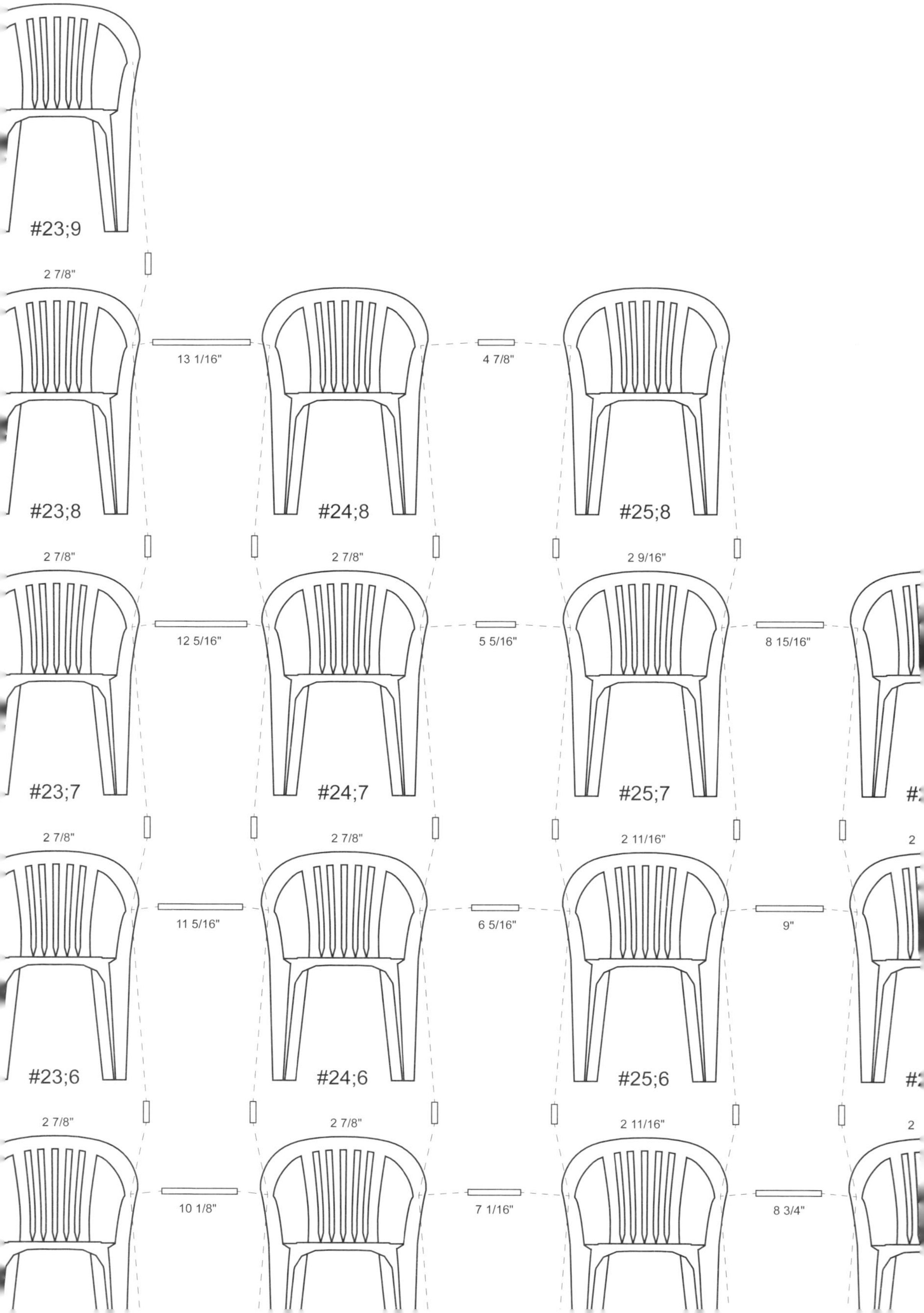
#23;9
2 7/8"
13 1/16"
4 7/8"
#23;8
#24;8
#25;8
2 7/8"
2 7/8"
2 9/16"
12 5/16"
5 5/16"
8 15/16"
#23;7
#24;7
#25;7
2 7/8"
2 7/8"
2 11/16"
11 5/16"
6 5/16"
9"
#23;6
#24;6
#25;6
2 7/8"
2 7/8"
2 11/16"
10 1/8"
7 1/16"
8 3/4"

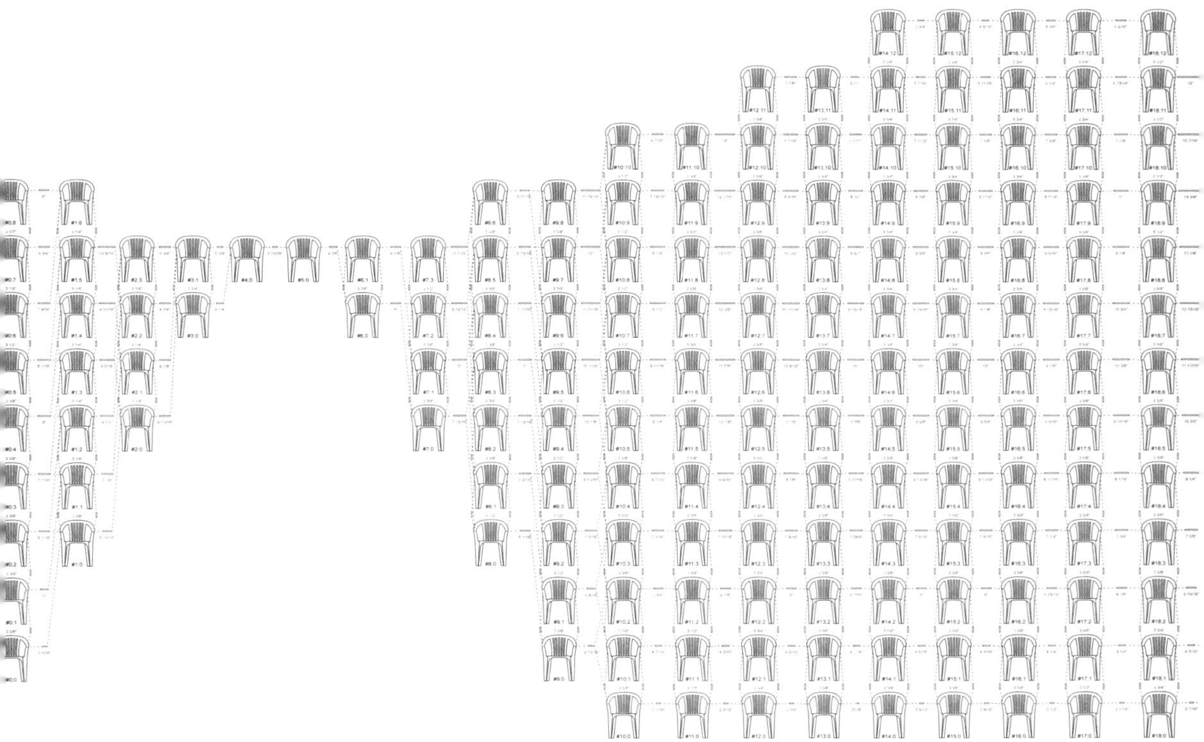

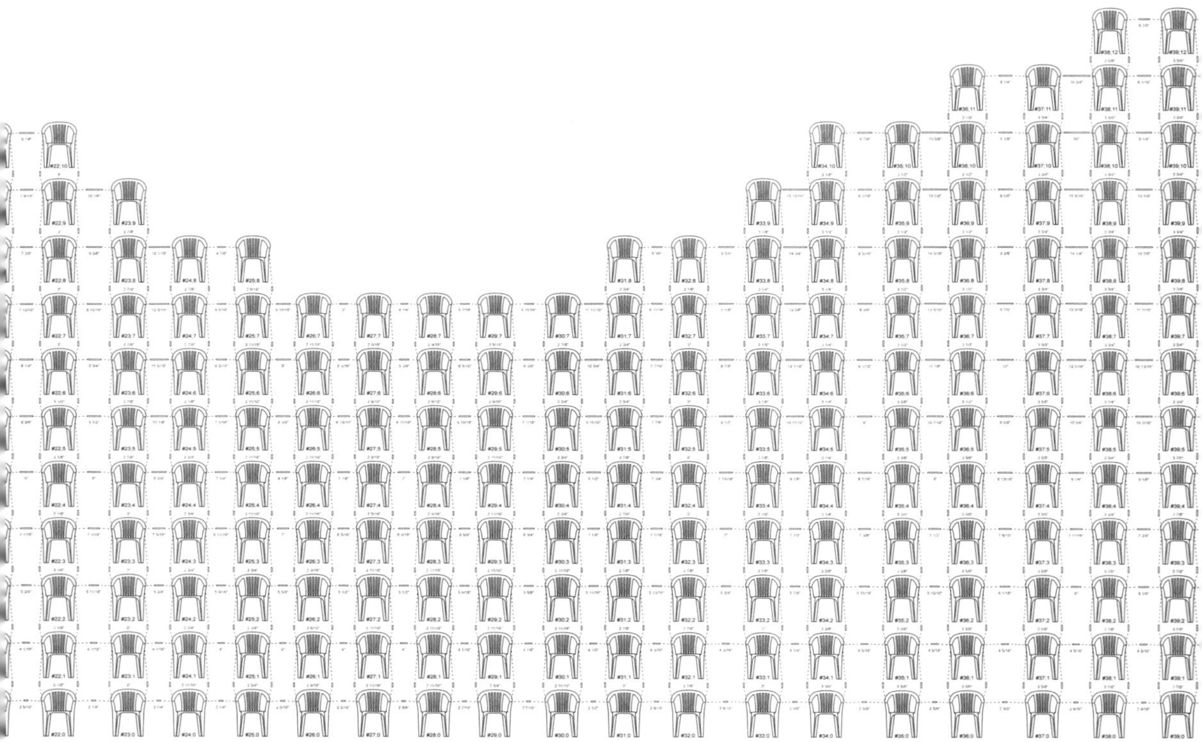

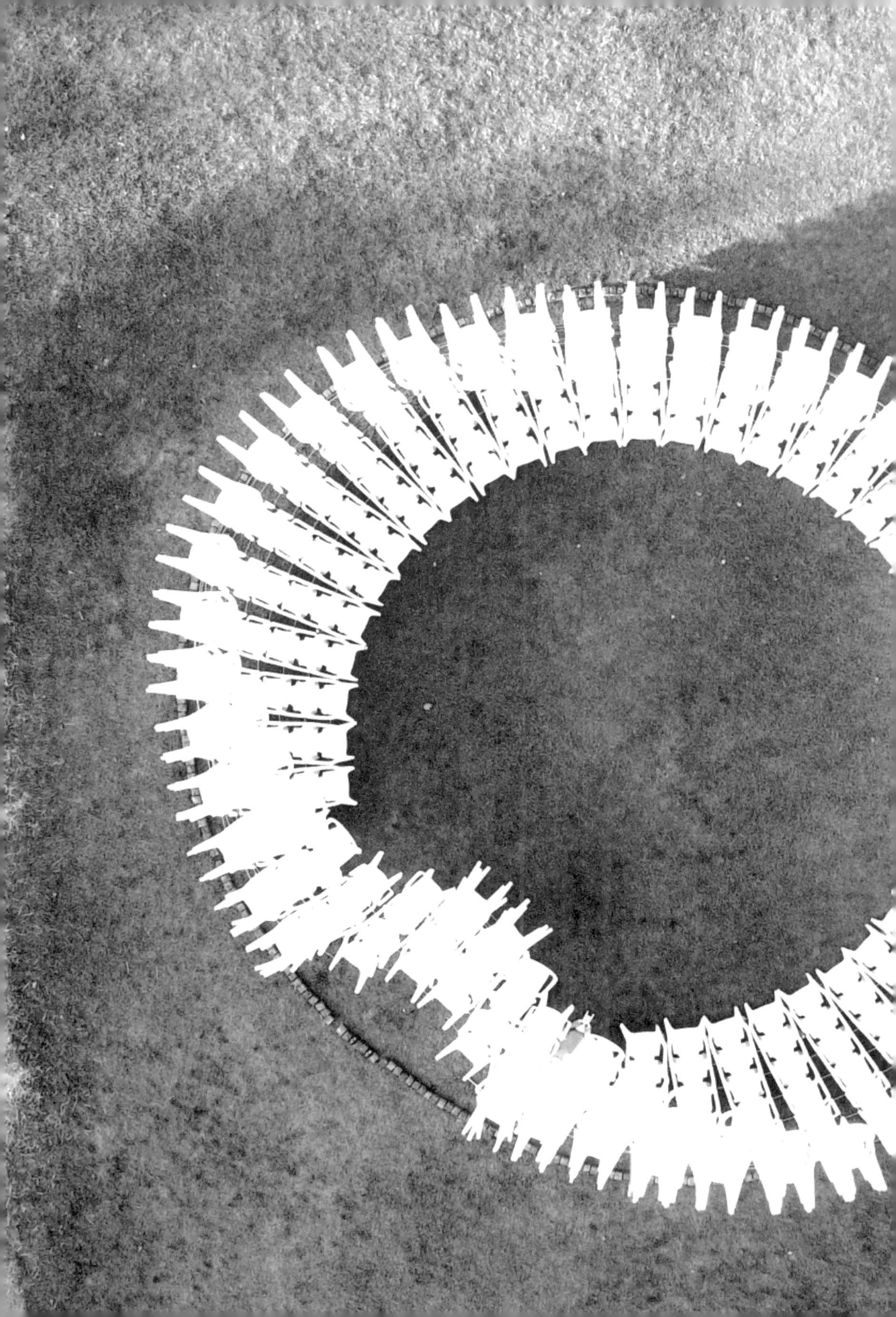

Urchin from the air. **Drone photograph by Thomas J. Campanella.**

Urchin, with John Lai. Photograph by Robert Barker.

Urchin. Photograph by Joe Wilsensky, Cornell University.

Urchin, 2016
Photograph by Starfish International

Chairs arriving: Girls' education in The Gambia. **Photograph by Starfish International Media House.**

Goosebumps

A Migration Pavilion
Winter Stations Competition, loser
Toronto, Canada
with support from Cornell Architecture/AAP
2019

Human migration, though sometimes welcome, is often met with bristling resistance. Some bird species are well known for their seasonal migration to warmer climes and they, too, are sometimes met with various forms of resistance. In the built environment, the ubiquitous bird-rejecting module is the bird spike. These pervasive devices cause the familiar scene of reverse-flying when the unsuspecting pigeon attempts to land on a spiked surface and is forced to recalculate its landing location at the last moment.

Goosebumps aligns the human's rejection with the bird's. A surface made entirely from bird spikes is woven into two cylindrical towers and oriented vertically with the spikes pointing toward the human body. Approaching the bird spike surface, the visitor empathizes with the bird's feelings when it is denied its prospective perch.

Studying tensile structures in 1987, Frei Otto made a sketch titled "Single Minimal Surfaces with three Rings of different sizes," for which a soap film would find the most efficient surface between the frames. *Goosebumps* adjusts the ring orientations to

harness the structure and height of an existing lifeguard station, thus accommodating inhabitation. Due to the inversion of the weave, two spaces are created. The first space has the spikes pointing outward and the translucent polycarbonate as the interior surface. The second space has the spikes protruding toward the inhabitant. Reminiscent of a *pigeonaire*, the two cylindrical spaces both welcome and expel the visitor to provoke thoughts on global migration.

Each 12" bird spike component is a demountable unit consisting of a polycarbonate base and metal spikes. By inserting the second-to-last spike into the second-to-last hole of a second spike, a pinwheel pattern is generated that allows the optimal flexure and density. This weave is suspended from three aluminum rings that use the existing lifeguard chair and the ground to hold them in position.

Goosebumps creates a hostile architecture, antagonistic at times to the outside and at times to the inside, asking us to reflect on the migratory populations of the world and our own agency to welcome or reject them.

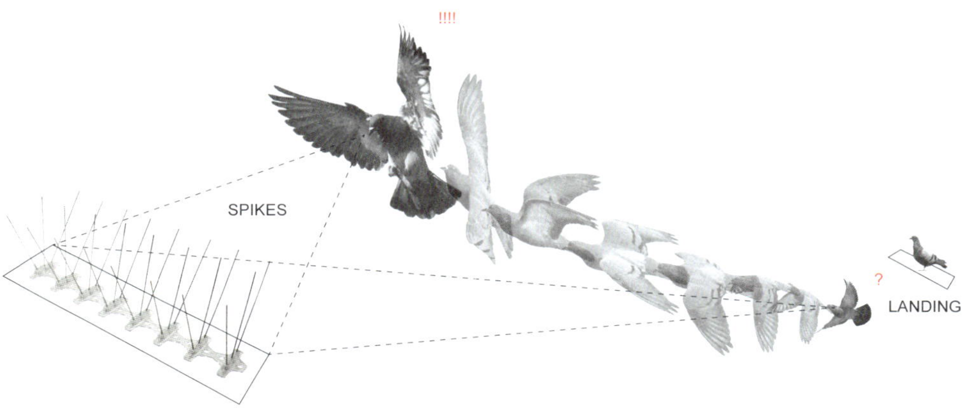

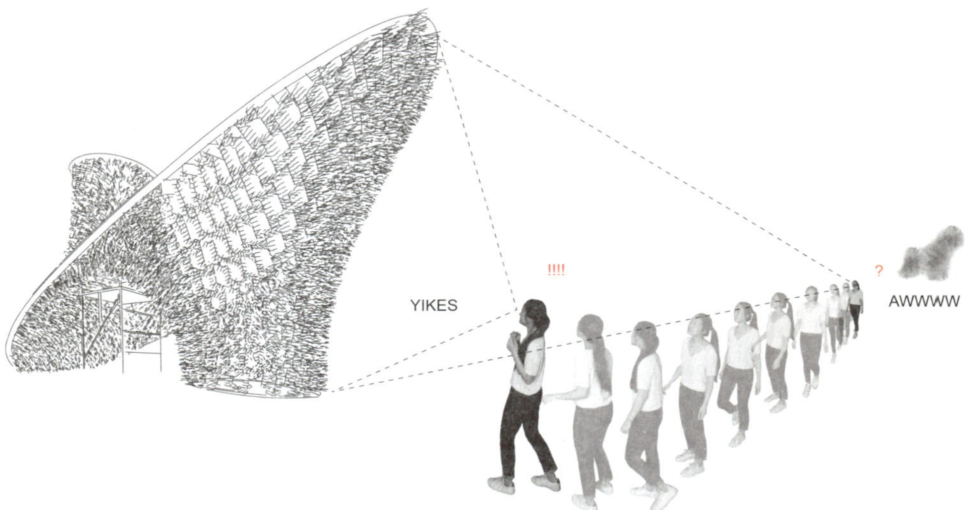
!!!!
YIKES
?
AWWWW

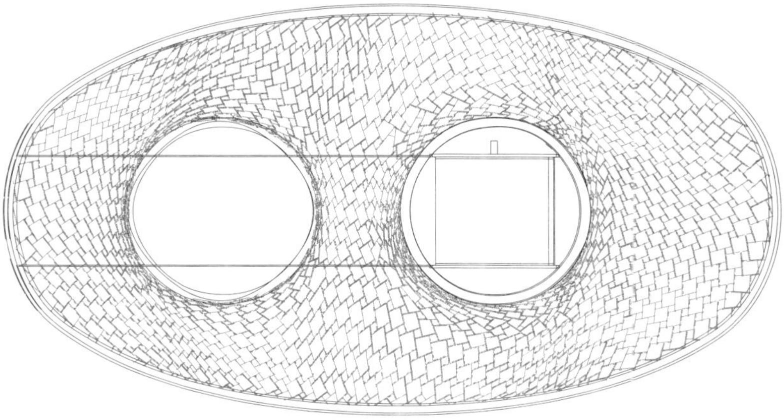

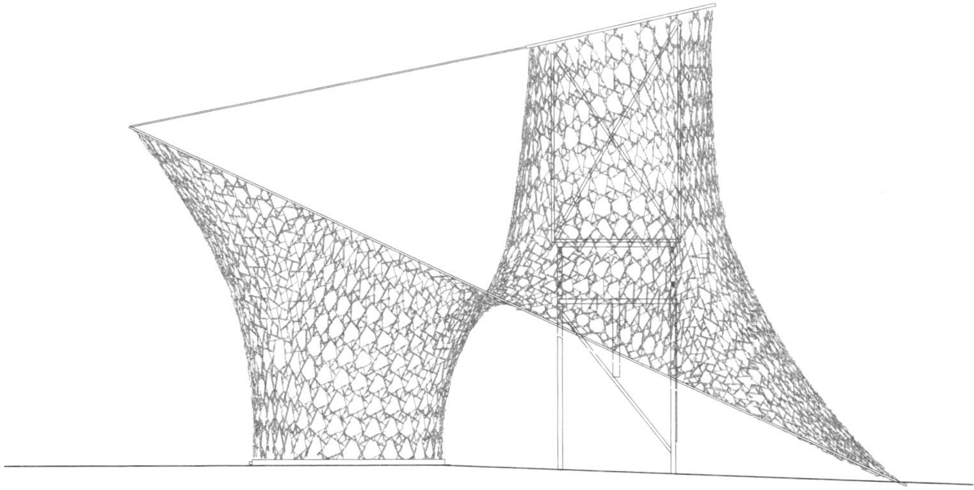

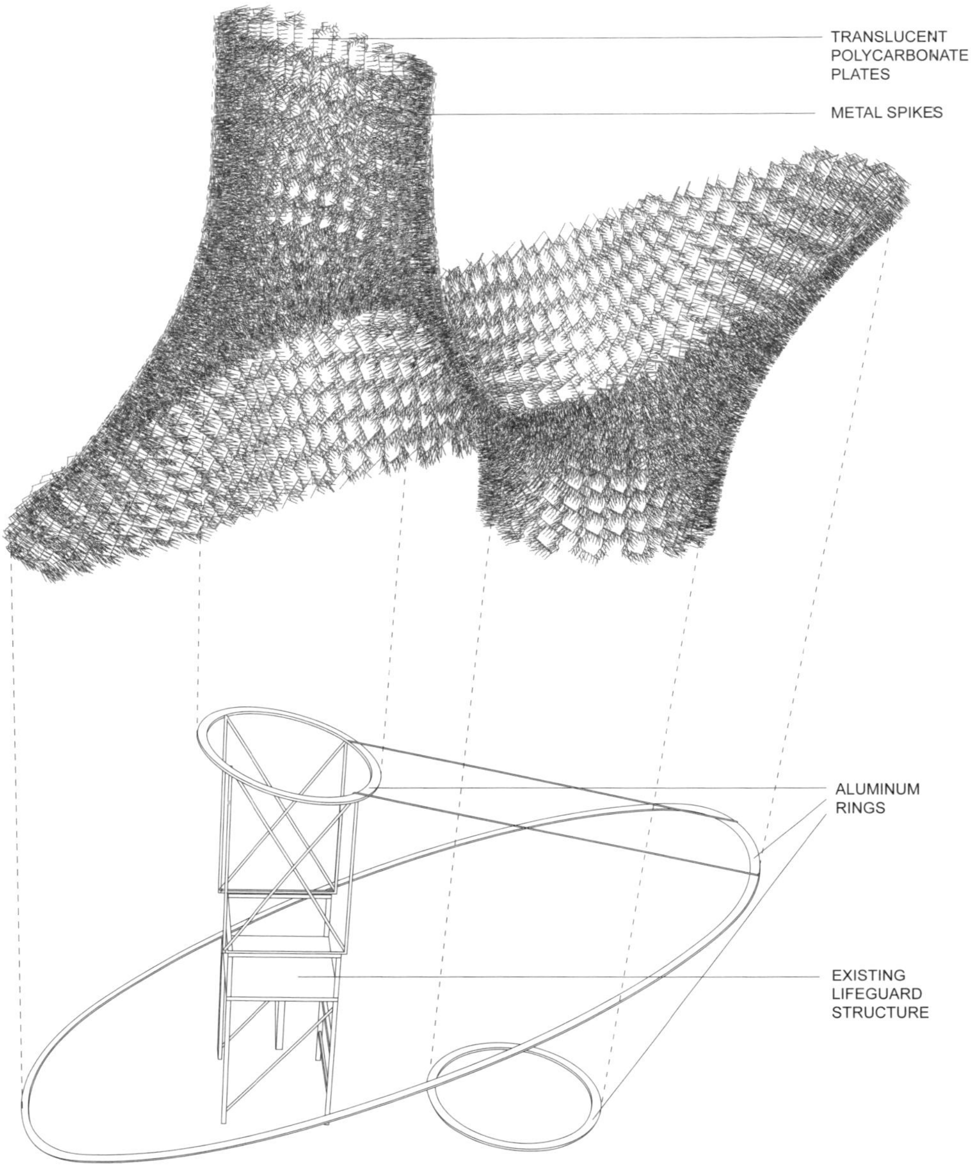
TRANSLUCENT
POLYCARBONATE
PLATES
METAL SPIKES
ALUMINUM
RINGS
EXISTING
LIFEGUARD
STRUCTURE

Wonderful

A Space of Dualities
It's a Wonderful Life Museum
private commission
Seneca Falls, NY, USA
2019–2020

Frank Capra's 1946 film, *It's a Wonderful Life,* follows the life of George Bailey, a man whose suicide is prevented by his guardian angel, Clarence. During the film, the angel shows George what the world would be like had he never been born.

Set in the fictional town of Bedford Falls, *It's a Wonderful Life* is believed to have been modeled after Seneca Falls in upstate New York. Throughout the film, themes of duality and conflict are ever-present. Bailey spends his whole life having to make a choice between sacrificing his own happiness for others and following his dreams. The narrative shows him as the embodiment of all that is good by contrasting him with a corrupt businessman, Mr. Potter, whose sole purpose in life is to make money at all costs. Appropriately, when Bailey's guardian angel shows him a world where he never existed, the idyllic town has been transformed into "Pottersville," now a den of crime and corruption.

Since 2010, the *It's a Wonderful Life Museum* has existed in Seneca Falls. This is one of only a handful museums in the world

focused on a single film, and the only one dedicated to a black-and-white movie. The museum exhibits a growing collection of film memorabilia ranging from film props to historical artifacts. Additionally, given the topics broached in the film, the museum doubles as the home of the local suicide prevention resource and idea center.

As the 75th anniversary of the film approaches, the museum seeks a new vision. Following the duality present in the film, the design proposes that the existing warehouse be gutted and that all new programs be amalgamated into a central object. This object-within-an-object communicates the tension between the two states present in the film. Generated based on the programmatic needs of the spaces (room recreations, exhibition spaces, and a small theater), the form creates secondary spaces between itself and the warehouse shell, while also making new connections to the town of Seneca Falls.

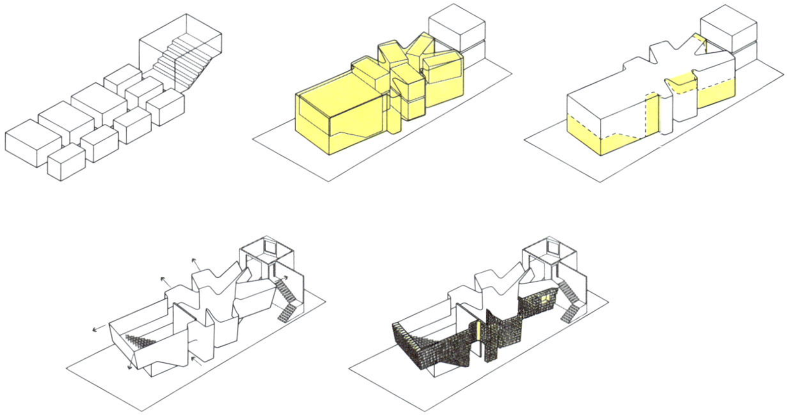

As an embodiment of the two worlds, the object can be read differently based on the perspective of the viewer. This is due to its skewed shelving skin, which is applied as a synthetic "fur" on all object walls. Through a precise and careful design, the position of the visitor vis-à-vis the object affects what they see and how they read the space. This draws a direct parallel with the film and places the visitor in the shoes of George Bailey, where the (literal) position they take can transport them to either Bedford Falls or Pottersville.

Within the shelving's unidirectional fur, the museum's large collection of memorabilia is exhibited. Meanwhile, the flat surface of the old building (or shell) houses the images and projections. Spanning between the object and the shell is a bridge that, for some distance, is a recreation of a structure in the film. In this case, however, the form melts into the *Wonderful* object at its midpoint. Additionally, all of the surfaces are painted in black and white tones to make palpable the black-and-white format of the movie and give users the feeling of being projected into the scenes. Indeed, it is only the visitors who are in color.

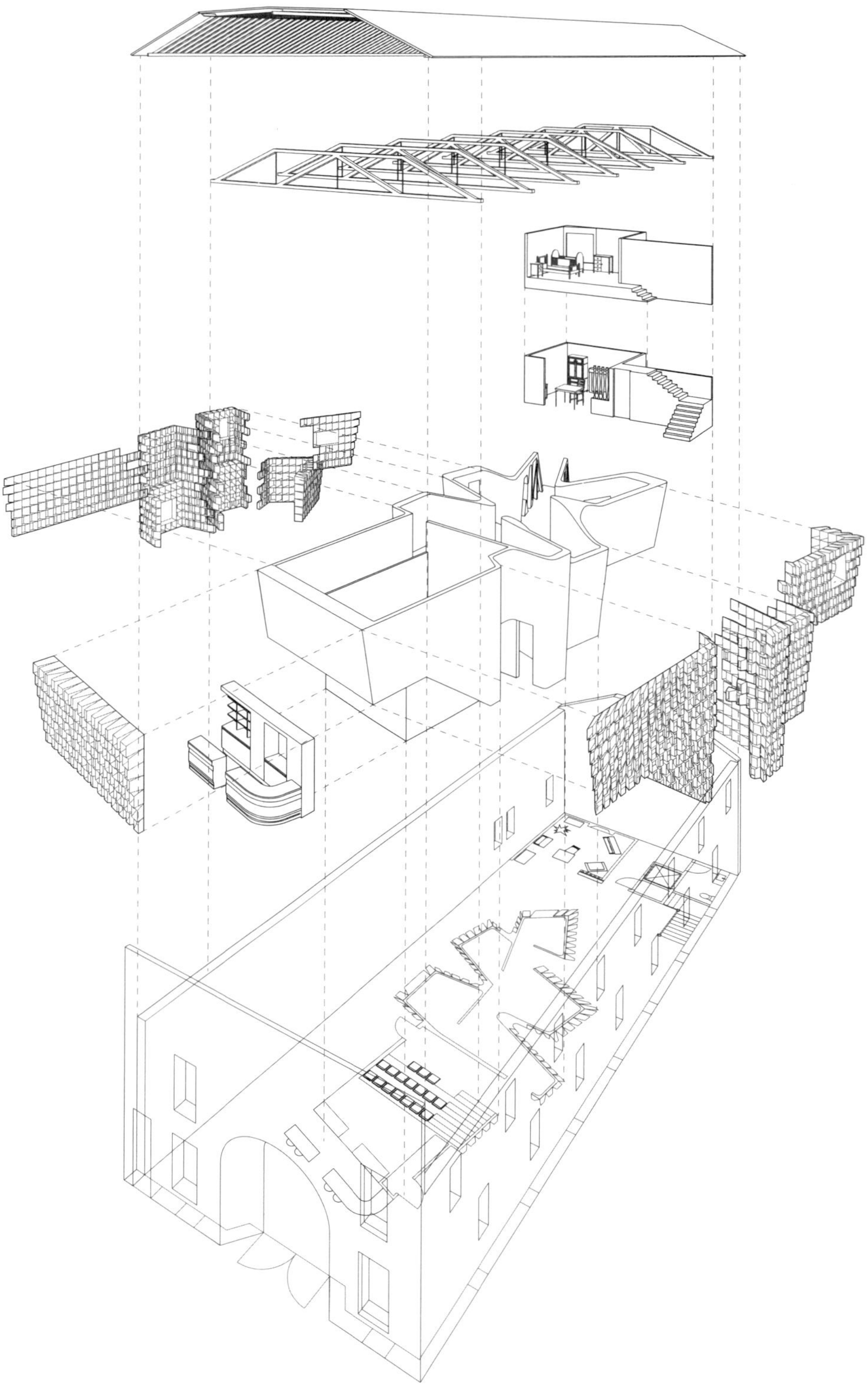

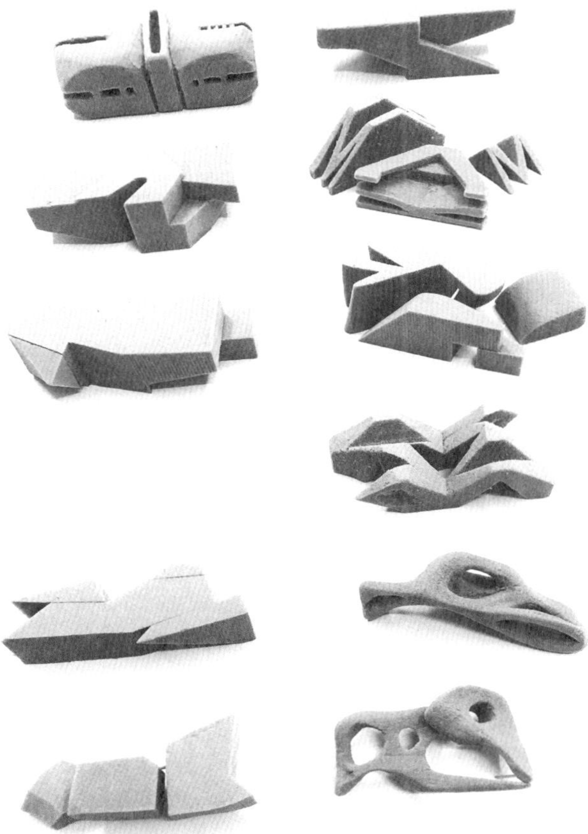

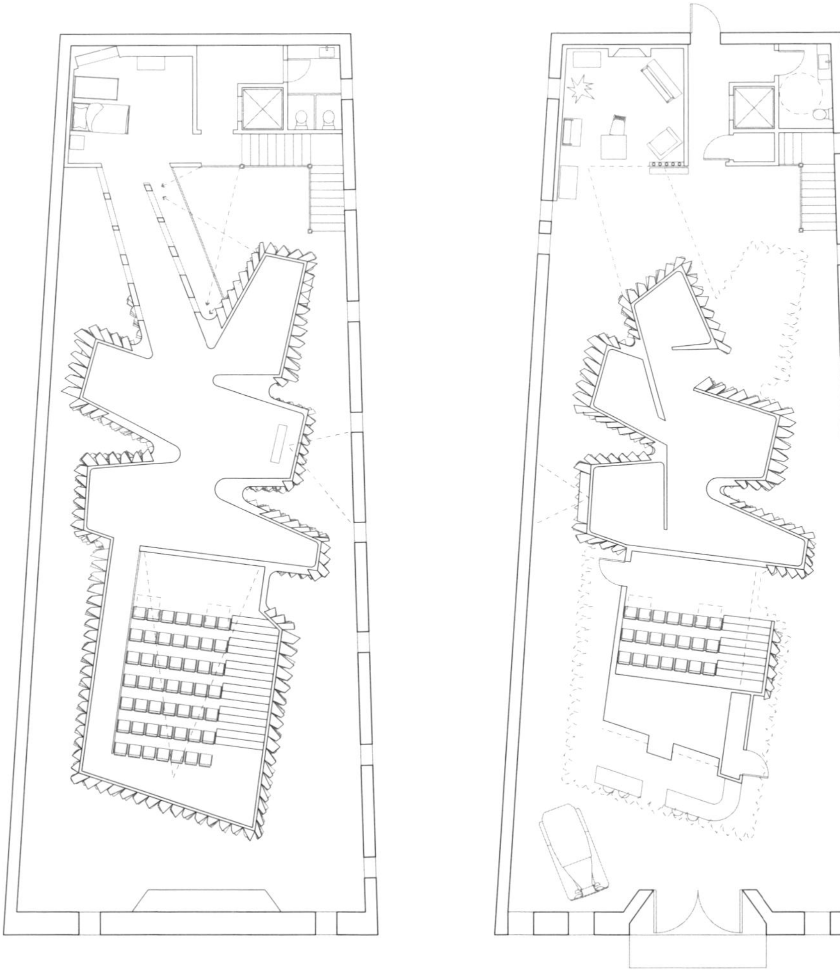

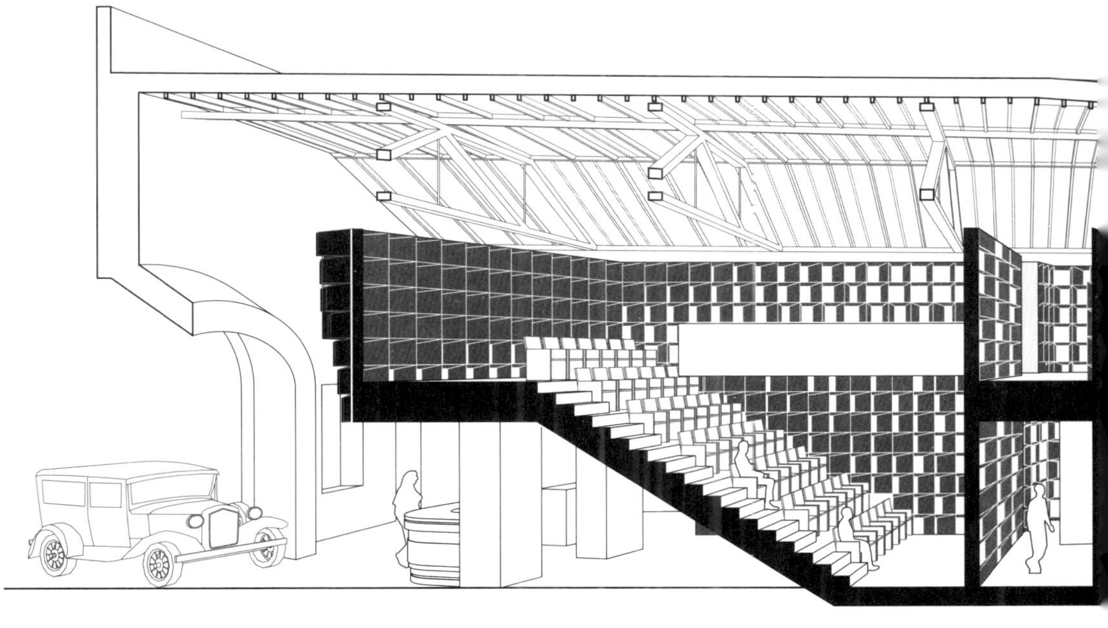

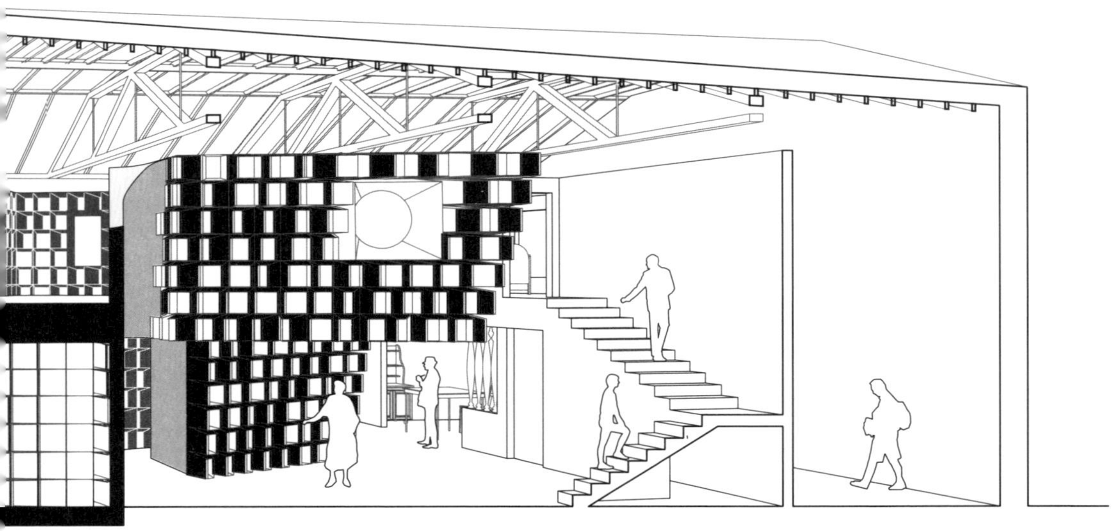

Coca-Cola
GOWER DRUGS

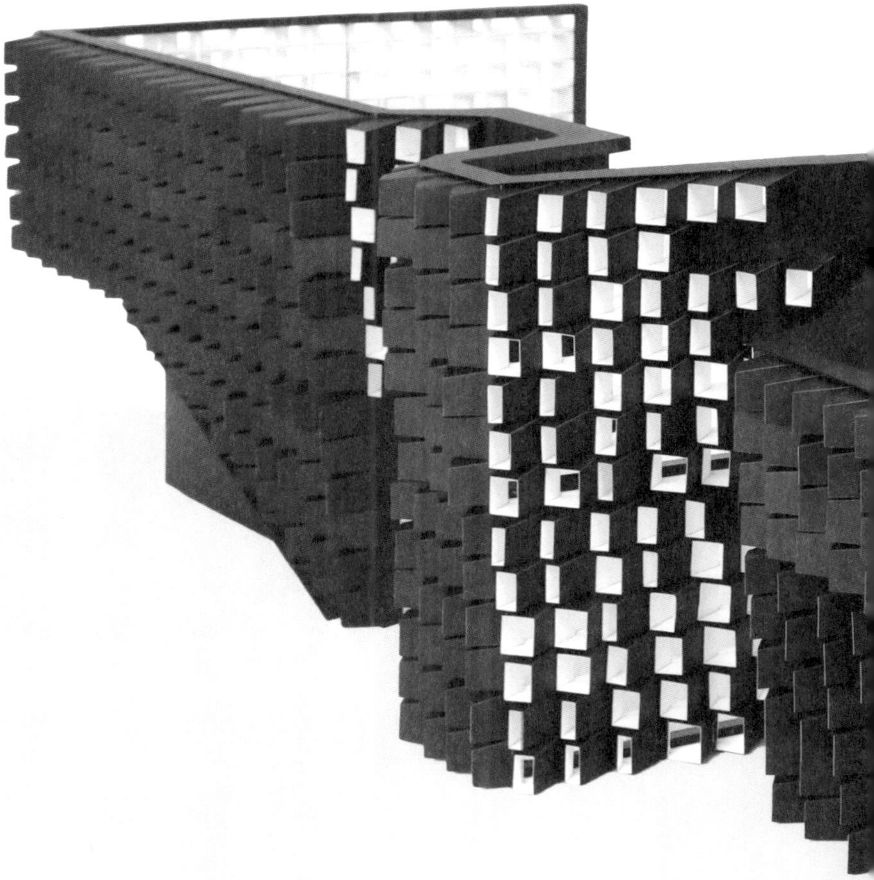

Confluence

A Park(ing)
in collaboration with **LMNOP (Lowder + Murata: Natures, Objects, Practices)**
Limited Competition for a riverside Parking Lot, shortlisted
Peterborough, NH, USA
2015

At the meeting of the Contoocook River and the Nubanusit Brook in Peterborough, New Hampshire, *Confluence* refers not only to its location but also to the act of programmatic stacking.

Perhaps the best example of multiple programs is conjured by Rem Koolhaas in *Delirious New York*, who proposes "eating oysters with boxing gloves, naked, on the ninth floor." The skyscraper, for Koolhaas, enables this stacking of completely unrelated programs that yield a "fantastic juxtaposition of its activities." In the Downtown Athletic Club, "each of the Club's floors is a separate installment of an infinitely unpredictable intrigue that extols the complete surrender to the definitive instability of life in the Metropolis."

Rem Koolhaas, *Delirious New York: A Retroactive Manifesto for Manhattan* (Oxford: Oxford University Press, 1978), 157.

A more practical application occurred in Rotterdam due to a political error. In 2004, the city's mayor made a promise to create a park near Marconiplein. His successor unwittingly signed into law a different plan to use the same site for parking. By 2006, two legal documents existed related to the site, one guaranteeing a park,

the other guaranteeing parking. The government's solution was to stack them.

In response to an equally bipolar brief, *Confluence* uses the natural topography to stack an urban park, a market, and a riverside balcony above 60 parking places. Additionally, a pedestrian bridge connects these new programs to the heart of Peterborough Town.

Conceived as a network of flows (cars, pedestrians, bikes) and eddies (farmers market shoppers, picnickers, audience/performance), the design facilitates fast currents of movement and slow pools of social interaction. Two paths widen and connect to form larger community balconies—one pushed into the hillside and another pulling out toward the river. Negotiating the existing slope, *Confluence* connects the deck level with the parking level by various ramps, stairs, and voids that lead down to a parking level

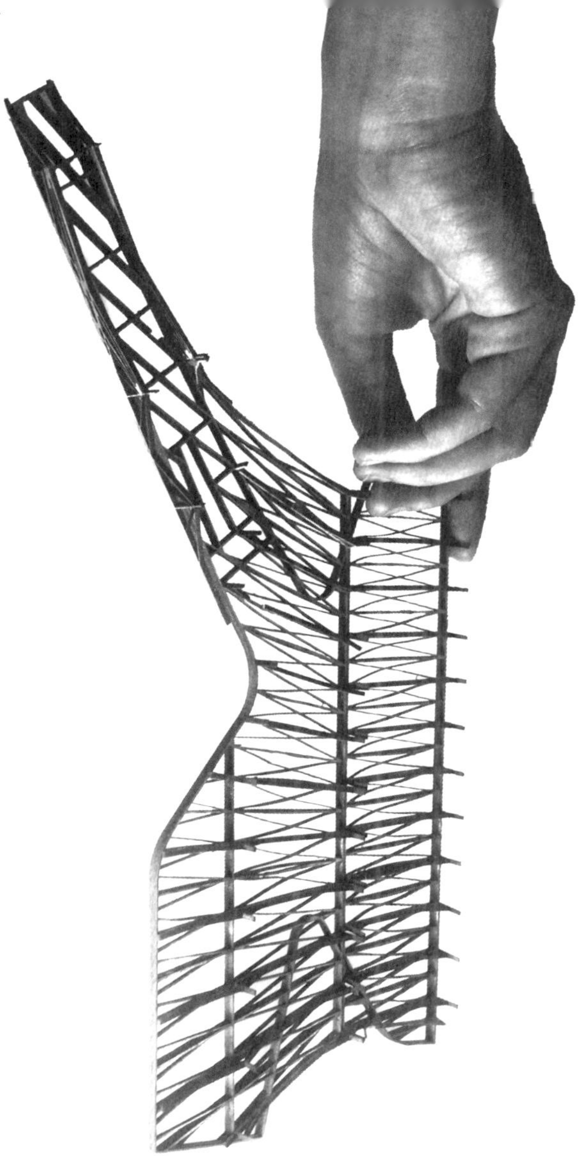

that is punctuated by light and greenery. The plants on both levels are a series of wild local grasses, which are low maintenance, and which also work to detoxify water from the deck and parking surfaces before it enters the waterway.

The design borrows its structural language from the mass timber bridges of the region, using locally reclaimed members. The exposed structure uses a trifurcating system that splits and deepens to create a variegated ceiling and bridge-truss articulation.

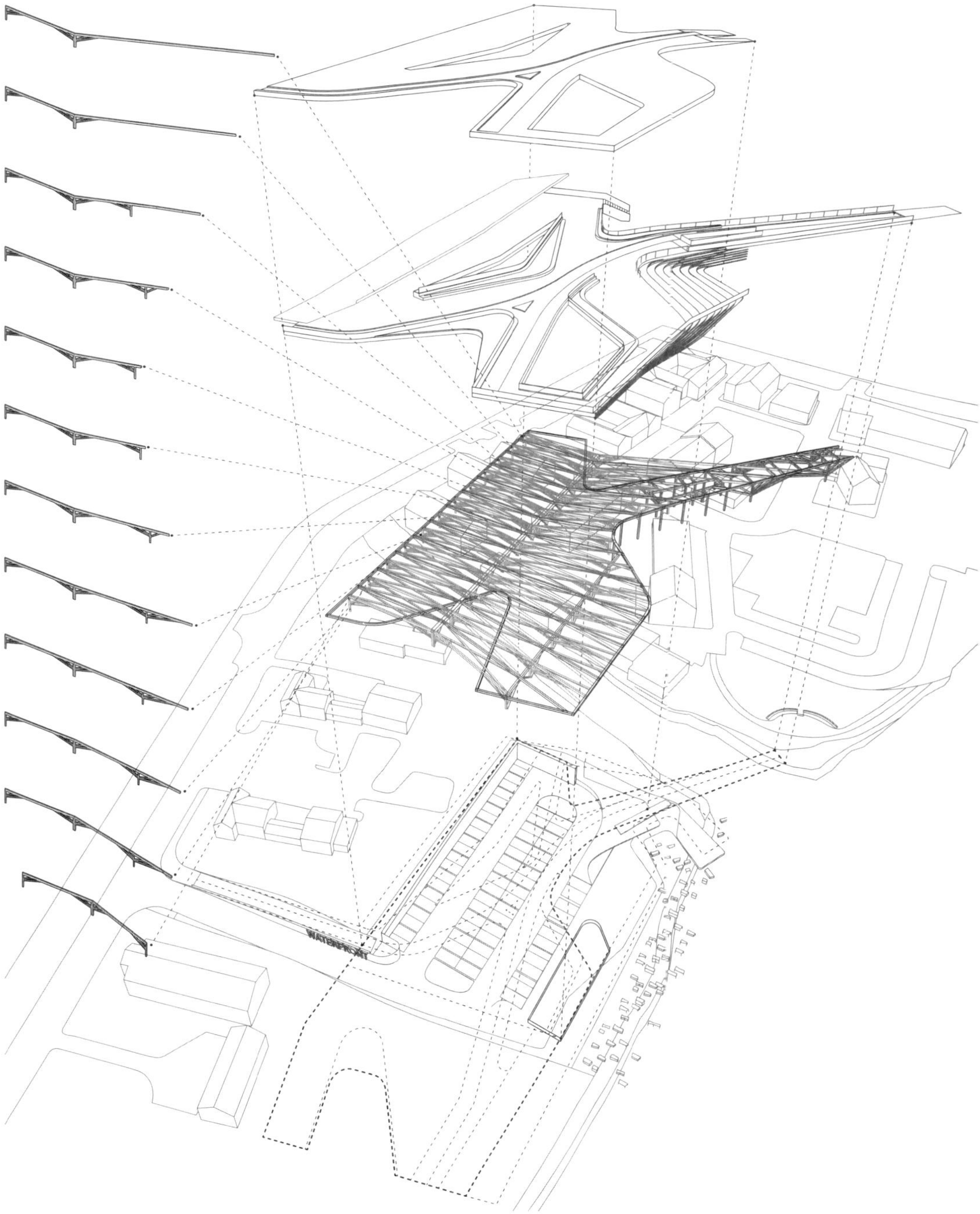
WATERFRONT

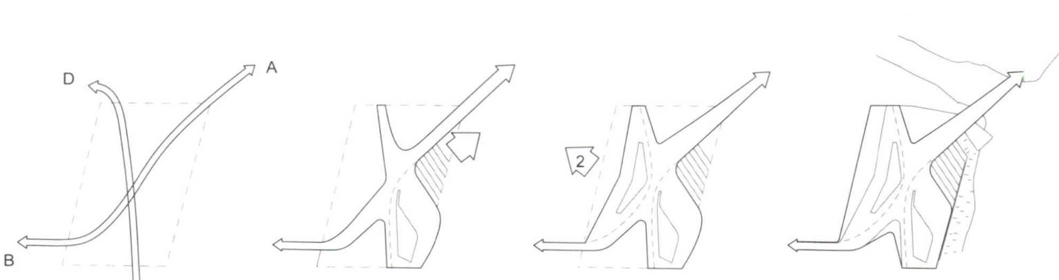

CONNECTIONS

PULL OUT 1 FOR AMPHITEHATER

PULL OUT 2 FOR MARKET

CONNECT OVER RIVER AND MARSH TO CITY CENTER

Janus House

A Two-sided House
private commission
Ithaca, NY, USA
2018–

The *Janus House* is a response to a site that has two radically different sides and a client who is a collector of art and antiques. A long drive through a dense forest ends abruptly, at the edge of a steep, grassy hill, overlooking Cayuga Lake to the west and a deep gorge to the north.

In response to this two-sidedness, as well as a desire on the part of the client for both modern and farmhouse aesthetics, the *Janus House* merges two antithetical models proposed by Pier Vittorio Aureli: Sebastiano Serlio's *Farmhouse for the Worker* (c.1541-47) and Le Corbusier's *Maison Dom-ino* (1914), each confronted with the other, as well as with the dichotomous site. For Peter Eisenman, the relationship between the *Maison Dom-ino*'s three slabs, six columns, six pads, and stair formed the basis of his argument for the self-referential sign. Or, as articulated by Pier Vittorio Aureli, "through the strict economy of means of the building, these moves produce an intentional redundancy that [Eisenman] identifies as the locus of architecture." This model is antithetical to Serlio's *Farmhouse for the Worker*, whose load-bearing stone peasants'

Pier Vittorio Aureli, "The Dom-ino Problem: Questioning the Architecture of Domestic Space," in *Log* 30 (Winter 2014): 153–68.

houses consist of a string of rooms for living and for animals, stretched along a masonry portico.

The *Janus House* similarly locates all of its functional programs in a heavy spine—the poché of the house, which includes the bathrooms, elevator, stair, and closets. This allows a portico-like space to transform into a more horizontal slab, with *Dom-ino*-like diagonals stretched between levels.

The view from the initial forest approach is a closed stone façade with minimal punctured openings. Windows are rotated 90 degrees from the plane of the façade to mask the openings from the face of the building. This twisting causes a shift to the façade planes and gives hints of a force beyond. As the ground drops steeply to

the west, toward Cayuga Lake, and vertically to the north, toward the gorge, a series of large terraces at the landing of each ramp cantilever out over the landscape. The diagonal walkways connect the terraces and protect the glazed west side from the harsh effects of the afternoon sun. The sinuous sloped landscape of the site is continued in the diagonal landscape of the façade so that the house reads more as an emergence from the landscape than an object on it.

Half farmhouse, half *dom-ino* slab, and fully embedded in site, the house transforms in the round from closed and vertical to open and horizontal, as the site, itself, radically transforms from forest to steep clearing to lake. The reverberations of the diagonal force of the landscape winding up into the house on the lake side are registered but resisted in the heaviness of the forest side. In between, the house stretches into horizontal floors and balconies, providing space for a large living level with garage, kitchen, dining and living spaces, a second level for guests, and an upper-level master suite with views over the trees and toward the lake.

Materials for the house are considered antiques that will contribute to the client's collection. In this way, recycled materials acquire the narrative of their provenance, and with that, a significantly increased value.

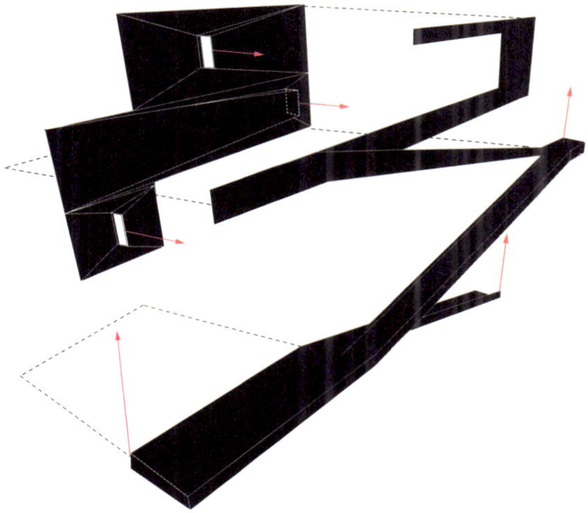

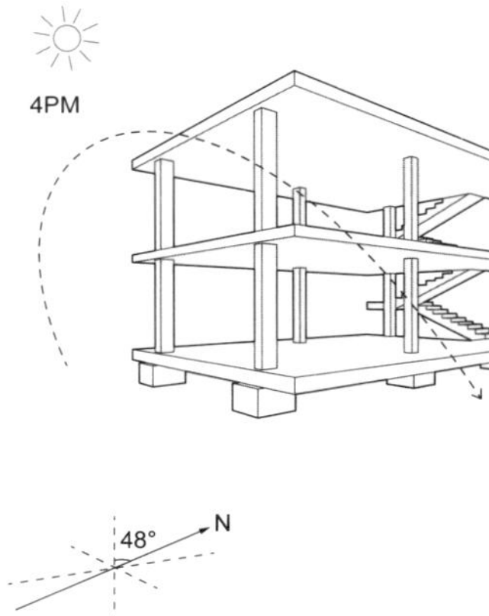
4PM
48°
N

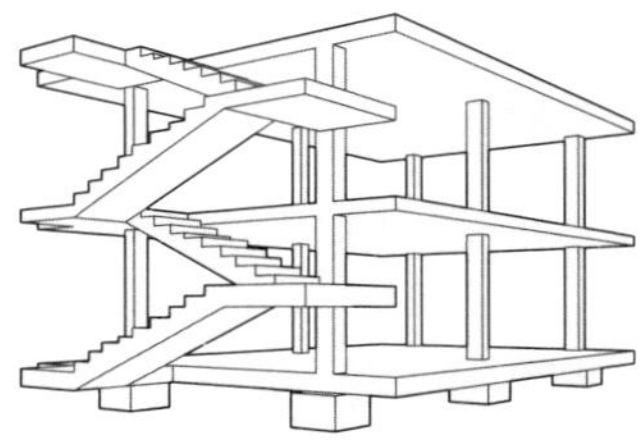

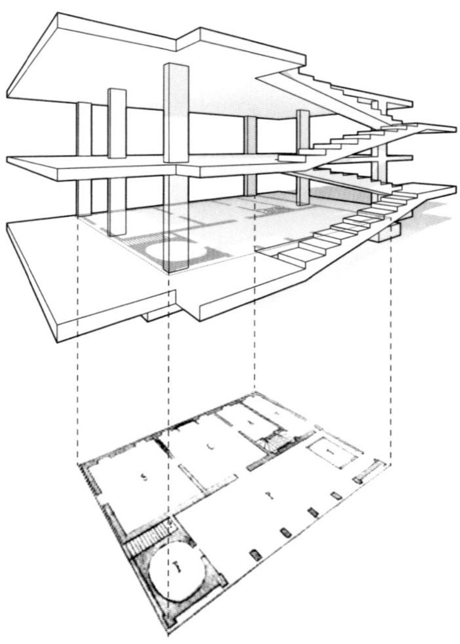

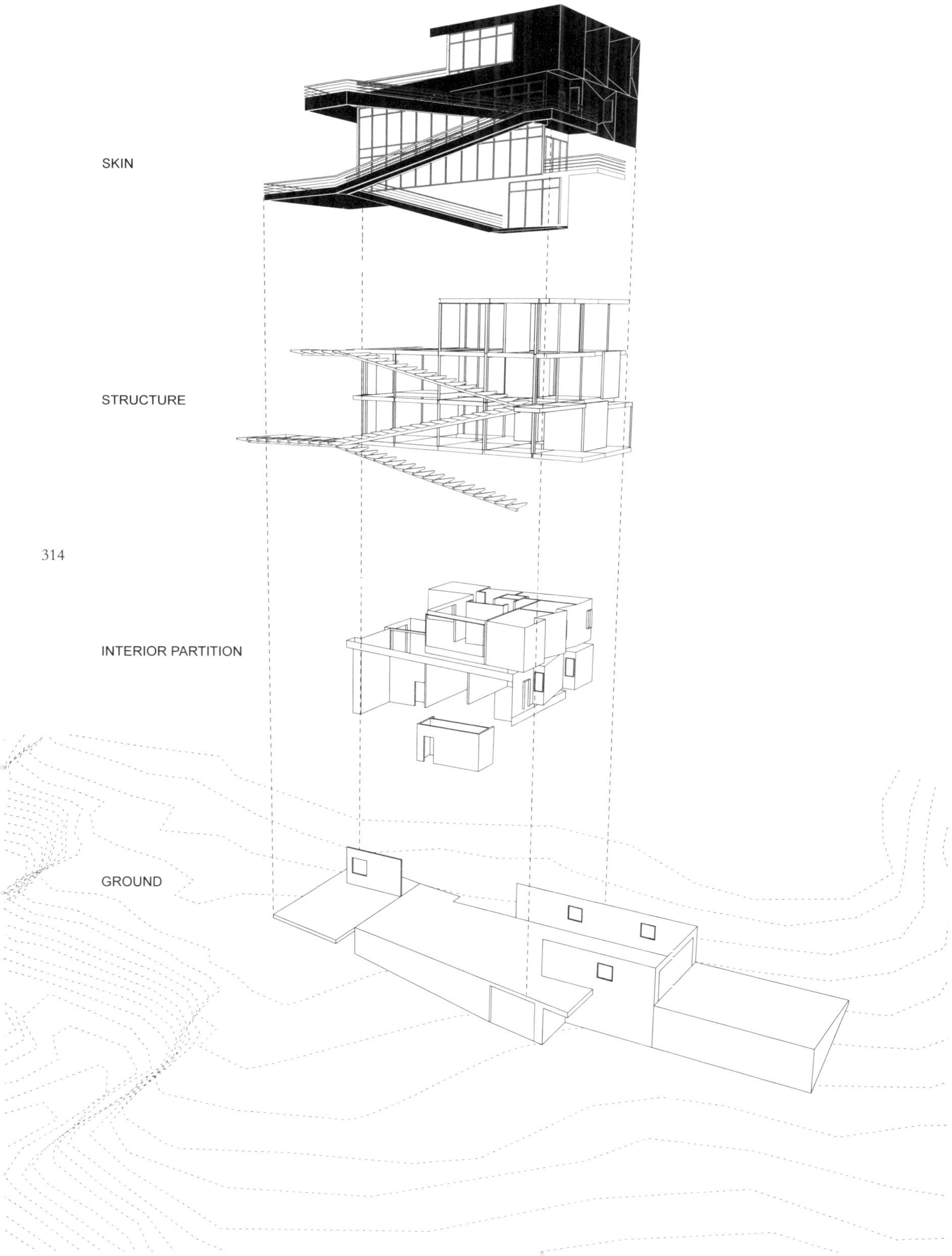
SKIN
STRUCTURE
INTERIOR PARTITION
GROUND

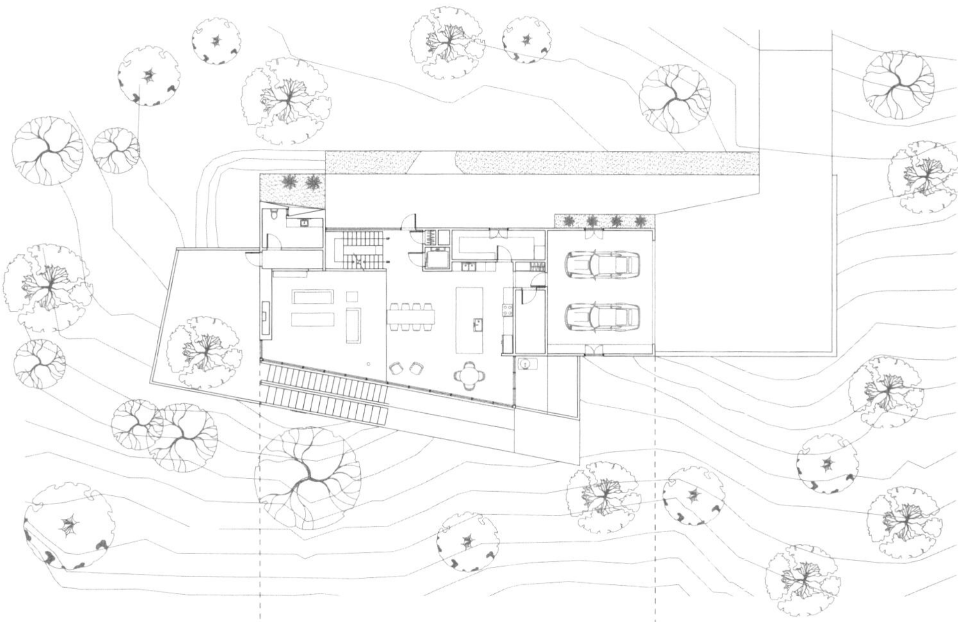

omg!

Zimmer

A Walking House
An OMG project: in collaboration with **Martin Miller**
with students from Cornell Mechanical Engineering and Architecture
with support from Cornell Architecture/AAP
2019

Zimmer is a conflation of the German word for "room" with the brand name of the metal device that assists humans with walking. Albeit a slow walker, its name also encourages a potential misreading as "zoomer."

In the 1960s, the space race and developments in mechanization provoked visions of a dynamic architectural future. Designs like Ron Herron/Archigram's *Walking City* or Cedric Price's *Fun Palace* speculated on movable and changeable structures. In 1965, Reyner Banham wrote that mechanical systems were too new to have been incorporated into the fundamentals of architecture. They simply were not embedded into the "proverbial wisdom of the profession: none of the great slogans—" he wrote, "form follows function, *accusez la structure*, Firmness Commodity and Delight, truth to materials, *weniger ist mehr*—is much use in coping with the mechanical invasion." Now that some time has passed, and mechanical systems have become more ubiquitous, how can these systems be incorporated into the language of architecture? Rather than allowing this area to be in the territory of the engineer, it is

Reyner Banham, "A Home Is Not a House," *Art in America*, April 1965, 75.

time for architects to think about legibility and meaning through dynamic and responsive structures.

Zimmer rethinks the house as a series of elements that harness energy. By considering its individual parts as physically dynamic and generative, *Zimmer* engages with nature and leaves a trace behind that impacts and is impacted by its surroundings. The installation is a small dwelling-like metal frame, with solar- and human-powered rooms that might be considered legs. As the legs move through a series of Chebyshev linkages, its spaces are also reconfigured.

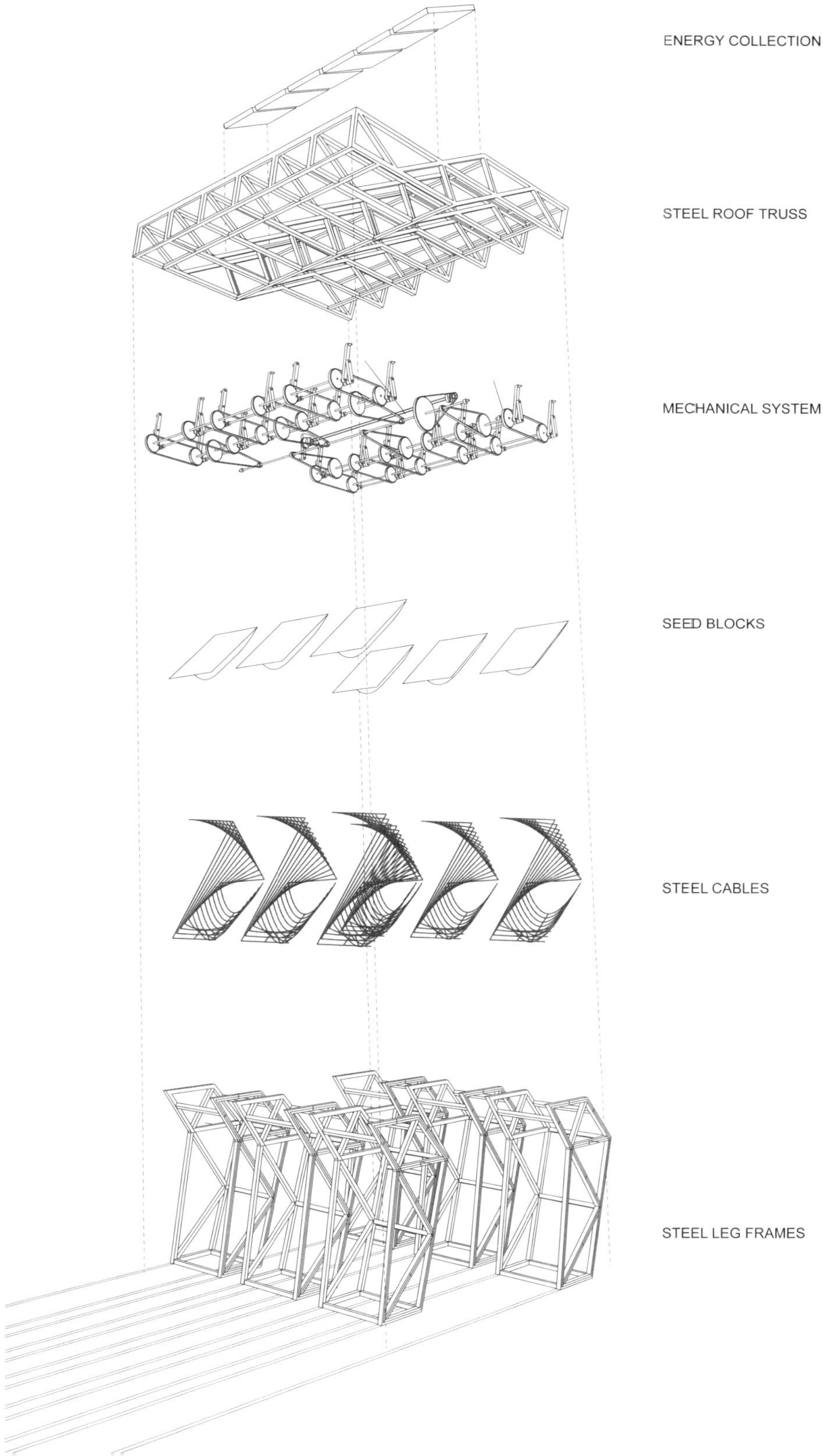
ENERGY COLLECTION
STEEL ROOF TRUSS
MECHANICAL SYSTEM
SEED BLOCKS
STEEL CABLES
STEEL LEG FRAMES

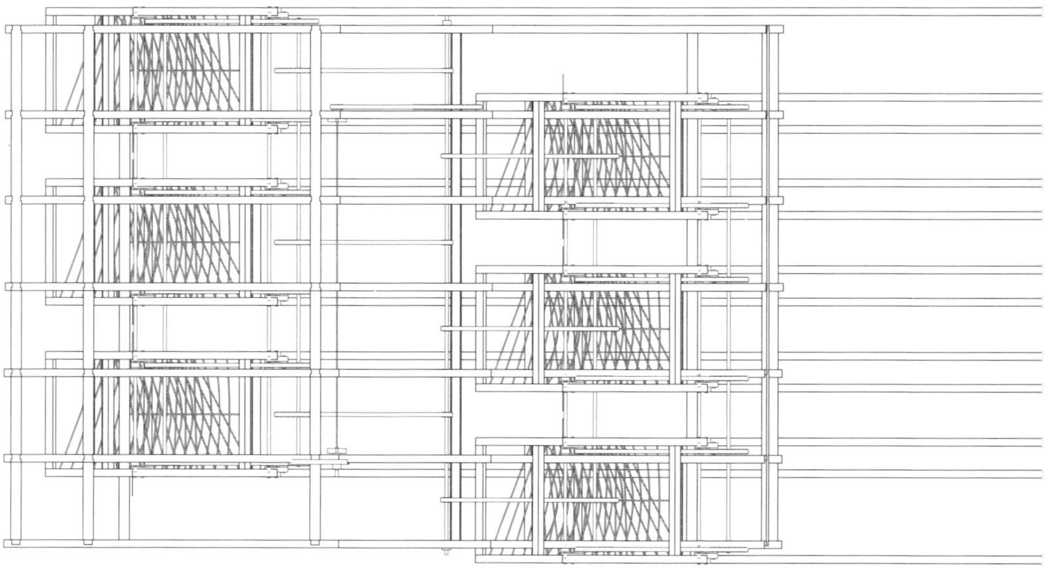

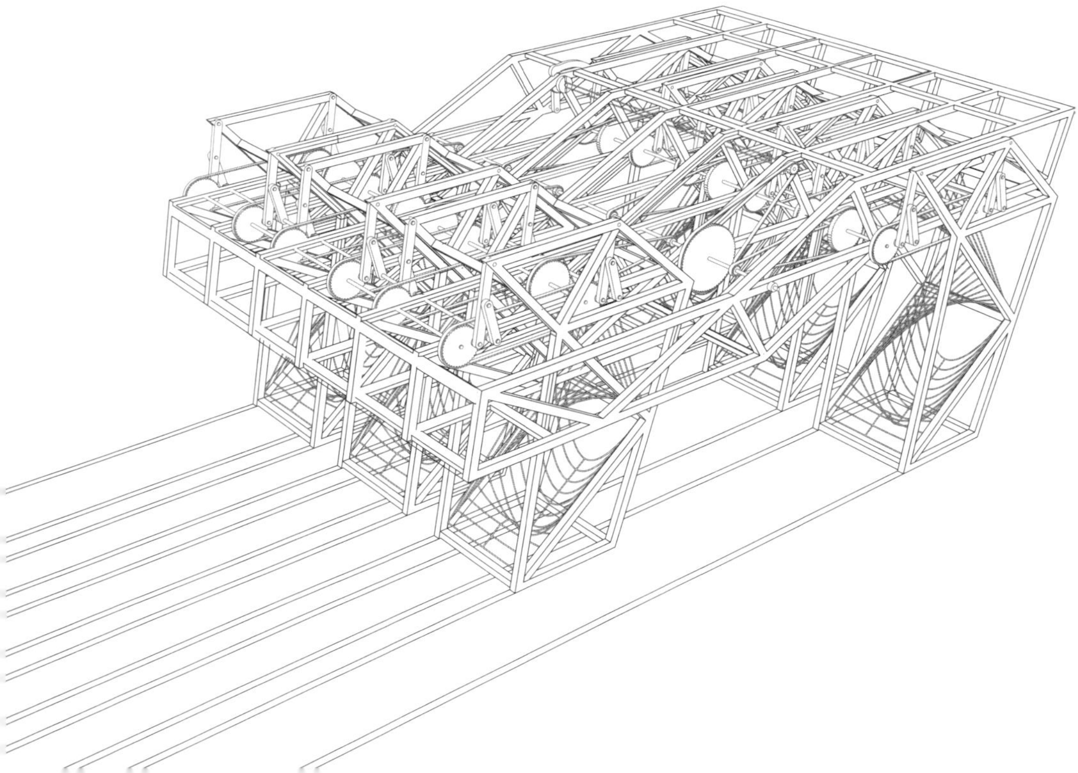

Constantly shifting the relationship between its rooms, this dwelling slowly walks across a field throughout the duration of a season. *Zimmer's* feet are embedded with seeds. As it lumbers seasonally, a trail of flowers is left as an index of its presence.

The project was undertaken in collaboration with Andy Ruina from Cornell's Department of Mechanical Engineering, as well as students from both Architecture and Mechanical Engineering. The team developed a series of prototypes using other mechanisms and forms beyond the original designs developed by OMG. The more iconic "Dinner Date" prototype used a simple crank mechanism, driving six legs in three rotation positions. In this iteration, the iconic form of the house is cut into six slices that not only reconfigure and fragment the overall image, but also split the main domestic programs in intentionally aggressive ways: the bed shifts from being a double to two singles; the dining chairs are at times at the table, and at times removed; the armchair is at times close to the hearth, and at times floating in space. Meanwhile, the more modern "Jeffrey" prototype used a Chebyshev linkage to shift four legs/rooms, which change their proximity to one another under a sleek planar roof.

Zimmer

A joint-effort between architects and mechanical engineers, Zimmer is a collaboration between Cornell Architecture, OMG, and Cornell Mechanical Engineering (Andy Ruina) with students: Mickey Ahi, Emma Boudreau, Isabel Brañas, Osehikhueme Etomi, Yanyang Hou, Erik Johnson, Eleanor Krause, Evan Spencer McDowell, Anbar Oreizi-Esfahani, Steven Song Ren John Andrew Scheeler, Alireza Shojakhani, Jiacheng Xu, Wyatt Yang, Derek Yi, Yue Zhang, Wangda Zhu, Magdalena Zink.

Zimmer version: *"Dinner Date."*

Zimmer version: *"Jeffrey."*

Ci-ça

A Tolerance Pavilion,
HMMD Competition, loser
The Red Square, Moscow, Russia
2015

Ci-ça (French for "this-that") is the origin of the English word "seesaw," the popular pivoting playground device that requires two players to push up and down at opposite ends of a long beam that is fixed at the center. The *Ci*-ça pavilion aligns 44 seesaws along a curvilinear spine. This provides a framework by which individuals can interact with others in the public space of Moscow's Red Square. Any individual must find a partner in the public space with whom to sit and seesaw. Their relationship will develop without words and perhaps strictly through gestures and expressions, requiring only the weight of each body and the spring in the legs of the other to enable a motion.

Like the seesaw, the overall volume of this pavilion balances at the center. Its 16 steel trusses of varied profiles are joined together to form a double cantilever, resting on the base podium and connected through the central three bays. On the underbellies, smooth mirrors reflect the movement of the people on the seesaws and in the square. Meanwhile, the vertical surfaces are clad with faceted tiles (derived from tiles on St. Basil's onion domes),

made to distort the reflection of the surroundings by breaking it up into fragments.

Beneath the seesaws, in continually fluttering light generated by the movement above, the café, workshops, meeting rooms, conference room, and reception are located. The galleries and auditorium are in the upper volume. Through them, the public can reach the roof deck, which overlooks the Red Square and the Kremlin beyond.

Designed to address the issue of tolerance, the pavilion uses the playfulness of the seesaw to provoke serious thought on

one's acceptance and reliance on others. Collectively, the seesaw landscape is constantly shifting. Its doubling and fragmenting effect creates an animated and constantly changing experience. The players on the seesaws and the inhabitants of the building become new active architectural components, without whom the building is incomplete.

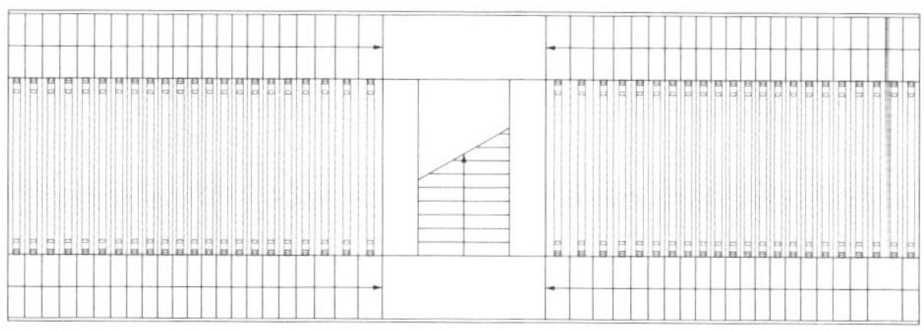

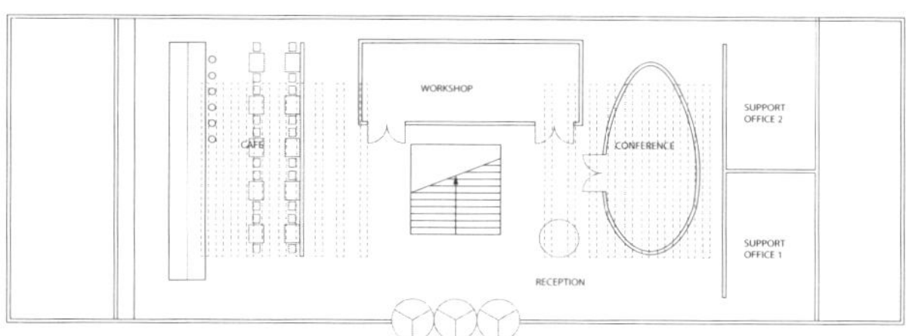

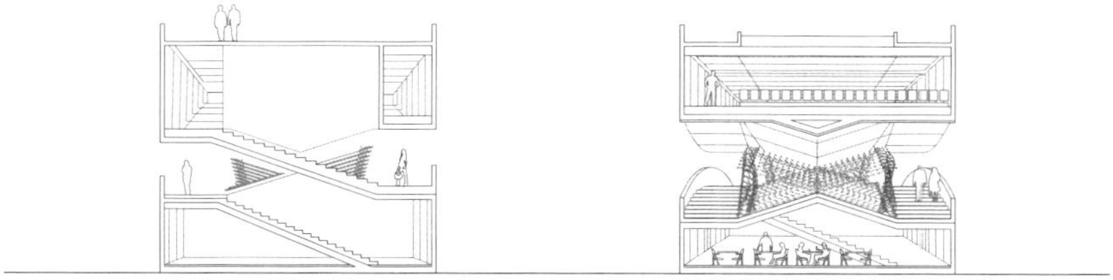

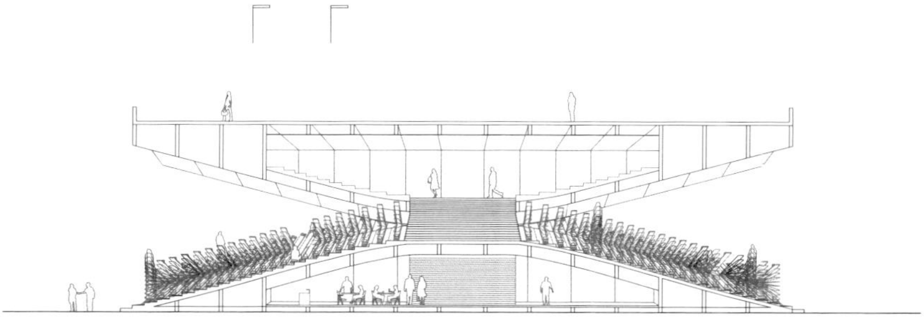

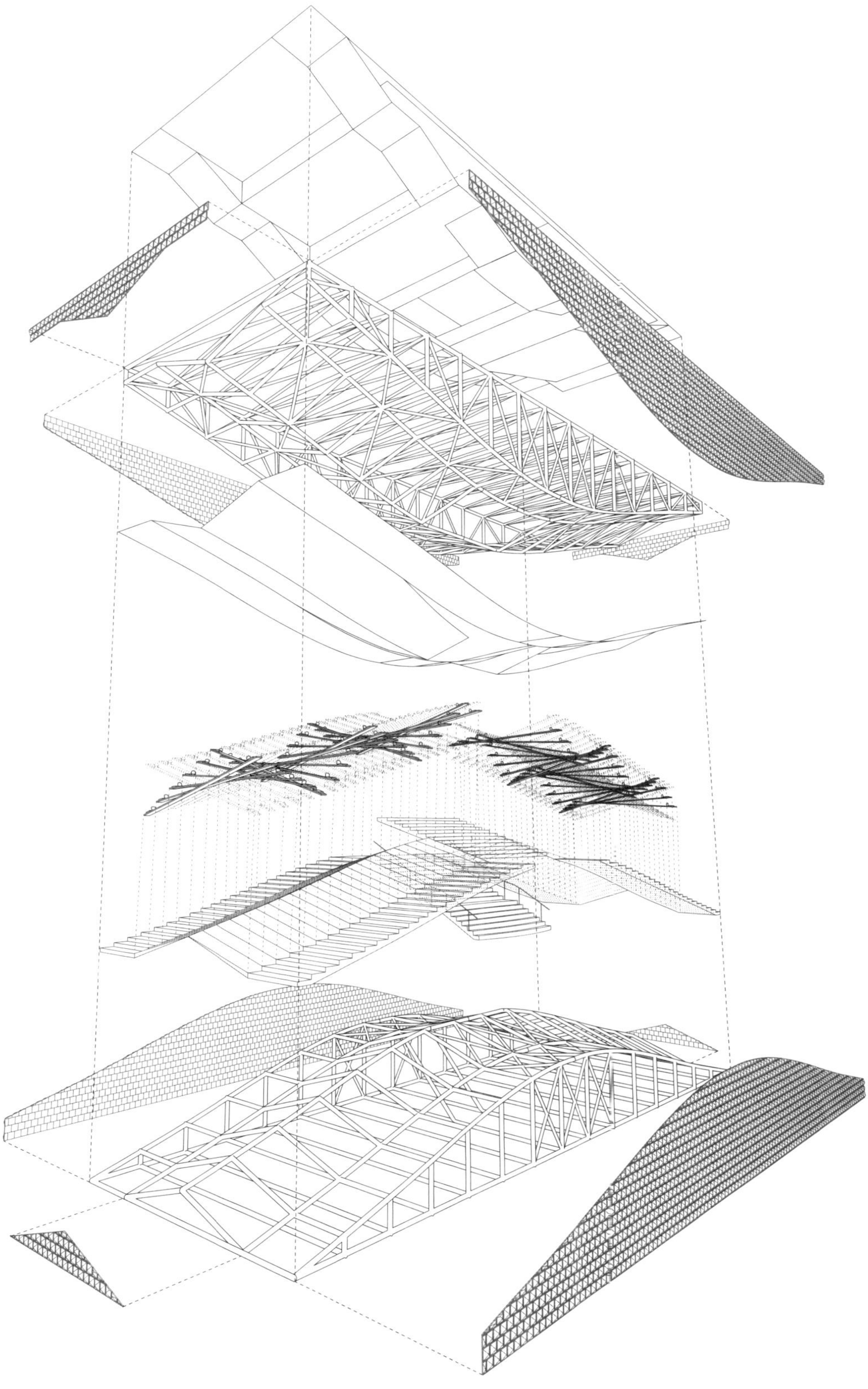

omg!

Art Dock

85% Museum, 15% Boat
An OMG project: in collaboration with **Martin Miller**
Guggenheim Museum Competition, loser
Helsinki, Finland
2014

This proposal for the Guggenheim Museum takes advantage of the harbor location and Helsinki's history of seafaring. *Art Dock* is 85% museum and 15% boat—a floating fragment of the museum that has detached and travels the world. This art boat takes the Guggenheim experience on the water to reach other audiences in the ports of Europe and beyond, as well as to gather work from other locations and bring them to Finland. When the boat returns from its voyage, the museum is completed, with all its galleries intact. The overall form and circulation of the building are generated by the presence (and absence) of this fragment.

Art Dock's volume produces three spaces: two of them public and open, and one private and enclosed (the museum proper). At the lowest level, the ground rises up, stretching thin sinuous columns between the building's body and the ground. Its polished Scandinavian obsidian underbelly reflects the activities of the harbor plaza. An orifice opens diagonally through the building to the entry, in a sideways, Carpenter Center-fashion, and onward to the roof plaza. Midway along this trajectory, the visitor enters into the museum.

The museum functions in a looped plan, with the lobby being a double-height space punctured by the boat's void to the east. Six large sub-dividable galleries are located in a C-shape around the main void, to the south, west, and north, along a spine of services. In addition to the indentation to be filled by the boat, a second indentation addresses an upper level bridge connection from Tähtitornin Vuori Park and the Olympia Cruiser Deck. When the boat is in dock, large doors open and the boat itself becomes a seventh gallery within the lobby.

Stained with pine-tar, a familiar sealant in the northern European fishing boat, the wood exterior is broken only by strategic large openings in the façade that connect the interior galleries to major landmarks in the city.

The literal penetration of the boat, the indentations into the form of the museum in plan, the doubling of public space, the voided diagonal through the museum, and the large windows to the city in the galleries are all moves that challenge the typical museum's hermetic response to the outside world. Instead, this museum is generated out of a series of external forces that shape it into its resultant form. Consequently, the museum shifts and cracks open under the pressure of the city and harbor, allowing the public to engage more fully even without buying a ticket or intentionally entering the galleries.

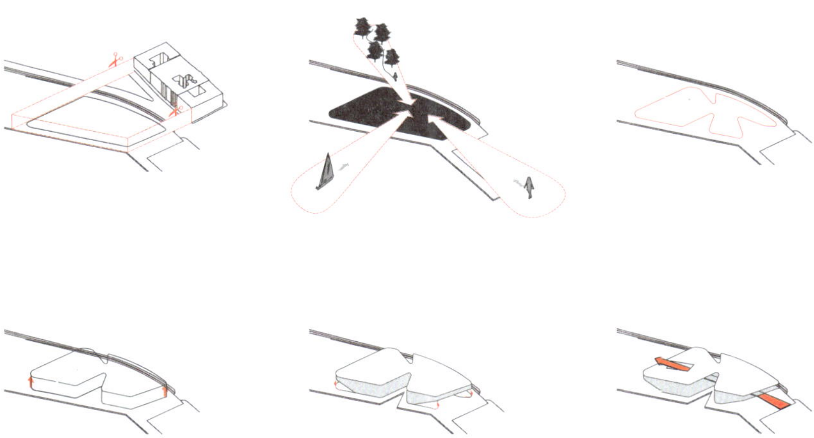

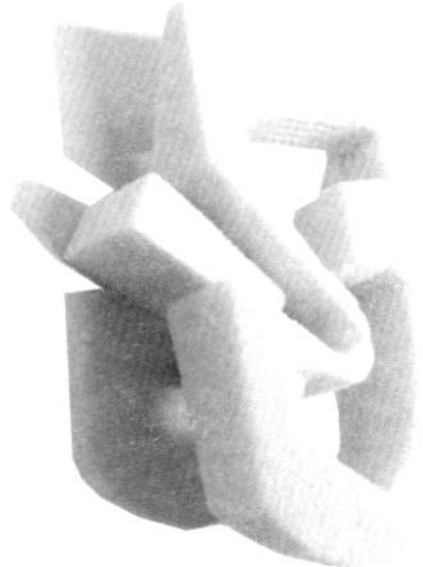

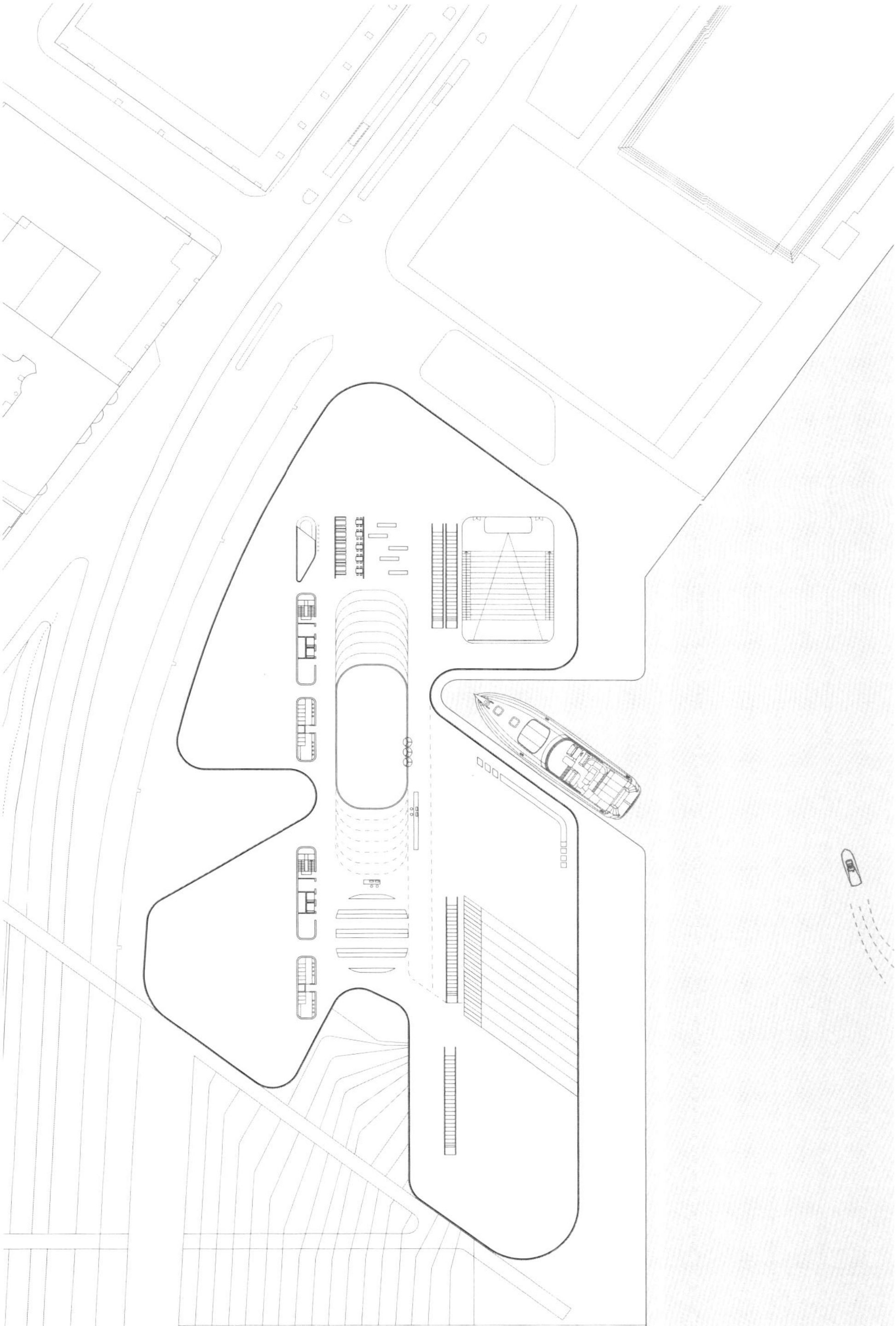

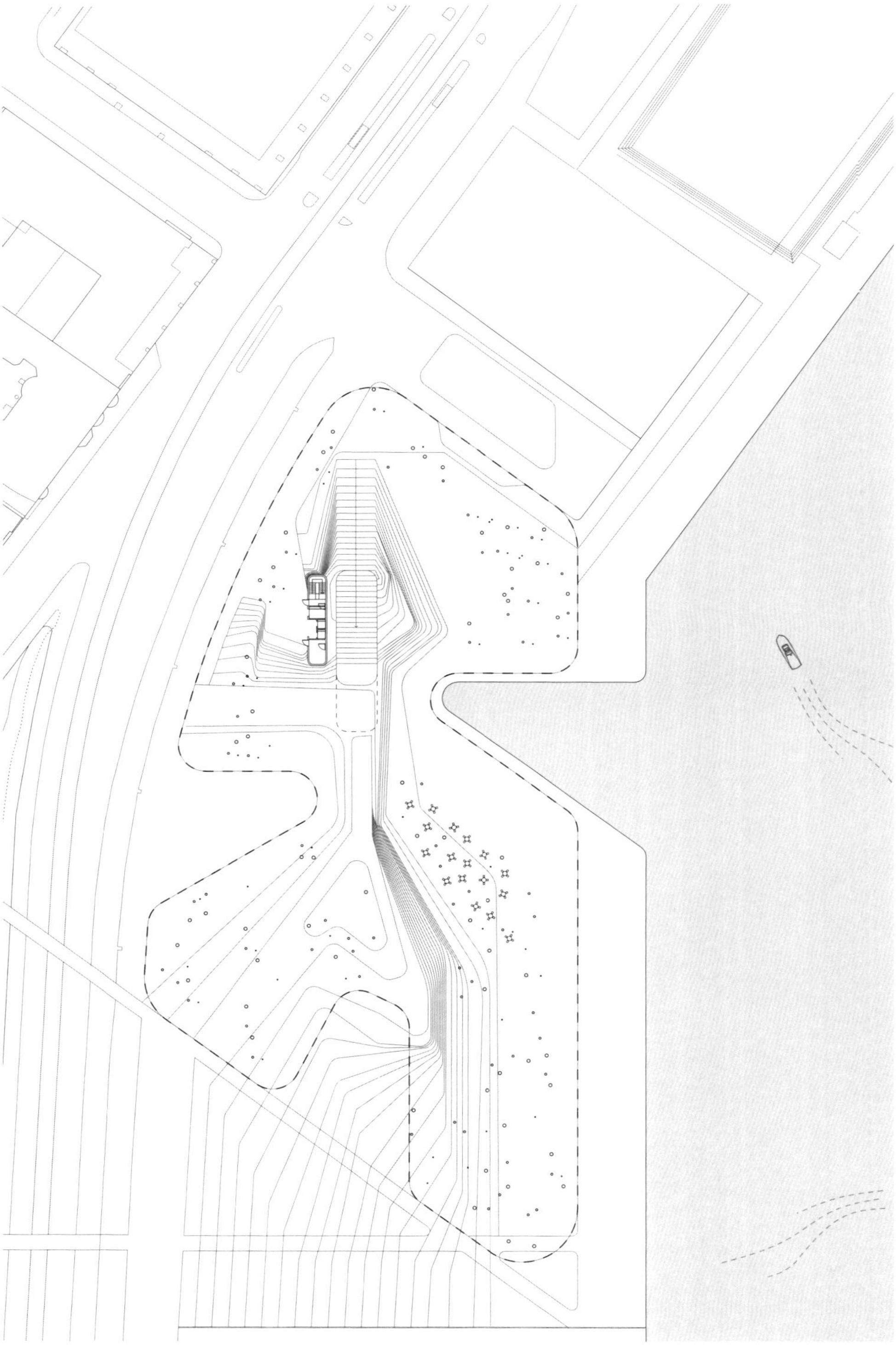

Recalculating:
A Conversation

Caroline O'Donnell, José Ibarra, and Martin Miller

Roscoe Diner, Route 17, halfway to Ithaca, NY.

Waiter: *White, wheat, or rye toast? What's your type?*

Caroline O'Donnell: *Wry*. (laughs).

José Ibarra: *Do you have pumpernickel?* Alright, Caroline … we are halfway to Ithaca and we have chatted enough about giraffes, genetics, and evolution. I want to hear about the nature and nurture that got *you* to where you are today. What's your earliest memory of space?

COD: To *were* I am today. Alright. My earliest memory is running in circles in an empty room; empty, except for a lush pink carpet. We were about to move into our new house in Athlone, in the geographic center of Ireland. This street became very important for my decision to become an architect. There was a man who was building the same house over and over again, more or less by himself, so it was a slow process. This meant that every year, a few new houses that looked just like mine (or its mirror image) would appear gradually: one house would exist as foundation trenches, another one as slabs, a third one halfway up to underneath the windows, and so on. They were totally open construction sites, and I would play there. As time went on, the man made slight adjustments; every new house would carry with it a little improvement. One could say they were evolving …

JI: Were there other important buildings or works of architecture in your childhood?

COD: Sure, but certainly not contemporary architecture. Castles, forts, and ruins. But I think the most important thing that I got from growing up in Ireland was the power of landscape and weather, especially on the northwest coast, where the edge of the continent is dramatic; the weather changes very fast and we burn the earth for heat because there's nothing else, no trees. In fact, the cottages in Donegal, where we used to go on vacations, are really a great demonstration of using what is available. The ground is very stony, so the fields are very small and enclosed by stone walls to clear the soil. The houses are also made of that stone and the roofs are thatched using the leftovers from the oats and barley.

JI: Tell me about your parents.

Waiter: *More coffee?*

COD: *Yes, please!* My parents were kind of opposites in many ways. My father was a mechanical engineer who ran a clothing factory, and my mother was a secretary, and somewhat of a performer. Normally, Northern Irish Catholics can agree on politics, but my parents had polar opposite views. You can tell it in the naming of their children. My brother, Fergal, was given an Irish name by my father. But my sister, Paula, and I have more international names, clearly my mother's choice. They were also different in many other ways. My dad was empathetic and easygoing, while my mum was exuberant and ambitious. But they danced well together, and they were both comedic. We were all northerners living in the south, so everyone was a bit out of place. I never really felt like I belonged there.

JI: You moved back up north when they split, right?

COD: Yes, back to Derry, with a southern accent at 12 years old. My new friends nicknamed me "Wexford," even though I was not from there, but that was the only place that someone knew of in the south. I always tried to fit in accent-wise, but I never really did.

JI: I just watched *Derry Girls* on Netflix. Have you seen the show? It is a comedy that portrays the normal frivolous obsessions of teenagers in Derry with the backdrop of The Troubles. How similar were your teenage years to that?

COD: An exact match. I was the wee English boy with the wrong accent. Just like in the show, we saw all the violence on TV … even though it was close, we never really witnessed it directly. Oftentimes, we heard bombs or could not go into town because of a bomb-scare, or a march, but it was not as bad as it had been in the 1970s, which is why my parents had left the city in the first place.

JI: What were you like as a student both in high school and at Manchester University?

COD: I was a nerd in high school. I did A-levels in Mathematics, Physics, Geography, and French. I went to Manchester because I didn't know anyone there and I really just wanted to be truly myself (as well as be a drummer in a band).

JI: Did you actually do that?

COD: Well, I had been in an all-girl band in high school called *Obsidian* ("the hardest rock known to humanity," we always clarified). We were influenced by L7, Hole, Throwing Muses, Veruca Salt, as well as some British bands like the Wedding Present. But no, the dream of being a rock star didn't pan out, not even an igneous one.

JI: (groans) And did you achieve your other goal of being yourself?

COD: I did. Very consciously. That was a really important thing to decide to do: to let myself express myself. I think I had been a bit restrained before then, but after this decision, if I thought of a joke or a design idea, I would just spit it out and say it.

JI: *Can we get the check, please?* And we should get gas while we're here …

Google Maps: *Head northwest on Old Route 17, then turn left to merge onto NY-17 W.*

JI: You've mentioned before that your work as an undergraduate student was not stellar in the beginning. But later, you became a star student. What changed? What and who were you exposed to?

COD: My first undergraduate year was pretty conservative, and I certainly did not flourish in that environment. But in the second year, there was an influx of professors from the Architectural Association (AA) in London. They were much more experimental, and something really clicked into place for me then. The first thing they did was have us work on two real competitions. One was an AIDS Memorial in Key West, FL. The other was a house for Princess Diana. I got first place in the AIDS Memorial competition. The Princess Diana House was a team competition that I did with Erana Samarasundera, and we won second prize.

JI: What were the big ideas in those early projects?

COD: The AIDS Memorial consisted of a colonnade of life-like forms; it wasn't clear what they were, but something alive … between an animal and a plant. The first component grew into almost an arch, but then each iteration degenerated as one traversed the beach, and it ended in what looked like the ruins of a pier in the water. The big idea here was to communicate the notion of growth and entropy—change of state—as an essential part of existence. And the second project, the Princess Diana House—she was still alive at the time—was three interlocked cylinders.

There were no floors, but the cylinders were elevators that constantly moved to create different alignments in the space so that she could manipulate the views of the paparazzi outside. The house created different levels of privacy and pose as she moved around the spaces so that she could, at last, have control over the press. So, it was like the *Fun Palace*, but the fun was for Diana.

JI: That's foresightful and very relevant to our discussion right now. What else came after that?

COD: In my third year, our school imploded and merged with Manchester Metropolitan University's Architecture department. I went to Sydney for my year out, worked in a couple of offices, and when I came back, I was much more energized. The new *Manchester School of Architecture* had four "colleges," basically different collectives of professors with different specializations. There was a landscape group, a history/theory group, a materiality group, and a bioclimatics one, which is what I selected.

JI: What was the conceptual and theoretical background behind the bioclimatics specialization?

COD: Bioclimatics is a term borrowed from biology. It's the study of the relationship between flora and fauna, and the climate of a specific region. My professors, Greg Keeffe and Geoff McKennan, borrowed the term to include architecture in that relationship. Actually, many of the texts we read in the program and some of the things I was exposed to are really fundamental in the book that I would write 15 years later—*Niche Tactics.* While many "sustainable" specializations are very technical, this program also emphasized the underlying theory. James Gibson's *Ecological Approach to Visual Perception*, for instance, remains a fundamental text for me in thinking about the world as an ecology, as a set of relationships.

Google Maps: *Recalculating.*

JI: There's always bad reception here but I'm pretty sure we're just meant to go straight … (nervous smile). Anyway, was it through the bioclimatics program and Gibson that you became interested in animals?

COD: I do love animals, it's true! But many interests started to come together in these years. Gibson's text looked at perception through the eyes of an animal. I was also interested in animals and aesthetics: does a beaver care what her dam looks like? Does a termite care? And I would say, "No, they are only interested in performance"; the termite is only interested in how the termite mound is ventilating. Even weaver birds, who have been reported to care about the aesthetics of their nests, are still thinking about the aesthetic project in terms of its performance—how to attract a mate. I proposed a thesis about animal architecture and aesthetics versus performance, but that was turned down.

JI: If that was turned down, what *was* your undergraduate thesis?

COD: My actual thesis also derived from Gibson's notions on perception and affordances. I was interested in how we, as architects, can subliminally direct people in our buildings. For example, imagine a corridor with a split in it. The user is confronted with two options. I wondered whether we could influence people to go one way versus the other. I wanted to design an entire building using those strategies, so I simplified the ideas of affordance and motivation to be about "needs" and "wants"—the needs corresponding to Gibson's notion of affordances (i.e., you

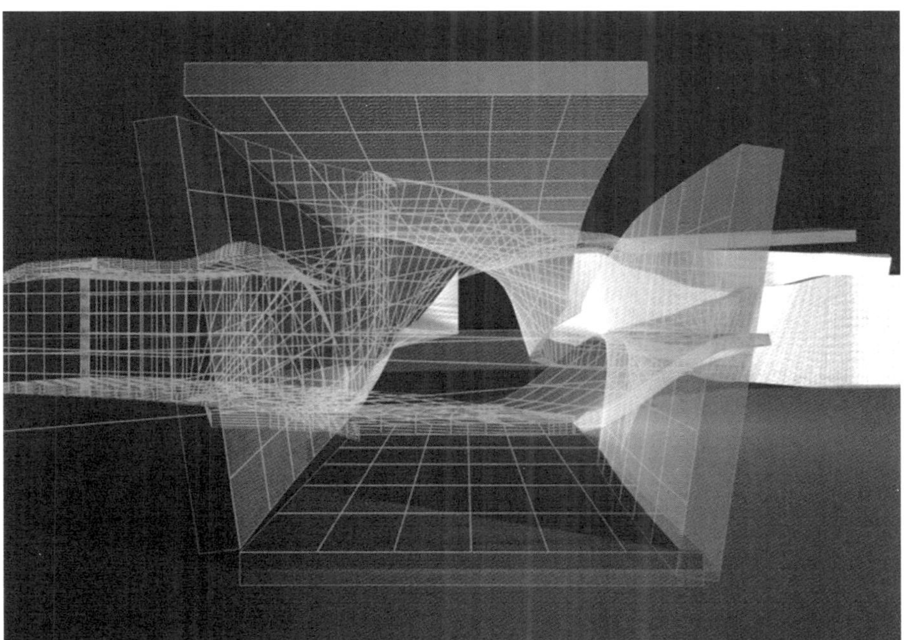

need a flat surface to be walkable on), and the wants corresponding to an object of desire at the end of the view. This last component drew in ideas about motive from Maurice Merleau-Ponty's *Phenomenology of Perception.*

But aside from these theories, I wanted my project to be somewhat scientific, to include real-life experiments. I did tests with objects and surfaces on the ground, and I recorded how people diverted their path based on the objects. This was a really simple experiment, but it demonstrated how one could motivate a change of path by something that didn't necessarily interrupt the walkability of the surface. I also asked visitors to the Kunsthal museum in Rotterdam to draw plans of the space that they were in, along with the series of spaces around them and how they moved through them. I analyzed those drawings to compare them to the actual plans. Then, I designed a new kind of museum based on that data.

> **JI**: *Niche Tactics* seems like a climax of all of the thinking, design, and teaching you'd done up until 2015. Tell me about the book and about the role of the giraffe as a spirit animal for the work.

COD: One of the reasons I'm interested in animals is because they look like the thing that they do—they are signs of their own performance. It can be as simple as feet being a response to meeting the ground or mouths being a response to specific foods. In Manchester, Greg Keeffe was talking about ecological theory and he said, "the better I can describe an environment to you, the sooner you'll be able to tell me what animal lives there." He was talking about the mutual dependence of an animal and its environment, and how one couldn't think of one without the other. Keeffe's metaphor used a lion, but I always found the giraffe to be a better example due to its exaggerated formal attributes.

Taking that claim seriously forced me to think about other aspects of the giraffe beyond the obvious elongated neck: the animal's circulation system had to respond to the big formal move of the head toward the treetops. In other words, there are both mechanical as well as material consequences to the stretching of the neck; the big formal gesture cannot happen without those other systems stepping up, too. The heart needs to be five times larger than a mammal of comparable size, because it needs to pump blood up so high. There need to be special valves in the neck so

that when the giraffe lowers its head to drink, it does not explode. And then on the outside, there are various parasites, predators, weather, and other factors that the animal must also respond to. So, when you start to diagram that, the giraffe stops being a figure and loses its boundary with the outside. One has to include all of the interior parts of the body as well as the exterior parts of the environment, resulting

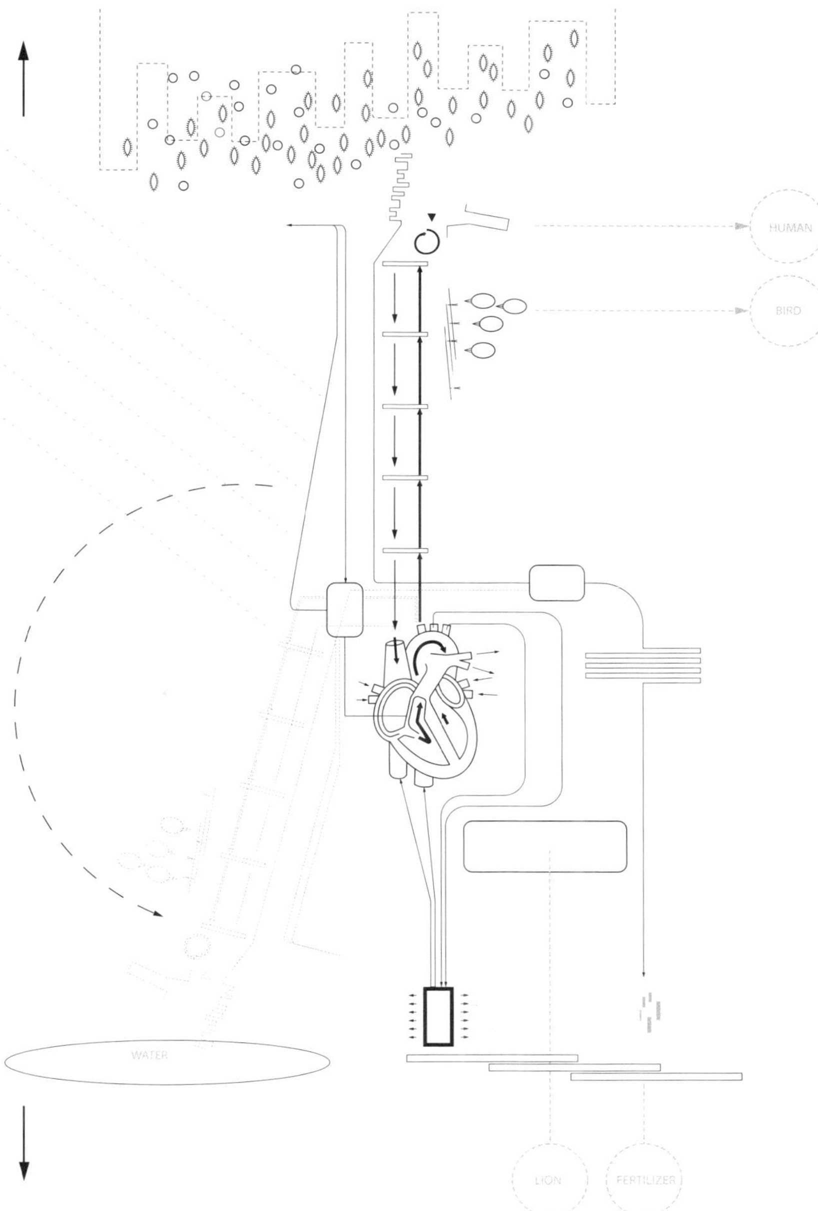

in a loss of the icon of the giraffe. Inevitably, when these ideas are approached through architecture, interesting questions arise: how does architecture communicate with its surrounding environment? Could architecture also erode its boundaries and lose its iconicity?

> **Google Maps:** *Continue onto I-86 W/NY-17 W for nine miles.*

> **JI:** It's clear that Gibson and Merleau-Ponty have played a crucial role in your career as architect and theorist since the beginning. I'm sure you were able to expand on some of these topics with someone like Spyros Papapetros during your M.Arch II training at Princeton University. How would you say graduate school complemented the background you already had?

COD: Spyros's seminar on architecture and psychoanalysis was actually the *only* point of connection between my previous life and the new, American, one. That class was very important in many ways, not least in the production of the essay, "Diagram as Remedy," which analyzed Freud's diagrams. But in general, the theory at Princeton was really hardcore US architectural theory: Colin Rowe, Rudolf Wittkower, Peter Eisenman, and so on; formal theory taught by both the formalists themselves, and those who were challenging them with more Koolhaasian questions of program (what they called the "projective"), like Sarah Whiting and Bob Somol, as well as other important counterpoints by some like Stan Allen and Jesse Reiser. That had little to do with my bioclimatics education and was more often than not directly at odds with it. They seemed to be the most opposite bodies of work possible. And I think what became exciting to me was precisely because of the incongruity of those two worlds. It was as if they could never meet each other; like oil and water. Peter, at one point, even made the joke that sustainability was like motherhood … it's great for some people, but not physically possible for him (laughs). But the eventual putting-together of those two worlds—the formal and the ecological—has become my project. In some ways, it can be put as simply as that.

One thing I began to fully understand in this country was the legibility of architecture. This was not something that was discussed much in Manchester and seemed to be everything that was discussed in Princeton. My thought was, "if architecture is legible, why is it always saying something about itself—self-

referential—to put it in Eisenman's terms?" Instead, wouldn't it be more interesting if architecture asked, "How are you?" or talked about some bigger picture? This is exactly what I started to think about in Peter's studio at Princeton, whose indexical project resonated with me. Troy Schaum, Brantley Hightower, and I were working on the design of something that looked like a big bar that had plowed into the ground. I remember making a diagram of sections through the building and the earth that they had "displaced," so you could see the result of the building's force in the landscape. It was a very indexical project where the landscape was doing as much of the communication as the architecture.

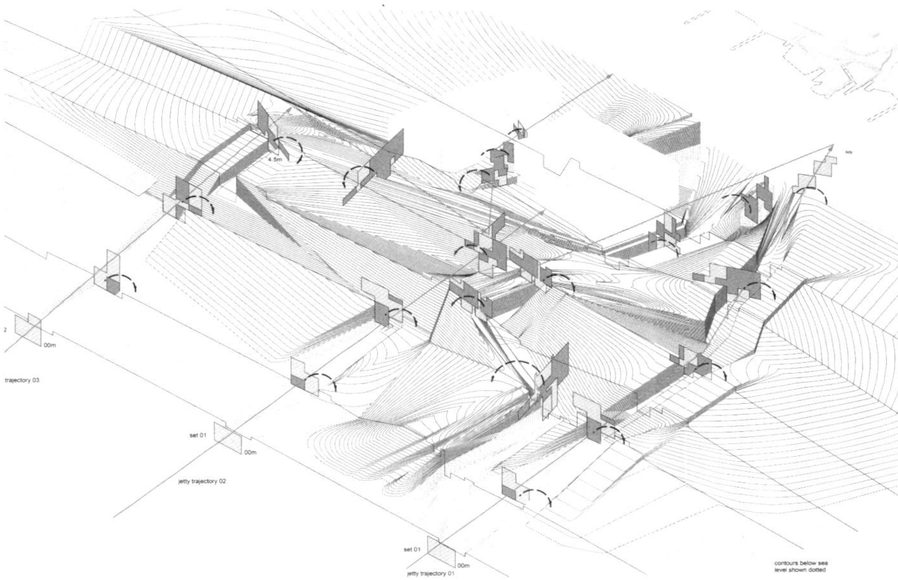

JI: What was your thesis at Princeton about?

COD: My M.Arch II thesis, advised by Sarah Whiting, was born out of my "lineage" to Greg Lynn, Peter, and all those who went before them. It was an ecological challenge to the formalist project. I was interested in Wittkower's diagrams of eleven Palladian villas and a twelfth "pattern" that Wittkover claimed was "in Palladio's mind" while he was designing. This, of course, aligns with Rowe's mathematically "ideal" villa. Greg Lynn, in his essays, had brought up a desire to consider the variations rather than the similarities, but he did not literally do it. So, that became the prompt for my thesis: to examine the villas in relation to their contexts while attempting to find rules by which they changed, rules which could then be applied

to other designs. I wanted to design an embassy for a divided US because I had arrived here just in time for Bush's re-election, which really opened my eyes to the political rift in the country. However, this idea was (again) shot down and I ended up designing an embassy for a united Europe. The logic was that embassies had originally been housed in villas, and a collective embassy, whether US states or EU countries, would be made of parts that related to a greater whole.

I recall Peter only seeing the project minutes before I defended it in my final review and saying I had ruined it by putting in floors. I argued that I needed those floors for the program itself … but that has haunted me ever since. In the end, I think Peter was right.

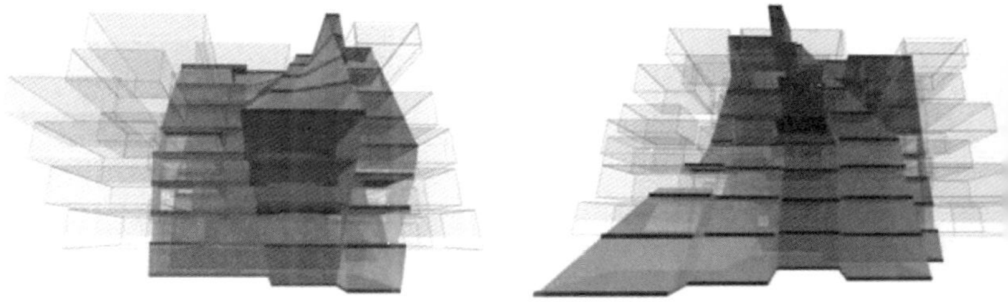

POCHÉ AS PUBLIC SPACE

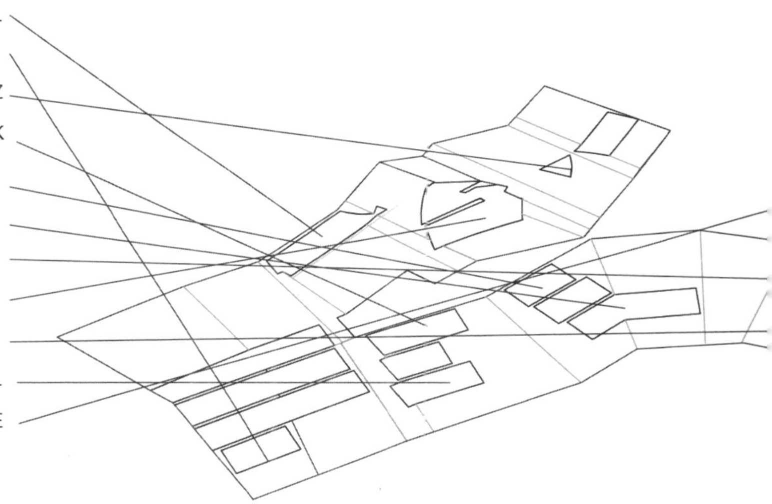

SURFACE INTERFACE

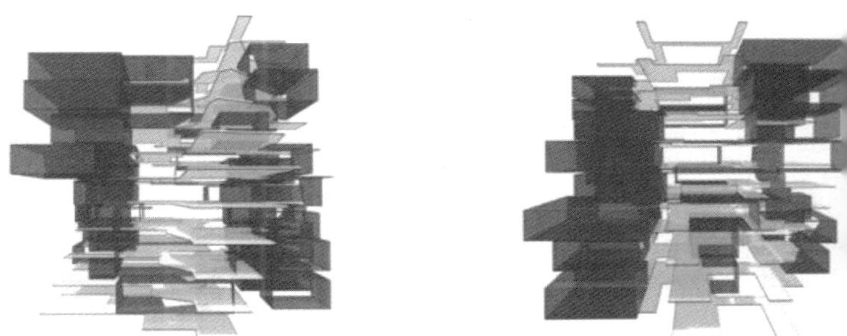

ROOMS AS PRIVATE SPACE

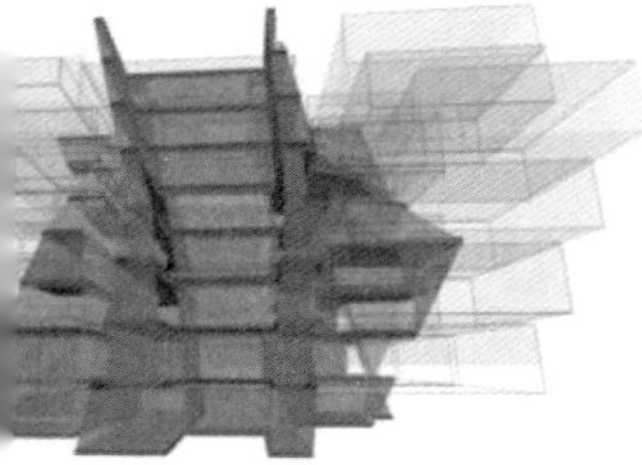

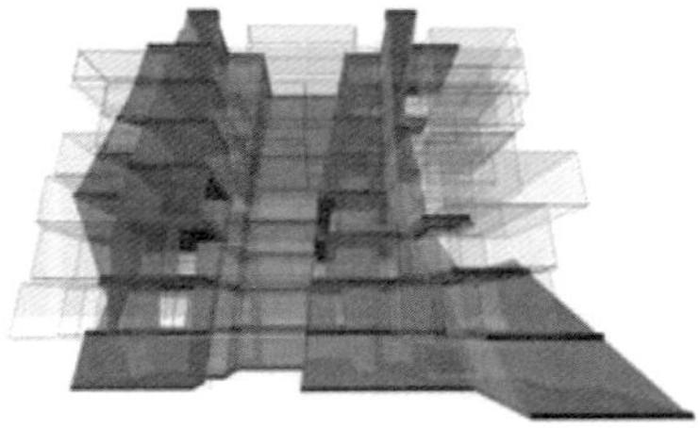

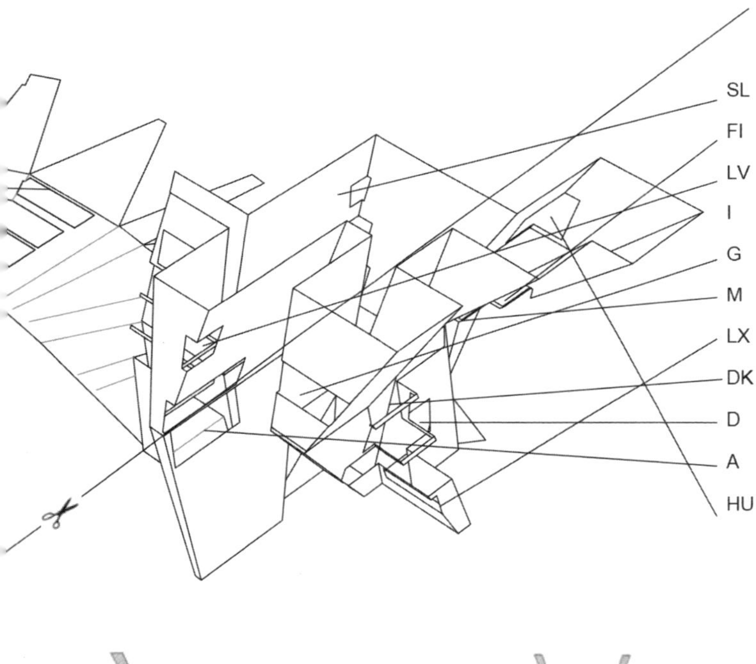
SL
FI
LV
I
G
M
LX
DK
D
A
HU

JI: After Princeton, you worked in Peter's office for a few years. Then, you and Troy decided to do some competitions together, right? Didn't CODA come out of that collaboration?

COD: Yes, after working on *Pompeii Santuario Station*, *Hamburg Domplatz Library*, and a few other projects at Eisenman Architects (while also teaching at The Cooper Union), I moved to Ithaca to teach at Cornell, and I was working with Troy on the Europan competition in Leisnig, Germany. We creatively put our last initials together and called ourselves "SODA," for Schaum O'Donnell Architects. Our project, *Urban Punc.,* rejected the brief of designing new housing and likened the city to a text that had been written long ago. What it needed, we claimed, was not a rewrite, just careful editing. We proposed so-called "apostrophes," which were rehabilitators added to the existing built fabric. We got second prize in that competition.

And then, after we stopped working together, I had to come up with a new name quickly for a new project, so I even more creatively used my own initials. CODA is kind of interesting as a word, though—it means always having the last word. It comes from the Latin *cauda*, which means "tail." It also connects to the words code and codex, which relate to deciphering and text. You know, before then, I had actually come up with a lot of great names for offices. I dated an architect in Manchester named Green, so our fictional office was called "GOD." And then we split up, and I wanted to have an office called "Two-Thirds of GOD." Or, in undergrad, my good friend's name was Nick Owen, and we wanted to have an office

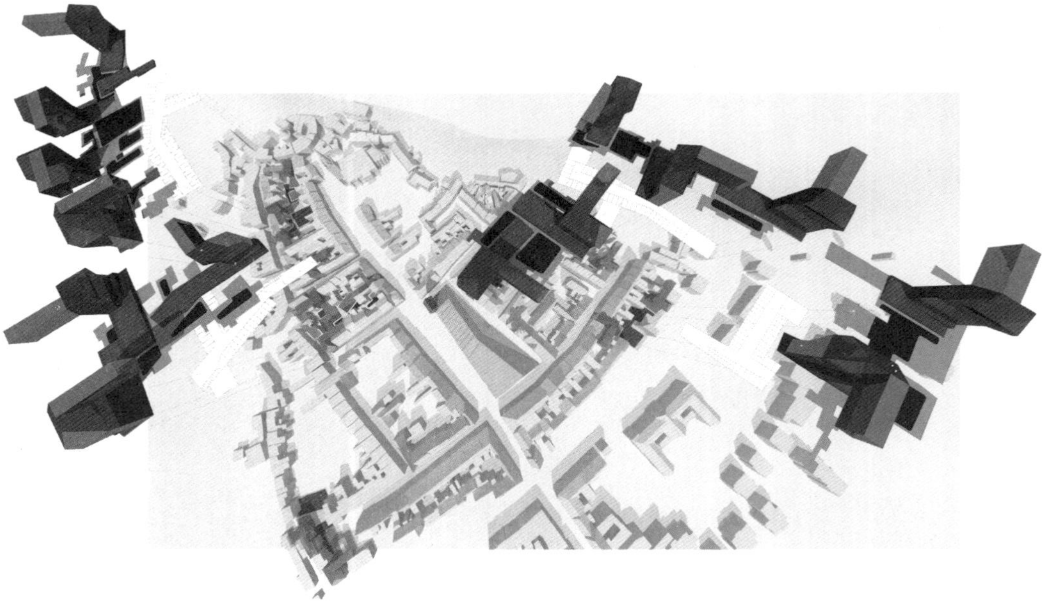

that would be a fish-and-chip shop at the front, with our architecture practice in the back: it would be called "NO COD."

The naming of things is a bit of an obsession of mine. We can communicate a lot in a name, like in an image, more so than in a text. *Tripe*, for example, communicates a lot in one little word, referencing nose-to-tail consumption. And *Primitive Hut* references the well-known image by Laugier, while *Evitim*, *Primitive Hut's* twin sister, is a partial inversion of the word "primitive." Years ago, there was a headline in some article about *Party Wall* that read, "*Party Wall* … It's not just one pun, it's two puns!" When I read this, I thought, "YES! Somebody got it."

> **JI**: (laughs) These are all great names, but I'll confess that "Two-Thirds of GOD" is my personal favorite. Now, let me ask you about the trajectory of your work. Your latest collaboration, with perhaps the trendiest of all names, is OMG. Can you tell me about this practice?

COD: Martin Miller and I started collaborating in 2014. First, with the Guggenheim Helsinki competition, *Art Dock*. We've done about one project per year together since then, under the banner of OMG (O'Donnell Miller Group).

I consider the projects we've done together to be amongst the most important works that I have been involved with: *Zimmer*, *Primitive Hut,* and *Evitim* have really pushed both of us. *Zimmer* continued the literally dynamic, almost vehicular or device-like

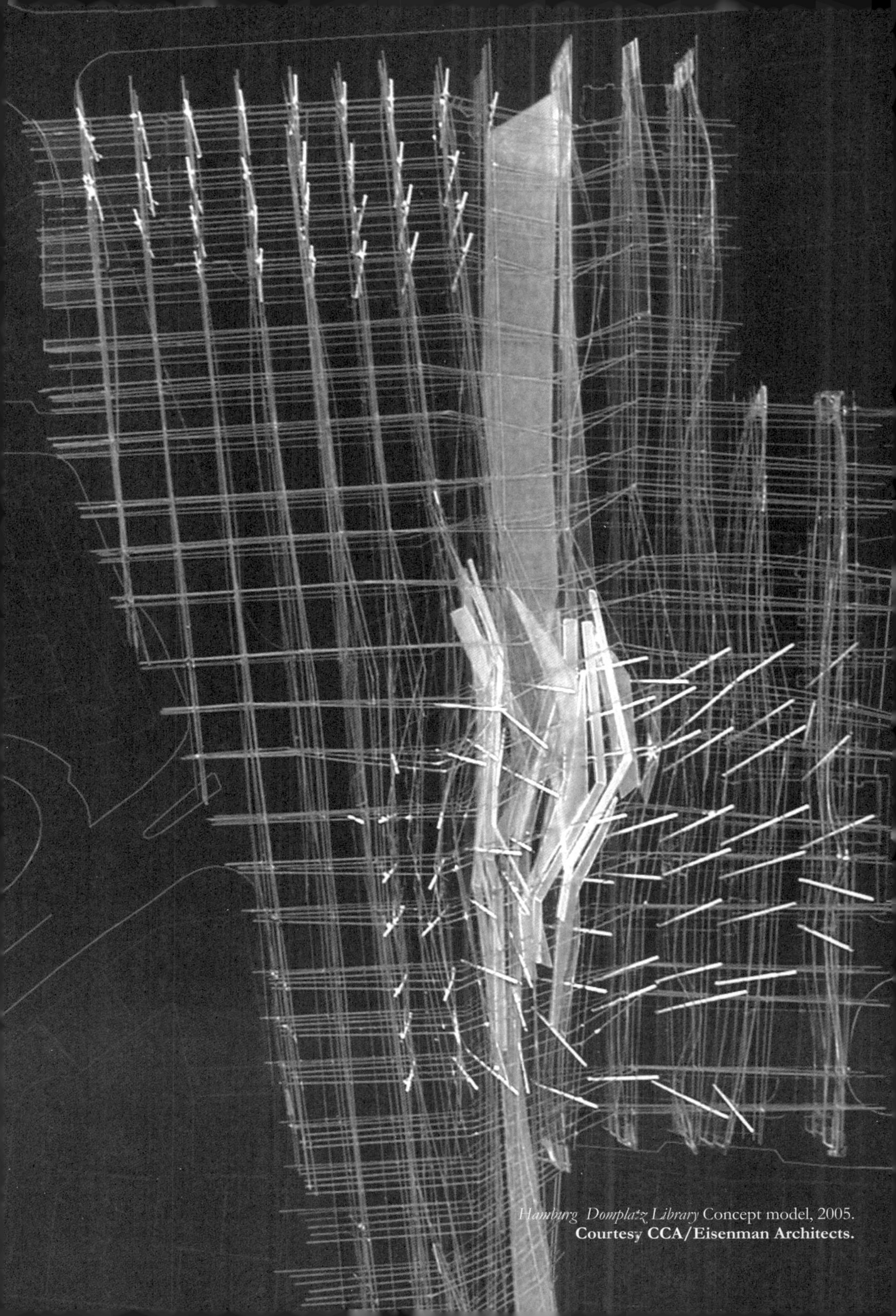

Hamburg Domplatz Library Concept model, 2005.
Courtesy CCA/Eisenman Architects.

trajectory that had existed in previous projects, but the latter two are transformative in other ways. *Primitive Hut* deals with decay and growth, referencing, as I mentioned, Laugier's etching about architecture as a continuation of nature. The pavilion uses custom bioresin components that allow it to partially decay around the trees, along with other more permanent components that allow it to grow with the trees. We designed interlocking components that needed no glue or fixings of any kind. Martin was interested in what he calls "the trace of the digital craftsperson," which prompted the question: how could we, by understanding the machine better, allow the form of the component to express the efficiency of such a machine? That meant not creating the smoothest surface that the modeling software Rhino could make but allowing a more gouged form that would be in a more productive dialogue with the tool for fabrication. I am often interested in looking outward and toward a dialogue with the environment, while Martin is often driven toward the building details, which have to negotiate with the tool. I think our interests certainly overlap in both the transformation and communication of the work, but our differences have been what propel the projects into worlds we might not have ventured on our own.

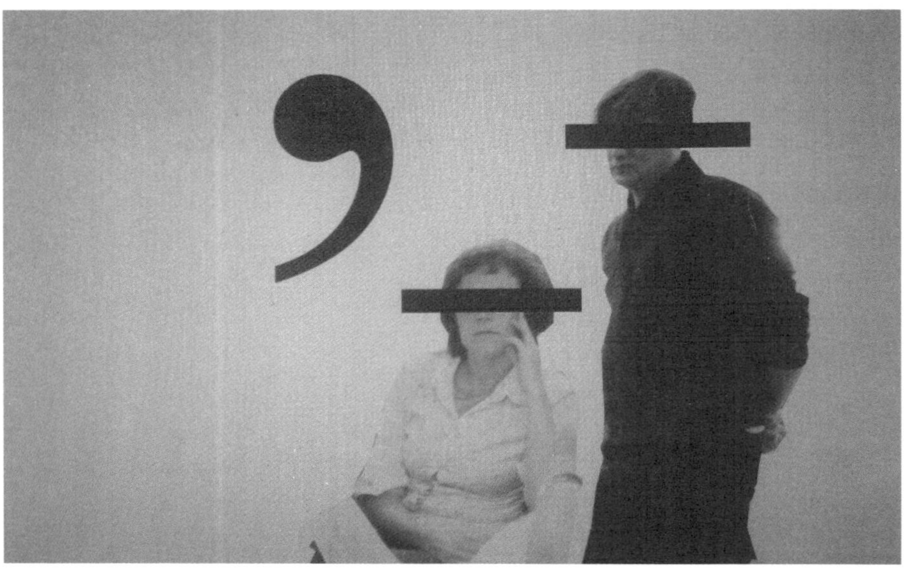

(Phone Rings) Phone display reads: Martin Miller.

JI: Speak of the devil!

COD*: Hello? Hey, great timing. We were just talking about you. Hold on, I'll put you on speaker.*

Martin Miller: *Huh? What? Wait no, don't put me on spea …*

JI*: Hey, Martin! Caroline was just telling me how OMG originated.*

MM*: What's going on? Who is this?*

JI: *This is José Ibarra, we're on our way to Ithaca and recording a conversation for* Werewolf …

MM: *Oh, hey José … what about a werewolf?*

JI: Werewolf, *the book that Caroline and I have been working on that explores architecture thr You know, like how a werewolf transforms between human and wolf, usually triggered by the M*

MM: *Or, like how Bruce Banner, the mild-mannered scientist, becomes the Incredible Hulk when he's a more of an internal state, whereas a full Moon is external. I mean, that guy probably just needed a f*

JI: *Sure … anyway, we were just talking about your collaborative practice with Caroline, the collaboration are really a combination of both your …*

MM: *What about Dr. Jekyll and Mr. Hyde? I am no expert in Gothic novellas, but what w I mean, Mr. Hyde is no werewolf, but there was definitely a transformation going on there .*

JI: *Good point, and yes, Dr. Jekyll and Mr. Hyde is another great exa architectural analog, and that's where you are relevant. As I was saying, O individual practices. I was wondering if you could …*

MM: *Hey, did you guys watch* Teen Wolf *for research? You know, that mo*

JI: *Of course, we watched all of the werewolf movies.*

MM: Teen Wolf *was pretty ridiculous. It was the '80s, so these movies into a werewolf and everyone is just cool with that and he becomes super would be pretty tough, you know? Everyone making fun of you, probabl Fox made it look like a pretty great way to experience one's teen y*

JI: *Okay.*

MM: *Same idea with this* Werewolf *book, right?*

JI: *Maybe?*

MM: *You know, the way you are looking at architecture transformative operations? I think Michael J. Fox conception of the werewolves in popular media. Bef of turning the werewolf into the popular kid in th there is no way it works without Michael J. Fox,*

JI: *(audibly disheartened) The m*

MM: *Nah, man, not the movie … I've ne*

JI: *Okay, well, thanks. Marti OMG.*

JI: Caroline, I guess we should go back to our interview.

Google Maps: *Take exit 8 for NY-26 toward US-11/ NY-79/NY-206/Whitney Point/Lisle, then turn right toward NY-26N.*

JI: Okay, we're almost there. We've established your connection to perception and semantics, as well as the leap you took forward and toward ecological thinking. How do you trace a line between these two "sides" of the discipline—the formal *Eisenmanian* thinking with the performative or functional agenda?

COD: Even though Peter would likely deny that he is interested in function, his question about the wall and the column is a functional one. In fact, in his analysis of the *Maison Domino*, he writes not just about the column, but the relationship between the column and other columns, between the column and the edge of the slab, and so on. He talks about the column not as an object, but as something whose meaning is embedded in relationships with other nearby objects and their functions. This is also ecological theory, or what Timothy Morton calls *hyperobjects* today. These theories are certainly related. When I write about *Urchin*, I approach it through Gibson's theory of affordances, but the same project can very well be described as a work about the sign and signified.

JI: This suggests that there is some type of universal truth behind the work (or behind *a* work, even), but it also preambles a readership or a legibility, which in turn implies an audience. Would you say that the architecture of CODA is meant to be legible, in a formalist way? Or, in other words, who is CODA's audience?

COD: Audience and readership are important factors for me. For Peter, only an elite, educated, architectural audience is the target. When he talked about "audience" in his seminars, his tongue-in-cheek question was, "Do you want to be Britney Spears or James Joyce?" Meaning, "Do you want your work to be understandable and consumable by the entire population, or do you want it to be high-level enough that only the best, most educated, literates in the world can understand it?" And of course, when phrased like that, the answer is James Joyce: you wouldn't want to be Britney Spears. But being Irish, I have a bit more insight into James Joyce, and from a very common perspective, not as a person who studied Irish literature. There's a famous line in *Ulysses* where the main character proposes to a woman. The response is written as, "Yes, she said yes, I will! Yes!" Of course, I can understand why people think that's a really poetic way of writing. But if you're from Dublin, that's actually just how you say "yes." When my mother from Derry said "no," she would say no at least five times. She said "naw, naw, naw, naw, definitely not, no." What that means to me is that James Joyce *is* Britney Spears. And that's what's so great about him. I think I want to be *that* James Joyce, who is able to communicate at the highest level to the most highly educated poets and writers, but also communicates to general audiences and maybe even has as good a beat as Britney.

JI: Caroline, in your opinion, have you achieved this multifaceted personality? Is there a project that might exemplify the elevated Joyce language paired with the catchy Britney beat?

COD: *Party Wall* is a good example of an object communicating something beyond itself. You could say it enters into the dialogue of Robert Venturi and Denise Scott Brown, reading architecture as "sign." In their famous

MM: *Sure, go ahead, but don't go too*

JI: *Caroline mentioned earl*
craftsperson." I wonder if

MM: *(exhales audibly) For me, thi*
arts of making, manufacturing, fab
deeply understands available tooling
manifestations of these variable combina
object that they are crafting.

Many people would argue that digit
removed craft and materiality from field
diminished authorship and control in th
to how a field like music has dramatically
to digital tools like Ableton *or* Garag
have immediate access to professional to
platforms has led to the greatest prolifer
majority of such outputs are amateu
which we produce, consume, and value m
architecture and other disciplines.

Despite my external personification
from a background rooted in handcraft:
art studio, earning a B.F.A. in sculp
pursuing my M.Arch. I try to operate
this sense, the idea of the "digital craf
entire process of making; they are the
and so on. The digital craftsperson un
not forget that digital objects will eventu
implies a translation of resolution:
of the digital realm to the material and

Within digital methodologies of form ge
only limited by the number of decim
achievable level of precision within buil
what is lost in the translation between a
To use a simple example, a designer
surface into the physical artifact via
achieving that level of accuracy involve
facing, and often excessive conversion
this case, the CNC-mill, and more s
can produce a less wasteful, and
understand things like corbeling and s
consider this novel relationship between
machine—and design for both of their
their specific parameters rather than rely
opens up new realms for expression o

drawing, *I am a monument*, the building is a sign, literally. This is counter to Peter Eisenman's *sign-as-index* and his ideas of *undecidability*. *Party Wall* is playing with these ideas by literally making a sign, but one that cannot be read by focusing only on the object. On the one hand, if you're looking at the object in order to decipher it, you're not going to get it. You need to look at the bigger picture to see what it has to say. You need to understand the relationship between the object, the sun, and the ground. And only then you can read that the shadow it casts spells "wall," which is what it perhaps wants to be, but also what it is not. On the other hand, in the Britney Spears sense, you can also simply understand the thing as a literal sign—a billboard, that is—that ties into the culture of large-scale steel signs around the site.

This multifaceted approach operates as jokes do. Martin mentioned the chapter "Duck Jokes" in *Niche Tactics* that introduces joke theory to architecture and, in particular, how context is relevant for the joke. First, you set up the context, and then the joke becomes funny because you subvert that context. Maybe that is the most important thing in any of this work: that there's humor. I mean that in all seriousness, because it gives the work an "aha!" moment, where something that has been set up is subverted. I'll tell you a joke by way of example …

JI: Great!

COD: It's a really bad joke though …

JI: I wouldn't expect anything less.

COD: Okay, so two goldfish are in a tank. One says to the other: you drive, I'll man the guns.

JI: (groans)

COD: It's a bad joke but imagine if architecture could make you groan like that, or even laugh. In *Niche Tactics*, I use the example of a scene in *Arrested Development* when Michael Bluth tells his colleague he forgot to say "away," as he speaks of his sister's first day in a new job where she "blew them all away." He repeats, as his employee reports via phone, "You mean 'away,' though, right? Because, otherwise, it sounds a little different." The turn of phrase makes the audience have to rethink what we thought we already knew; it makes us have to overthrow the original context.

> **JI:** Subverting the norm is a crucial part of your work: "Let's use skateboards to make a wall … let's use chairs to make a theater … let's split the nave of a church in two." But this desire for subversion has also generated a love for the rejected, which you sometimes describe as "ugly" and "Fugly" in *Niche Tactics*. For instance, using trash or recycled materials to build; what does that have to do with architecture and also with subversion? And why is that important to you?

COD: I've been thinking recently about Mary Douglas's statement that waste is just "matter out of place"; matter that does not belong where it is, which goes back to joke theory and the desire to subvert a context. In the beginning, what I was most interested in was the perceptual trickery of waste as an out-of-place material. For instance, for PS1, the original idea was to use plastic chairs, not skateboards. The brief called for both seating for film screenings and performances, as well as an empty courtyard. This seemed impossible to achieve at once. So, we thought of the wall/sign/Trojan horse-object as a chair storage device. But we could not afford 3,000 chairs, and environmentally, that also seemed immoral. We had to find an alternative that was, in Gibson's terms, sittable-on, and that's how we arrived

—it really makes you see the "digital" manifested in any of the projects you've

·, we first created perfectly smooth, ents of the final installation in order to Iowever, pragmatic constraints of time, ine the production of the 4,000+ parts anding the CNC-mill and its method of ıce between the costly and time-intensive, mething which could be rapidly produced IC can only cut away so much material ss do we need to achieve the design without ıcing effects and textural conditions emerge es that operate at both the scale of the re assembly?

one that precisely cut the joints of the t to the scalloping of the material to create o form a continuous registration across whole. The latter might sound ornamental, indset: what does a robot want to make? otive traces in the components: indexical d visible.

al marks important to you?

nanship, David Pye talks about how ion of the object itself. Good woodcarvings, e of it within the final piece, rather than n sculptors such as Auguste Rodin, who ess the materiality and process explicitly ıccurate and precise to the human form, g and texture of the sculpture. It's a g the crafted object to retain a dialog with Ve do not think enough today about how rested in making that explicit, considering atch production methodology.

background rooted in handcraft. How did ın studying architecture?

rking as a very young child; too young ıe occasion (laughs), but these are such on of what my grandfather and I might hear Grandpa's voice explaining how to ıre I have an entire plan before executing. on an old table-mounted foot-powered encouraged me to create things (drawing,

at the skateboard waste, by looking for cheaper and more eco-friendly sittable-on objects. I was interested in how the viewer might see this object and have to mentally reconstruct

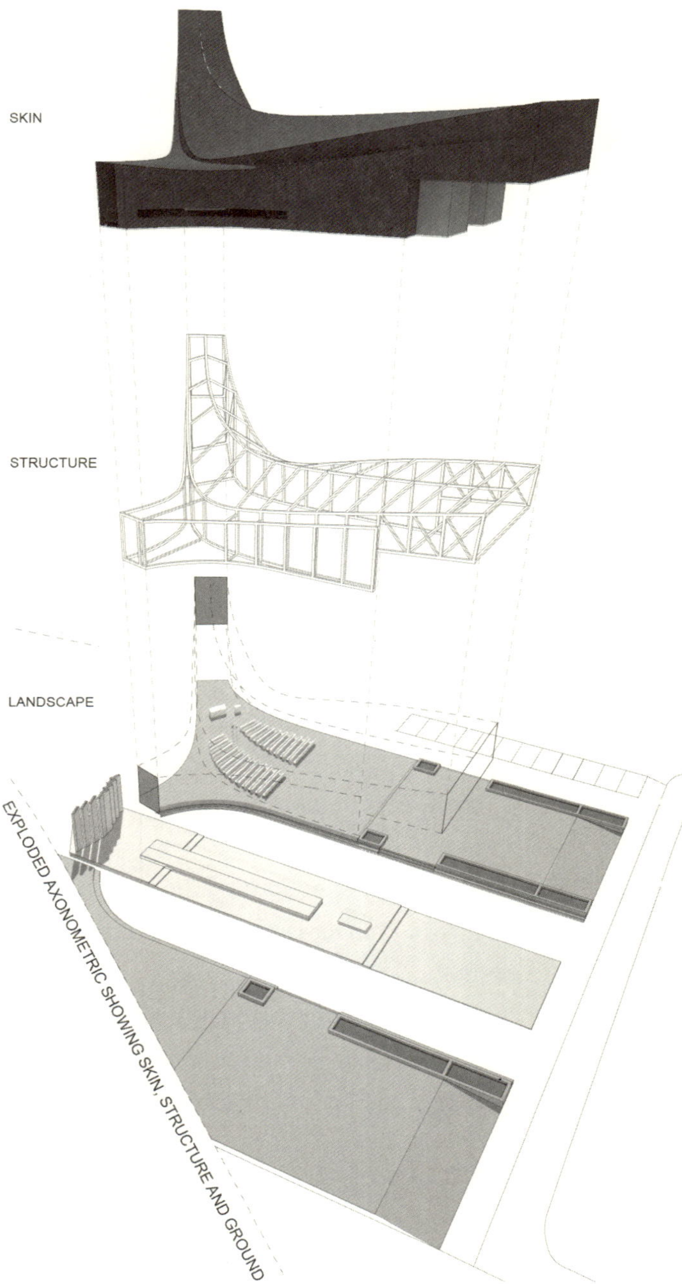

EXPLODED AXONOMETRIC SHOWING SKIN, STRUCTURE AND GROUND

its provenance, step-by-step, a little like Eisenman's House diagrams, but now relative to the *true* origin story of the material component.

But that project, and several after, made me think about waste more pointedly. I developed design studios at Cornell and Harvard alongside Dirk Hebel, Felix Heisel, and Dillon Pranger, which really opened up the world of waste and the potentials of circular systems. Thinking about material reuse in a temporary pavilion is always part of competition briefs these days. This makes sense for a temporary pavilion but, in working with waste materials for the last few years, I have also inevitably become more conscious of the wastefulness of our still-temporary but longer-lasting "architecture proper." The question now becomes, how do we design with time in mind? Or, where were our materials before they were here, where will these materials go, and how will they be used when they are no longer part of our buildings?

Google maps: *Merge on the left onto NY-79 W/Main St*

JI: Alright, we're getting close to Ithaca … Speaking of "architecture proper," it seems that, at first, you

sculpting, building), and my father helpe
the making, I was kind of over it. While
was the act of problem-solving and figu

When I began my M.Arch at UPenn
my classmates had some knowledge or ex
carpenter after college, basically had no id
drawing upon my background, I saw p
environment that would be exceedingly
familiar. As I began to learn about pa
actually program material behaviors t
deformational behaviors inherent to m
than cutting a curve, I could bend a cur
simplifying the fabrication in the proce
is not a new one; in fact, it is prev
upon an intuitive and in-situ construction
of the architect, who is typically respon
and translated by engineers, contracto
use material behaviors in digital space
in programming only the essential con
material behaviors to resolve their own g

JI: *It seems that even if your t*
interested in the material world

MM: *You could say that. I never real*
fabricated. It might make me a control fr
is to produce an elegant set of instruction
this reason, I have been very interested
instructions for a robot, usually expressed
the assembly. It's in the architect's jurisd
for both processes to define more elegant an
by Roland Snooks, a serious digital in
production: sometimes what is good for t

JI: *This is interesting, because*
designers working in digital spa
this sense, a lot of fiction actu

MM: *Right. I think the more purel*
contemplate its potential physical manif
provocations. I have done several purel
the translation from digital to physical is
should write a counter-book to Adolf
Crime and Gravity.

COD: *I consider Martin to be*
late '90s fictional ornamen
that is pretty interesting, bec

treehouse. Still, when we were done with
e things and certainly play with them, it
ess of making that was most interesting.

ely overwhelmed by the digital. Most of
e digital tools and I, having worked as a
oing (laughs). It was a disaster. However,
to draw and test things in the digital
the analog means with which I was
and computation, and I discovered I could
r, it became clear that I could use the
lement of the design. For instance, rather
erial behavior to my advantage and thus
using material behaviors for construction
lar architecture, though often dependent
opinion, this is antithetical to the role
ng a set of drawn instructions to be read
ors elsewhere. My solution was to try to
" and intuitive environments. I believe
elements and allowing the simulated
tations.

are digital, you are ultimately always
built.

g without thinking about how it would be
believe that the primary role of the architect
tation of space in the material world. For
elops novel drawing techniques: a set of
ths and g-code, and another set to express
nd reduce the manipulation of materials
s. I was recently listening to a talk given
talked about defining optimization of
od for the assembly team and vice versa.

d age, the primary motivation of many
ily its translation to the physical world. In
ed into digital model making.

great—I find it inspiring to see and to
projects can bring up truly wonderful
but with my background and upbringing,
n. I've been thinking for a while that I
and Ornament, *but mine would be*

on digital, the first generation being this
ornament kind. I think his criticism of
generation was not at all interested in

were working at a much more urban scale. How did you go from buildings (at Eisenman), to urban projects (at SODA and CODA), to pavilions (at CODA and OMG)?

COD: I actually have quite a background in urban design. Between undergraduate and graduate schools, I had worked for several years in Rotterdam at KCAP (Kees Christiaanse Architects and Planners) on urban scale projects. After hours, I also did many competitions, most of which were at an urban scale.

I continued to participate in the *Europan* competitions when I came to the States, as I mentioned. After SODA's success in Leisnig, I tried my luck in the next cycle, this time as CODA. I hired my first student assistant, Leslie Mignin, and we cranked out two sites that summer in the basement: one in Dubrovnik and one in Dublin. We got shortlisted for *1000 Cranes*, the Dubrovnik design—a gradient of transformation over a large parking structure, from plaza to skylight to pavilion. But Dublin, that one, we won. That project, *Counterspace,* was about transforming the vernacular row house into a kit of familiar parts that could be recomposed to respond to their environment. *Counterspace* is a term from typography and was used in reference to the monkish illuminations in the Irish manuscripts, in which the monks cared as much about the space between the letters as they did about the letters themselves.

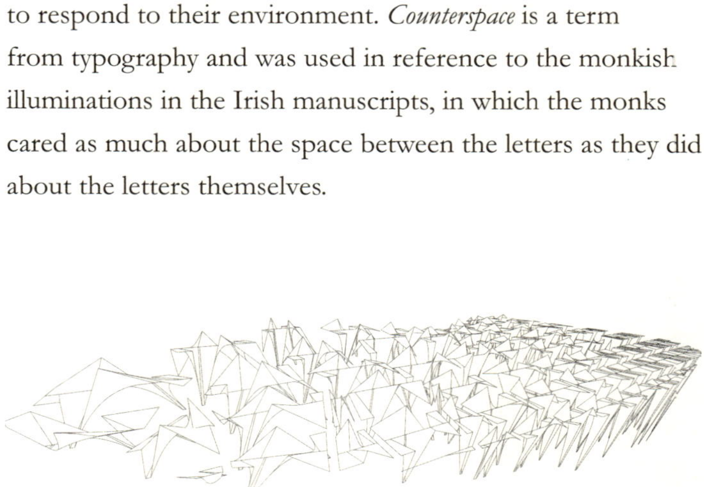

Later, I worked with Suzanne Lettieri on a competition to redesign the town of Klaksvik in the Faroe Islands. We lost that one, but it's crucial for us to have done it. We developed an urban strategy where each block was a loop that began from an existing building and the form of the block maximized sunlight and minimized wind within the courtyard, generating strange but highly tuned urban forms.

After many urban scale competitions in Europe, we looked for competitions in the US. They were almost all at a much smaller, pavilion, scale, but it didn't really matter, because the CODA approach that we had developed could be applied to any scale. And when we got nominated for PS1, we were very ready.

JI: And how has the more recent transition in your practice from pavilions back into building scale been?

COD: We try to keep the big agenda constant: generate from site, maintain a dialogue with the environment, think about the relationship between time, function and materials, make things that can change, and make some serious "aha" moments.

JI: And give it a good title?

COD: For sure. *Charolina House* (with Dillon Pranger) is a recycled house for a woman called Karolina, using the charred remains of her family's log cabin. *Salt Inc.* is an inclusive and accessible addition to an artists' residency called the Constance Saltonstall Foundation for the Arts, which provides spaces and surfaces that can transform their programs depending on season and use.

JI: (laughs) Is that an obscure joke about seasoning, seasons, and salt?

COD: It wasn't, but it is now.

> **JI:** Sometimes in your practice the jokes are "gettable" in the name or the object itself. Oftentimes, you'll also accompany your work with a set of diagrams that will unpack the work somewhat or, perhaps, decode the hidden joke or meaning behind the work. For example, it is unlikely that anyone knows of the saltire on the inside of *Combust*—which is a fantastic political statement, by the way—without the diagrams. I'd like to hear about diagrams and other representational techniques in your practice. Last night, I was re-reading that Freud essay, "Diagram as Remedy," and then took another look at some of your drawings. Perhaps for the first time, I realized there was something curious but consistent about what I've been calling your "exploded axons": they were, in fact, not axons at all, but perspectives. I found some other deliberate monstrosities here are there. What is the reason behind these perceptual tricks, and how do they resonate with what you are trying to do now?

COD: Flicking through the entire collection of Freud for Spyros's class in the Bobst Library during the winter of my first semester at Princeton, I found a handful of diagrams. I was daunted by all the text, but I was much more comfortable reading diagrams. They even seemed architectural, perhaps because both psychoanalysis and architecture coincide in their attempt to draw both the virtual and the real. This is something I always ask my students to do these days, to draw things that are not there, or to draw things that are not so tangible, like sunlight, rain, temperature, and so on. These virtual things are as present in a site as their physical counterparts. My thinking always is, if you don't draw it, then you're never going to bring it into

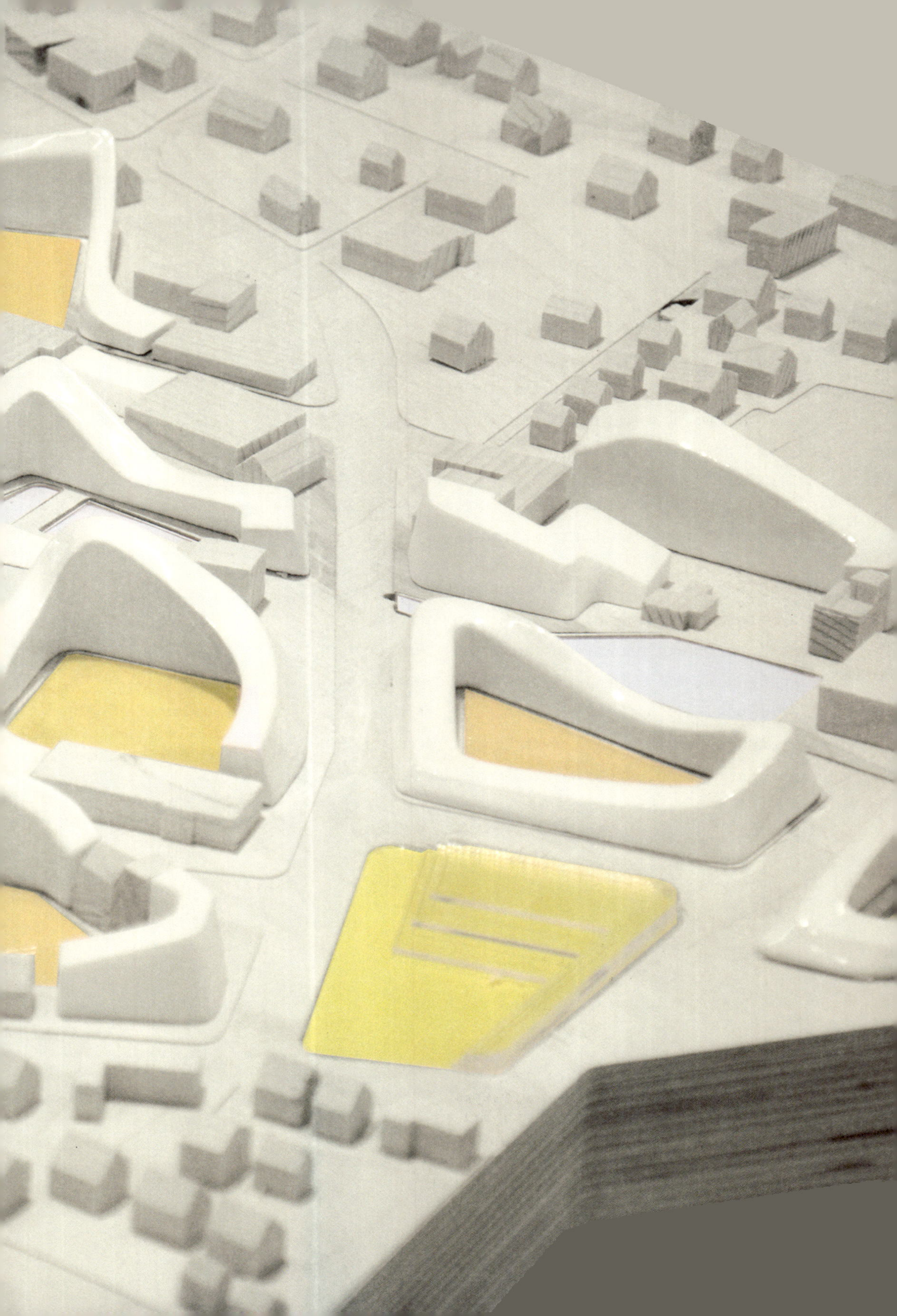

the conversation. In the diagrams, Freud was drawing things that were in virtual (mental) and physical space with equal conviction. They were both circles of the same size: one was black, one was white, but they were both just as important as each other. Some of the representation employed in this book relies on these ideas. For instance, the exploded perspectives privilege the attention that is given to certain parts of a project over another. Similarly, the diagrams of transformation that appear throughout the book call out visible and invisible forces that modify—and oftentimes generate—the architecture itself.

> **JI:** You mentioned the task to "represent what is not there." Where does that come from?

COD: Maybe it's an Irish thing. I explained how material or volumetric the weather is, so I think the tendency is culturally engrained, in a way. But intellectually, Eisenman first enlightened me to this in his story about *Santa Maria della Pace*, where the rosette in the corner suggests that there are actually two ionic pilasters which have slid beyond the corner, and we happen to be looking at the tail-end of

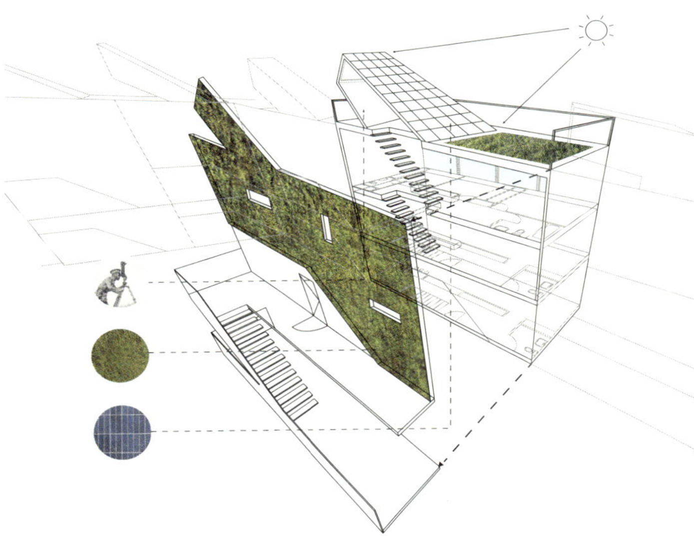

ferent. There is no way to do anything the c is constantly evolving and expanding: we dology. What's the fun in that?

nematic interactive installation for the ation on the theme of air. The project They appeared as softly draped fabric point they took on the form of the catenary luence of users to manifest and transform involved digitizing user inputs and their s similar to the way in which Gaudi used ation of the compressive stone columns,

it is difficult to bring literal kinematics to ctural scale. Maohaus *is a good example ses very dynamic effects. It's a façade project The form was found through the simulation understanding the inherent strength within 0th century. In our case, we strove to embed ade through rippling. The geometry of the a crucial role in the strength of the façade, e UHPC panels, which were 2 meters We incorporated an array of thousands of save weight and, most expressively, to hide h the parametric variation of the precise hat hidden and mostly just visible when ment on a public façade, which would ask lves.*

d Caroline both have in common, as people umor have to do with architecture?

ally impossible within architecture. Our of our lives, but I find the best social and more powerful points through humor. Dave George Carlin are probably amongst the personal heroes. With regard to architecture, ild up to it that I find interesting.

architecture, but there is clearly humor in you mentioned all contain a moment of I get it."

ly … this whole thing is a joke, and you Evoking that humorous response through nts of reveal are what invite the laughter: se. There's this chapter called "Duck ..

them at their moment of intersection. I really appreciate the idea that architecture can play with the mind in that way. In a couple of my projects, I have dealt with absence explicitly. For instance, the drawing for Storefront for Art and Architecture called *Missing You*, or the disappearing banknote, *Globo*. For *Missing You*, we were asked to make a drawing of Storefront and decided to draw the old tin ceiling that was always in the photos but never the object of anyone's attention. It had been there, but in a way, was always unseen. When we got there to document it, it was gone … it had been removed and was in storage. We tracked it down and photographed it in pieces, and then mapped them back to their original location on the ceiling. The second project, *Globo,* is a banknote for zero dollars that was designed to accompany my "Architecture on Money" essay. That essay notes the popularity of the image of architecture on multiple currencies around the world and aligns the disappearance of physical money with the becoming-virtual of architecture itself.

I am interested in the representation of things that we don't see in order that they be included. In a way, this is a

MISSING YOU

A DRAWING OF AND FOR STOREFRONT

Commission: Storefront for Art and Architecture
Year: 2013
Size: 17" x 24"

Storefront's pressed tin ceiling, visible but never the subject of the numerous photographs in which it appeared, once hovered above the eye's cone of attention and gathered marks of time, weather, and events. In 2012, the ceiling was removed and stored. This image documents the 91 pieces missing from Storefront today. When the ceiling was in place, it was often missed perceptually. It was present yet almost invisible, forgotten, unseen. When we looked for it, we missed it, in other ways.

continuation of what Eisenman started as drawings of lines of force. Indeed, sometimes his force lines did come from the site, as in the diagram in his Cambridge dissertation of the *Casa Del Fascio* and the Como Cathedral's force on it. But that is still connected to contextualism—in this case, context is understood only as the built environment. I am interested in context being thought of as the dynamic environment, which is much harder to represent, but just as present.

JI: Thinking about these absences reminds me that, at the end of the same Freud text, you mention Cedric Price and how he has a business card stating that he was "Anti-architect No. 1." This is something you still talk about today in your classes. But your essay also claims that Price's *Fun Palace* is (rummages) an "attempt to erase the traditional sense of architecture in favor of an ephemeral architecture that can interact, wear, and eventually disappear." Is this what CODA aims to do?

COD: No way, don't read while you drive, José … especially a quote from such a long time ago. Maybe CODA aims to do this partially. I am interested in an architecture that can interact. But maybe rather than disappear, I'd prefer that it *appear more*: that the architecture could become more active and operative. I also mention Bernard Tschumi's event diagrams in that essay. Recently, I was reading Sanford Kwinter's *Architectures of Time,* where he says that the opposite of an object is an event, and I started to understand Tschumi better—he is also an anti-object architect. I would not put myself in the same category as Price and Tschumi because I am interested in events *and* objects equally, and I want them to interact. That's where the werewolf thrives.

Google Maps: *In 500 feet, take exit 8 to Ithaca, NY*

COD*: Working with Martin at*
I might also need to reference M

MM*: You are simply referencing the ranti*

COD*: Many of the things th*

MM*: Not a book …*

COD: *Ahem … are much*
robotics, self-driving cars, ar
projects after the OMG collabor
these issues—specifically how we e
and machines—as well as how
conversations we have had abou

MM*: Maybe the best part of OMG*
For each OMG project, Caroline has come
one." My mind starts to race at the first

COD: *You just stop listening …*

MM*: Probably, but to give an ex*
started with some goofy idea to make a
various walking mechanisms and underst
constituent elements of the home is what m
there, too. For me, it is hilarious to make a
the mechanical engineer. For instance, the
Archigram's A Walking City*; it was all*
is about making an outrageous prov
consciously need to consider the actual impl
Spaces *began airing in 2000, and three*
with a sketch called Trading Spouses.
of the show, but with less hilarity and c
finds balance between the gag of a hous
and development to make that a reality
continuously reconstitutes itself thoug

I think ArtDock *is a funny projec*
a ship into the museum? To have this p
it's off on a world tour, where the art wo
humor as a social commentary. To me, tru
statements, and I think OMG is both,
Teen Wol …

static noises

JI: *Martin? Hello??? Is this a*

JI: Alright, I'd like us to talk quickly about your many other roles in the discipline: as educator, editor, and writer. You are the director of the Professional M.Arch program at Cornell University and have been teaching for over ten years now. How does teaching complement your practice, or why do you do it?

COD: I hope I can make a difference in the world by educating architects who will ask important questions and be equipped to make bold and creative responses, which will yield a better future for everyone. Teaching also makes me a better designer. I learn from my students, and by asking tough questions of them, I have to ask those same questions of myself. Teaching, writing, designing … I think it's important to be doing it all. Everything nudges everything else forward, even though those same things are always taking time away from one another. As Michael Young would say, I am sticking lots of sticks in my brain and stirring them all around.

JI: What about *Pidgin* and your involvement with architectural texts and publications, in general. How is that connected to your own post-indexical/ecological work?

COD: Brian Talbot, Marc McQuade, and I started *Pidgin* together at Princeton. The main idea was that we saw a lot of polished, finished work being put out into the world, but we knew that there was a lot happening in seminars and other aspects of our lives that was really "meaty," and we were interested in producing something that was rougher and faster than the official prospectus. The name *Pidgin* summed this up: a quick dispatch (pigeon) or a language in constant development by many (pidgin). The concept was really strong, but even so, the fact that the magazine is still very

BIRDSHIT

COVER FOR PIDGIN MAGAZINE

Produced for Pidgin 24.

Year: 2018
Size: 7" x 3"

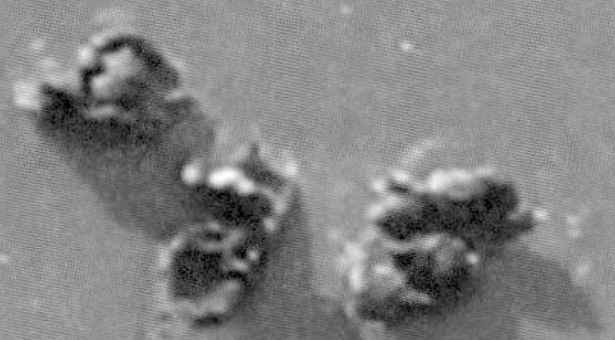

At *Pidgin's* conception, alternative names were tossed around—Beef, Frank, Medium-Rare, and Asparagus-Asparagus—but the final choice won out because its phonetic captured the spirit of two of the little journal's key concepts: a language formed by many, and a low-tech dispatch. This dispatch was to be rough and ready, dirty, unfinished. And of course with pigeon mail comes pigeon shit. In fact, everything leaves a trace and we, in this era and culture have been too ready to ignore the traces that we are leaving.

Pigeon excrement in cities is considered a nuisance, eroding façades and staining car paint jobs. In the countryside, the same material is collected as a valuable nitrogen-rich fertilizer. Depending on your standpoint, this is waste or resource, nuisance or nourishment. While Eisenman's indexical project brought the notion of the trace of the past into architecture (and birdshit is certainly an index of the bird's former presence), can the trace of the future be embedded into our present? Rather than hiding our waste in the feel good realm of single-stream recycling, and designing buildings out of materials yet to be defined, can we think of our building's dismantling in our designs? As the EPA slowly disappears, can we think about the waste for which we designers are responsible, and the future resource that it could be if properly considered?

Can we talk about that shit?

The heights are in feet above
SOUNDINGS IN FATHO
Pidgin
24
Nautic Miles
0
1
2
3

much alive is incredible. You know, one of the highlights of my career was actually doing the *Pidgin* shit cover for issue 24, where at first the image appears to be an island in the ocean, and only upon closer examination does the reader potentially see what it really is. It's the simple things in life …

I think the connection to my work is not so much in terms of content, but in methodology. I like to approach all projects via their DNA and their site, and these qualities are just as real for books as for buildings. Reviving the *Cornell Journal* was like operating on a beloved historical building. The team and I needed to understand that DNA before we could evolve the publication.

Usually, the process of developing a journal is very much *like* designing, but recently, the book literally became the installation. *This Is Not A Wall* is a compilation of 70 contributions around the design and construction of the project *Party Wall.* It's a book that tells one story through many small stories, in many different voices, including the MoMA director, the PS1 janitor, fabricators, children, and so on. Because the publisher had a surplus of copies they were unable to sell after some time, we felt it necessary to build a wall with the leftover copies of the book.

> **JI:** You transformed your *This Is Not A Wall* book waste into a wall. Very CODA, very werewolf. It's not one of the examples that is literally kinetic or that changes its material states, but the function of the book, the affordance,

changes. In this case, the rolled paper returns to a log-like state. Why don't you expand on this shift toward werewolf-thinking … whatever happened to the giraffe?

COD: The last chapter in *Niche Tactics* is about monsters. Monsters exist outside of the notion of species because they break the rules. There's a seventeenth-century explanation of the difference between species, monsters, and artificial, or what Francis Bacon calls "liberty, errors, and bonds." Liberty (species) is described as free and developing ordinarily, while bonds (or the artificial) are constrained and molded by human intervention. But the definition and distinction of errors (monsters) is fascinating. The monster is, Bacon says, "forced out of her proper state by the perverseness and insubordination of matter and the violence of impediments." That is to say, monsters are so erroneous as to exist separately, outside the "proper" category of the species. They are no longer a bad copy of a platonic model but, beyond simply a variation: monsters have crossed into another realm.

I always knew that if I moved beyond the giraffe, I would be moving into the monster world. The monster is outside the norm, yet it potentially drives an evolutionary process. The werewolf is of particular interest to architecture because the transformation is, first, motivated by the context, and second, more than formal—it is material and performative.

COD: José, since I've talked almost all the way here, why don't *you* tell me how this werewolf experience has affected *your* practice?

Google Maps: *Recalculating*

JI: *I think we may have taken a wrong turn …*

COD: Let's just keep going and see where we get to?

JI: Okay …

In a similar way as you describe your innate understanding of Peter's indexical project, your ecological approach and *Niche Tactics* in particular are both extremely formative for me, and also felt intuitive since the beginning. As you might recall, my undergraduate thesis at Cornell tried to "psychoanalyze" the

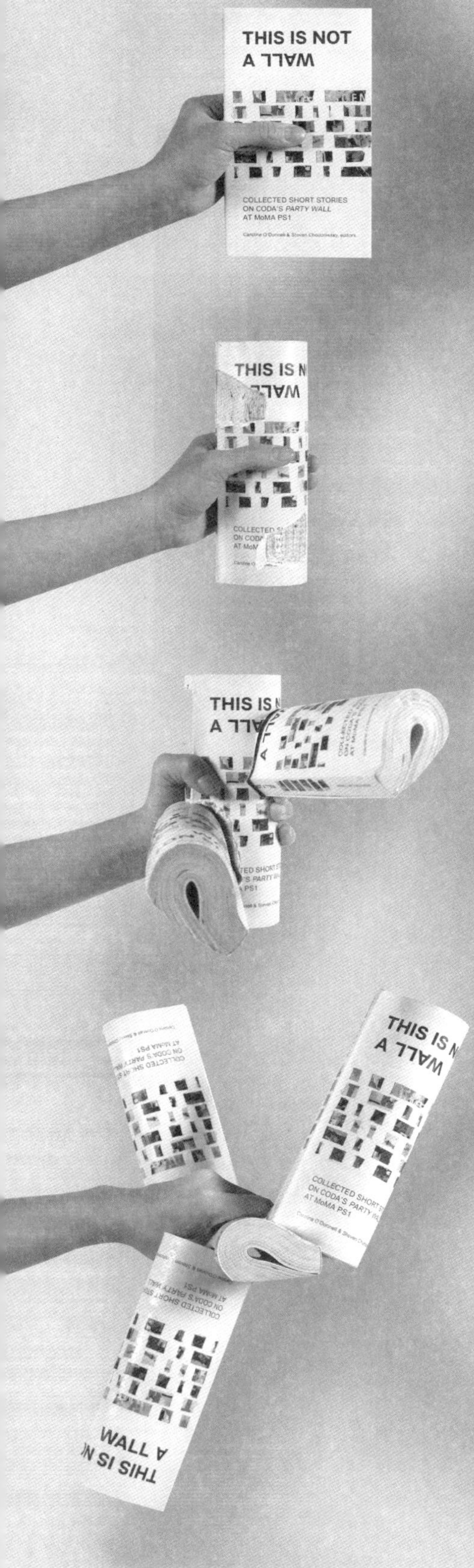

THIS IS NOT A WALL

ANOTHER WALL

Self commission.

Year: 2020
Size: 6' x 6'

In 2017, *This Is Not A Wall*, edited by Caroline O'Donnell and Steven Chodoriwsky, was published. Through acts of reportage, recollection, and remix, the book assembles a total of 75 individual contributors in the form of 75 unique stories, told in chronological order, which, combined, tell the story of a project made by many.

In 2020, Actar notified O'Donnell that 20 boxes of books remained in the warehouse and, either the storage would need to be either paid for, or the boxes would be returned.

While a book most often affords reading, it also has structural properties, especially when rolled. In this state, it returns to the wood-like quality from whence it came.

The This Is Not A Wall *Wall* was produced by rolling each book to reveal a log-like effect via the partially visible pages, and by CNC-notching books together via a connector book. As the angle of the notch is rotated, the rolled books rotate across the length of the wall, creating a change in porosity.

This project continues CODA's trajectory of explorations in material misuse, and the ways in which novelty might be found in materials previously considered waste.

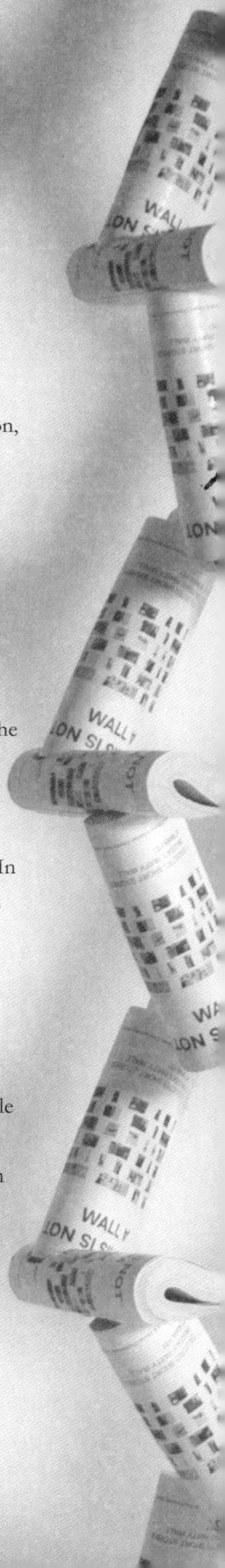

Berlin Wall, understanding it to be an object that could say things (it could talk about its traumas) and was in need of an architectural intervention. Your work helped me to see that the visible and invisible forces of "trauma' could be mapped and would derive an architecture with and for its environment. My work since then has taken a turn toward ecology, which has felt incidental, and yet entirely natural and necessary: after all, what larger traumas might there be now than mass extinction and climate unrest?

Our collaboration in *Werewolf: The Architecture of Lunacy, Shapeshifting, and Material Metamorphosis* has blurred certain boundaries in my perception of our individual approaches. Still, I find myself increasingly working with Morton's concept of *hyperobjects*. Hyperobjects transcend specificity and are massively distributed in space and time. While some in the discipline have taken this as an opportunity to make architecture out of anything and everything, I am more interested in the implication that things are entangled *with* everything else, and the idea that the temporal scales of objects are completely enmeshed. This prompts us to look at architecture as slower paced, lasting anywhere from a few seconds to deep (geologic) time. This requires a focus on process (rather than form), as well as an embedded capacity for change in the form, function, performance, and even users of architecture. This ecological entanglement also demands empathy with biological and geological beings, which I'm calling *geoempathy*. This is a term I use to describe a design of process, which yields new objects that respond to and interact with other things (objects, rocks, plants, animals, humans, and so on) in the world. Approached in this light, architecture becomes rhizomatic: non-linear and non-hierarchical, operating more as field than as object.

Who knows, maybe in a few years there will be another *monofesto*?

COD: Festigraph?

Google Maps: *Recalculating*

Moon Phases, António Cidadão (Amateur Astronomer), 1999.

184

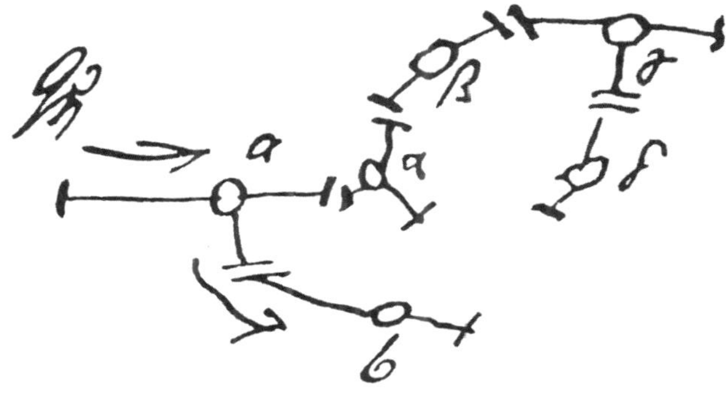

Caroline O'Donnell
Diagram as Remedy
Decoding Freud's Diagrams

The territory of the psyche, though influenced by real events in space and time, is not spatial. However, it must be spatialized in order to be represented. Freud was troubled by "the problem of how it will be possible to give a two-dimensional picture of anything that is so much of a solid as our theory of hysteria." [1]

The problem of visualization and space in psychoanalysis is one that Freud grappled with throughout his life and his complete works contain around twenty diagrams that illustrate his writings. For Freud, the diagram is used as a way of representing the psyche and its relations with the external world. In '*An Infantile Neurosis*', after a meandering explanation of the complex connection between the series '*faeces, penis, baby*', Freud utilizes the diagram for additional clarity, explaining: "I feel sure that by this time the manifold interrelations of the series...have become unintelligible, so I will try to remedy the defect by presenting them diagrammatically and in considering the diagram, we can view the same material in a different order." [2] Freud essentially sees the diagram as a remedy – a means of temporary mediation between the unintelligible psychic realm and the spatial realm.

In his discussion of hysteria, Freud describes the components of a hypothetical diagram representing the three strata of hysteria, without ever drawing it: "While two [strata] would be represented in a spatial diagram by a continuous line, curved or straight, the course of the logical chain would have to be indicated by a broken line which would pass along the most roundabout paths from the surface to the deepest layers..." [3] Here, without having set eyes on a diagram, we are struck by the concept of the diagram as an aid to mediation between two realms. The broken line itself is a remedy—an in-between condition of the complete line and the absence of line which exists in both the real and the virtual worlds and that appears time and again in the Freudian diagram.

The diagram is the tool which mediates between the concept and the form

Pidgin 1, Princeton School of Architecture, 2006.

and therefore links virtual space (the space of desires, trajectories, events, histories, projections) and real space (the tangible, visible elements of the world such as objects, persons, and places) to reveal the meaning inherent in the structure.

Freud's diagrams are idiosyncratic, rarely have a key or index, and lack any one convention or standard, "composed creatively in [his own] unique combination or superimposition of conventions."[4] However a close reading of the diagrams reveals that the notations (arrows, annotations, circles, continuous and dashed lines) though slippery and flexible, do have enough consistency to be decoded. The diagrams are reminiscent of contemporaneous drawings from the disciplines of medicine, science, architecture, and archaeology. The diagrams of the Ego Organization (title page), for example, show Freud's use of the electrical diagram as a metaphor for the transfer or neurons in the ego organization. What would be the flow of current and the capacitors represent the flow of neurons and the inhibitors in the ego.

The representation of the unintelligible seems to be an irreconcilable paradox which is also faced by architecture as a discipline that inherently swings to and fro between real and virtual space. What Freud draws as hatched areas, solid lines, and blackened circles, the architect reads as poché, walls, and objects. Other Freudian symbols denote the virtual condition; Freud's broken line, for example, which often represents a line of desire or a virtual trajectory, appears to varying extents in the architectural drawing, from the temporal line of a sliding door at one end of the spectrum, to the dashed lines which denote event or movement in work like Bernard Tschumi's *Manhattan Transcripts* or ephemerality in the case of Cedric Price's *Fun Palace*. The catalogue which follows attempts to decode the notations in Freud's diagrams, and makes a start at providing an index, which Freud never did. Through the deciphering of the sign, we can begin to speculate on the way in which this oscillation between the virtual and the real engages with the process and production of architecture.

Diagram of the Phobia in a 5-year old boy

Little Hans, mainly psychoanalyzed by his father, with written assistance from Freud, develops a nervous disorder at the age of 5. He has been obsessed with his *wiwimacher* from the age of 3, inferring, for example, that his mother should have a large *wiwimacher* since a horse's was so much bigger than his own.[5]

When out with a nursemaid one day, Little Hans has a nervous attack on the street, (to which he later attributes a fear that 'a horse will bite him'), and insists on going home to be cuddled by his mother. Later that day, Little Hans is afraid that the horse will come into his bedroom. As the phobia develops, it becomes clear that Little Hans' fear of horses and of the outside is strongly related to his desire to be intimate with his mother inside the house, in the bedroom, and in the bed. The desire for the mother and the anxiety that she will abandon him had existed before as evidenced by dreams and by flirtatious behavior from Hans in his father's absence. The horse merely becomes the 'object' to which the fear is transferred.

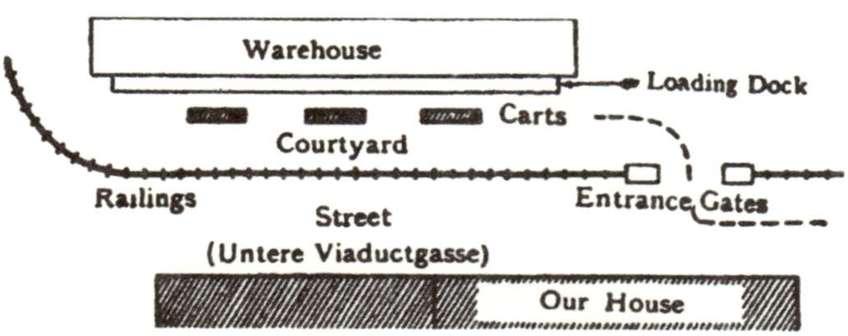

186
187

Diagram of Phobia in a 5-year old boy: SE Vol. X 1909 *Analysis of a Phobia in a 5-year Old Boy* p.46

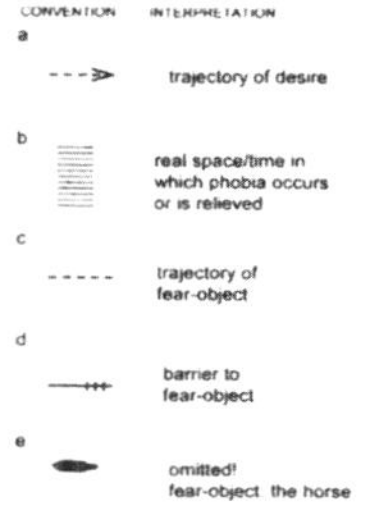

The spatial aspect of Little Hans' fear is not emphasized by Freud. Though Jacques Lacan later takes up this case in particular and its connection to the urban context, he is in many ways equally dismissive of Hans' spatial environment (as noted by Anthony Vidler in his essay *Agoraphobia: Psychopathologies of Urban Space*). The intimacy of the inside and the possibilities of cuddling with his mother become sharply contrasted to the exterior world in which such behavior is not permitted, and in which the approach of horses and carts (which pass the house frequently to enter the warehouse opposite) come to objectify Little Hans' anxiety of losing his mother. The horses and carts represent the factors which are an obstacle to Little Hans and his mother: the father (with his *large penis, 'moustache', 'lack of eye-glasses'*) and the birth of his new baby sister (*the heavily loaded cart, the possibility of falling*, and—from the series faeces, penis, baby—*the penis*).

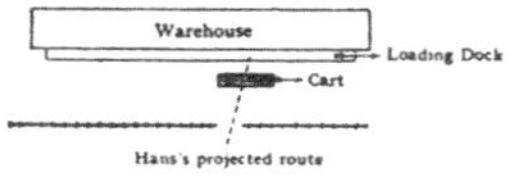

Diagram of Phobia in a 5-year old boy: SE Vol. X 1909 *Analysis of a Phobia in a 5-year Old Boy* p.48

Freud's diagram is a plan representation of the scene outside Little Han's house, showing the warehouse opposite with its loading dock and courtyard where three carts stand, all fenced off by railings. The trajectory of the carts as they leave the courtyard and pass through the gates onto the street is represented by a dashed line. Little Hans' own house, the relief from his fears and place of intimacy, is hatched, as are the carts, the representation of the object of fear.

The horses, though supposedly the 'object', are not represented at all. This is particularly curious since Freud, in his summary, stipulates that Little Hans' case is not agoraphobia because the phobia, "...soon ceased having any relation to the question of locomotion and became more and more clearly concentrated upon horses." [9]

In an additional diagram, Freud maps not only the real space but the virtual: one dashed line of desire connecting Little Hans to the warehouse. This line not only traces Little Hans' expressed wish that he would like to cross over the carts in order to play on the dock, but also the latent content of his wish to 'penetrate'; to pass into prohibited ground.

Despite the simplicity of these diagrams, the dotted lines representing the virtual condition of desire and the movement of the horse are apparent. Little Han's greatest fear, of course, is that these trajectories would intersect. In real space, the horse would move off as he climbed over it, and he would be injured. In virtual space (the fantasy), the father or the baby sister would prevent him reaching intimacy with his mother. The two scenes, real and virtual, become overlaid.

Diagram of Emma's Hysterical Repression: Project for a Scientific Psychology, 1895

In the case of Emma, Freud diagrams his patient's fear of shopping. Two memory systems collide in this diagram, the memory from the age 12 (upper portion) when Emma was mocked on account of her clothes by two shop assistants one of whom attracted her, and an earlier memory from the age of 8 (center) when Emma's genitals were fondled through her clothes by
a shopkeeper. These combined thoughts of clothes-shopkeeper-assault, 188
though introjected separately, are combined by displacement and re-pro- 189
jected in a form that merges shopping and aloneness with anxiety. Emma's actual experience of shopping (top right) occupies a small proportion of the drawing at the 'recent' end of Freud's time-axis.

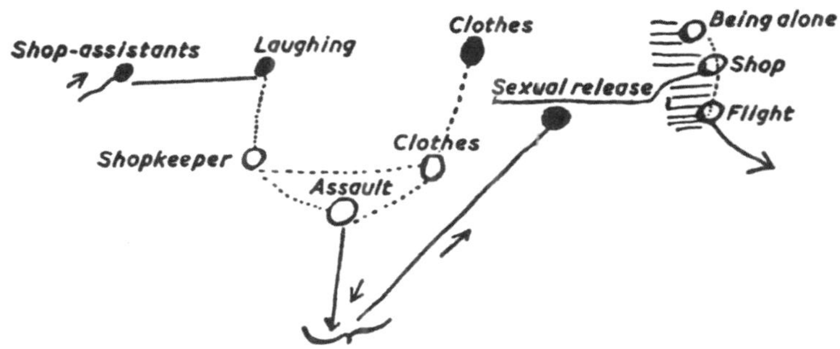

Diagram of Emma's Hysterical Repression: SE Vol I *Project for a Scientific Psychology*, 1895, p.354

In the diagram, elements are arranged above and below an invisible line according to the recentness of their occurrence. Certain elements (shop-assistants, laughing, clothes, sexual release) are represented by a black circle, whereas the others are represented by a white or voided circle. Another overlapping grouping occurs between the elements of laughing, shopkeeper, clothes (1), clothes (2), and assault, as connected by the dotted line. The meaning of these groupings may lie in the discrepancy between virtual and real space, the dotted line, for example, representing the virtual processes of the mind (thought), and the solid line representing Emma's real experience (content).

Note that here, as in Freud's diagram of Little Hans' phobia (and also in the Sexualschema (right)), the hatched area represents the real space of fear and escape. The arrow of 'Flight' moving diagonally towards the bottom right is comparable to the arrow of 'Defiance' in the series - faeces, penis, baby which could be read either as a trajectory but also as a z-axis. This possibility not only brings the diagram into the third dimension, but specifically brings the real or spatial part of the diagram towards a potentially more realistic representation of space.

The repetitions here work in the same way as the theory of condensation

in dreams. The objects "shop keeper/assistant" and "clothes" both appear twice in the different experiences that are the 'content'. These repeated elements, that is, more numerous though no more important, become "over-determined" to form the conscious focus of the hysteria. These elements are the substitute for the repressed fear of assault.

The "{" appears to represent the screen of the ego which receives the image of earlier shopkeeper. This image is introjected and subsequently that (negative) image is projected back onto the shop-assistants (top left arrow). The condensed experience is re-projected as sexual release when shopping. This '{' is a miniaturization of Freud's Ego Organization diagrams, but here - crucially - unlike the Ego Organization diagrams, the ego projects outward.

Diagram of the Architecture of Hysteria

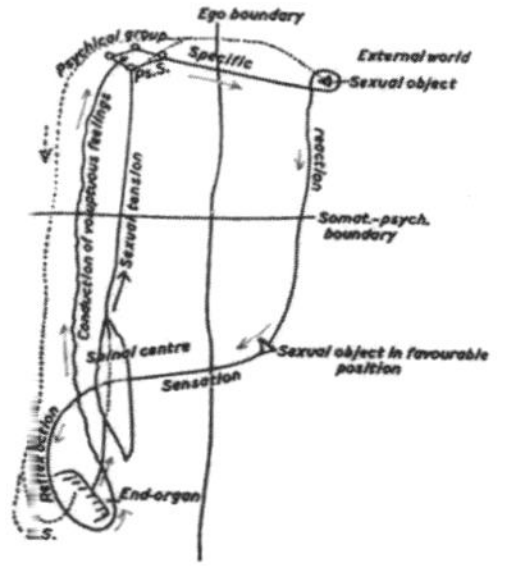

Diagram of Sexuality (Sexual-schema): SE Vol I 1895, *Draft G: Melancholia*, p.202

"Since most of the scenes converge on the few symptoms, our path makes repeated loops through the background thoughts of the same symptoms".[11]
Freud explains the process of psychoanalysis in this cryptic diagram. Whitney Davis describes this 'work' as a process of recovery wherein "the present history of analysis (from right to left) is 190
mapped onto or over the past history of repres- 191
sion (from left to right)." The thick horizontal lines ('f' in the key) represent the 'scenes' which are reached by analysis. With each analysis (1, 2,

3...), the repressed scenes (I, II, III...) are reached, each scene deeper than the previous. The path of analysis (dashed - red in the original) is described as a loop which travels to the scenes and then deeper, then up to a symptom, then to a deeper scenes and so on. These dashed lines travel back over the path of the black solid lines of repression. The diagram is actually two diagrams superimposed and woven into each other: the real history of the patient and the virtual history according to the analyst.

Here, the orientation shows time moving from left to right, along an invisible x-axis, the analyst going 'back in time' to reach the repressed "thought". Depth into the unconscious, (up-down) is shown along the y-axis, again, the analyst having to go down to reach the repression.

This diagram is about movement between the unintelligible dream thought deep within the psyche and the dream content closer to the surface. It is about layers, depth and digging, and so, in a way the language that we use in the discussion of this diagram is a particularly architectural language. The process of psychoanalysis mapped out here is comparable to the process of architectural design; the movement between the conceptual and the tectonic, the constant oscillation between the idea and the building. In con-

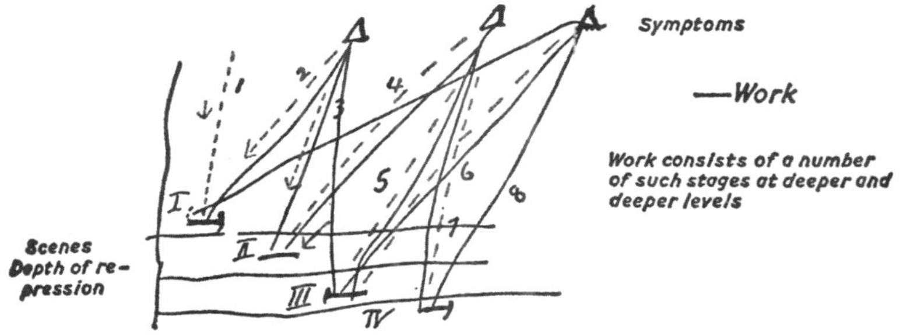

Diagram of the Architecture of Hysteria: SE Vol. I 1895 *Extracts from the Fliess Papers*, p.251.

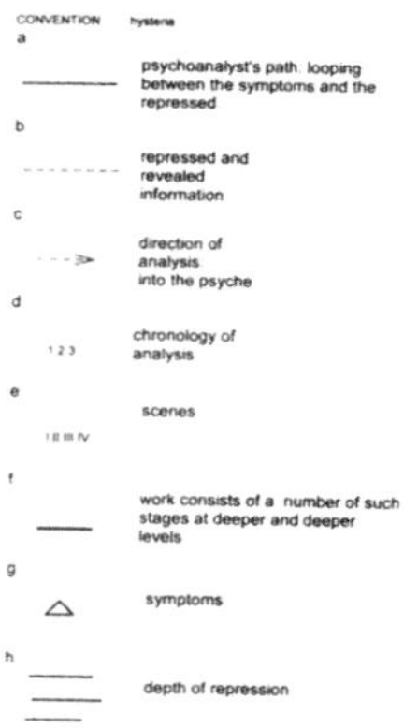

sidering the diagram as a generator—the diagram becoming architecture. What type of architecture would the diagram of hysteria produce? What would become of the layered and convulsive promenade that is the physical manifestation of the realm between the spatial and the unintelligible?

Although the three diagrams describe different scenarios, they all deal with the coexistence of real and psychical space and the negotiation between them. Little Hans' and Emma's cases focus more on mapping geographic space (the warehouse, the shop) - the physical site of the phobia. Though the diagram of hysteria charts mainly psychic space, it does reference an imaginary line or surface which bounds and orientates this virtual space. Freud is allowing real space and psychical space to coexist while remaining distinct. Real space is denoted by a hatched area or by a line that acts as a screen between the two realms. Freud, in considering the pysche as a three dimensional solid, necessarily collapses the structure into a two dimensional representation in order to create a diagram in the same way that real space must be flattened in an orthographic projection.

The table on p.195 shows a key for seven of Freud's diagrams discussed in the original version of this
text. 192
193

The Psychoanalytic Diagram and Architecture

The diagram, in its location between the actual and

the virtual, has the ability to become both the architectural dream-thought and the post construction self-analysis (the building on the couch). Furthermore, the diagram can dominate to the extent that the building behaves as diagram. The diagram of Colin Rowe's ideal villa or Rudolf Wittkower's geometric pattern, for example, is a virtual condition that can never come into being but carries as much conceptual weight as the masonry structure that is its final representation . Similarly, within the same lineage, Peter Eisenman's Cardboard Houses imply the virtual cube that pre-existed the house and the process of transformation that led to its coming into being. The reading of the building then necessitates a reading of the virtual condition and the (fictional) process that links the virtual with the real. The deep structure of psychoanalysis, the "truth" revealed through reading down through the layers in the psyche -- may be compared to the deciphering of the certain "truth" of the geometric platonic object.

For a discipline that necessarily oscillates between the unintelligible virtual realm and the spatial, though, the architectural palette for the visualization of the unintelligible is limited. In *The Manhattan Transcripts*[13] , Bernard Tschumi makes a series of diagrams, photographs and drawings whose purpose is to transcribe things normally removed from conventional architectural representation. For Tschumi, there is no architecture without event, but architectural representation is caught in a 'prison-house of language' that excludes certain concerns that are not the real physical stuff of architecture.

In MT1, which narrates a murder in central park, Tschumi uses two types of lines – solid and dashed - to notate the movement of two subjects – the victim and the murderer – that are not themselves represented. The vectors are not aligned with the frame and in diagram 3 (top right), and they are not extended across the frame anymore but end with arrowheads two-thirds of the way across the frame. The simple notation communicates an increase in movement which is reinforced by a much more frenetic composition of the

CONVENTION		FORGETTING NAMES	FAECES, PENIS, BABY	HYSTERIA	SEXUALSCHEMA	LITTLE HANS	EMMA	
a	———	connectivity	connectivity	psycho-analyst's path looping between the symptoms and the repressed	connectivity		connectivity	connectivity/path both real and virtual
b	- - - - - -			repressed and revealed information	contrary flow/undefined path	trajectory of fear object	repressed connectivity	repressed connectivity contrary flow undefined path trajectory (real)
c	——→	direction of flow	direction of flow	direction of analysis into psyche	direction of flow		projection-introjection/ movement in real space	direction of flow projection-introjection movement in real space
d	- - - ->			direction of analysis into psyche	direction of opposing flow	trajectory of desire		direction opposing direction virtual/projected trajectory
e					end organ	real space of relief from fear	real space in which phobia occurs	real space in which phobic event (or relief) takes place
e	{	part of a series of groupings					ego surface	real space in which phobic event (or relief) takes place
e	● ○				part of a series of groupings	objects	objects	objects
e	△			symptoms	objects in motion			objects in motion

194
195

vectors in the following frames that lead up to the event of the murder. Comparing this sequence to Emma's Hysterical Repression diagram, many of the same notations can be read. The two line-types now represent two paths through the psyche, the solid and blackened dots now represent psychical objects rather than objects in the park landscape. The plans of the park that appear begin to reiterate the Freudian language of objects and connections that appears in Emma's diagram.

In neither diagram is the subject represented, rather implied by the presence of the vectors. The rigid square frame in the sequence is comparable to the'screen' of the ego that bounds the space that is to be diagrammed. In Tschumi's sixth diagram (bottom right) the vector actually breaks out of its frame. The line of flight, that vector that breaks out Tschumi's fourth and sixth diagrams or at the bottom left of Emma's diagram, clearly denotes a change of pace, a panic, a break from the system. Event in both cases is represented not only by a moment but by a sequence of interrelated and constantly shifting connections in the past and in the future.

In MT4, the movement of acrobats, ice-skaters, dancers, soldiers and football players is diagrammed and eventually reconstructed. The white circle, the dashed line and the arrowhead are the main notations which describe the subjects and their movement in relation to one another. Again, looking back to the diagram of Emma's Hysterical Repression and to the diagram of Hysteria, the relations between both these figures and the objects in the psyche is through movement and forces between the parts. There is a constant fluctuation between the parts, up and down, or back and forth, from the surface to the deepest layer. In MT4, Tschumi describes the arrows as more than just directional indications – as having an effect outside themselves so that they 'carve out space'. The diagramming of the intrusion of the bodies in space becomes synonymous with the process of development of architecture. Tschumi writes : "it started by deconstructing the city, today it explores new codes of assemblage".[14] In a way, Tschumi considers this methodology of

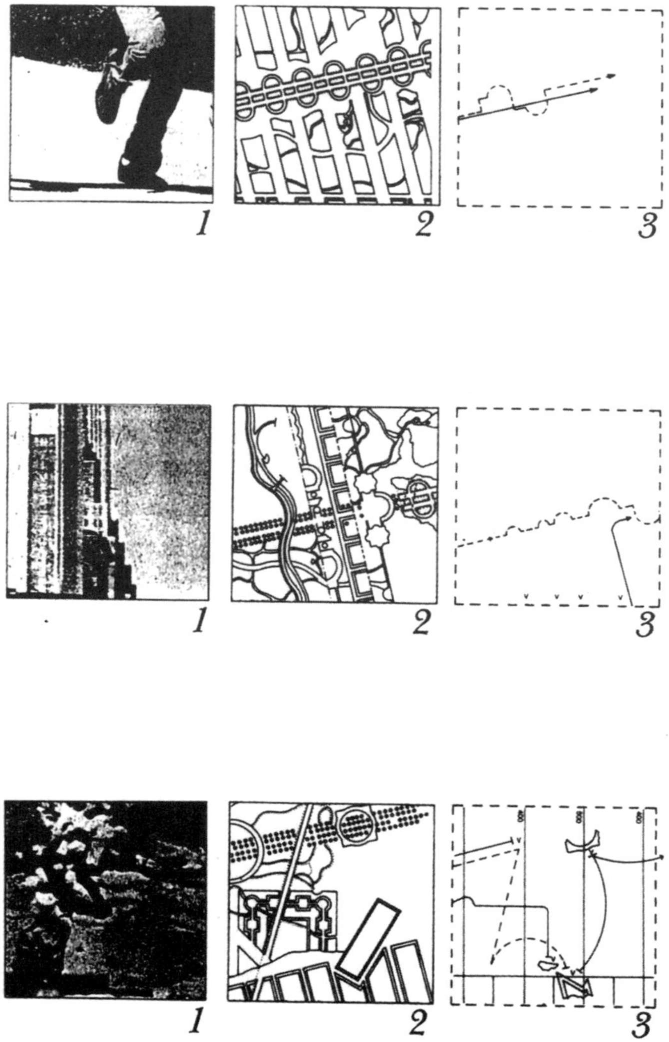

Diagrams from *The Manhattan Transcripts: MT1*, Bernard Tschumi: Academy Editions, New York and London, 1981.

diagramming to be a remedy for the issues he has with architectural representation and process.

The dashed line of desire appears in the architectural project most notably in Cedric Price's perspective for the *Fun Palace* in which all lines are dashed. For Price, the self-titled 'anti-architect no.1', the desire was that the building would not exist. His *Fun Palace* is an attempt to erase the traditional sense of architecture in favor of an ephemeral architecture that can interact, wear, and eventually disappear. Visitors to the building are expected to make their own path, create their own narratives through the building much in the way that the psychoanalyst must read deep into the structure of the psyche to unravel his own plot. Also seen as a kind of remedy, Price's architecture was an attempt to reconsider the problems of architecture through research and notation, or as Mark Wigley puts it, "his way of destabilizing architecture was just to go deeper and deeper into each of its most basic operations." [15]

In a note late in his career, Freud suggests real space as a projection – a flattening of three-dimensional space into the two-dimensional space of the diagram:

> Space may be the projection of the extension of the psychical apparatus. No other derivation is probable. Instead of Kant's a priori determinants of our psychical apparatus. Psyche is extended; knows nothing about it.[16]

The space of the psyche and the space of the real world become collapsed and entangled. Though they both occupy different spaces, they are constantly influencing each other. There is no hierarchy between the two. It is perhaps this temporary collapse that is allows Freud to diagram the two realms in one flattened space.

The flat space of the architectural drawing – a projection, in both the technical and the design senses of the word - should open up the possibili-

ties for the virtual, the unintelligible, to become part of the language of representation, and furthermore, to become generative in the production of architecture.

Notes

1. Sigmund Freud, Letter to Breuer, "*The Standard Edition of The Complete Psychological Works of Sigmund Freud*", 24 volumes, London, Hogarth Press, 1955. (hereafter: SE) vol. I ,1895 , p.147

2. Sigmund Freud, *An infantile Neurosis and other work*, SE Vol. XVII 1917-19, p.132

3. Sigmund Freud, *Studies on Hysteria*, SE vol. II,1893-5 , p 291-2

4. Whitney Davis, "*Drawing the Dream of the Wolves*", Indiana University press, 1995,p.82

5. Sigmund Freud, SE vol. X, 1909, *Two Case Histories*, p.10

6. Sigmund Freud, SE vol. X, 1909, *Two Case Histories*, p.40-41

7. Anthony Vidler, *Warped Space Art, Architecture, and Anxiety in Modern Culture*, Massachusetts Institute of Technology, Cambridge 2000, p. 148.

8. Sigmund Freud, SE vol. X, 1909, *Two Case Histories*, p.115

9. Sigmund Freud, *Diagram of The Architecture of Hysteria: SE Vol. I 1895 Extracts from the Fliess Papers*, p.251

10. Sigmund Freud, SE Vol I, Draft G, *Melancholia*, 1895 p.201

11. Whitney Davis, "*Drawing the Dream of the Wolves*", Indiana University press, 1995,p.82

12. Bernard Tschumi, *Manhattan Transcripts*, London : Academy Editions 1994.

13. Bernard Tschumi, *Architecture and Disjunction*, MIT Press, Cambridge MA, 1996

14. Mark Wigley, Cedric Price's Fun Palace, *Domus*, 2004 Jan n.866 p.14 – 23, p. 22

15. Sigmund Freud, *Findings, Ideas, Problems*, 1941 [1938], SE vol. XXIII 1937 – 1939, p.300 (August 22)

This is a summary of the paper Representation of the *Virtual and the Spatial: In-between Worlds in Freud's Diagrams* written for the "Architecture and Psychoanalysis" Seminar in Fall 2004 under the instructorship of Spyros Papapetros. The author wishes to thank Spyros Papapetros and Andreas Quednau for their advice and patience with this paper.

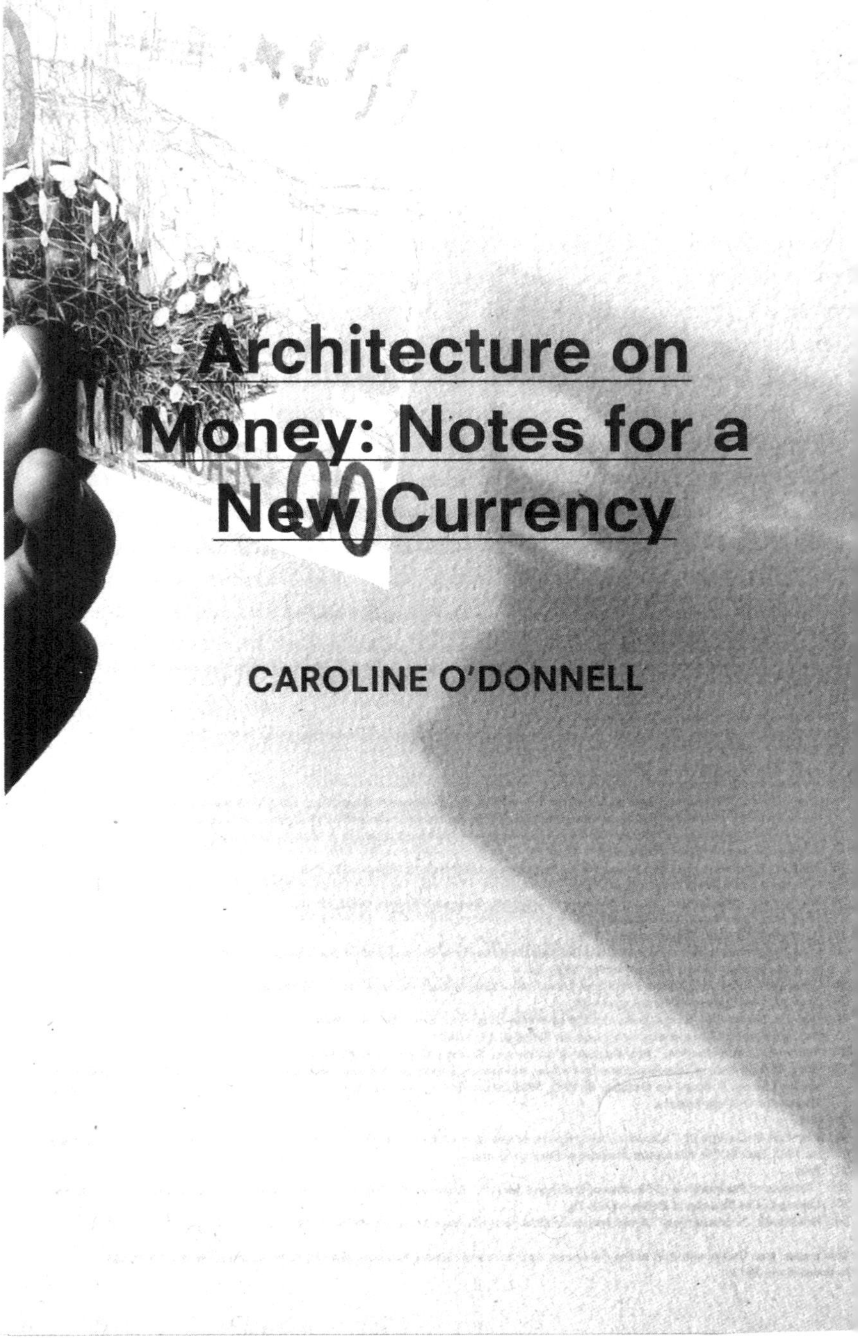

Architecture on Money: Notes for a New Currency

CAROLINE O'DONNELL

More than one hundred years ago, Georg Simmel raised concerns over the increasing disconnect between the value of money and its symbolism. Simmel's understanding of money as both "a concrete and valued substance and, at the same time, as something that owes its significance to the complete dissolution of substance into motion and function" reads as a poignant prophesy of the demise of paper currency.[1] Today, through the increasingly ephemeral transactions brought about by electronic banking, our money travels at the speed of Simmel's anxiety in a state of "complete dissolution."

Architecture, a discipline caught between physical reality and immaterial ideas, mirrors the simultaneous concreteness and ephemerality of money. Yet despite the radical transformations in both architecture and money, a familiar and nostalgic architecture continues to adorn some of the world's major banknotes.

Real Money

Underlying the development of money is the notion of exchange, an activity most simply exemplified by barter. While the concrete reality of such exchange has clear advantages, its limitations are perhaps best illustrated by nineteenth century opera singer Mademoiselle Zélie who, after her performance in the Society Islands, received the contractually stipulated one third of the takings: in this case, three pigs, twenty-three turkeys, forty-four chickens, five thousand coconuts and innumerable bananas, oranges, and lemons; payment that the singer had great difficulty in bringing with her on the remainder of her world tour.[2] Barter depends on the double coincidence of wants: the desire by both parties for the commodities of exchange. Failing this unlikely coincidence of desires, a few highly tradable commodities began to be used as media of exchange. Materials that were portable, durable, and had high value density, including amber, axes, beads, cowry shells, drums, eggs, feathers, gongs, hoes, ivory, jade, kettles, leather, mats, nails, oxen, pigs, quartz, rice, salt, thimbles, vodka, whale's teeth, and yarns, often gained ornamental and symbolic value—in addition to their intrinsic value—through their exchange.[3]

In the western world, the transformation from irregular and unmarked silver blobs to standardized coins occurred in the first half of the first millennium BCE. These "dumps"—a natural gold-silver

405

amalgam washed downriver and deposited in the flats of Lydia and Ionia—were punch-marked and stamped with inscriptions that came to guarantee purity and weight. Finally, these developed into rounded coins stamped with deep indentations on both sides. Their use spread rapidly throughout the Mediterranean, the stamp or punch usually depicting the Ruler in a symbolic declaration of both of their power and the coin's authenticity.[4]

Representative Money

The invention of the printing press in 1440 prompted Leonardo Da Vinci to make detailed drawings of the first mechanical mint intended to produce uniform metal coins. It took two centuries, however, to fully transition from the idea of the metallic coin press to paper money itself, as increasing world trade finally rendered coinage unfeasible.[5]

Initially, this "representative money" was backed by a government or bank's promise to exchange it for a certain amount of silver or gold. For example, the British Pound Sterling was redeemable for a pound of sterling silver, and in the U.S., before the establishment of the Federal Reserve in 1913, the Gold Certificate was redeemable in gold, which was, as the note declared, "payable to the bearer upon demand." But the situation could not persist at the rapidly increasing volumes of international trade: after 1933, U.S. notes could only be redeemed in in treasury debt, not gold, and from 1963 onward, no statement of redeemability whatsoever appeared on U.S. notes.[6] It was this abstraction from precious metal to paper note that Georg Simmel had feared: "more and more a mere symbol, neutral as regards its intrinsic value."[7]

Architecture on Money

All money is a promise. The implied trust is not simply between two parties in an exchange, but rather encompasses all of society: there must also exist a confidence that the value given in exchange for an interim value (a coin) will be replaced without loss. The inscription in the sixteenth century coins of Malta: *non aes sed fides* (not copper but faith) demonstrates this necessity for the economic community to have trust in the continuity of the currency. On the coin, this trust became pictorialized through the image of the sovereign.[8]

With notes replacing coins en-masse in the nineteenth century, the issue of trust became imperative.[9] The image of the recognizable face (whether figurehead or other trusted personality) became the standard on notes all over the world. In 1929, the U.S. dollar was reduced in size and standardized for consistency across the nation, and, with some adjustments, it is this design with which we are familiar today. One side of the current U.S. note is engraved with portraits of well-known Americans, mostly, though not always, former presidents.

The Lincoln Memorial. Photo by Brandon McKeon.

And on the reverse: architecture. The one-dollar note depicts the most fundamental essential architectural form: the pyramid. Missing its cap, the truncated form signifies incompletion. The remaining denominations follow suit: the Lincoln Memorial on the $5, the US Treasury on the $10, the White House on the $20, the US Capitol on the $50, and finally, Independence Hall on the $100.

For the special committee appointed by the U.S. Secretary of the Treasury in 1929, the Neoclassical architecture of U.S. government buildings seemingly had all of the qualities that money needed to communicate: solidity, tangibility, value, permanence, and perhaps most importantly, trustworthiness.[10] As both money and architecture have evolved in real time, the architecture of the dollar has remained reassuringly static and retrospective.

Architecture on the Euro

In February 1996, the European Monetary Institute, the forerunner of the European Central Bank, launched a competition in which nominated designers were asked to submit proposals for a series of seven banknotes. The competition brief suggested two themes: “Ages and Styles of Europe” and “Abstract or Modern Design.” In the design brief for the former category, suggestions were made for architectural works that might adorn the reverse sides of the notes as well as portraits of significant and recognizable Europeans for the obverse.

Austrian Designer Robert Kalina's winning designs featured depictions of actual bridges, including the Rialto Bridge in Venice and the Pont de Neuilly in Paris. Eventually, these were abstracted into more anonymous architectural fragments, when it was noted that each architectural work is inevitably related to a country of origin, while the note itself represents a value that spans across the Eurozone. Identifying particular monuments together with particular values implied a hierarchy that was clearly unacceptable to an institution charged with representing equality amongst nations.

The designs with which we are now familiar erase the specific and the detailed in exchange for the generic. Instead of well-known European landmarks, the notes display stylized representations of architecture typical of each period: Classical (€5), Romanesque (€10), Gothic (€20), Renaissance (€50), Baroque and Rococo (€100), Art Nouveau (€200), and Modern (€500). While the obverse sides present windows and doorways that symbolize “the European spirit of openness and cooperation,” the reverse sides feature bridges “symbolizing the close cooperation and communication between Europe and the rest of the world.”[11]

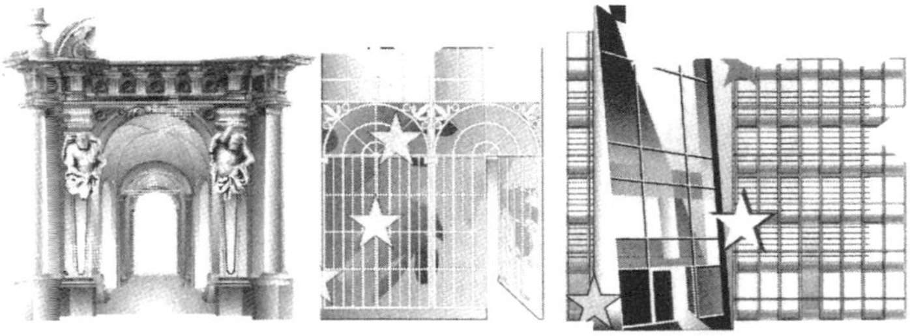

FROM LEFT TO RIGHT: Classical (€5), Romanesque (€10), Gothic (€20), Renaissance (€50), Baroque and Rococo (€100), Art Nouveau (€200), and Modern (€500)

As is typical on paper currencies today, the Euro features a variety of security devices in the form of holograms, watermarks, magnetic ink, and other devices, which render the note's imagery different in varying light conditions and orientations. Beyond the pragmatics of security, these images within images, these ghosts of images, are tentative steps towards the note's dissolution.

From Paper to Information

In the Renaissance, architecture became an intellectual discipline distinguished from construction. In his recent defense of architecture versus design at Cornell University, Peter Eisenman described Leon Battista Alberti's discourse in *De Re Aedificatoria* as "the first conscious human mediation to differentiate architecture from building, to see architecture as the sign of something as opposed to merely something."[12]

Similarly, much as money was abstracted from material to paper, the term "paper architecture" emerged to describe an architecture that remained unbuilt and, in many cases, not intended for construction. Cuts in federal aid to cities and high inflation during the 1970s debilitated the construction industry, but architectural design flourished. According to sociologist David Gartman, this lack of funds increased competition, putting "the dissenting trends pioneered in the 1960s into a hothouse, accelerating the process of innovation."[13] These paper projects were often liberated from financial, material, and technological constraints. Archigram's *Walking City*, for example, envisioned a future in which hi-tech, amphibious vessels perambulated above the existing city.[14] Inspired by space travel, and the potential effects of that technology on society, the project proposed new nomadic lifestyles and collective ways of interaction, in which

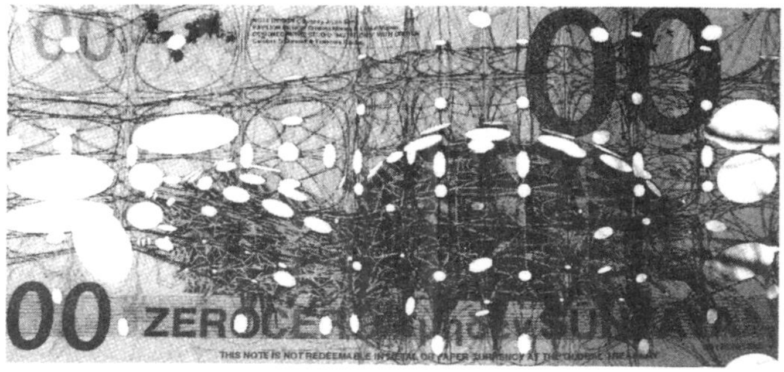

Globo designed by CODA (see also p. 30). Project Designer: Courtney Song. The bill features a study for a series of Pigeon Pavilions by Cristina Marais and Leslie Mignin as part of the studio "Mutations" at Cornell in Spring 2011, taught by Caroline O'Donnell and François Roche.

architecture was the hyper-present accomplice. And despite its existence only on paper, the power of this project, and others like it, is certainly greater than many of its material interpretations.

Following this, in the 1980s, under the deanship of Bernard Tschumi, Columbia University began a series of "paperless studios," which used animation software to explore dynamic and surface-based processes in architecture. According to Greg Lynn, one of the studio instructors at the time, the geometries produced did not operate according to a fixed model, but through "animations and dynamic modeling based on differentiation, multiplicity, continuous variation, and transformation."[15] Clearly, the computer was considered to be more than another drafting tool: it enabled new modes of thinking and production, an architecture formed by algorithmic operations that are radically different from the processes of sketching or drawing.

Like paper architecture's transition to the digital, money has become increasingly electronic, existing on our screens and flowing through our networks as pure information. Yet the meaning of money remains, as Simmel predicted, when he observed the tendency of the populus "to disregard the substance entirely, and to regard the effects as the only important matter."[16]

End Notes

While the trajectory of money is surely headed towards complete dematerialization, we exist in an interstitial moment where notes are still a vital component of exchange. In this in-between

period, the introduction of a new note may be neither material nor virtual: it may express its ambivalence through the architecture it bears, through its materiality, and other devices.

A retrospective architecture is no longer an appropriate metaphor for something increasingly understood as more volatile than stable, more virtual than solid, and more imaginary than real. Given the parallel trajectories of money and architecture from material to paper to pure information, all the while maintaining the sanctity of idea above substance, what if some of the virtual architecture produced today could find its place on new notes?

Until the moment when global currency becomes completely virtual, the "Globo" is proposed as a temporary expression of economic and architectural unpredictability. The Globo at last aligns the ephemerality of architecture and money in one transparent, flimsy, holey, and barely-there bill. Following tradition, the note features architecture: now a dynamic and digital architecture that communicates little stability or trustworthiness. On the contrary it suggests change, ephemerality, and the increasing dominance of effect over substance.

NOTES

Thanks to Courtney Song for her editorial comments.

1. Georg Simmel, *The Philosophy of Money* (Routledge NY, 1978), 176. First published 1900.
2. William Stanley Jevons, *Money and the Mechanism of Exchange*, (D. Appleton and Company,1875), 1.
3. An exception to the "portability" criterion is the Rai, a currency on the Micronesian island of Yap. The Rai is a piece of limestone whose value is dependent, amongst other factors, on size. The largest Rai stone is 3.6 m in diameter. Though the ownership of the stones changed, they were not physically exchanged. For more information, see William Henry Furness, *The Island of Stone Money, Uap of the Carolines*, (Philadelphia: J.B. Lippincott Company, 1910).
4. Philip II, as an symbol of power and influence, issued gold coin depicting his victory in the chariot race of the 356 BC Olympic Games on one side and the head of Zeus on the other. These coins spread to celtic tribes, where the head of Zeus was mistaken for Philip close-up and prepared the way for the issue of coinage to be accepted as the personal right of the king.
5. Learning of the paper notes from travels to the Orient, European banks began printing paper money in the seventeenth century. China had produced block-printed notes first on leather (118 BC) and then on paper (806 AD), primarily due to a shortage of copper. From 960 AD on, paper money was in regular circulation, by 1020 AD, inflation had spiraled out of control. The populus, having lost their trust in money, returned to coinage.
6. In his book *End the Fed*, Ron Paul, chairman of the House of subcommittee on domestic monetary policy, which oversees the Federal Reserve as well as the currency and the valuation of the dollar, embraces Austrian economic through which holds that the government has no role in regulating the economy. He advocates a return to the gold standard as a response to the uncertainty of the economy in the U.S. In an interview on the "Colbert Report" January 4, 2011, Paul argues "The main reason we want gold is, over six thousand years gold has always been picked over paper. Paper is always destroyed. There has been no example of paper lasting for long, long periods of time. Money has always evolved out of the marketplace of something of real value."
7. Simmel, *The Philosophy of Money*, 176.
8. The inclusion of "In God We Trust" on all currency became required by law in 1955. The national motto first appeared on paper money in 1957 on $1 Silver Certificates, and on all Federal Reserve Notes beginning with Series 196.
9. Simmel argues that trust is necessitated equally in metal coins, as the recipient has no means of testing the validity of the metal upon receipt.
10. Ironically, this style is an adoption of the architectural style of European monarchies which the fledgling democracy so clearly opposed.
11. "Design Competition for the First Series of Euro Banknotes," European Central Bank, accessed March 1, 2013, http://www.ecb.europa.eu/euro/banknotes/html/design.en.html.
12. Peter Eisenman, "RE:RE: Design or Architecture: Wither the Discipline?" *The Cornell Journal of Architecture*, (2011): 179.
13. David Gartman, *From Autos to Architecture: Fordism and Architectural Aesthetics in the Twentieth Century* (Princeton: Princeton Architectural Press, 2009), 323.
14. This claim is made as a response to the avant-garde imagery, and despite Dennis Crompton's insistence on pragmatism and realism. While the projects are developed in many pragmatic ways, including structurally, the author maintains that these projects are primarily visionary, conceptual projects.
15. Christopher Hight, *Architectural Principles in the Age of Cybernetics*, (Routledge, 2008), 43.
16. Simmel, *The Philosophy of Money*, 169.

Survey

One or Several Wolves

1. What is a werewolf,
in the most basic terms?

2. How is the werewolf different from its horror relatives, such as the vampire or Frankenstein's monster?

3. What might werewolves have to do with architecture?

turns

full moon

turn a back

transform

recognizability hybrid

Transformability perception

furriness

teenager

hair

414

crazy

full

architectural, aesthetic, and general

life decisions based on the moon heavy shedders

power

capacity to transform shape

Esra Akcan
1. A werewolf is believed to be a human that turns into a wolf especially during the full moon. In the language that I grew up with, werewolf is translated as Kurt Adam, which can easily be confused with the proper name Kurt Adams in English and German.
2. You can turn a werewolf back to human if you bite and hurt it. It is a creature whose antidote is the same as its virus. You have a better chance to survive if you are attacked by a werewolf.
3. Some architects are like werewolves.

Tei Carpenter
1. A human that can transform into a wolf and vice versa.
2. It's about recognizability. A werewolf is a hybrid and isn't immediately recognizable since it exists as either human or wolf so that it (he/she?) otherwise blends in.
3. Transformability with perception—an architecture that can be doubly read. Maybe furriness?

Josh Greene
1. A werewolf is most likely a teenager and cannot be any older than 21. They have a tremendous amount of hair on the backs of their hands and on their faces. Their hirsute faces cannot be mistaken for your average hipster dude with a beard in say, Portland or Brooklyn. They are really into the moon.
2. They are all about the moon and care tremendously about their clothes. They prefer to wear tight fitting jeans and plaid shirts. They get crazy when the moon is full.
3. This is just a guess, but given their commitment to lunar cycles and all things moon, I am certain that they make a ton of architectural, aesthetic, and general life decisions based on the moon. Additionally, they may be heavy shedders so I imagine that they are concerned about crafting environments that keep the constant hair loss in mind. A lot of non-werewolves get grossed out by hair everywhere and werewolves are sensitive to that.

Javier Hinojosa
1. A werewolf is a man with enormous will and power, his strength is so complete that is compared to the strength of a wolf and usually is feared by its own community.
2. The werewolf is not a horror character, it is a misunderstood man of power in the collective imaginary, just as women of power are called witches.
3. Architecture understood as whole, as a body, has the capacity to transform shape from the interior through will and power used as structures, just as a werewolf.

turns into hybrid full moon
most of the time

transform
full moon

defined by the things around it

hairy, vicious, dog-man super fast
Struggles with self-identity endearing
inevitable lack of control

changes full moon
forced to shapeshift
burden of returning back

metamorphosis (material transformations)
unintended consequences

full moon

never been dead

transforms feral engages with its
environment

combination

Dasha Khapalova
1. A human that turns into a human/wolf hybrid when there is a full moon.
2. For most of the time it's human (which is not the case for vampires, for example, who are always in their "horror" form and are never just human).
3. I guess they also need a place to live.

John Lai
1. It has to do with the moon. Creatures that look like you and me transform into their lunar selves at full moon.
2. A werewolf is a dual creature. The others are always a vampire or a zombie. A werewolf is two, and sometimes they don't even know. Also a werewolf is tragic.
3. A werewolf is defined by the things around it.

Suzanne Lettieri
1. A hairy, vicious, dog-man that can run super fast using its hind legs.
2. Struggles with self-identity in an endearing way (i.e., Remus Lupin).
3. The inevitable lack of control, but recalls what occurred.

Paul Lewis
1. A human who changes into a wolf at night, triggered by a full moon.
2. A werewolf's distinction is its ability (or curse) of being forced to shapeshift, and the burden of returning back to human form to witness the consequences of its actions.
3. Parallels might exist with issues of metamorphosis (material transformations), and the fear of facing the unintended consequences of what one has wrought.

James Lowder
1. Somebody who is normal most of the time, but then when there's a full moon becomes a wolf.
2. The four big ones are the werewolf, the vampire, Frankenstein's monster, and the mummy, which is a particular case of zombie. Unlike the other three, a werewolf has never been dead. Vampire is dead in a coffin, Frankenstein's monster is parts of dead people sewn together, and zombies are dead-undead.
3. Buildings might begin to be throught of as werewolves. Due to cyclical external pressures, architecture transforms into something more feral and engages with its environment in a different manner. Alternatively we could think about architecture for the werewolf, a wild post-human subject that architecture needs to accommodate.

Andrew Lucia
1. A werewolf is a half-human half-animal (human-beast) creature that is a combination of a human and a wolf. Although human for most of its outward life,

transforms full moon

transformer

Michael J. Fox Michael Jackson

morphology and appearance from one state to the next do to contextual stimuli

architecture that adapts its morphology or appearance to contextual constraints and input through time

triggered

transform voracious external stimulus

contingency

internal struggle

Michael J. Fox

different states

provoking alternative and unforeseen outcomes

good guys

wholesome lad with good intentions

banging into the ground

extra hair

sharp teeth bloodshot eyes run around

bitten

superpowers

the creature transforms into a werewolf upon exposure to a full moon.
2. A werewolf is a transformer, and so is similar in kind to a vampire who can transform into a bat (if one is so inclined to believe in that mythology). On the contrary, Frankenstein's monster is an assemblage and does not transform into anything.
3. I'm not entirely sure, but both Michael J. Fox and Michael Jackson are coming to mind. Joking aside, as transformers, werewolves act to seamlessly change their morphology and appearance from one state to the next do to contextual stimuli. This transformation of the human-beast brought on by external stimuli could be taken as a corollary or model for an architecture that adapts its morphology or appearance to contextual constraints and input through time.

Ryan Ludwig
1. A werewolf is both man and beast—the seemingly mundane individual triggered to transform into a voracious creature by external stimulus.
2. Werewolves are elusive, hidden, repressed, and even tortured, bonded to a contingency they cannot reign into control. Most, if not all other horror relatives are self-serving, out for blood, destruction, or vengeance. The werewolf's erratic behavior is borne out of an internal struggle with the self, an interior battle against that which cannot be tamed. Unlike his horror relatives, the werewolf can also be fun, even a hero like Michael J. Fox's character in the 1985 film *Teenwolf*.
3. Perhaps the werewolf could be a good model for architecture. Operating along the edge of different states, triggered by stimuli into transformation toward various orders of unmitigated emotion capable of provoking alternative and unforeseen outcomes.

Aleksandr Mergold
In Russian folklore, these creatures are the good guys, literally—something along the lines of "the werewolf banged himself into the ground and became a "**добрый молодец**" (AKA, a wholesome lad with good intentions) and saved the day." So I have a hard time relating these things to the horror relatives as you suggest. As far as Architecture goes—well, there is that banging into the ground part.

Martin Miller
1. A man or a woman who during the full moon grows a lot of extra hair and their face becomes like a dog's with sharp teeth and bloodshot eyes and they run around trying to catch people and turn them into a werewolf.
2. It's similar to a vampire in that it has to be bitten to become what it is. It has different goals: it doesn't want to suck blood, it's just angry at the moon. It's different in its superpowers: it has the superhuman strenth of the hulk, and like the hulk, it's

exhausted and confused

wild full moon

lives in the forest part man part wolf pointy teeth strong and vicious

dirty animals
skulking

actually exist

420

Teen

rather be part wolf

transformation
dueling identities

turns nights full moon
no control
phase of the moon

always exhausted and confused about what happened: there is some memory loss that goes with that frantic wolfing about.
3. Their transformation is contexual. Some people in architecture are interested in that.

Pauline Morrow

1. A mythical ferocious wild creature that comes out at full moon and eats people. Seen in scary movies.
2. It howls, lives in the forest, is part man part wolf, has big pointy teeth. Very strong and vicious.
3. It would force people to lock themselves in a building, afraid to come out. Forest habitat can be used for building.

Ben Nicholson

1. Werewolves are dirty animals, not very good at keeping their coats clean. Facial expressions are in the skulking category, all the time, as they always eat something that they know they should not have, like babies out of prams and crows eating roadkill. Their howl is not quite as blood curdling as a coyote's.
2. Vampires and Frankenstein's monster are not real, they are mythical creatures, whereas werewolves actually exist.
3. Not much. They might be hanging around diabetes hospital dumpsters sniffing out sawn-off legs or in handkerchief gardens looking for human veal—babies in prams—their favorite. They rarely go into cities, as no one would take them seriously. They enjoy the company of alligators and crocodiles on beaches.

William O'Brien, Jr.

1. Honestly, I only think of Michael J. Fox and *Teen Wolf*. I was seven when that movie came out and with older sisters who had posters of MJF on their walls, it is the image that comes to mind given any mention of werewolves … or teen-werewolves, as it were.
2. Way better than any of those other ones … I'd much rather be part wolf than part bat.
3. I suppose notions of "transformation" and architecture's potential to contain dueling identities comes to mind.

Fergal O'Donnell

1. A werewolf is a person who turns into a wolf-like creature on nights with a full moon.
2. The werewolf has no control over its transformation to/from wolf and human. This is dependent upon the phase of the moon.

faster

social packs

transform full moon
bites

bites

strong

half half
every 28 days
change depending on changes around them
422

full moon

transforms only during a full moon

something most of the time
something else occasionally

unibrow extra furry sharp teeth

full moon

night
fur

3. Wolves have different skills than humans. They run faster, and they have a very well developed sense of smell. Wolves also have similarities with humans. Wolves are monogamous for life, but they are social animals, moving and living in family packs. These characteristics can influence the architect's vision.

Christopher Pickles *(Age 8)*
1. An animal that you can get bitten by. When you get bitten, you automatically transform into one when there is a full moon.
2. It bites people and has a more harmful bite than a vampire. Werewolves can bite you anywhere on the body. It could give you rabies.

Milly Pickles *(Age 13)*
1. A mythical dog-like creature that bites humans.
2. It is dog-like, most others are human-like.
3. Werewolves are known for being strong, (architecture is meant to be strong).

Paula Pickles
1. A mythical creature that is half-wolf and half-man.
2. It only appears every 28 days. Its horror relatives are always ready to pounce.
3. They change, and appear different, depending on changes around them. No one really understands either (except other architects and werewolves).

Shane Pickles
1. A mythical creature that is human until a full moon shines, then it turns into a wolf-like humanoid.
2. It transforms into the monster only during a full moon whereas the others are always monsters.
3. Architecture is designed to be something most of the time but can transform into something else occasionally.

Dillon Pranger
1. Half man, with a unibrow. Half extra furry dog, with really sharp teeth.
2. Werewolves don't have any really great superpowers, they're essentially just big dogs that come out during a full moon. Vampires can fly, Frankenstein's monster is undead/immortal …
3. Everyone (thing) needs a place to live.

Jenny Sabin
1. A werewolf is a human-dog and a dog-human of the night.
2. A werewolf has fur.

of the landscape

part part

divide natural/wild cultural/tame

have never been modern

architecture is part culture part nature

more

wild more threatening

as if it were a wolf has-been

transformation I wish I were sometimes

ambitions powers

changes

at night

split personality

transforms

full moon

scary transformations

3. They are of the landscape, not dwelling.

David Salomon

1. A werewolf is a creature who is part human, part wolf.
2. Werewolves are unique monsters because they are part animal, part human. As such they challenge the divide between the natural/wild and cultural/tame realms. You might say that werewolves have never been modern.
3. Hmmm. Like werewolves, architecture is part culture part nature, though it likes to think it is only the former. It would be interesting if architecture was a little more wild, a little more threatening, like a werewolf. Too much culture and not enough nature can make for a timid discipline.

Peter Stec

1. Were-wolf: as if it were a wolf, at night. A has-been wolf too, perhaps. Cursed both ways, to initiate the transformation. I wish I were a wolf, sometimes. But in reality both human and lupine, wer-wulf.
2. Clearly, different animals—different fears: of contagious bites, out of control ambitions, transformations into vast powers. Different genealogies as well: resurrection and un-death, recursive creativity, cross-speciation—the Plague, the Golem, the *Metamorphosis*.
3. Some, Wolf, are becoming architects in the daytime. "Architects are dog breeders" is a memorable lecture by Prix. If casting architectures as werewolves, would the Coop Himmelblau projects *Falkestrasse*, *Pavilion 21*, or *Confluences* make the cut?

John Zissovici *(possible vampire)*

1. Are you asking me because I am a vampire? The werewolf is a human that changes into a wolf at night.
2. He has a split personality, the others don't.
3. I'm too angry to talk about that.

Zikowwwic

1. Child, don't be afraid; a werewolf is a mere fantasy creature that transforms from person to wolf, usually during full moon.
2. It is presumably harder to spot, as it is only active one night a month.
3. At times, both experience scary transformations (which additionally also hurt a little).

Afterword

Cynthia Davidson

426

If an afterword were just that, a single word after some thing or some event, then allow me to choose just one for this volume titled *Werewolf*.

So.

What? you might ask. Think of the particle's many forms—adverb, conjunction, adjective, pronoun, even its occasional masquerade as the fifth note on the major scale (that is, as a noun) or appearance as an abbreviation. *So* is the ultimate lingual transformer: Do you really think so? So much to do. You did so say it. So what!

But my use of *so* here comes from the Irish poet Seamus Heaney's translation, in 2000, of the epic poem *Beowulf*—not a werewolf, but not without resonance. The first word of the Anglo-Saxon in which *Beowulf* was written, which scholars estimate was between the mid-seventh century and end of the tenth, is *Hwaet*. As Heaney explains in his introduction to the translation, previous translators have interpreted this word as "lo," "behold," and even "listen," among other words. Being Irish, Heaney brought another language to bear: "In Hiberno-English Scullionspeak, the particle 'so' came naturally to the rescue, because in that idiom 'so' operates as an expression which obliterates all previous discourse and narrative, and at the same time functions as an exclamation calling for immediate attention. So, 'so' it was."[1]

I, too, offer *so* in the spirit of obliterating all previous discourse and narrative, of sweeping out the stories that come before this one, to start again, at the end, with the possibility of another narrative, another transformation or translation of lunacy, shapeshifting, and material metamorphosis embedded not only in the work of CODA but also in the language used to describe that work. Even the language used to describe this book. Hidden in footnote ten of the Introduction, for example, O'Donnell and Ibarra write: "If a manifesto is a mission statement and a monograph is the study of a body of work, then this is both and neither a manifesto and a monograph; a monographic manifesto, or, perhaps, a monofesto, a manigraph, or a festigraph." Ugly terms, all of them, at first reading (as an editor/writer, I struggle not to suggest "improvements"). But such transformations and the acceptance of ugly as a possible outcome are at the heart of CODA's philosophy.

Transformation, however, does not always produce ugly nor produce monsters. Arresting, perhaps unfathomable, but not ugly. *Combust*, for example, the

"architectural bust" CODA produced in 2015 for the Los Angeles exhibition "Bust," is such a transformation. The generic bust of base, neck, and head was rotated and elongated to produce a form that seemed to metamorphose the long neck of an Amedeo Modigliani portrait with the mouth in Edvard Munch's *The Scream*, and then make a passing reference to Meret Oppenheim's *Object*. The resulting form's thin skin was punctured and punctuated with wooden matches, expanding its presence with what seemed to be a porcupine-like array of sticks until one peered into the mouth and saw the matches' red tips, which, O'Donnell writes, were "always threatening to combust and cause the [gallery smoke-detector] to sound." Threatening, but not a monster. Simply unfamiliar, even beautiful.

Aligned with the other commissioned architectural busts, each exhibited on a traditional gallery pedestal, *Combust* was decidedly different, negotiating the divide between the art of the bust and the sign of architecture to produce neither. After the exhibition, *Combust* was ignited, teasing a fire alarm to sound, and then disappeared in a cloud of smoke only to emerge as an ashy husk. The trace of its transformation, like that of several other CODA works that involve fire, is recorded here, reifying the importance of the book, not just in poetry, but in architecture.

It is a fire-breathing dragon that leads to the warrior Beowulf's demise, but not before he has slain the "man-eating monster" called Grendel and then beheaded Grendel's vicious mother in a battle to the death. Mother and son, in Heaney's translation, are the subject of "the country people's tales about the monsters."

> *. . . One of these things*
> *as far as anyone ever can discern,*
> *looks like a woman; the other, warped*
> *in the shape of a man, moves beyond the pale*
> *bigger than any man, an unnatural birth*
> *called Grendel by country people*
> *in former days. They are fatherless creatures,*
> *and their whole ancestry is hidden in a past*
> *of demons and ghosts. They dwell apart*
> *among wolves on the hills, on windswept crags*
> *and treacherous keshes, where cold streams*

pour down the mountain and disappear
under mist and moorland.[2]

This narrative, handed down for centuries, translated multiple times by those who can still read Anglo-Saxon, or Old English, has itself been transformed over time. The most recent translation, by Maria Dahvana Headley and published in 2020, once again reconsiders that important opening word, *hwaet.* As Irina Dumitrescu writes in the *New York Review of Books*, Headley's translation of the word "lobs the poem into contemporary slang like a ping pong ball into a red Solo cup: 'Bro.'"[3]

I began this afterword by reaching back to a centuries' old reference. Similarly, O'Donnell and Ibarra cite Alberti—that ever-present presence in architecture—clearly reconsidering the architect's warning, in the *Ten Books of Architecture*, that the "errors of excess" could produce a "monster with limbs disproportionate." In responding to Alberti and other historical precedents, the authors' own contemporary slang may be their reference to the Shakira song *She Wolf*—"There's a she-wolf in disguise, / coming out, coming out, coming out." *Werewolf* is not so much a transformation of the past as it is a new interpretation grounded in the realities of the present. In other words, this "festograph" is a bit like a ping pong ball in a red Solo cup. It is also a "lo," a "behold," a "listen."

So. Always starting over again.

Notes

Foreword

Peter Eisenman

[1] Peter Eisenman, in an initial conversation about the book with Caroline O'Donnell & José Ibarra.

[2] Shape-shifting sounds semantic to me. Form is absolutely different.

[3] Ferdinand de Saussure, *Course in General Linguistics*, trans. Wade Baskin (New York: New York Philosophical Library, 1916), 121–22.

[4] Jacques Derrida, "*Signature Event Context*," in *Limited Inc* (Evanston: Northwestern University Press, 1988), 3.

Introduction

Caroline O'Donnell and José Ibarra

[1] Robert Bloch, "The Man Who Cried 'Wolf!'" *Weird Tales* 38, no. 5 (May 1945).

[2] The werewolf, in literature, is not exclusively male, as the quote from Robert Bloch's "The Man Who Cried 'Wolf!'" exemplifies (see note 1). The earliest literary mention of a she-werewolf is in Gerald of Wales's twelfth-century *Topographia Hiberniae,* in which a female is part of a wolf-couple. In 1839, a female werewolf appears in *The Phantom Ship* by Frederick Marryat and in 1896, the title character of *The Were-wolf* by Clemence Housman, a female writer, is a disarmingly beautiful woman dressed in white furs. Today, she-werewolves are gaining a stronger foothold in popular culture: *Monster High* by Lisi Harrison, *Lonely Werewolf Girl* by Martin Millar, *Maneater by* Thomas Emson, *Otherworld* by Kelley Armstrong, and *The Wolves of Mercy Falls* by Maggie Stiefvater, to name a few in literature; *Ginger Snaps* (2000, directed by John Fawcett) in film; the character of Debbie Pelt in *True Blood* (HBO, seasons 3-5) in television; and more. In the 2009 song, *Loba,* Shakira sings, "A domesticated girl, that's all you ask of me, darling it's no joke, it's lycanthropy." Female writers of werewolf tales have been similarly present. In fact, one of the earliest and most influential werewolf novels, *Bisclavret,* was written (transcribed from folklore) by medieval poet Marie de France (1160 to 1215), although in this case, her wolf was male. While the werewolf in literature has been predominantly male, the creature's lunar cycle and relationship to the moon confirms the werewolf of this book to be a she.

[3] Hannah Priest, "Introduction," in *She-Wolf: A Cultural History of Female Werewolves,* ed. Hannah Priest (Manchester: Manchester University Press, 2015), 1.

[4] Christa Agnes Tuczay, "Into the Wild – Old Norse Stories of Animal Men," in *Werewolf Histories,* ed. Willem de Blécourt (London: Palgrave Macmillan, 2015), 64.

[5] Snorri Sturluson, *Heimskringla,* ed. Erling Monsen, trans. A. H. Smith (Cambridge: Heffer & Sons, Ltd, 1932), 64.

[6] Guillaume de Lavigne, *Les Chiens célèbres, réels et fictifs, dans l'Art, la Culture et l'Histoire* (Raleigh: Lulu Press, 2015), 62.

[7] Herbert de Vries, "Werewolves: A Reconsideration of Hobbes's State of Nature from the Perspective of Biopolitics," in *The Animal Inside: Essays at the Intersection of Philosophical Anthropology and Animal Studies,* eds. Geoffrey Dierckxsens, Rudmer Bijlsma, Michael Begun, and Thomas Kiefer (London: Rowman & Littlefield, 2017), 153.

[8] de Vries, "Werewolves," 154.

[9] Brian J. Frost, *The Essential Guide to Werewolf Literature* (Madison: University of Wisconsin Press, 2003), 6.

[10] If a manifesto is a mission statement and a monograph is the study of a body of work, then this is both and neither a manifesto and a monograph; a monographic manifesto, or, perhaps, a monofesto, a manigraph, or a festigraph.

[11] de Vries, "Werewolves," 154.

From Caged Human to Cageless Monster

Caroline O'Donnell and José Ibarra

[1] Vitruvius, *The Ten Books on Architecture*, trans. Morris Hicky Morgan (Cambridge: Harvard University Press, 1914), 1.

[2] Aristotle, *Poetics*, 1459 a20, trans. Ingram Bywater (Overland Park: Digireads Publishing, 2017), 37. Cf. also Vickers (1989), 345, who gives a list of organic unity in classical works. A similar position is displayed in Plato's writing of Socrates's belief that a speech "should be like a living being, with a body of its own, as it were, and neither headless or feetless, with a middle and with members adapted to each other and to the whole." See Plato, *Phaedrus*, 264c, trans. Benjamin Jowett.

[3] Vitruvius, *Ten Books on Architecture*, 72.

[4] See Caroline van Eck, *Organicism in Nineteenth-century Architecture: An Inquiry Into Its Theoretical and Philosophical Background* (Architectura & Natura Press, 1994), 42. The text references Francesco di Giorgio Martini, *Trattato di architettura, ingegneria e arte militare* (Turin), 1481-84.

[5] Le Corbusier, *The Modulor: A Harmonious Measure to the Human Scale Universally Applicable to Architecture and Mechanics*, trans. P. de Francia and A. Bostock (London: Faber & Faber, 1956), 37.

[6] Jacques Derrida, *The Animal that Therefore I Am*, ed. Marie-Louise Mallet, trans. David Wills (New York: Fordham University Press, 2008), 29.

[7] Kari Weil, *Thinking Animals: Why Animal Studies Now?* (New York: Columbia University Press, 2012), 13.

[8] Manfredo Tafuri, *Interpreting the Renaissance: Princes, Cities, Architects* (New Haven: Yale University Press, 2006). Extracted from Ingraham, *Architecture, Animal, Human*, 19.

[9] Leon Battista Alberti, *The Ten Books of Architecture*, trans. J. Leoni, (New York: Dover Publications, 1986), quoted in Catherine Ingraham, *Architecture, Animal, Human: The Asymmetrical Condition* (New York: Routledge, 2006), 183

[10] Caroline van Eck, *Organicism in Nineteenth-century Architecture: An Inquiry Into Its Theoretical and Philosophical Background* (Amsterdam: Architectura & Natura Press, 1994), 48.

[11] Aside from the evolutionary revolution, the animal's challenging of the human could not have been possible without the destabilization of notions of objective beauty found in the aesthetic theories of David Hume, as well as William Hogarth and Edmund Burke.

[12] Catherine Ingraham, *Architecture, Animal, Human: The Asymmetrical Condition* (New York: Routledge, 2006), 224.

[13] Leon Battista Alberti, *The Ten Books of Architecture*, trans. J. Leoni, (New York: Dover Publications, 1986), 13–14.

[14] For instance, Susan Doubilet called the Neue Staatsgalerie a "'faceless' monster, a grotesque exotic animal." See Susan Doubilet, "The Talk of the Town," *Progressive Architecture* 10 (1984): 74. Similarly, self-proclaimed architecture critic, Prince Charles, referred to Peter Ahrends's design for the extension to the National Gallery in London as a "monstrous carbuncle on the face of a much-loved and elegant friend." See Alastair Jamieson, "The Prince of Wales on architecture: his 10 'monstrous carbuncles,'" *The Telegraph* (May 13, 2009).

[15] In his "Aphorisms on the Composition of the Primary History" (1620), Francis Bacon separates nature into three parts: Species, Monsters, and Artificial; or by another set of names: liberty, errors, and bonds. The first and last are described plainly enough: as free and developing ordinarily, and as constrained and molded by human intervention, respectively. The monsters' description, however, is more arresting: the monster is "forced out of her proper state by the perverseness and insubordination of matter and the violence of impediments." That is to say, monsters are so erroneous as to exist separately, outside the "proper" category of the species. They are no longer a bad copy of a platonic model, but, beyond simply a variation, monsters have crossed into another realm.

[16] Reiser + Umemoto, *Atlas of Novel Tectonics* (Princeton: Princeton Architectural Press, 2006), 85.

[17] Erwin Panowsky, "The History of the Theory of the Proportions as a reflection of the History of

Styles." Extracted from Greg Lynn, "Body Matters," *Folds, Bodies and Blobs* (Brussels: La Lettre Volée, 2004), 141.

[18] Today mutations are understood as the basis of evolution. In evolutionary terms, the monster or mutation is exactly that which makes steps, whether large or small, toward a more symbiotic or "hopeful" relationship with its environment. The term "hopeful monster" was coined by Richard Goldschmidt and has been written about in the chapter "Hopeful Monsters," in Caroline O'Donnell, *Niche Tactics: Generative Relationships between Architecture and Site* (New York: Routledge, 2015), 186–206.

[19] In some cases, this multiplicity also comes as one species inside another, as is the case with the Werewolves of Ossory.

[20] Weil, *Thinking Animals*, 15.

[21] Sanford Kwinter, *Architectures of Time: Toward a Theory of the Event in Modernist Culture* (Cambridge: MIT Press, 2002), 4.

[22] Kwinter, *Architectures of Time*, 4.

[23] *The Wolf Man*, directed by George Waggner, written by Curt Siodmak, (Universal, 1941).

[24] The vampire, often considered a relative of the werewolf, is in some narratives prone to transform their incisors by the scent of blood of a nearby, juicy human. Meanwhile, the Incredible Hulk transforms due to the stimulus of anger. While these stimuli may be said to be external, there is also an internal emotional condition that is the true trigger. This is not the case with the werewolf who transforms regardless of emotion.

[25] Arbiter Petronius, *Satyricon* (Cambridge: Harvard University Press, 1975).

[26] The return to human form can be triggered by diving into water or rolling over and over in dew, kneeling in one spot for one hundred years, and so on. See Brian J. Frost, *The Essential Guide to Werewolf Literature* (Madison: University of Wisconsin Press, 2003), 9.

[27] Other transformations that take place in the book are due to evil pacts and spells.

[28] Count Eric Stenbock, "The Spirit Lamp" in *Periodica,* June, 1893.

[29] Reflection in water recurs in the werewolf fiction, including the film *Curse of the Werewolf,* Terence Fisher (Director) Hammer Films, 1961.

[30] *The Wolf Man*, Wagner.

[31] See informal survey at the end of this book.

[32] Riva, M. A.; Tremolizzo, L.; Spicci, M; Ferrarese, C.; De Vito, G.; Cesana, G. C.; Sironi, V. A., "The Disease of the Moon: The Linguistic and Pathological Evolution of the English Term 'Lunatic,'" *Journal of the History of the Neurosciences* 20, no. 1 (January 2011): 65–73.

[33] R.D. Laing, *The Divided Self: An Existential Study in Sanity and Madness* (London: Penguin Books, 1960), 68–69.

[34] Timothy Morton, *Hyperobjects: Philosophy and Ecology after the End of the World* (Minneapolis: University of Minnesota Press, 2013), 27–28.

[35] Morton, *Hyperobjects*, 27–31.

[36] Gilles Deleuze and Félix Guattari, *Kafka: Toward a Minor Literature,* trans. Dana Polan (Minneapolis: University of Minnesota Press, 1987), 22.

[37] Morton, *Hyperobjects*, 65.

[38] George W.M. Reynolds, *Wagner, the Wehr-Wolf* (New York: Cosimo, Incorporated, 2008), 64. Originally published 1857.

[39] Gerald of Wales, *The History and Topography of Ireland,* trans. O'Meara (London: Penguin Classics, 1983), *143–44*.

[40] Coined in 1852 in an anonymous critique of the work of Claude-Nicolas Ledoux. The critique was written for *Magasin Pittoresque* in 1852 and entitled "Etudes d'architecture en France."

[41] Germain Boffrand, *Livre d'Architecture contenant les Principes Generaux de cet Art* (Paris: Guillaume Cavelier Père, 1745), 11.

[42] Even before he became associated with Jacques Derrida, Eisenman's syntactical thinking was founded on Colin Rowe's notion that architecture was like a code that could be deciphered. Rowe too understood architectural form as "a continuous dialectic between fact and implication." That is to say that beyond the *real* building, there was a *virtual* building—*literal* and *phenomenal,* in Rowe's own terms—a phantom, constructed by the reading subject, (a theory that echoes Vitruvius's original statement on the sign and the signified). See: Colin Rowe & Robert Slutzky, "Transparency: Literal and Phenomenal," in *Perspecta* 8 (1963): 45–54.

[43] Rosalind Krauss, "Death of a Hermeneutic Phantom: Materialization of the Sign in the Work of Peter Eisenman," *House of Cards,* (Oxford: Oxford University Press, 1987), 174–75.

[44] Peter Eisenman, "The End of the Classical: the End of the Beginning, the End of the End," *Perpspecta* 21 (1984): 154–73.

[45] Bruce Elliot, "Wolves Don't Cry," in *Triple W: Witches, Warlocks, and Werewolves*, ed. Rod Serling (New York: Bantam, 1967).

[46] Brian J. Frost, *The Essential Guide to Werewolf Literature* (Madison: University of Wisconsin Press, 2003), 13.

[47] Robert Louis Stevenson, *The Strange Case of Dr. Jekyll and Mr. Hyde* (London: Longman, 1886), 9.

[48] Stephen King, *Danse Macabre* (New York: Everest House, 1981), 72.

[49] Juhani Pallasmaa, *The Eyes of the Skin: Architecture and the Senses* (London: Wiley, 2005), 11.

[50] "She Wolf," Spotify, track 1 on Shakira, *She Wolf,* Epic Records, 2009. The song was written by Shakira, John Hill, and Sam Endicott. Originally a Spanish language song called "Loba," with additional lyrical contributions by Jorge Drexler.

[51] Clemence Housman, *The Were-wolf* (New York: Arno Press, 1976).

[52] See Caroline O'Donnell, "Duck Jokes," in *Niche Tactics: Generative Relationships between Architecture and Site* (New York: Routledge, 2015), 155–73.

[53] Giorgio Agamben, *Homo Sacer* (Palo Alto, CA: Stanford University Press, 1998), *105.*

[54] Agamben, *Homo Sacer*, 105.

[55] Herbert De Vriese, "Werewolves: A Reconsideration of Hobbes's State of Nature from the Perspective of Biopolitics," in *The Animal Inside: Essays at the Intersection of Phliosophical Anthropology and Animal Studies,* ed. Geoffrey Dierckxsens, Rudmer Bijlsma, Michael Begun, and Thomas Kiefer (London: Rowman & Littlefield, 2017), 154.

From Strategy to Tactic

Caroline O'Donnell and José Ibarra

[1] Reyner Banham, Studio Brief, School of Architecture and Environmental Design, SUNY AB, Department of Design Studies, DSN 230: Architecture and Environmental Design: History and Concepts. From the Banham Archives, Buffalo. Remembered incorrectly by James Lowder in conversation with Caroline O'Donnell in January, 2018. The actual text reads: "A building is one way to solve a comfort-problem. It can keep the rain off your head or spears out of your back. It is also an expensive, but rather permanent, way of solving problems that might have been solved by simpler, less durable means (like wearing a hat or making a peace treaty with your enemies)." Banham continues by discussing the "commitment," "values," "legacies," "records," "ideals," and stories embodied in the solidity of architecture.

[2] Reyner Banham, "A *Home* Is *Not* a *House*," *Art in America* (April 1965): 70.

[3] "The mechanical invasion is a fact and architects—especially American architects—sense that it is a cultural threat to their position in the world." See Banham, "A *Home* Is *Not* a *House*," 70.

[4] Florian Idenburg, Jing Liu, and Ilias Papageorgiou, *Solid Objectives: Order, Edge, Aura* (Switzerland: Lars Müller Publishers, 2017), 479.

[5] Lydia Kallipoliti, "Return to Earth: Feedback Houses," *The Cornell Journal of Architecture*, no. 8 (2010): 115–18.

[6] Cedric Price's *Fun Palace*, another fictional work from the UK in the same period, featured an infinitely reconfigurable series of boxes on tracks, rearrangeable depending on the desired program. In the US, rotating and revolving buildings proliferated in the 1940s and 1950s, most notably with the rotating restaurant phenomenon.

[7] Chip Lord, interview by Rebecca Cleman, *Electronic Arts Intermix*, n.d., http://www.eai.org/resourceguide/exhibition/singlechannel/interview_lord.html

[8] Molly Wright Steenson, *Architectural Intelligence: How Designers and Architects Created the Digital Landscape* (Cambridge: MIT Press, 2017), 131.

[9] John McHale, *The Future of the Future* (New York: George Braziller, 1969), 177–78.

[10] Banham, "A *Home* Is *Not* a *House*," 75.

Perceptual Metamorphoses: Becoming With

Kari Weil

[1] Ursula K. Le Guin, "The Wife's Story." https://frielingretc.files.wordpress.com/2013/03/the-wifes-story-ursula-k.pdf

[2] Jacob von Uexküll, *A Foray into the Worlds of Animals and Humans.* Trans. Joseph D. O'Neil (Minneapolis: University of Minnesota Press, 2010).

[3] Temple Grandin suggests that persons with autism are unable to screen out certain stimuli and thus perceive the world in ways that are closer to some animals. See her *Animals in Translation: Using the Mysteries of Autism to Decode Animal Behavior* (New York: Scribner, 2005), especially Chapter 2.

[4] Wolfgang M. Schleidt, Michael D. Shalter, "Co-evolution of Humans and Canids: An Alternative View of Dog Domestication: Homo Homini Lupus?" in Evolution and Cognition 9, no. 1 (Oxford: Oxford University Press): 57–72.

[5] Franz Kafka, "The Metamorphosis," trans. Willa and Edwin Muir, in *The Complete Stories*, ed. Nahum N. Glatzer (New York: Schocken Books, 1971), 89–139.

[6] Gilles Deleuze & Felix Guattari, "Becoming Animal," in *Animal Philosophy*, ed. Peter Atterton and Matthew Calarco (New York: Continuum, 2004), 88–100.

[7] Deleuze & Guattari, "Becoming Animal," 88.

[8] Franz Kafka, "A Report to an Academy," in *Collected Stories*, ed. Gabriel Josipovici (New York: Knopf, 1993): 195–205.

[9] Such a need to prove his "human" abilities is an interesting foretelling, if not ironic critique, of contemporary animal rights movements that would argue for the legal standing of certain species—especially great apes—on the grounds that they are like us—that they also have consciousness, thought, or language.

[10] Kafka, "A Report to an Academy," 203.

[11] Kafka, "A Report to an Academy," 198.

[12] Kafka, "A Report to an Academy," 199.

[13] Kafka, "A Report to an Academy," 199.

[14] Kafka, "The Metamorphosis," 101.

[15] Kafka, "The Metamorphosis," 115.

[16] Caroline O'Donnell, *Niche Tactics: Generative Relationships Between Architecture and Site* (New York: Routledge, 2015), 24.

[17] Kafka, "The Metamorphosis," 130–31.

[18] Kafka, "The Metamorphosis," 134.

[19] Donna Haraway, *When Species Meet* (Minneapolis: University of Minnesota Press, 2008), 244.

[20] Donna Haraway, *Staying with the Trouble: Making Kin in the Chthulucene* (Durham, NC: Duke University Press, 2016), 4.

[21] R.C. Lewontin, "Gene, organism, and environment," in D.S. Bendall (ed.), *Evolution from molecules to men* (Cambridge: Cambridge University Press, 1983), 273–85. This text is also cited in Kevin Laland and Michael J. O'Brien, "Niche Construction Theory and Archeology, Springer Science and Business Media LLC," 2010, https://pdfs.semanticscholar.org/b88f/eda47a93e873b2464061abc3db9de0a84b9f.pdf

[22] James J. Gibson, *The Ecological Approach to Visual Perception* (Boston: Houghton Mifflin, 1979).

[23] James J. Gibson, *The Ecological Approach to Visual Perception* (New Jersey: Lawrence Erlbaum Assoc. Inc. Publishers, 1986), 7.

[24] See chapter 5, "An Ecological Approach to the Picturesque," in Caroline O'Donnell's *Niche Tactics: Generative Relationships between Architecture and Site* for more on affordance theory in architecture.

[25] Tim Ingold, "Point, Line and Counterpoint," *Being Alive, Essays on Movement, Knowledge and Description* (New York: Routledge, 2011), 79. Makes reference to J. von Uexküll, *The Theory of Meaning*, trans. B. Stone and H. Weiner from Bedeutungsslehre, ed. T.von Uexküll, *Semiotica* 41, 1 (1982), 25–82.

[26] For more on the difference between affordance and Umwelt, see Tim Ingold, "Point, Line and Counterpoint," *Being Alive, Essays on Movement, Knowledge and Description* (New York: Routledge, 2011), 79–80.

[27] Deleuze & Guattari, "Becoming Animal," 96.

Lunar (Re)Turns: Cosmology, Ecology. and Extraterrestrial Influence

Spyros Papapetros

[1] Rudolf Wittkower, "The problem of harmonic proportion in architecture" in *Architectural Principles in the Age of Humanism* (1st edition 1949) (London: A.D. Academy Editions, 1998), 104–53.

[2] Reyner Banham, "The New Brutalism," *The Architectural Review* 118 (December 1955): 354–61.

[3] Alina Payne, "Rudolf Wittkower and Architectural Principles in the Age of Modernism" *Journal of the Society of Architectural Historians* 53 (1994): 322–42; and Spyros Papapetros, "MICRO/MACRO: Architecture, Proportion, and Cosmology in a Modern World," in *PROPORTIO*, ed. Daniela Ferretti et. al. (Ghent: MER. Paper Kunsthalle & Axel and May Vervoordt Foundation), 92–117.

[4] Fritz Saxl, "Microcosm and Macrocosm," in *Lectures* 1 (London: The Warburg Institute, 1957): 58–72.

[5] Aby Warburg, "Pagan-Antique Prophesy in Words and Images in the Age of Luther," in *The Renewal of Pagan Antiquity*, ed. Kurt W. Forster, trans. David Britt (Santa Monica: Getty Research Institute 1999), 597–699.

[6] For a definitive study of this theme in the circle of the Warburg Library, see Raymond Klibansky, Erwin Panofsky and Fritz Saxl, *Saturn and Melancholy: Studies in the History of Natural Philosophy, Religion, and Art* (London: Nelson, 1964).

[7] Warburg's essay was eventually published in 1920 and mentioned with admiration in Binswanger's correspondence with Freud. See *Letter from Ludwig Binswanger to Sigmund Freud* November 8, 1921 (available on Psychoanalytic Electronic Publishing: https://www.pep-web.org/document.php?id=zbk.050.0155b).

[8] Albrecht Dürer, "The Sow of Landser," engraving, 1496, described in Warburg, "Pagan-Antique Prophecy," 637.

[9] Albrecht Dürer, *Melencolia I,* engraving, 1514, described in Warburg, "Pagan-Antique Prophecy," 641–44; for the identification of the lunar rainbow in the background of Dürer's engraving, see Erwin Panofsky, *The Life and Art of Albrecht Dürer* (4th ed.) (Princeton: Princeton University Press, 1955), 156.

[10] Warburg, "Pagan-Antique Prophecy," 650.

[11] To be sure, Wittkower is the co-author of a study on the "influence" of Saturn on artists and their art: Rudolf and Margot Wittkower, *Born Under Saturn. The Character and Conduct of Artists – a Documentary History* (New York: Norton, 1963).

[12] See woodcut drawings on "bloodletting" from a 1499 calendar from Basel and a 1724 *Historienkalendar* from Hamburg in panel B of the *Mnemosyne Atlas,* Aby Warburg: Der Bilderatlas Mnemosyne (Gesammelte Schriften, vol. 2.1), ed. Martin Warnke and Claudia Brink, Berlin 2000, 10–11.

[13] See the entry on "Lunacy" in *The American Cyclopaedia: A Popular Dictionary of General Knowledge* edited by George Ripley and Charles A. Dana, Second edition (1879), Vol. 10, 715–18.

[14] For legal definitions and practices related to lunacy see N. Arthur Haywood and Arnold S. Massey (solicitors), Lunacy Practice (London: Stevens and Sons Law Publishers, 1900).

[15] "House Approves Eliminating 'Lunatic' From Federal Law," *The New York Times*, 5 December 2012.

[16] Joseph Melling and Robert Turner, "The road to the asylum: institutions, distance and the administration of pauper lunacy in Devon, 1845–1914," in *Journal of Historical Geography* 25, no. 3 (1999): 298–332.

[17] Andrea Stone, "Lunacy and Liberation: Black Crime, Disability, and the Production and Eradication of the Early National Enemy" in *Early American Literature* 52:1 (2017): 109–40.

[18] The very identification between the legally proclaimed "lunatic" and the law occurs on the body, or rather "two bodies," of Freud's well-known patient Judge Schreber: on the one hand demonstrably mad exhibiting a series of psychotic behaviors, and on the other assessed capable to adjudicate by a legal panel in spite of his mental infirmity. See, Peter Goodrich "The Judge's Two Bodies: The Case of Daniel Paul Schreber" in *Law Critique* 26 (2015), 117–33.

[19] Lauren Farquharson, "A 'Scottish Poor Law of Lunacy'? Poor Law, Lunacy Law and Scotland's parochial asylums" *History of Psychiatry* 28, no. 1 (2017): 15–28.

[20] See the study of mechanicist Wilhelm Roux on "the strife of parts in the organism: Wilhelm Roux, *Der Kampf der Theile im Organismus. Ein Beitrag zur Vervollständigung der mechanischen Zweckmässigkeitslehre* (Leipzig: Engelmann, 1881).

[21] Charles Darwin, *The Expression of The Emotions in Man and Animals* (London: Murray, 1872), 132–37 and 249–51.

[22] Darwin, *Expression of The Emotions*, 297–98.

[23] For a mid-19th-century overview of werewolf legends, see Sabine Baring-Gould, *The Book of Were-wolves being an account of a terrible superstition* (London: Smith, Elder, and Co., 1865).

[24] See my "Darwin's Dog and the Parasol: Cultural Reactions to Animism," in *e-flux journal* 36, (July 2012).

[25] For a recent clinical view of several historical cases of lycanthropy see Jan Dirk Blom, "When doctors cry wolf: a systematic review of the literature on clinical lycanthropy," *History of Psychiatry* 25, no. 1 (2014): 87–102.

[26] Frederick J. Kiesler, *Magic Architecture. Origin and Future. The Story of Human Housing*, unpublished book manuscript (ca. 1946), Archive of the Austrian Frederick and Lilian Kiesler Private Foundation in Vienna. The first publication of Kiesler's manuscript is forthcoming in an edition by Spyros Papapetros and Gerd Zillner supported by the Kiesler Foundation and published by the MIT Press.

[27] Frederick J. Kielser, drawing (ca. 1944), Archive of the Austrian Frederick and Lilian Kiesler Private Foundation in Vienna, SFP_6615_0.

[28] See my "The Birth of Design" published in the e-flux *Supehumanity* online articles: https://www.e-flux.com/architecture/superhumanity/68709/the-birth-of-design/

[29] See my "Magic Architecture: Caves, Animals, and Tools in the Atomic Era," in *Friedrich Kiesler: Lebenswelten / Frederick Kiesler: Life Visions*, ed. Dieter Bogner, a.o. (Basel: Birkhäuser, 2016), 58–71.

[30] See the conversation between Caroline O'Donell and José Ibarra in this volume.

[31] Mario Carpo, "Introduction" in Bernard Cache, *Projectiles* (London: AA Books, 2011), 5–14.

[32] On the "prerarchitectonic" condition see my "Pre/post/erous histories, or histories and theories of the *prearchitectonic* condition," published in e-flux: https://www.e-flux.com/architecture/history-theory/225184/pre-post-erous-histories/

[33] In addition to the 1951 exhibition *Growth and Form* by Richard Hamilton in London's ICA, see the recent collection of essays edited by Philip Beesley and Sarah Bonnemaison, *On Growth and Form: Organic Architecture and Beyond* (Halifax, NS: Tuns Press and Riverside Architectural Press, 2008).

[34] See among others, Edward Robert De Zurko, *Origins of Functionalist Theory* (New York: Columbia University Press, 1957).

[35] See, for example, the article published in CNN while I was writing this text: "Scientists bid farewell to the first Icelandic glacier lost to climate change. If more melt, it can be disastrous," by Harmeet Kaur, CCN.com, August 18, 2019: https://edition.cnn.com/2019/08/18/health/glaciers-melting-climate-change-trnd/index.html

[36] For an ingenious account of the cataclysmic perspective of the history of architecture, surviving from Biblical times to the Enlightenment and to September 11, see Hubert Damisch, "Prologue: Noah's Ark" in *Noah's Ark: Essays on Architecture*, ed. Anthony Vidler (Cambridge: The MIT Press, 2016), 1–24; and for the first publication of the essay, see Damisch, "L'Arche de Noé," in: *Critique* 476–477 (1987): 5–22.

[37] Narimen Yousfi a, Raouf Nader Rekikb, Cristiano Eirale, a.o: "Lunacy revisited – the myth of the full moon: are football injuries related to the lunar cycle?" *Chronobiology International* 35, no. 10 (2018): 1385–90.

[38] Wally Barr, "Lunacy revisited: The influence of the moon on mental health and the quality of life" in *Journal of Psychosocial Nursing & Mental Health Services* 38, no. 5 (May 2000): 28–35.

[39] Barr, "Lunacy revisited," 30.

[40] Barr, "Lunacy revisited," 30.

[41] For the presence of the "Children of the Planets (*Planetenkinder*)" in Renaissance cosmological iconography and imagination, see again Aby Warburg, "Italian Art and International Astrology in the Palazzo Schifanoia, Ferrara" in *The Renewal of Pagan Antiquity*, 563–92.

Awry of the Plan

Jesse Reiser

[1] Per Philip Guston, this was said to him by John Cage during the 1950s. Guston published this memory in a statement in *It is: A Magazine for Abstract Art* 5 (Spring 1960).

[2] Le Corbusier, *New World of Space* (New York: Reynal and Hitchcock, 1948), 123–24.

[3] Let us not forget the becoming animal, so celebrated by Deleuze, also has a dark side. The SS colonel Otto Skorzeny celebrated these animalistic impulses through the naming of his *Werewolf* band of confederates, who smuggled ex-Nazis out of Europe and South America while promulgating Nazi ideology in the Middle East and elsewhere. He could assign responsibility for his atrocities to an animal spirit rather than himself, denying authorship of his own acts. Something architects reading post-structuralism should keep in mind.

Shape Shifting: Intelligent Animism

Greg Lynn

[1] Greg Lynn, *Animate Form* (New York: Princeton Architectural Press, 1999), 10.

[2] Lynn, *Animate Form*, 10.

[3] Greg Lynn, "Multiplicitous and Inorganic Bodies," in *Folds, Bodies, and Blobs: Collecged Essays* (Brussels: La Lettre Volée, 1998), 34.

[4] Colin Rowe, *The Mathematics of the Ideal Villa, and Other Essays* (Cambridge: MIT Press, 1976).

[5] A version of this diagram had appeared in 1944 in his essay, "Principles of Palladio's Architecture," *Journal of the Warburg and Courtauld Institutes,* 7 (1944), but contained only ten villas and the pattern, and excluded Villa Capra (Rotonda).

[6] Greg Lynn, "Multiplicitous and Inorganic Bodies," 39. See also Greg Lynn, "The Renewed Novelty of Symmetry," in *Folds, Bodies and Blobs*, 76.

[7] Lynn, "Multiplicitous and Inorganic Bodies," 56.

[8] Published originally in *Assemblage* 26:4, and later in Lynn, *Folds, Bodies and Blobs.*

[9] (Touch IOS™)

Hair Dos and Don'ts: A Brick Problem

Jimenez Lai

[1] Not everything is about Michael Meredith—in this case, low- and high- resolution simply refer to an image's readability at multiple scales, its sharp details, dots per inch (DPI), and verisimilitude.

[2] The more recent production's photorealistic depiction of *The Lion King* has been criticized by many for lacking the character's ability to emote. Perhaps, with the loss of abstraction, something more was lost. Meanwhile, in the low-tech 1994 analogue, the fur-as-surface lion gains in character what it lacks in resolution. See Roger Eber (https://www.rogerebert.com/reviews/the-lion-king-2019) and Molly Freeman (https://screenrant.com/lion-king-2019-movie-reviews/).

[3] James J. Gibson, in *The Ecological Approach to Visual Perception* (New York, NY: Psychology Press, 2013), 156.

[4] In fact, the film renders 600 million strands of hair in total (on 9,063 characters of 63 species). See: Insider, "How 'The Lion King' Remake Was Animated | Movies Insider," YouTube video, 10:54, August 29, 2019, https://youtu.be/DlJkEe315mM

[5] Jason Payne, "Hair and Make," in *Log* 17: Superficial, guest ed. Mark Foster Gage and Florencia Pita (Fall 2009).

[6] In his SCI-Arc exhibition opening discussion with Eric Owen Moss, Payne had to defend questions about a potentially postmodern vernacular whole that he did not intend to do. The meta-brick was the project, not the accidental house.

[7] Robert E. Somol, "12 Reasons to Get Back into Shape," in *Content: OMA/AMO, Rem Koolhaas*, ed. Rem Koolhaas (London: Taschen, 2004), 86.

[8] Somol, "12 Reasons," 86.

Afterword

Cynthia Davidson

[1] Seamus Heaney, "Introduction," in *Beowulf*, trans. Seamus Heaney (New York: W.W. Norton & Company, 2000), xxvii.

[2] Heany, "Introduction," 95.

[3] Irina Dumitrescu, "Dudes Without Heirs," *New York Review of Books* (December 3, 2020).

Competition Phase for PS1/MoMA Young Architects' Program, Rand Hall, January 2013.

Urchin, 2016, under construction. Photograph by Thomas J. Campanella.

Office, 2018, working three times as hard. **Photograph by Robert Balder.**

Editors

Caroline O'Donnell is an architect, educator, and writer. She is the sole principal of CODA—an internationally recognized practice focusing on the application of ecological thinking through form, systems, and materials—and an occasional collaborator with OMG. O'Donnel is an associate professor, holding the Edgar A. Tafel Professorship, and chair of the department of architecture at Cornell University, and recently a visiting associate professor at Harvard GSD. She holds a B.Arch from Manchester University (2000) and a Post-Professional M.Arch from Princeton University (2004). She was the editor-in-chief of the *Cornell Journal of Architecture* (2009–2017), and co-founder of *Pidgin* magazine. Her book, *Niche Tactics: Generative Relationships between Architecture and Site* (Routledge, 2015), describes a design agenda that looks toward natural and local resources to produce meaningful architecture. O'Donnell has also co-edited and contributed to *This is Not a Wall* (AAP/Actar, 2017) and *Design for a Circular Economy: The Architecture of Waste* (with Dillon Pranger, Routledge, 2020), as well as numerous publications and exhibitions worldwide.

José Ibarra is an architectural designer, researcher, and educator whose interdisciplinary work focuses on the intersection between architecture and environmental uncertainty. He is an assistant professor of architecture at the University of Virginia, director of transformation and research of CODA, and was formerly the 2019–2020 Urban Edge Fellow at the University of Wisconsin-Milwaukee. Ibarra holds a B.Arch from Cornell University and a Post-Professional M.Arch from Princeton University, where he received a Certificate in Media and Modernity, and was awarded the 2019 Robert Geddes Post-Professional Award and the 2018 Howard Crosby Butler Fellowship. Ibarra's work comprises curation and editing, most recently having co-curated *TOO FAST TOO SLOW*, and edited the UVA *Architecture Reading Group* series, *Pidgin* magazine, and the *Cornell Journal of Architecture*. Ibarra's work has been published and exhibited at several global venues of art and architecture.

Contributors

Cynthia Davidson is an architecture editor, writer, and critic based in New York City. She is the founding editor of *Log: Observations on Architecture and the Contemporary City* as well as the *ANY* series of conferences and publications. She was co-curator of the American Pavilion at the Venice Architecture Biennial in 2014.

Peter Eisenman is a world-renowned architect and educator. He has designed a number of structures throughout the world, including the Memorial to the Murdered Jews of Europe in Berlin, the City of Culture of Galicia, Santiago de Compostela in Galicia, the Wexner Center for the Arts in Columbus, OH, among others. Eisenman currently teaches architecture at Yale University.

Jimenez Lai works in the world of art, culture, and education. Before founding Bureau Spectacular, Lai worked for various international offices, including MOS and OMA. Lai is widely exhibited and published around the world, including the MoMA-collected White Elephant. His first book, *Citizens of No Place*, was published by Princeton Architectural Press with a grant from the Graham Foundation. Lai has won various awards, including the Architectural League Prize for Young Architects and Debut Award at the Lisbon Triennale, and the 2017 Designer of the Future Award at Art Basel / Design Miami. Alongside MoMA, Lai's work has been collected by SFMOMA, Art Institute of Chicago, and LACMA.

Greg Lynn is an innovator in redefining the medium of design with digital technology as well as pioneering the fabrication and manufacture of complex functional and ergonomic forms using CNC (Computer Numerically Controlled) machinery. The buildings, projects, publications, teachings, and writings associated with his office have been influential in the acceptance and use of advanced materials and technologies for design and fabrication. As design opportunities today extend across multiple scales and media, his studio Greg Lynn FORM continues to define the cutting edge of design in a variety of fields. His work is in the permanent collections of the most important design and architecture museums in the world including the CCA, SFMoMA, ICA Chicago and MoMA. He is a Studio Professor at UCLA's school of Architecture and Urban Design where he is currently spearheading the development of an experimental research robotics lab.

Martin Miller is primarily concerned with how the digital onslaught will define our future realities, both physical and virtual. He is an assistant professor of the practice at Cornell University, an occasional collaborator with OMG, and the cofounder of the design office AntiStatics Architecture based in Beijing and New York City. Defining a mantra which is ever adaptive to emerging technologies, AntiStatics' work seeks to find a balance between our convergent existences. Recent works include *MaoHaus*, a thin-shell concrete façade with hidden embedded imagery; *Pussy Hut*, an inhabitable pussy hat that's a tribute and monument to the Women's Rights movement; and CatenAIRies, a responsive installation provoking the impact of air as a driver for spatial definition. Miller received his master of architecture from the University of Pennsylvania after receiving a B.F.A. in sculpture with

a minor in mathematics. He currently teaches graduate studios as well as seminars focused on the implementation of computational design techniques including artificial intelligence, simulation, and robotic fabrication.

Spyros Papapetros is an art and architectural historian and theorist whose work focuses on the historiography of art and architecture, the intersections between architecture and the visual arts, as well as the relationship between architecture, psychoanalysis, and the history of psychological aesthetics. He is the author of *On the Animation of the Inorganic: Art, Architecture, and the Extension of Life* (The University of Chicago Press, 2012) and the editor of *Space as Membrane* by Siegfried Ebeling (London: AA Publications, 2010). Papapetros is an associate professor at Princeton University School of Architecture.

Jesse Reiser is an architect and educator whose work has been published and exhibited widely. He was a fellow of the American Academy in Rome in 1985 and he worked for the offices of John Hejduk and Aldo Rossi prior to forming Reiser + Umemoto with partner, Nanako Umemoto. Among several other recognitions, the firm was awarded the Chrysler Award for Excellence in Design in 1999. Currently, Reiser is a Professor of Architecture at Princeton University School of Architecture.

Kari Weil is University Professor of Letters at Wesleyan University. She is the author of *Androgyny and the Denial of Difference* (University Press of Virginia, 1992), *Thinking Animals: Why Animal Studies Now* (Columbia UP, 2012), *Precarious Partners: Horses and their Humans in Nineteenth-Century France* (University of Chicago Press, 2020), and numerous essays on literary representations of gender, feminist theory and, more recently, on theories and representations of animal otherness and human-animal relations. Her current research moves between theories of animal magnetism, biosemiotics, and the power of touch.

Acknowledgments

We are deeply grateful to our contributors Cynthia Davidson, Peter Eisenman, Jimenez Lai, Greg Lynn, Martin Miller, Spyros Papapetros, Jesse Reiser, and Kari Weil. Their arguments not only advance important theories, but in many cases, they give words to ideas we have been trying to formulate for several years.

We are also grateful for the inspiration, guidance, and support of so many important people in our lives. Thanks to Martin Miller for his creativity, his wit, his constant insistence on excellence, and his dissatisfaction with mediocrity. Thanks to Daniel Peacock for his precise comments and remarks, so many of which prompted important discussions and decisions that made this a better project. Thanks to Xiaoxue (Iris) Ma and Meng Ma for their unfailing dedication and creativity throughout the process. And to James Lowder, Ryan Ludwig, Daniel Peacock, and Tao Du Four for their editorial comments and insights.

We acknowledge the support from different institutions and our colleagues within them. Thanks to Cornell University College of Architecture, Art, and Planning and to the department of architecture, especially Gale and Ira Drukier Dean J. Meejin Yoon and former Chair Andrea Simitch, as well as former Dean Kent Kleinman and former Chair Mark Cruvellier. Thanks to the University of Wisconsin-Milwaukee, the School of Architecture and Urban Planning, and the Office of Undergraduate Research, in particular Chair Mo Zell and student Ben Zerrien. Thanks to the University of Virginia School of Architecture and the department of architecture, especially Edward E. Elson Professor and former Dean Ila Berman, as well as Vincent & Eleanor Shea Professor and Chair of Architecture Felipe Correa.

We also thank the Harvard University Graduate School of Design students who participated in the seminar, "Werewolf: Architectures of Change," taught by Caroline O'Donnell in Fall 2018: Giorgos Chatzopoulos, Sichuan Chen, Fang Fan, Trent Fredrickson, Anirudh Gurumoorthy, Xiao Han, Linda Just, Johanna Kasubowski, David Kim, Proey Liao, Zlatan Sehovic, Vaissnavi Shukl, Aime Vailes-Macarie, and Ever Vargas.

We are grateful to our clients, curators, and other friends of architecture: MoMA/PS1 (Pedro Gadanho, Sean Anderson), Art Omi (Warren James), MacDowell (David Macy), the Constance Saltonstall Foundation for the Arts (Lesley Williamson), the Buffalo Architecture Foundation, the *It's a Wonderful Life* Museum, Jai and Jai Gallery, Karolina Grunberg, William O'Brien Jr., Andreas Quednau, Sabine Muller, John + Pat Novarr, Nick Owen, Erana Samarasundera, Troy Schaum, Brantley Hightower, Adam Frampton, Marc McQuade, Ajay Manthripragada, Dillon Pranger, Felix Heisel, Whitney Moon, Michael Jefferson, Suzanne Lettieri, Trudy Watt, Nikole Bouchard, Paola Cuevas Báez, Deborah Garcia, LMNOP, Michael Young, and Hayley Eber.

Special thanks to Elise Jaffe + Jeffrey Brown, Phillip Eisenberg, Jody Gorton, Dan Kaplan FAIA and Amy Graydon, Mr. & Mrs L.P. Kwee, Alison Levasseur, Helene Lindenfeld, Gene and Pamela McGuire, Jon and Nancy Pundyk, Celeste Robbins, Susie Rodriguez, Paul Rubacha, Rene Dake Wilson, Silman Engineering, Banker Steel, Pennwood Construction,

Fluidity Design, Comet Skateboards, Datadraft, American Apparel, JC Steel, Component Assembly Systems, SFDS, Extra Packaging, Emeco, Soft Trucks, Langan, Hydro-composites, Koolfog, Krinner Screws, Armory Fabrication, E2E, Cowpots, Olollo, Home Depot, Starfish International, Ryan Paxton, Frank Parish, Tyler Williams, and Kurt Brosnan. We are also grateful to the Arts Council of Ireland and the Fonds BKVB (Netherlands), who supported Caroline's voyage into the unknown many years ago.

We are indebted to each other, too. We have spent many moons conceptualizing and crafting this monstrosity, and we are deeply grateful for the positivity and support, as well as sharp critique, that we have given one another through all these years.

Werewolf: The Architecture of Lunacy, Shapeshifting, and Material Metamorphosis would not have been possible without our publisher, Applied Research and Design Publishing, especially founder, Gordon Goff, who believed in this project since the beginning, and our managing editor, Jake Anderson, who saw it through each of its iterations.

Finally, we are grateful to all those who, knowingly or unknowingly, are embedded in the narratives of this book. In particular, none of this work would have been possible without a fluctuating and growing team of collaborators and researchers: Juan Carlos Artolozaga, Isabel Brañas Jarque, Mwanzaa Brown, Lin Sen Chai, Jully Chen, Stephen Clipp, Farzad (Freddo) Daneshvaran, Nick Doermann, Vanille Fricker, Nathan Friedman, Brian Havener, Kate Heath, Iroha Ito, Michael Jefferson, John Lai, Suzanne Lettieri, Iris Xiaoxue Ma, Maria Ma, Meng Ma, Alex Mecattaf, Chris Morse, Travis Nissen, Min Keun Park, Laura Stargala, Hana Svatoš-Raznjevi, Rachel Mei-Lan Tan, Jessica Tranquada, Courtney Jiyun Song, Alireza Shojakhani, Derek Yi, *with* Edward Aguilera Perez, Basak Akman, Zahid Alibhai, William Trey Anderson, Dylan Arceneaux, Bushra Aumir, Nils Axen, Michael Babcock, Jordan Berta, Emma Boudreau, Kun Bi, Sarah Bujnowski, Nicholas Cassab-Gheta, Jimmy Hong Ji Chen, Kun Chen, Vivien Shao Chen, Joon Choe, Richard Nelson-Chow, Tess Clancy, Stephen Clond, Jacob Cohen, Gretchen Craig, Tianqi Cui, Ryland Dandretta, Joseph Diamond, George Distefano, Eliana Drier, Ruan Drummond, Olivier Ducharme, Luke Erickson, Gary Esposito, Osehikhueme Etomi, Bari Felix, Lucy Flieger, Aurelie Frolet, Andrew Fu, Diego Garcia Blanco, Laura India Garinois, Ramses Gonzalez, Lucas Greco, Yue (Lancer) Gu, Andrew Hart, Sarah Haubner, Ben Hoffman, Farzana Hossain, Poyen Hsieh, Isabella Hubsch, Noah Ives, Eleanor Krause, Joseph Kennedy, Ben Kessler, Jerry Lai, Spencer Lapp, Varya Larionova, Wachira Leangtanom, Siobhan Lee, Nicolas Leonard, Mark Leskovec, Jessica Levine, Mark Yu-Chen Lien, Jason Lin, Lauren Lochry, Linzhe Lu, Le Luo, Maria Yue Ma, Roger Mainor, Daniel Marino, Heather Mauldin, Evan McDowell, Alexandre Mecattaf, Ashley Mendelsohn, Leslie Mignin, Jamie Mitchell, Melanie Monastirsky, Hafsa Muhammad, Brad Nathanson, Sophie Nichols, Maureen O'Brien, Fergal O'Donnell, Juanito Olivarria, Giffen Ott, Anbar Oreizi-Esfahani, Ximeng Pan, Leroy Patterson, Shane Pickles, Max Piersol, Dillon Pranger, Chris Ray, Ashley Reed, Zelmira Rizo-Patron, Heriberto Rodgriguez, Daniel Salomon, David Salomon, Olivia Salomon, Shovan Shah, Yeung Shin, Stephen Max Silverstein, Peter Stec, Alexander Terry, Daniel Torres, Daniel Toretsky, Kashyap Valiveti, Haoran Wang, Xueting Wei, Arthur Yang, Christopher Yi, Linjun Yu, Jenny Zhang, Yang Zhao, Maggie Zou.

Published by Applied Research and Design Publishing, an imprint of ORO Editions.
Gordon Goff: Publisher

www.appliedresearchanddesign.com
info@appliedresearchanddesign.com

Edited by:
Caroline O'Donnell and José Ibarra.

Design and research assistance from:
Xiaoxue (Iris) Ma, Meng Ma, Nicolas Leonard, Alexandre Mecattaf, Freddo Daneshvaran, and Benjamin Zerrien.

Project Manager:
Jake Anderson

Front cover:
"Wrinkled Apple," James Nasmyth, from *The Moon: Considered As A Planet, A World, And A Satellite*, 1874.
Courtesy of National Galleries of Scotland. Gift of Mrs. Riddell in memory of Peter Fletcher Riddell 1985.

Back cover:
"Back of Hand," James Nasmyth, from *The Moon: Considered As A Planet, A World, And A Satellite*, 1874.
Courtesy of National Galleries of Scotland. Gift of Mrs. Riddell in memory of Peter Fletcher Riddell 1985.

All images by CODA unless otherwise noted. Photography by Caroline O'Donnell, Martin Miller, Alireza Shojakhani, Maria Yue Ma, John Lai, Brian Havener, and Xiaoxue (Iris) Ma.

10 9 8 7 6 5 4 3 2 1 First Edition

ISBN: 978-1-951541-13-2

Color Separations and Printing: ORO Group Ltd.
Printed in China.

AR+D Publishing makes a continuous effort to minimize the overall carbon footprint of its publications. As part of this goal, AR+D, in association with Global ReLeaf, arranges to plant trees to replace those used in the manufacturing of the paper produced for its books. Global ReLeaf is an international campaign run by American Forests, one of the world's oldest nonprofit conservation organizations. Global ReLeaf is American Forests' education and action program that helps individuals, organizations, agencies, and corporations improve the local and global environment by planting and caring for trees.